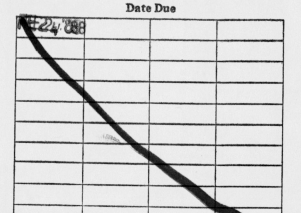

# THE GOVERNMENTS OF
# FOREIGN POWERS

# The GOVERNMENTS of FOREIGN POWERS

PHILIP W. BUCK
STANFORD UNIVERSITY

JOHN W. MASLAND
DARTMOUTH COLLEGE

HENRY HOLT AND COMPANY · NEW YORK

# PREFACE

IN a time of rapid change, there is need for a book which gives an account of the chief governments of the world. While the method and purpose of this book are discussed in Chapter 1, a few words may be added here.

The government of England receives more space than do the governments of France, Italy, Germany, Russia, Japan, and China. Present conditions of uncertainty and difficulties of access to information of necessity curtail the discussions of other states. Every effort has been made to give a simple but accurate description, though often the appraisal of institutions and practice must be tentative.

While the authors have frequently consulted with each other during the preparation of the book, Philip W. Buck wrote the first twenty-two chapters and John W. Masland the last seven. Both wish to make acknowledgment to the friends who gave them aid and counsel, particularly to Professor Charles Fairman of Stanford University; to Manfred Vernon, graduate assistant in the Department of Political Science at Stanford; and to John M. Maki of Harvard University. Mr. Vernon's help was most valuable in the preparation of the chapters on Germany. The comments of Mr. Maki contributed greatly to the improvement of the chapters on recent developments in Japan. The authors, of course, must take responsibility for any errors in fact or interpretation.

*Stanford University, Calif.*　　　　　　　　　　　P. W. B.
*Hanover, N. H.*　　　　　　　　　　　　　　　　J. W. M.
*January 6, 1947*

# CONTENTS

# THE GOVERNMENTS OF
# FOREIGN POWERS

# CHAPTER 1

# GOVERNMENTS, POLITICS, AND NATIONAL POLICIES

THE American citizen of the twentieth century, whether he likes it or not, has become a citizen of a world community. The problems of peace and security, of economic and social welfare, of social and racial minorities, are now so pressing that every citizen must interpret the significance of his government's action in terms of its effect upon foreign as well as domestic policy. World War II and the difficulties of reconstruction in the post-war period have forced these global responsibilities not only upon the political leader when he formulates a program but upon the voter when he casts his ballot.

The gravity of the international aspects of national policy has been amply explained to the citizen by lengthy discussions in public meetings, by articles in periodicals and newspapers, and by many widely read books dealing with the problems of international organization. International relations and the drift of foreign policy of the great powers of the world are constantly brought to the notice of every interested person.

**One World of Sovereign States.** Behind all these problems of international adjustment and cooperative action, however, lies the fact that the "One World" of this century is still organized in sovereign national communities. The associated action of national states is surely becoming increasingly important; but on the most hopeful estimate the probabilities of establishing a truly effective world government are still relatively remote. And even if a world federation could be successfully organized within the near future, the member-states of such a federation would retain a wide range of freedom of action, just as California and Massachusetts continue to exercise very substantial powers within the framework of American federalism.

To put the matter bluntly, an American citizen should not only understand the government of the United States thoroughly but also possess a working knowledge of how the Russians run the government of the Soviet Union and how the British make use of the English constitution and manage the machinery of association within the Empire-Commonwealth. Ideally, this knowledge should include something about all the states of the world, but that clearly would be too large a task. The terms "Big Four" or "Big Five" suggest the nations about which some knowledge is most necessary.

The aim of this book is to furnish the essential information needed to interpret the policies and action of the great states of the world. Its true subject might be described as "contemporary government," since its purpose is to make available significant facts about the operation of the great states of the world. Comparison and contrast between governments may often be helpful in understanding the working of each, and will be used occasionally to explain how institutions function in any particular country. Reference will often be made to the government and politics of the United States, in order to illustrate problems of administration, or characteristic political attitudes.

The method used, therefore, is that of description. This does not preclude analysis and interpretation, but the chief concern of this book is to *describe* the institutions of the great powers and some near-great powers, and to characterize the working of their institutions.

## THE GREAT POWERS AND THE SMALL NATIONS

The choice of governments to be described requires some explanation. Five states have been designated by the United Nations Charter as permanent members of the Security Council: England, the Soviet Union, China, France, and the United States. Since this book is intended for American students, the

United States here appears only as a basis for illustrative comment on the assumption that the student's concern is chiefly with foreign governments.

It should be remembered that, although they were defeated in World War II, the three Axis states, Germany, Italy, and Japan, remain of importance in world affairs. All three have populations as large as some of the five, and all are important industrial and trading communities. Though their governments are disorganized by recent defeats, it is worth while to analyze the pattern which is taking shape in each of them. The United States, moreover, is contributing to the reorganization of political affairs in each of these former enemy nations, and it is essential for the American citizen to appreciate these undertakings.

The exclusion of many governments should also be explained. Spain, Switzerland, the Scandinavian states, the Balkans, the Baltic states, the republics of Latin America—these and others are not discussed. The simplest reason for their exclusion is the inclusions. While the smaller nations occasionally make the headlines, and are always pursuing policies which have great importance for their own citizens and at times for others elsewhere, it is, nevertheless, the great powers which carry weight in the modern world. The pattern of government and politics in the seven—England, France, the Soviet Union, Italy, Germany, Japan, and China—then, is the concern of this book.

## THE SIGNIFICANT ASPECTS OF MODERN GOVERNMENTS

**Constitutional History.** For each of the governments to be considered, there are certain aspects of modern states which must be understood.

The constitutional development in each community has a powerful influence upon its present political organization. Every American student realizes that the Constitution of the United States has to be interpreted in the light of the story which lies behind its adoption and amendment, and that the present performance of our Congress, our President, and our administrative agencies, can be fully understood only in terms of our governmental history. The same is true for any state, great or small. Therefore, in dealing with each state, a summary will be given of its political and constitutional growth, in order to explain its present institutions and practices.

**Constitutional Framework.** The framework of institutions needs also to be described. The significant features of legislative bodies and their procedures in making laws and guiding policy, the powers of executive and administrative agencies, the organization and training of the civil service, the pattern of local administration—all these institutions in action govern the conditions of life and shape national policy in each of these communities.

**Political Parties and Public Opinion.** A further aspect is fully as important as the history and the institutional framework: the organization of political parties and the movements of public opinion. American students realize that an understanding of the policy of the United States at any given moment requires a knowledge of the tradition, the programs, and the character of the membership of the party in power. This is equally true for the many parties acting in coalition in the Fourth Republic in France, or for the Communist party in Russia which monopolizes the field of political action. In every state, the principal parties must be identified, and their tradition and program must be characterized.

**Recent Policies.** One final subject requires attention in each of these states. The recent history of leadership and policy has a powerful effect upon the present and future programs of any community. The course of events in the immediate past both limits and initiates the kind of program which may be adopted for the future. Referring once more to American experience—the Republican party, should it succeed in the elections of 1948, would nevertheless maintain and extend, in all probability, the social security legislation placed upon the statute books by the Roosevelt administrations. In the same way, a Conservative government in England would be forced to accept much of the present policies of the Labour Cabinet. And it is hard to imagine a leadership in the Soviet Union which would attempt to abolish the results of the three five-year plans!

The subjects of chief concern, therefore, are: constitutional history, viewed always with the intention of explaining contemporary practice; constitutional and administrative framework and the powers of institutions and agencies of government; political parties, with special emphasis on their programs and leadership; and the recent history of policy and action in the community.

## By-products of the Study of Modern Governments

The study of contemporary governments yields more than the first important purpose declared in the preceding pages, to understand how the British, French, Russians, Italians, Germans, Japanese, and Chinese run their national affairs. Since all these states, with the exception of China, are large industrial and commercial communities, with great urban populations, the problems faced by all of them are similar to those of the United States. Therefore, an understanding of how these communities organize and operate their own governments, of how their public policies are arrived at, can be provocative to the American citizen. Knowledge of how other communities do things can suggest improvements in our own country, or demonstrate the advantages of our present types of action.

Besides understanding the operation of governments, some comprehension of the temper of other communities can be gained from the study of their political institutions. It might be said that governmental institutions constitute a sort of bony framework which gives some indication at least of the character and potentialities of peoples.

Finally, it must be admitted that the actions of governments, at present, profoundly affect the lives of every citizen. In a modern industrial world, public control of personal action has a much greater significance than it had in the nineteenth century. The more the citizen knows about the working of his own government and the performance of other governments in the world, the more intelligently he can express his opinions and exert his influence.

## READINGS

The following are a few of the standard and classic works by distinguished scholars in which comparative studies of government have been made:

Bryce, Viscount, James, *Modern Democracies*, 2 vols., London, 1921.

Finer, H., *The Theory and Practice of Modern Government*, 2 vols., New York, 1932.

Friedrich, C. J., *Constitutional Government and Politics*, New York, 1937.

Marriott, Sir J. A. R., *The Mechanism of the Modern State*, 2 vols., Oxford, 1927.

Some books of fairly recent date which deal with these governments are:

Beukema, Herman, William M. Geer and associates, *Contemporary Foreign Governments*, New York, 1946. Colonel Beukema and Major Geer, with their associates of the U. S. Military Academy, made valuable use of the records of American military government authorities in occupied territories.

Buell, R. L., ed., *Governments in Europe*, rev. ed., New York, 1938.

Heinberg, J. G., *Comparative Major European Governments*, New York, 1937.

Hill, N. L., and H. W. Stoke, *The Background of European Governments*, rev. ed., New York, 1940. A very useful collection of readings.

London, Kurt, *Backgrounds of Conflict*, New York, 1945.

Munro, W. B., *The Governments of Europe*, 3rd. ed., New York, 1939.

Ogg, F. A., *European Governments and Politics*, New York, 1939.

Rappard, W. E., and others, *Source Book on European Governments*, New York, 1937. Documentary materials with explanatory comments.

Shotwell, James T., ed., *Governments of Continental Europe,* New York, 1940.

Spencer, H. R., *Government and Politics Abroad,* New York, 1936.

Zink, Harold, and Taylor Cole, eds., *Government in Wartime Europe,* New York, 1941.

In addition to the foregoing suggestions, the student can find illuminating comment in books which deal with the problems of modern government in general. A few books of interpretative comment should be listed:

Becker, Carl L, *Modern Democracy,* New Haven, 1941. The late Professor Becker was one of the most distinguished of American historians, and this essay is representative of the penetrating quality of his mind.

Merriam, Charles E., *The New Democracy and the New Despotism,* New York, 1939; *Systematic Politics,* Chicago, 1945. These two books, by one of America's most distinguished political scientists, discuss the problems of government in general.

Finally, mention should be made of a few periodicals which contain articles on various aspects of government, written by scholars:

*The American Political Science Review,* published bi-monthly by the American Political Science Association.

*Foreign Affairs,* New York, published quarterly by the American Council on Foreign Relations.

*Foreign Policy Reports,* New York, published twice a month by the Foreign Policy Association.

*The Political Quarterly,* London, published four times a year.

Two annual publications are of importance for the factual data they contain:

*The Statesman's Year Book,* published in New York and London.

*Political Handbook of the World,* Walter H. Mallory, ed., New York, published by Harper and Bros. for the American Council on Foreign Relations.

Each of the above lists might be indefinitely extended, but the intention here is to offer suggestions of useful and authoritative writings, and sources of information, which the student may find of value in pursuing his interests further. Succeeding chapters will conclude with similar listings of references for more extensive reading.

# ENGLAND

# CHAPTER 2

# THE CONSTITUTIONAL DEVELOP-
# MENT OF BRITISH GOVERNMENT

MOST Americans realize that the government of the United States cannot be fully understood unless something is known of its historical development. The Presidency, the powers of Congress, the work of administrative agencies, in fact most of the actual operations of contemporary government, are the result of constitutional provisions around which have accumulated customs, judicial interpretations, and various popular influences. As citizens we may be only dimly conscious of this, but at least we have learned that the performance of government today is the product of powerful historical traditions, growing out of our colonial past, our experimentation with the adoption of a federal form of government, and our nineteenth- and twentieth-century experience in meeting the problems of society.

The same is true of British government. The American student is puzzled by the fact that the British have no written constitution such as we have; actually there is a British constitution. Not a single document, it is instead a series of documents, over which has grown the same encrustation of tradition, precedent, and custom which surrounds our Constitution. The English constitution is indeed all history, hence the necessity of beginning the study of the government of Great Britain with a review of its constitutional development.

In a text such as this any review of English constitutional history must be brutally condensed—for it is a long and complicated history. The story begins as early as 55 B.C. with the Roman occupation of the islands, continues through Anglo-Saxon times, and then runs from the Norman conquest to the present. Tennyson was speaking in poetic hyperbole when he said that "through the ages one increasing purpose runs," but it is not exaggeration to say that the growth of English political institutions and practice is fairly steady through all these centuries. It is, moreover, a history full of exciting episodes—battles, wars, and revolutions.

Clearly it is impossible to tell the whole story—the constitutional changes alone have been the subject of volumes [1]—but a useful account can be given in terms of the growth of the chief operating institutions of present-day English government: (1) the Crown and the administrative agencies, (2) the Parliament and the voting electorate, and (3) Cabinet leadership and the formulation of national policy. This amounts to telling the story backward: we look at the contemporary action of institutions, and study their history in order to understand how the functions of government are carried on today.

## THE CROWN AND THE ADMINISTRATIVE AGENCIES

The administrative acts of English government are done in the name of the Crown, or the king. When the traffic policeman stops a speeding motorist, when the income-tax collector sends a bill to the taxpayer, the official performs this duty by virtue of the power of the Crown. The citizen obeys because he recognizes, however dimly, that the king symbolizes the national government of England, though no subject thinks that his majesty has actually ordered the performance of each administrative act. The institution of the Crown is dramatized at the opening of a session of Parliament, when the king tells the assembled Lords and Commons what the plans are for forthcoming legislation and administrative policy. Some of the phrases from George VI's address at the opening of Parliament, August 15, 1945, show the traditional pattern: "My Ministers will submit to you the Charter of the United Nations. . . . In the Far East my Ministers will make it their most immediate concern to ensure that all prisoners in Japanese hands are cared for and returned to their homes.

[1] Some of the standard works on English constitutional history are listed in the bibliographical note at the end of this chapter.

. . . It will be the aim of my Ministers to bring into practical effect at the earliest possible date the educational reforms which have already been approved. . . ." [2] While these pronouncements on policy and on legislation have actually been written by the ministers, the king reads the speech, and by so doing expresses the intention of the English government to act in the ways indicated.

**William the Conqueror.** At times in the early history of England the king was the true originator of policy and the director of administrative action. Anglo-Saxon kings, from the fifth century to the Norman conquest, did not possess great powers because they were usually regarded as merely the most important of the great earls who were the heads of the governments of the local districts, or shires. When William the Conqueror established his rule over England after the battle of Hastings, he made the kingship a much more powerful institution. By creating a national system of taxation, by putting his appointed lords lieutenant in charge of the shires, by making himself head of the English church, and by other methods of centralization of authority, he took charge of the government of the realm. Not all of his successors could equal him in force of personality, industry, and administrative skill, so the importance of the Crown as an "estate of the realm" fluctuated through the reigns of succeeding kings. Contests between various competitors for the kingship, for example the Wars of the Roses, likewise diminished the prestige of the office.

**Tudor Absolutism.** In 1485 the first of the Tudor monarchs, Henry VII, came to the throne; and during his reign and that of Henry VIII and Elizabeth, the king, or queen, acted as a powerful monarch and a popular national leader. The Tudors governed England, making use of Parliament and the high administrative officials. Consequently their reigns have been called "practical absolutism." When Elizabeth died the crown went to her cousin, James Stuart, king of Scotland, who became James I of England. James I and Charles I made the mistake of asserting the divine

[2] *New York Times,* August 16, 1945.

right of the king to rule without gaining support in Parliament
for their policies. The Tudors had ruled England without saying
they were doing so; the Stuarts declared they possessed a divine
right to rule England, but finally failed to accomplish their purpose. Two revolutions in their reigns, the Puritan revolt
(1640–60) led by Oliver Cromwell, and the Glorious Revolution (1689), finally placed James II's daughter, Mary, and her
husband, William of Orange, upon the throne. Subsequent
family relationships led to the present reigning house of Windsor
(originally Hanover). Eventually the slow changes of history
established the situation expressed in the foregoing quotation
from the king's speech—that the king reigns, but does not rule.

**King's Clerk to Secretary of State.** While the place of the Crown
in English government was slowly evolving, a corresponding
growth of administrative agencies occurred. When William the
Conqueror began to rule England he needed, of course, the aid
of officials to carry out his policies. In feudal government there
were two classes of high officers of the state which he could employ for this purpose: the officers of the royal household and
the members of the feudal councils. He could, and did, make use
of the officers of the royal household, for a feudal kingdom resembled a family run on a national scale. One of the very useful,
though not exalted, officials was the king's clerk. The clerk was
a private secretary, indispensable in those days because ordinarily
the king could not read nor write. By entrusting his signet, or
personal seal, to the clerk as a symbol of royal authority, the king
could give directions to his ministers and transmit the royal will.
A modern administrative descendant of the king's clerk is the
minister of foreign affairs, whose formal title is "His Majesty's
Secretary of State for Foreign Affairs." Other feudal officers of
the Norman household similarly achieved administrative authority; the justiciar might be properly regarded as the feudal an-
cestor of the present lord chancellor, the chief legal officer of the
government and the custodian of the Great Seal of the Realm.

*Curia Regis* **to Courts and Exchequer.** Besides the royal household, the feudal councils made up of great lords and important

feudal officers, could be converted to administrative agencies. In Norman times there were two councils which exerted influence by advising the king and by participating in the actual administration of policy. The *Magnum Concilium,* composed of all important members of the nobility, served chiefly as an advisory body, and because of its size and diverse membership functioned also as a sort of legislative body. The smaller council, called the *Curia Regis,* included the greater feudal lords, many of them exercising real administrative authority; its members began to take over direction of some of the functions of government. What might be called committees, the Board of Exchequer and the Lords of the Admiralty, assumed duties of administration. From the *Curia Regis* some members with knowledge of the law went out to administer justice in the king's courts throughout the land. Thus it can be said that the modern High Court of Justice, as well as the Exchequer and the Admiralty, is the product of this development of feudal governing councils into administrative agencies. During the reigns of the Tudors the Privy Council advised the king, and its members often functioned as his ministers.

In this way, under the leadership of able and active kings, there were gradually built up in the feudal organization of English government the great administrative offices and boards, many of which still carry on similar functions under modern conditions. The process was slow but steady, and changes took place in response to practical day-to-day necessities. The final result was the establishment of the administrative machinery by which tasks of government, first under medieval and later under modern conditions, were fulfilled.

## THE PARLIAMENT AND THE ELECTORATE

It has already been said that not all the English kings succeeded as well as the Tudors in getting Parliament to support their policies. The tradition that a great council, representing the feudal estates of the realm, should have a share in the determination of policy began in Anglo-Saxon times. The Saxon kings were under an obligation to ask for the advice of the Witan, a council made up of the great officers and the high nobility. Its membership was never precisely defined and its meetings were never regular, but its existence was accepted by kings and nobles. After the Norman conquest the *Magnum Concilium*, with much the same sort of membership, continued this function. In 1215 the assembled barons of the kingdom exacted from King John a pledge, expressed in the document of Magna Carta, that he would always use his royal powers in accordance with the laws and feudal customs which had been established. Magna Carta was hardly a charter of human liberties. It was an assertion by the barons that no king could exceed the customary and legal limits on royal authority, and King John agreed because he urgently needed the support of these powerful nobles in order to raise taxes. None the less the presumption was created, however limited the provisions of the charter, that every king had to obey the traditional rules of the kingdom. One of these rules was that he was required to assemble his barons, including the spiritual lords, and give heed to their advice. Fifty years later a similar contest between barons and king led Simon de Montfort, the leader of the great lords at that time, to assemble a Parliament which included representatives of the lesser nobility and even the freemen, the knights of the shires from the counties, and the burgesses from the towns and cities. Other partially representative assemblies followed this one, and in 1295 the "Model Parliament," called together by Edward I, gave authority to this pattern of a great assembly of the estates of the realm.

**Lords and Commons.** From the thirteenth century forward the story of the growth of a representative assembly is one in which the form of representation approached more and more closely that of the Parliament of modern times. About this time most of the great lords of the clergy withdrew because they had an assembly called Convocation, in which they could transact the business of special interest to them. In the times of the Tudors the voting franchise for the qualified electorate was slowly defined by law. The active leadership of the Tudor monarchs enhanced the prestige and the importance of the assembly, even though the monarchs, and especially Queen Elizabeth, were able to induce it to follow royal leadership in policy. A curious aspect of this development is that the body became an assembly of two houses—instead of three houses reflecting the three feudal classes of those who fought, those who prayed, and those who worked—because the representatives of counties, towns, and the lesser clergy came to regard themselves as "the Commons," while the members of the higher nobility, including some of the bishops, could claim a seat in the House of Lords. Democratic legislatures of other nations now reflect this bicameral structure, imitating the fortuitous growth of a representative assembly in two houses in England.

**Parliament's Powers.** During the centuries that the pattern of representation became established, there was a simultaneous definition of the powers of Parliament. The right to grant taxes dates back almost to Magna Carta; the hearing of petitions gradually led to full rights of legislation. The pliability of the Tudor Parliaments really increased the powers of the body. Since the king could secure what he wanted in taxes or legislation, he was not averse to asking for it.

**The "Glorious Revolution," 1688–89.** In the seventeenth century the Stuarts precipitated a struggle between king and Parliament by disregarding these traditional rights of representation and legislation. The final result of the revolution was victory for the representative assembly, and when William and Mary came to the throne it was by virtue of parliamentary consent, and with guarantees for the powers of legislation and taxation. While William and his successors still retained considerable powers of leadership and administration, the principle was clearly established that Parliament was the supreme sovereign body of the kingdom.

**The Reform Bills.** Once this sovereignty was clearly recognized, it was only natural that there should be popular demand to make the legislative body more truly representative of the whole nation. The successive parliamentary reform bills of the nineteenth

century achieved this result. The unreformed House of Commons, with its limited franchise for citizens in the counties, its eccentric feudal qualifications for voting in the towns and cities, and its antiquated distribution of seats leaving the new industrial cities unrepresented, was changed by the acts of 1832, 1867, 1884, and 1918 to the present legislative body. The present House of Commons is elected from roughly equal districts called constituencies, in which all adult citizens with residence qualifications cast ballots for a member of Parliament. The first reform bill of 1832 was the result of a widespread popular movement, and, while it did not greatly enlarge the existing electorate, it popularized the principle that the House should be fully representative of all classes of the nation. Later measures steadily reduced voting qualifications and equalized constituencies.

### Cabinet Leadership and the Formulation of Policy

Charles II had to admit, when the Stuarts were restored to the throne, that Parliament was sovereign. The real problem of making this authority practical, in terms of control of national policy, lay in establishing effective and continuous control of the king's ministers. Impeachment by Parliament proved to be a clumsy way of directing the action of ministers. The final solution of the difficulty was achieved by a process of adjustment in which both king and Parliament participated.

**Cabinet and King.** The revolutions produced an alignment of parties: the Court or Tory party which had supported the king, and the Parliament or Whig party which had asserted the authority of the legislative assembly. When William of Orange came to the throne, he found that the simplest way of avoiding conflict with the Whig majority in his Parliament was to choose his ministers from that parliamentary group. The first two Georges, uninterested in English politics and unskilled in the English language, made continuous use of this device for reducing friction and inconvenience. George III, though he attempted to make the king once more an "estate of the realm"—affected by the concept of a Patriot King—employed the devices of party and parliamentary politics to increase his influence.

**Cabinet and Parliament.** Before George III came to the throne Sir Robert Walpole was prime minister for the better part of twenty years. When he lost the Whig majority in the Commons, his resignation in 1742 established the conventions of Cabinet leadership and Cabinet responsibility to Parliament for administration and proposal of policies, and the obligation of resigning office, or dissolving Parliament and calling an election to choose a new Parliament. The effect of these customary arrangements—for such ways of doing things were not embodied in laws— was to link together the executive and legislative activities of government. This is the distinguishing feature of Cabinet government: the true leadership in legislative and executive action is in the hands of a group of ministers who are actually the leaders of the majority party in the national legislature.

During the nineteenth century these conventions were firmly fixed in the minds of the general public. The contests between two great leaders, Mr. Gladstone for the Liberals and Mr. Disraeli, (later Lord Beaconsfield) for the Conservatives, dramatized the process by which a majority of the people choose a majority party in the House of Commons, and what might be called a small executive committee—the Cabinet—formulates policies and carries them out, assured of control of the House of Commons. Whenever the Commons refuses to support the Cabinet, either a new House of Commons or a new Cabinet must be found. This is secured by dissolving the House and holding an election, the result of which must be either to return a majority for the Cabinet formerly in office or to require the designation of a new set of ministers who will reflect the will of a new and different majority.

## SUMMARY: THE NATURE OF THE CONSTITUTION

This brief sketch of a long, slow development—it is worth repeating that it spans the centuries from the Anglo-Saxon kingdom in the sixth century to present-day Great Britain—suggests a few generalizations about the nature of the British constitution.

**Adjustment in Practice.** First of all, it is clear that the constitution is the product of practical solutions of concrete problems. The problem of converting the feudal, decentralized government of Anglo-Saxon and Norman times into an effective, national government was achieved by making use of the power of the king, and developing his household and his councils and councilors into working officers and agencies of administration. The problem of whether king or Parliament should be the ultimate sovereign was solved, after the revolutionary episodes of the seventeenth century, in favor of Parliament. The problem of making Parliament fully representative of the people—dimly foreshadowed in the early great councils of the feudal estates—was solved by the extensions of the franchise in the reform acts of the nineteenth and twentieth centuries. The problem of making the acts and policy of government truly representative of the will, first, of the legislature and, then, of the people, was solved by the slowly evolving practice of ministerial responsibility to Parliament and party majority. To a very large extent, therefore, the constitution is a mass of traditional ways of carrying on government. Customs and precedents are fully as important as laws or charters.

**The Great Documents and Constitutional Statutes.** Nevertheless, while the conventions of the constitutions are very important, there are some documents that have a great influence. Magna Carta, the Petition of Right which was presented to Charles I in 1628, and the Bill of Rights which William of Orange agreed to when he accepted the crown, all have an important place in the constitutional history and form a significant part of constitutional law. Similarly there are some statutes passed by Parliament, like the Reform Act of 1832, or the Parliament Act of 1911 restricting the legislative powers of the House of Lords, which have a determining effect upon English government. In addition to these there are the principles of the common law, enunciated throughout centuries by the courts, which control the relations of government authorities to each other, and which define the liberties of the English citizen. Finally, as in the United States, judicial decisions form a part of the rules which govern the action of the government.

The British constitution, then, is a set of rules under which government is carried on from day to day, and these rules are to be found written in the great documents, in statutes, and in judicial decisions. Many are obeyed though they are unwritten customs and precedents or principles of the common law. Except for the fact that there is no all-inclusive single document like the Constitution the situation is much the same as in the United States. In this country, laws, customs, and judicial decisions, as well as the text of the Constitution, are important in defining the action of government authorities.

The British constitution can hardly be regarded as the product of a political theory or philosophy. This fact is worth noting. It does not mean that the great English political philosophers like Locke, or the great jurists like Blackstone, did not influence the development of the constitution. Most English political thought, however, comes after the event, and the problem of determining that the sovereignty should ultimately be in the hands of Parliament was achieved before Locke published his *Two Treatises of Civil Government*. If it is at all true to say that the British empire was built in a fit of absence of mind, as much can be said for the British constitution. It evolved through practice. A series of practical solutions for governmental difficulties were developed during the long course of its history. In large part, this explains its durability. The processes of development began long ago, and change is still taking place.

**Parliamentary Sovereignty and Constitutionality.** An important aspect of this constitution should be explained to the American student. Because the Parliament is truly sovereign, and expresses the will of the people as authoritatively as that will can be formulated, there is no technical difference between ordinary statute law and constitutional law. An act of Parliament is by definition constitutional. English courts may interpret and refine the meaning of such an act, but the judges cannot declare it unconstitutional. The authority of the Parliament is unrestricted by constitutional limits; in fact, the Parliament may make both ordinary and constitutional law. The simplest token of this situation is that the Reform Acts, and the Parliament Act of 1911, though clearly having the nature of constitutional law, are simple acts of Parliament, passed in the same way—though with more public interest and discussion—as other legislation.

One other general aspect of this constitutional development should be noticed. The phrase "Mother of Parliaments" which is applied to the British Parliament is not merely poetic exaggeration first uttered by Englishmen. In actual fact the governments of such British dominions as Canada and Australia are quite closely modeled on the government of the mother country. The continental parliamentary governments, such as the Third French Republic, and the postwar government in Japan were organized in a form frankly imitative of British cabinet government. England was one of the first great national states to develop this democratic pattern, and as such it is worth close study, for the democratic principle of government by the people achieved one of its earliest practical forms in the British Isles. Though American government is very different, still we owe much of our pattern of legislative bodies, popular control of policy, and system of laws and courts to our British political ancestry.

This preliminary review of the constitutional development must be kept constantly in mind as our study proceeds to the contemporary institutions and practice of English government. The most fundamental and consistent aspects of the relationships of people to Parliament and of Parliament to Cabinet, depend upon the traditions which have been given such solidity by the long centuries of practical experience. Every English citizen has been taught this history in school, has heard it discussed in private family conversations and public political meetings. Thus, although "there was no constitution in England," actually there is deeply settled in every English citizen's mind the historical relationship of the agencies of government.

## READINGS

Suggestions for further reading begin with references to a few small works which state this constitutional development in brief space:

Adams, G. B., *An Outline Sketch of British Constitutional Development,* New Haven, 1918.

Clokie, H. McD., *The Origin and Nature of Constitutional Government,* London, 1937.

Brebner, J. B., and Allan Nevins, *The Making of Modern Britain,* New York, 1943.

A few of the classic and standard histories are:

Maitland, F. W., *The Constitutional History of England,* Cambridge, 1908.

White, A. B., *The Making of the English Constitution,* New York, 1925. Deals with the development up to 1485.

Keith, A. B., *The Constitution of England from Queen Victoria to George VI,* London, 1940. Two volumes handling the institutions topically.

May, T. E., and F. Holland, *The Constitutional History of England,* 3 vols, London, 1912.

Some recent valuable works are:

Adams, G. B., and R. L. Schuyler, *Constitutional History of England,* New York, 1934.

Kier, D. L., *The Constitutional History of Modern Britain, 1497–1937,* New York, 1938.

Numerous other standard and classic works might be mentioned, but the foregoing give many suggestions for further study, particularly on more specialized aspects of the development.

## CHAPTER 3

# "THE GOVERNMENT": THE CROWN, THE CABINET, AND THE CIVIL SERVICE

WHEN an Englishman referred in 1940 to "the Churchill Government," or spoke in 1945 of "the Labour Government," he meant much the same thing that an American meant when he spoke of "the Roosevelt Administration," or "the Democratic Administration." What is referred to in both cases is the existing leadership of the nation, and the phrases imply that the executive officials who are responsible for conducting the regular daily work of administering laws and regulations are also responsible for proposing policy. The Englishman and the American both realize that a leadership is in charge of affairs; they criticize or praise "the Government," or "the Administration," according to their opinion of administrative actions and the announcements of policy. Blame or applause may be equally undeserved, but the leaders cannot evade full responsibility.

Unless he were remarkably ignorant or naïve, a British citizen would not attribute these actions to the king; he would realize that the constitutional history had made the king the least important agency of the government so far as determination of policy is concerned. Nevertheless, the royal family and the Crown continue to take up a considerable amount of newspaper space, especially rotogravure, and the coronation of George VI in 1937 was made into an immense public celebration.

A typical Englishman, if cross-examined on what he thought were the effective agencies of British government, would probably identify the Crown, the Cabinet, and the Civil Service. In order to understand his meaning, each of these institutions should be described for the student.

## THE CROWN AND THE KING

A shrewd nineteenth-century observer of English government, Walter Bagehot, remarked that government had to have its dignified and impressive side as well as its practical working agencies.[1] This need is met by the institution of royalty. The pageantry of the opening of a session of Parliament, when the king in the royal coach drives through London to Westminster; the military spectacle of the changing of the guard at Buckingham Palace; the occasional appearances of Princess Elizabeth at regimental dances, the queen's visits to hospitals or charitable institutions, all serve to give the English citizen a pleasant, familiar picture of the formal aspects of government in his country. In the United States, the President has to perform similar ceremonial duties, and also carry the real responsibilities of administering the laws and consulting on policy—this might explain the fact that the lives of many American Presidents have been short while most English kings serve for a long time and keep their health.

The easiest way to understand the function of royalty in Britain is to distinguish between the powers of the Crown, and the powers of the king. The Crown is an institution, and by its authority the acts of government are carried on—as a result of the historical development which was sketched in the preceding chapter. The Cabinet ministers are formally appointed by the Crown; defense regulations for the conduct of the war were issued as Orders in Council under the authority of the Crown; officials perform their duties in the name of the Crown. The Crown is a permanent and continuous institution; the traditional announcement, "The King is dead, long live the King!" typifies the immortality of government authority. The king, however, merely serves as a symbol of national and imperial power.

[1] Walter Bagehot, *The English Constitution*, essays III and IV.

He has little personal influence on what is actually done in the name of the institution.

Because George V was a sensible and public-spirited man, he was able to exert some influence on the course of government policy. The same thing is true of his second son, the present king. The powers of the king depend upon his ability and skill as a person not as king, to make suggestions to his ministers. From his youth he has always had the opportunity to learn about government and politics from the inside. The present king, as Duke of York, had wide acquaintance with the leaders of the nation, and naturally learned a considerable amount about the problems of the empire and the British community. Now he is informed regularly by the prime minister about all important affairs of state, and whenever he offers advice it must carry weight because of his patriotism and experience. It is impossible to say how much influence he can exert upon the Cabinet, but the limits are very narrow. The prime minister and the Cabinet are in office because their party won a popular election, and they are obligated to fulfill a substantial part of their campaign promises. No suggestion the king could offer would overweigh the compelling force of this general obligation; but the Cabinet ministers might welcome his advice on many details of policy, even on matters of some significance. The real responsibility for acts of state, however, rests upon the Cabinet and the ministry.

The powers of the Crown, then, are the formal expression of the sovereign authority of the government, and are exercised by the responsible ministers. The powers of the king are the informal opinions of a well-informed and devoted man who has great opportunities to learn about current problems, and to express his viewpoint concerning them. It is true that there have been a few occasions, when the opinion of the monarch had some effect upon policy. When England faced a financial and economic crisis in August and September of 1931, George V is credited with having suggested to Mr. MacDonald and to Mr. Baldwin that it would be desirable to form a ministry in which all the English parties participated. Since the consultations between the leaders and the monarch were confidential, it is impossible to say how much influence the king's suggestions carried, but consultations did occur, and a national government was finally formed.

Like the Crown—an institution and a symbol—the monarch serves as an agency of government, and administrative action is carried out by virtue of traditional authority. In former times and as late as the eighteenth century, the king was advised by his ministers; at present, the ministers are advised by the king.

### THE CABINET: THE LEADERS OF "THE GOVERNMENT"

The nature of the Cabinet can probably be understood best by reference to the recent Cabinet formation. A parliamentary election was held on July 5, 1945, and when the results were finally published just over three weeks later, it was clear that the Labour party had won a majority of the seats in the House of Commons.[2] The Conservative party, under the leadership of Mr. Winston Churchill, had contested the election; and when the results were known, Mr. Churchill and his Cabinet resigned, so that a new Cabinet, reflecting the new Labour party majority, could be chosen. The king called Mr. Clement Attlee, the leader of the Labour party, to consult on the membership of a new Cabinet, and on July 27, the first appointments were announced. Mr. Attlee was named prime minister, first lord of the treasury, and minister of defence, the same offices which Mr. Churchill had held as head of the national government in wartime; and five other important Cabinet posts were filled, all the men being leaders in the Labour party and having had public experience in Parliament and in the Cabinet. Since these appointments were representative of the personnel of the new leadership, a brief description of a few of the offices and the persons is helpful:

*Secretary of State for Foreign Affairs*: Ernest Bevin
*The Office*: This is the headship of the Foreign Office. It cor-

[2] *London Times,* July 27, 28, 1945.

responds roughly to that of Secretary of State in the American federal government. It requires constant attention to the diplomatic problems of Britain and the Empire, and it imposes heavy responsibilities for the formulation of lines of foreign policy.

*The Man*: Mr. Bevin, at the time of his appointment, was sixty-four years old. He was a self-made man, having been a farm boy, a shop clerk, a streetcar conductor, a secretary of the Dock Workers Union, and a member of government committees for labor and transport services in World War I. After that war he was the organizer of the Transport and General Workers Union, and became its national secretary. He had had a long career in the House of Commons, and Winston Churchill appointed him minister of labour and national service in the War Cabinet of 1940. His great vitality, his organizing and administrative skills, his long experience in the Labour party, made him one of the important leaders, and therefore he was appointed by the king, upon the advice of Mr. Atlee and other party leaders, to one of the most important Cabinet posts.

*Lord President of the Council and Leader of the House of Commons*: Herbert Morrison

*The Office*: This is one of the medieval heritages of modern British government. Unlike the office of foreign secretary, this post carries no specific administrative responsibilities. It is usually given to an important leader of the party, and entitles its occupant to participation in cabinet meetings. The incumbent helps to formulate general policy but does not assume administrative tasks with respect to any particular government activity. Since the post has this formal character, it can be combined—as in this case—with the task of defending and explaining the government's policies to the House of Commons, and with serving as an aide to the prime minister in holding the support of the majority.

*The Man*: Mr. Morrison's experience has been like that of Mr. Bevin. He is the son of a policeman, and his life has been spent as a Labour party organizer and official, as an active and effec-

tive member of the London County Council (the governing
council of metropolitan London), and as a Labour member of
the House of Commons. In the War Cabinet he was secretary of
state for home affairs and minister of home security. The latter
post he administered with energy and skill, organizing the
civilian defense of Britain.

*Chancellor of the Exchequer*: Hugh Dalton
*The Office*: Though the title is medieval, the office is modern in
its functions. It is analogous to that of the Secretary of the
Treasury in the United States government. The incumbent must
assume responsibility for formulating and defending the financial
policy of the Cabinet, and for the collection of taxes, the borrow-
ing of money, and the expenditure of funds. Since this is a vital
aspect of policy, "the Treasury," as it is often called, influences
the policies of other departments of government, and the chancellor is therefore one of the most important officers in the
Cabinet.
*The Man*: To call Mr. Dalton a "mastermind" is a brief and but
slightly misleading characterization. He had a distinguished
record as a student at Eton, one of the famous and exclusive
English schools, and at Cambridge University. He has been a
member of the faculty of the London School of Economics and
Political Science, has published scholarly works in the field of
economics and public finance, has had a long experience in the
House of Commons, and served in the MacDonald ministries in
the period between the two World Wars.

*President of the Board of Trade*: Sir Stafford Cripps
*The Office*: The title of this position reflects the English government organization of the eighteenth century, when these
functions were carried on by a committee of the Privy Council.
The present functions of the office are comparable to those of
the Secretary of Commerce in the American President's Cabinet.
Government regulation of many aspects of foreign and domestic
business activity, supervisory powers over municipally owned

public utilities, collection and publication of economic statistics and data, and many aspects of economic policy, particularly reconversion from war conditions, all fall within the jurisdiction of this department.

*The Man:* Sir Stafford Cripps is a distinguished barrister—what Americans would call a trial lawyer—and has had wide business connections and experience. He was educated in both science and law, has had a long record in the Labour party, holding government positions of importance in Mr. Churchill's Cabinet during World War II.

**Membership of a Cabinet.** Besides these four important appointments, two others were announced on the same day: Arthur Greenwood, one of the chief leaders of the Labour party, was appointed to the Cabinet without portfolio; Sir William Jowitt, a distinguished barrister and former Cabinet minister, was made lord chancellor, the head of the system of courts and chief law officer of the government.

A week later, nineteen more appointments were announced, and a fairly complete cabinet list could be published two days later.[3] It included twenty members of the Cabinet: the six already named, and other offices of comparable importance, such as six secretaries of state in charge of departments dealing with dominions, colonies, India and Burma, home affairs, war, air, and Scotland. Twenty ministers, in charge of such activities as supply and aircraft production, war transport, food, pensions, and town and country planning, were designated as ministers of Cabinet rank, and thereby entitled to participate frequently in discussion of general policy. In addition, there were thirty-two junior ministers, all having the function of assistants to the ministers, like financial secretary to the admiralty, parliamentary undersecretary of state to the colonial office, or assistant postmastergeneral. The men and women who held these offices were less important leaders of the Labour party, with experience in various business, trade-union, or professional occupations. One of them,

[3] *London Times,* August 6, 1945.

J. H. Wilson, was a member of the faculty of University College at Oxford. He was designated Parliamentary secretary to the Ministry of Works because of his academic training and expert knowledge.

This description of the personnel of the Labour party Cabinet gives some insight into the general pattern of English Cabinet government. Mr. Attlee, after consulting with other leaders of the party, proposed this list of ministers to the king, who then announced the appointments. Except for the limits imposed on the number of ministers and junior ministers by the Ministers of the Crown Act,[4] passed in 1937, the leaders may exercise their discretion as to the number of offices in all categories, and the distribution of government functions among them. What really happens is that the most important leaders decide that they need to have a certain list of offices, and place key men of the party in these positions. Experienced and influential men, with long experience in government, Parliament, and party, are assigned to important and responsible posts; promising younger men are given the responsibilities of junior ministries.

**The Cabinet Team.** The net result is the formation of a Cabinet or Ministry, which is in effect a team of administrators and leaders, led by the prime minister, each of them having in a sense, a dual personality. As chief administrators, or junior assistants to chief administrators, they take charge of a government department; as party leaders they propose legislation and make announcements of policy, and defend such proposals in the House of Commons. The prime minister, whose position has long been defined as "first among equals," acts as a chairman of the Cabinet meetings in which the lines of policy are discussed and agreed upon, and assumes the chief responsibility for explaining and defending these policies to the Parliament and the nation.

**American and English Cabinets Contrasted.** While it is possible to compare the administrative functions of particular English Cabinet ministers with those performed by the corresponding

[4] Ministers of the Crown Act, 1937. 1 Edw. VIII and 1 Geo. VI.

members of the President's Cabinet in the United States, the collective responsibilities of the two bodies are different. The President selects the members of his official household to assist him in performing executive and administrative duties. They are responsible to him, and he may enforce that responsibility by asking for their resignations or removing them from office. Often they are relatively unknown to the general public— President Truman's appointment of Thomas C. Clark as Attorney-General in May 1945 is a recent instance of the choice of a man who had administrative experience but was not widely known. American Cabinet members may advise the President on policy, but he is not obliged to accept their counsel. While they frequently appear before committees of Congress, they are not required in any direct way to defend policies before the legislature. Their public statements may sometimes be the means of announcing policy, but final decisions rest with the President. English Cabinet ministers, as has just been explained, collectively assume the duty of declaring, defending, and carrying out the chief actions of the government.

In wartime the organization of the Cabinet has changed to fit the needs of such a period. In World War I a small War Cabinet, including only the most important officers, was organized; in World War II, Mr. Chamberlain and then Mr. Churchill adopted the same organization. Mr. Churchill's War Cabinet after 1940 fluctuated between seven and nine members, including the chancellor of the exchequer, the secretary of state for foreign affairs, the minister of labour and national service, and other key men. Vital decisions were made by this group, which met almost daily; other ministers were consulted when plans significantly affected their departments. Mr. Attlee's Cabinet shows the more normal peacetime pattern: a Cabinet group of twenty discusses the main lines of policy, and other ministers of Cabinet rank, and even junior ministers, are called in occasionally to have a share in framing plans for future action.

**Nature of Cabinet Government.** At the risk of tiresome repetition, it is worth restating a general characterization of the nature of Cabinet government. A national party wins an election, and thus establishes a majority in the House of Commons. The leaders of this party, after consultation among themselves, choose a team of key men and enterprising and promising younger men to be an executive committee in charge of the policy and the administration of the government. The king formally appoints this group to Cabinet positions, and each member of the group assumes a double responsibility—the task of directing the work of a government department, and the duty of sharing in the formulation of legislation and policy and in defending proposals in the House of Commons, for each Cabinet minister retains his seat in the House, or is elected to a vacant seat. If no seat is vacant, some loyal member of the party disqualifies himself by accepting the Wardenship of the Chiltern Hundreds, thus vacating a seat. In the ensuing by-election the new minister wins a place in the Commons.

This team of leaders is assured of the support of the party majority so long as it is able to retain the confidence of the members of the party, both inside and outside of Parliament. If that confidence is lost, and the proposals of the Cabinet are defeated because of adverse public opinion and unwillingness of the majority to vote for legislation to carry out policies, the Cabinet resigns, a new general election is usually held, and the action of the voters results in either a new majority and a new Cabinet, or the endorsement of the old Cabinet by a more loyal majority.

It is evident from this brief description of these vital relationships that Cabinet government is very different from the traditional American pattern. In the United States there is the presumption that executive and legislative functions are separate. In theory the Congress passes laws and resolutions on policy, the President and his Cabinet administer them; in practice, the two situations are not as different as they seem—every American citizen expects the President to propose policies, and every President who possessed any initiative has tried, with varying success, to exercise functions of political and party leadership.

The American citizen, carefully taught in his school days to subscribe to the theory of separation of powers between executive, legislative, and judicial functions, finds it a little hard to understand the intentional combination of policy formulation and policy administration which exists in English Cabinet government. If he applies close observation to the working of American institutions, however, he can recognize that both the American President and the British prime minister are national leaders, bearing responsibility for proposing and executing national government policy.

## THE CIVIL SERVICE: SKILLED PRACTICAL ADMINISTRATORS

The brief character sketches of a few of the members of the Labour government in 1945, show that none of the ministers can claim to be expert in the field of his departmental responsibility. Mr. Bevin, able and well-informed as he is, cannot bring to the problems of foreign policy the background and experience of the trained diplomat. Mr. Dalton, though he has a scholarly command of the field of economics, can hardly be regarded as a skilled official in the practical aspects of governmental finance. Other members of the Cabinet have even less claim to specialized knowledge of the work of the departments they administer.

**Amateurs and Experts.** Cabinet government, in existence for well over a century, has taught both the citizen and the political leader to expect that the members of the ministry will be amateurs, not experts. The ministers are laymen who possess the confidence of the public and the party because they are widely experienced in public affairs and are reliable interpreters of the wishes of the public. But to carry on the complex tasks of public administration, the ministers must depend upon the experience and training of the permanent officials of each department. There is a small army of civil servants—the phrase the Englishman uses to describe the trained public officialdom—in each ministry of the national government. These civil servants are forced, both by law and by the necessities of their careers, to be nonpartisan in their attitude. The same official, during his government service, will act under different ministers pledged to different party programs. The tax expert in the Treasury, who in the spring of 1945 advised Sir Kingsley Wood, a member of the Conservative party holding orthodox views on business and finance, had in the fall to put his training and experience at the command of Mr. Hugh Dalton, chancellor of the exchequer in a Labour government which proceeded immediately to nationalize the bank of England.

**The Civil Service: Recruitment and Classes.** For nearly a century the English government has recruited into its permanent civil service a very high quality of personnel, and since the civil servant has so much to do with the effectiveness of government action, every private person and public official recognizes the need for a competent government staff.

The service is classified into five groups: the administrative class, open by competitive examination to candidates who usually have university training; the executive class, usually recruited by promotion from people in the service who have had secondary school training and experience; the clerical class, recruited by examination from candidates who have finished the major part of secondary school training; the clerical assistant class grade I, recruited from people with less training than the other classes; and the class of copying typists and shorthand typists, whose qualifications are what would be expected from their title. During 1944 a committee was set up to examine the civil service.[5] It recommended a plan of training for people already in the service, to be directed by the Treasury, which has always had considerable powers over the supervision of government personnel.

**A Typical Civil Service Career.** The members of the administrative class form the most responsible part of the government service, and occupy the important positions in the various government departments. A brief sketch of a typical career, combining aspects of several individual performances, will serve

[5] Cmd. 6252, 1944

to show what sort of people hold these jobs. Our imaginary candidate is eligible to compete in the examinations held by the Civil Service Commission, a semi-independent agency of the government, when he (or she) has completed a university degree and is still within the age range of twenty-one to twenty-four years. Invariably the candidate has studied at the university in what are called the "honours schools," and holds a degree with distinction, a recognition of superior scholarship. Every year many young people enter this competition; the examinations are general, covering the subjects of history, philosophy, economics, and the like. Our candidate has specified an interest in some particular branch of the service, and so takes some of his examinations in general subjects which apply to his chosen field. Very little specialization is required, however, so he is able to enter a wide field of competition. The examiners are members of the university faculties, or have comparable training and background. Our candidate, let us say, makes a good showing in the examinations and stands high on the list of successful competitors. He is therefore allowed to name the particular branch of the service to which he aspires, and is assigned a job as an assistant to an experienced administrator (who entered the service years before in the same way). He serves for a probationary period of about two years, during which time his personal qualities are assessed by his superiors. If it seems desirable, he is transferred to some other branch; if he fails to demonstrate the necessary qualifications, his connections with the whole service may be terminated.

However, our young man is fortunate, and impresses his superior officers as a person of promise. He performs his duties meticulously, displays intelligence and even originality in memoranda and reports which he prepares, and is watched with kindly attention, mixed with rigorous judgment, as he progresses in the official hierarchy. He meets a few minor emergencies with poise and discretion, and finally is recommended for promotion. After this, the limit on his career is largely dependent on his length of life. If he lives long enough, he rises to the position of a bureau head or a division chief, and may even attain the really significant and responsible post of chief under-secretary of the department. By this time he has had dealings with various ministers who have been in charge of the department, and has had the opportunity of making suggestions and arguing aspects of proposed government policy.

**Advancement in the Civil Service.** He may serve a number of years in the important and responsible position of chief permanent under-secretary. A woman has ceased to be promoted before this stage is reached, the principle executive positions being still reserved for men. During the past few years there has been considerable discussion in the House of Commons of the opportunities for women in the hierarchy, but there still exists a limit on their promotion. Our man, then, by this time has matured into being something of a bureaucrat; though he does not display all the undersirable qualities which the term connotes to the uninitiated. He has had a long experience in the work of a particular ministry; he has had opportunities to master his job in terms of books and study as well as in routine office procedures; he has matured intellectually during the passage of the years. When he reaches retirement age at about sixty-five, he receives a pension, and often a knighthood or even a barony, as a mark of the appreciation of the government and the people; and he is likely to spend his remaining years—of which there are usually many—leading a healthy and quite happy life in some English village or suburban town, still actively associated with public affairs as a solid citizen and a member of local government councils and committees.

**Prestige of the Service.** The prestige of the government service in England is still incomprehensible, in part, to the American student. Recently, however, we in the United States began selecting responsible permanent government officials on the basis of general educational and intellectual qualifications; with the passage of time we may come to recognize the important part played in modern government by the well-trained and assiduous civil servant. In England the selection, training, and promotion of administrative officials which are illustrated by this hypothetical career result, as one might expect, in a very high level of respectability, and even of intellectual initiative and inventiveness. Naturally there cannot be much expectation of the latter qualities, because brains of real creative power are very scarce in any human activity; but, for the daily performance of the endless routine of administrative work, reliability and competence are virtues well worth securing. "He was good, poor fellow, and let who would be clever, and was therefore promoted to an under-secretaryship," might well be placed as an epitaph on our man's modest tombstone in the village cemetery where his ashes finally repose.

**Ministers and Under-secretaries.** The relationship of these experts with the various laymen who hold ministries should receive a few words of comment. Ministers are vigorous men, politically effective in the rough and tumble of partisan debate in the House of Commons, and in handling hecklers in the party meetings during electoral campaigns. They are men who know what they want, and even have a fairly good comprehension of what the public wants. All of them come into office pledged to their party's program, and each of them often seriously disturbs the calm routine of established activities—as did Leslie Hore-Belisha as secretary of war, with his plans for a new English army just before the outbreak of World War II. The brass hats at the War Office—and every office has its brass hats —swamped him with reports and memoranda; but eventually the official hierarchy yielded to the energy and public influence of the political leader, while it successfully defended some of the cherished, and useful, routine procedures which were worth preserving. The co-operation of expert official and lay political leader has been remarkably fruitful of good results for modern English government. It is making its appearance in other modern governments, particularly in the national and state governments of the United States.

## The Growth of Ministers' Powers

The widening range and the increasing complexity of the functions performed by government in England, as elsewhere, has produced the phenomenon analyzed by an investigating committee as "The Growth of Ministers' Powers." [6] The work of the committee was begun partly because the executive departments' use of rule-making powers, and of hearings on cases of administration which had a judicial character, had increased to the point where it was sharply criticized by Lord Hewart, then lord chief justice, in a book with the suggestive title, *The New Despotism*. Stated briefly, the chief substance of the criticism was that many administrative departments (and officials in those departments) were empowered to make rules and to decide cases, neither of which were subject to review in the regular system of courts. This was regarded by the lord chief justice and by other able jurists as a dangerous invasion of citizens' rights. [7]

**Rule-making and Quasi-judicial Powers.** The practices which were criticized can be illustrated by an example. A physician in a small town in England usually takes a certain number of patients under the provisions of the Health Insurance Acts, and is paid from government funds. The Ministry of Health places his name on a published list of doctors of the community, called a panel. The legislation empowers the minister to strike the doctor's name from this panel, if after investigation it appears that he is not giving proper attention to his "panel patients," or is in other ways failing to meet fully the requirements of the law. The minister of health, in such a proceeding, has power to make a final decision, whatever effect it may have upon this particular doctor's professional standing or income. Similarly, the powers of the Railway Rates Tribunal to set railway rates, or the power of the Board of Trade to grant permission (in the form of a provisional order, later formally confirmed by Parliament) to a town or city to operate an electric light plant, may

[6] Cmd. 4060, 1932.

[7] C. K., Allen *Bureaucracy Triumphant,* 1931. A similar study was made for the United States a decade later—quite closely paralleling the *Report on Ministers' Powers*—by the Committee on Administrative Procedure, appointed by the Attorney General, *Administrative Procedure in Government Agencies,* Senate Document no. 8, 77th Congress, 1st session.

have far-reaching effects. Naturally, the legal profession, whose business consists in large part of defending private rights in the courts, looks with disfavor upon these extensions of administrative and executive authority.

**Conclusions of the Committee.** The report of the committee on the general subject was a disciplined and careful effort to analyze the whole phenomenon, and its general conclusions are worth summarizing. After hearing much expert testimony, the committee reported that the growth of these powers was a natural consequence of the complexity of the tasks of modern government. Executive or administrative action was prompt, flexible, and based upon specialized knowledge. The members of the committee made various recommendations for improving procedures, but they agreed that the necessity for this extension of executive and administrative authority was inescapable under the economic and social conditions of the twentieth century.

## The Growth of Ministers' Powers in Wartime

The conditions imposed by total war, particularly the hazards of the bombings during the winter of 1940–41, tremendously extended this use of administrative authority. Legislation adopted in 1939, anticipating the possibility of war, conferred upon the government the power to issue orders for the defense of the realm, and Parliament renewed this legislation from year to year. Under this grant of power the Defence Regulations were issued as Orders in Council—which means that these general regulations were promulgated by the king in council, though actually formulated by the Cabinet and issued under the authority of the Crown. These regulations were published from time to time, and are collected in the official volumes of the Statutory Rules and Orders.[8]

**Wartime Powers.** As might be imagined, the range of subjects covered by the regulations is very broad, but the dimensions

[8] *The Defence (General) Regulations,* published yearly as a separate volume of the *Statutory Rules and Orders, 1940–1945.*

can be indicated by some statistics: in 1940, the first full year of war, about 2223 orders were issued, and those bearing upon problems of war and defense totaled 1552 pages; in 1943 there were 2149 pages of orders issued concerning war and defense activities. All sorts of subjects appear in these pages: the organization of civilian defense; the imposition of central control, through regional commissioners, upon the work of local government authorities; extensive regulation of prices, supply of goods, labor conditions; and all the other fields of government supervision made familiar to the American citizen by the Office of Price Administration (OPA), the War Production Board (WPB), or the Office of Civilian Defense (OCD).

Sometimes the wartime rule-making power was diffused through three levels of authority. Orders were made conferring upon ministers the power to make orders granting to regional commissioners or other subordinate officials the power to make orders regulating the activities of the civilian population. Quaint situations are frequently revealed in the succession of administrative rules. One slightly frivolous example will serve to illustrate the complexity of the problems handled during these years. The sport of falconry has had its devotees in England since medieval times; but in 1940 it was necessary to empower the secretary of state for air to permit any person to destroy peregrine falcons, or their eggs, because the birds were imperiling the lives and the patriotic services of homing pigeons carrying important military messages. This order revoked the legal protection given these birds under a series of Wild Birds Protection acts running back as far as 1880. Ardent lovers of the sport protested; and, as a consequence, orders issued in subsequent years defined carefully particular areas in which the falcons might be destroyed, leaving some less vital sections of the kingdom open for the flight of these interesting, but dangerous, birds of prey.[9] This is an amusing minor instance of the range of authority exercised. Page after page was issued specifying prices, wage levels, factory

[9] S. R. O. 1940. nos. 1016, 1078, 1164; and similar orders in 1941 and 1943.

lighting, living conditions, fire defense, control of dangerous explosives, blackout regulations, and all the multitude of controls necessitated by the war.

These controls are being cautiously and slowly lifted during the transition period from war to peace conditions. In mid-October 1945 the Labour government introduced a motion to continue the pattern of wartime controls for a period of five years, and it was passed after a sharp debate. The difficult problems of postwar Britain will undoubtedly require the continuance of this type of regulation; even the Conservatives proposed that the period of extensive regulation should last as long as two years.[10]

**Parliamentary Scrutiny of Rules.** The members of the House of Commons have understood for some years that this development of administrative authority might well require modification of the regular procedure of the House, if the exercise of executive authority was to be closely watched and criticized. In May 1944, while the war was still going on, a motion was introduced to subject departmental rules to the scrutiny of the special committee of the Commons, and after a good-tempered debate the Churchill Ministry accepted the suggestion.[11] The probable result will be that such extensions of executive power will receive in future much more rigorous investigation and discussion by the Commons, but the use of these devices will surely continue.

## "THE GOVERNMENT"; SUMMARY

A single chapter can do no more than suggest the subtlety of the many interlocking relationships in the practice of English Cabinet government. The broad fundamentals should be kept in mind, and can be stated in terms of the evolution of public policy.

First, during an electoral campaign conducted with a great deal of public discussion, both enlightened and unenlightened,

[10] *New York Times,* October 16, 1945; *London Times* of same date.
[11] *London Times,* May 18, 1944.

each party proposes a program. This campaign results in the election of a majority in the House of Commons committed to accomplishing its own program. Then, by the actual choice of the real leaders of the majority party, and with formal designation and appointment by the Crown, a committee (Cabinet) of the leaders of that party is entrusted with the responsibility of devising and administering the actual substance of the program. While these leaders are formulating policy in terms of administrative action and legislative proposals, they hear and often heed the advice and counsel of the king; and they are constantly subject to the vigilant criticism and comment of the House of Commons. With respect to administrative and legislative details, they confidently depend on the ability, integrity, and experience of the civil service, so that what is accomplished is done with care and skill. When the people feel the effects of government action, they evince approval or, as in wartime, acqui-esce with fortitude. Should they disapprove, the grumbling may rise to a roar of disapproval in the press, in public meetings, and in tea and dinner conversations; a motion of censure is made and carried in the House of Commons; an election takes place; and the opposition party may find itself responsible for a new Ministry with a more popular program. The net result is responsible and responsive government, even though the recent growth of ministers' powers has invested the Cabinet with great authority.

### READINGS

The suggestions listed below refer to the subjects discussed in this chapter.

The Cabinet and the Crown:

Bagehot, W., *The English Constitution*, 2d ed., New York, 1924, or later editions. A classic set of essays, very stimulating and interesting in style.

Jennings, W. Ivor, *Cabinet Government*, Cambridge, 1937. A standard recent work.

Keith, A. B., *The Constitution of England from Queen Victoria to George VI,* London, 1940, vol. I. chs. I-V. A detailed work by a famous scholar.

Muir, Ramsey, *How Britain Is Governed,* 3rd ed., Boston 1935. This might be regarded as a modernized version of Bagehot's book.

The Civil Service:

Cohen, Emmeline W., *The Growth of the British Civil Service,* New York, 1942.

Dale, H. E., *The Higher Civil Service of Great Britain,* New York, 1942.

Jennings, W. Ivor, *op. cit.* ch. V.

Keith, A. B. *op. cit.* vol. II, chs. XIII-XX. Chapter XX particularly deals with the selection and training of the service.

*Report of the Royal Commission on the Civil Service,* 1929. Cmd. 3909.

Stout, H. M., *Public Service in Great Britain,* Universtiy of North Carolina Press, 1938.

The Growth of Administrative Authority:

Note the works of jurists and the committee given in the footnotes in preceding pages.

Carr, Sir Cecil Thomas, *Concerning English Administrative Law,* New York, 1941. An interesting series of lectures.

Gordon, Lincoln. *The Public Corporation in Great Britain,* New York, 1938. An account of this type of agency, with the British Broadcasting Corporation as an outstanding example.

Hankey, Lord, *Government Control in War,* New York, 1945.

Robson, W. A., *Justice and Administrative Law,* London, 1928. The careful work of a distinguished scholar.

# CHAPTER 4

# THE ELECTORATE AND THE PARLIAMENT

$A$ PARLIAMENTARY election in England is like a Presidential election in the United States. The reason for this is clear, if the pattern of Cabinet government is kept in mind. When the English voter participates in the choice of the members of a Parliament he does much more than designate the member from his own locality. He fully realizes that his vote will contribute to the support of a majority party, to the program of legislation which that party has promised in its election manifesto, and to the selection—when a cabinet is chosen—of the leaders who will carry out policies. If his ballot has been cast for the candidate who belongs to one of the parties which lost the election, he then understands that he has expressed himself in support of "His Majesty's loyal opposition" and can reasonably hope that the members of that party will criticize the government, and keep it from doing the things he dreads the most.

This is similar to the position of the American voter during a Presidential campaign. He works for his Presidential candidate, his party, and his program. If his candidate was Mr. Willkie in 1940, or Mr. Dewey in 1944, he treasured the hope that his vote would impose restraint on the reforming zeal of the Democrats and their leader, and that at some future time—less than sixteen years away!—the policies he was backing would receive a majority vote from the people. In England this general decision by all the people at a parliamentary election is referred to as "the mandate," and parties offer platforms, candidates, and leaders in the hope of securing a "mandate" to carry out their policies.

47

To appreciate the importance of the House of Commons it is necessary to describe the voter, the candidates, and the legislative and critical functions of the Parliament as a body representative of the electorate.

## The Voter and the Parliamentary Constituencies

**The Suffrage.** The qualifications for voting have changed a number of times during the nineteenth and twentieth centuries. These changes were referred to in the introductory sketch of English constitutional development; but their significance should be explained a little more fully.[1] The House of Commons before 1832 was seriously unrepresentative of the people; and the effort to extend the limited electorate showed some of the characteristics of a popular revolution. The Reform Act of that year admitted the middle classes to the franchise by reducing and simplifying the property qualifications which had been in force for centuries. Thirty-five years later, by the Act of 1867, the working classes in the towns were allowed to vote. By the act of 1884 practically all men were enfranchised, and in 1918 women were given the voting privilege. When women were given the vote, a curious reluctance to declare their age as thirty years or more, as required by the law, limited their participation, and in 1928 the "flapper vote"—to use the slang of that ancient time—was legalized. Women achieved the age of political discretion, or indiscretion, as soon as men—when they were twenty-one years old.

The suffrage in England now is much the same as in the United States. Felons, idiots, and lunatics—when legally certified as such, and not allowed at large—are not qualified. Aliens, persons guilty of corrupt election practices, and peers—because they may claim a seat for themselves in the House of Lords— are likewise disqualified. Aside from these limitations, any citizen may vote if his or her name appears on a voting register —the equivalent of registration as a voter in the United States.

[1] See Chapter 2, pp. 19–20.

The register of voters is prepared by the clerk of the county or town in which the voter has resided, or has had a business for at least three months. The list is published; the citizen must see to it that his name is on the list, and procedures are open to him to establish his claim. Great difficulties, and some special legislation to overcome them, occurred in preparing the lists for the election of the summer of 1945, because the last election had been held ten years before, and the majority of voters had been in the armed services, war work, or defense services, or had been bombed out of their former residences. Regulations applying to registration will change probably before the next election in order to make the system more accurate and complete, but there was no really serious dissatisfaction in 1945.

A small number of people in England possesses the right to vote more than once. The most common form of plural voting continues to exist with regard to the universities, which possess the standing of parliamentary constituencies. A voter who has maintained his university standing, and has also a residence in some other part of England, may cast a ballot in both places. This is surprising to the American voter; and it seems likely to disappear in England, so that the classic democratic principle of "one person, one vote" would be fulfilled.

**Parliamentary Constituencies.** For the purpose of electing members of the House of Commons—they are referred to as M.P.'s, signifying Members of Parliament—England, Wales, and Scotland are divided into districts of approximately 50,000 to 70,000 inhabitants, called constituencies. Most constituencies elect— "return"—one member to the House of Commons, but several of the university consituencies may elect two. In December 1944 a Representation of the People Act was passed, providing for the creation of twenty-five new constituencies by a boundary commission, which finished its work in the following January. This was an emergency measure, passed in preparation of an anticipated election, and the results will doubtless soon be subjected to a systematic revision. The act increased the number of members in the House elected in July 1945 to 640 and corrected the most glaring population inequalities between districts. Final determination of the representation pattern must wait until every voter in England returns home, or decides never to return, but to live and vote wherever the conditions of wartime have finally placed him.

The system of elections by constituencies which return only one member has consistently underrepresented some parties and overrepresented others. The usual effect has been to exaggerate majorities, and to injure minorities.[2] As a result, there has been a persistent demand for some form of proportional representation, but so far no significant change has been made. The defects of the existing system operate to the advantage of the party which wins an election, and therefore none of the elected governments has taken up the problem.

### THE ELECTION OF AN M.P.

**Candidates.** It is difficult to get elected to the House of Commons but it is easy to become a candidate. A petition, signed by a proposer, a seconder, and eight other persons, serves to place any qualified person's name on the ballot as a candidate. Qualifications for candidacy are substantially the same as for voting, except that they exclude a very considerable number of administrative officials and judicial officers. So long as the candidate has a residence in the United Kingdom, he or she need not be a resident of the constituency in which the campaign is made; a tradition which has tended throughout the history of Parliament to raise the standard of performance of members. Every candidate is required, in a sense, to gamble on the campaign: an election deposit of £150 is required (to discourage frivolous candidacies) and is not refunded unless the candidate polls at least one-eighth of the votes cast. The real practical limit on candidacy is the action of the parties in choosing and supporting a good representative. This will be explained in the following chapter.

[2] Ramsey Muir, *How Britain Is Governed*, 1935, Ch. V.

**Campaigning.** Once nominated, the candidate conducts an active personal campaign—though the English phrase says he "stands" for Parliament, he really "runs" more perseveringly than the American representative. There is a great deal of what might be called face-to-face campaigning: small street-corner meetings addressed from the rear of a motorcar or motor truck (called in England a lorry); a great deal of "heckling" (questions to the candidate in public meetings); a great deal of visiting of voters at their homes (the English word is canvassing) by the candidate himself or his active supporters; and a number of garden parties (almost always held in drawing rooms because of inclement weather).

A national campaign goes forward at the same time and the candidate benefits from the efforts of his national party organization. Here all the familiar devices of an American Presidential campaign make their appearance: posters and slogans; radio broadcasts by party leaders (radio time is distributed among the parties with as much equity as possible by the British Broadcasting Corporation); newspaper publicity and support of all kinds; sound films and big city public meetings. It is a period of intense political activity, made all the more hectic because there are usually big and important issues to be decided, as well as the choice of M.P.'s. Ordinarily an election follows the fall of a government on an important question of public policy; and that question bulks large in the public mind. In the summer of 1945 the Labour party's proposals for socialization of key industries competed with the Conservative "Four-Year Plan," and the dominant problem in the voter's mind was the question of transition to peace conditions after the stress of wartime.

**Money and Elections.** Naturally, all this activity requires financing, and the use of money in elections is controlled with a good deal of success by the regulations embodied in the Corrupt Practices Acts. Usually every candidate hires an election agent, who sees that the legal restrictions on the use of money are carefully observed. If later it can be demonstrated in a prosecution in the courts that money was used improperly, the candidate, if he is successful, is deprived of his seat in Parliament and never allowed to contest that constituency again, nor any other for seven years. The Corrupt Practices Acts are too technical to permit exact explanation here, but it can be said that they set up strict limits on the amount of money which may be spent, as well as restrictions on the improper use of funds in bribing or treating. The standard of respectability, as well as the liveliness of performance, is very high; and the degree of participation by the electorate is indicated by the fact that in July 1945 nearly 87 per cent of the eligible voters cast ballots.[3]

**Dissolutions and General Elections.** Fortunately for the nerves of both voters and candidates, English elections are brief. They may be frequent, for dissolution of Parliament may occur at any time, and no Parliament (unless it prolongs its own life during a period of crisis, as did the wartime Parliament which sat from 1935 to 1945) may stay in office for more than five years. The dissolution of the Parliament in 1945 occurred on June 15 and the election was set for July 5, which allowed nineteen days of campaigning. Mr. Churchill, to cite one candidate, made that a hectic period, with an active and successful performance in his own constituency, and a busy tour of speaking throughout the country. Two to three weeks of campaigning, however, is ample, for Cabinet government is of such a nature as to attract and hold the interest of the general public and to prepare the voters for the questions of policy which receive discussion during the campaign.

**By-elections.** Every election does not take place because of the fall of the government. Vacancies occur in the House from time to time, by death or by elevation to the peerage. While resignation is not permitted, a member may vacate his seat by disqualifying himself through accepting a small sinecure post under the Crown, usually the wardenship of the Chiltern Hundreds. When a vacancy occurs, a special election (called a by-election) is held to fill it. By-elections are actively contested because, though they take place in only the one constituency in which a

[3] *London Times,* July 28, 1945.

seat is vacant, the results often reflect nation-wide changes in public opinion. English journalists compare the vote in the by-election with that of the preceding general election in the district, and draw conclusions about the political strength of the government's following. A series of defeats, during months or years, may seriously damage the prestige of a Cabinet.

## THE HOUSE OF COMMONS AT WORK: ITS GENERAL TASKS

Once selected, the members assemble, when called by the king's official proclamation, in the Houses of Parliament in the borough of Westminster in London. Since the historic meeting rooms were damaged during the war, there are plans in progress to build a new chamber for the Commons. The discussion of these plans reveals a characteristic conflict between those, like Mr. Churchill, who wish to preserve the traditional arrangements with all their inconveniences (of which the chief was simply lack of space to seat all the members) and those iconoclastic modernists who dream of an air-conditioned room with a public address system. Whatever happens to the meeting place, it is safe to predict that the ceremony of opening Parliament will remain unchanged in all its feudal pageantry. The king and queen drive in state to Parliament, and the Commons are summoned to the meeting room of the Lords where they stand humbly uncovered. The Speech from the Throne is read; and in subsequent sittings of the House the wording of a humble Address to His Majesty is debated, in which formal thanks for his consideration and kindness is barbed with all the criticism of his ministry's program that an active and alert opposition can introduce into the motion.

**Scrutiny of Administration and Questions.** The business of the House falls roughly into two major categories: watchful criticism of administration, and lawmaking on important questions of policy. The first function is performed in large part in what is called "the question hour." The House sits daily—except Saturdays, Sundays, and holidays—and begins its session usually at

2:45 P.M. Monday through Thursday, and at 11 A.M. on Friday. The meeting usually adjourns at 11:30 P.M. (4:30 P.M. on Friday)—the social weekend or the political business weekend, or the more frequent combination of the two, shortening the Friday sitting. After a brief amount of business concerned with private bills (which will be explained below) questions are addressed to the ministers concerning the administration of public business, or more general matters of policy. Ordinarily the question period is lively, with the member putting the query and the minister replying with what retorts he can muster. This is one of the best opportunities for eliciting information on matters of administrative action. Not infrequently the opposition introduces a motion which criticizes government action or policy. Expressions of viewpoints in the subsequent debate provide guidance for the action of government departments.

With the growth of ministerial powers, described in the preceding chapter,[4] the concern of the House with the range of administrative authority led to the creation of a special committee with powers to call for records and testimony on administrative orders having the force of law.[5] A select Committee on Procedure was created on August 24, 1945, and while its chief concern is methods of expediting the business of Parliament in general, it recommended in its first report the creation of a joint committee to consider administrative action.[6] It seems very likely that the Parliament will devote a larger portion of time in the future to the job of scrutinizing and criticizing the action of ministers and their subordinate officials.

**Types of Bills.** The traditional function of the Parliament is to pass laws. There are three kinds of legislation which the House and its committees must consider: (1) *Private bills*. Matters of  business, or of local government, which affect only a part of the nation (though that part may be a city as big as Birmingham, which may wish to build a municipal electric plant). These bills

[4] See Chapter 3, pp. 41–44.
[5] *London Times,* May 17, 1944.
[6] Cmd. 189, 1946.

are handled by select committees, with usually four members, which deal with the matter in the manner of a judicial hearing, calling witnesses, hearing counsel both for and against the measure, and finally recommending action to the whole House. The recommendations of these committees are ordinarily adopted with little debate. Sometimes a similar procedure is applied to provisional orders issued by a government department. (2) *Private members' bills or motions*. Matters of general national concern (like Mr. Herbert's Marriage Bill, passed in 1937, changing the divorce laws), introduced by a member of the Commons without the backing or support of the Cabinet. (3) *Public bills*. Big projects of legislation, introduced by a member of the Cabinet or the Ministry, backed by the leadership, and commanding the attention of the Parliament and the country. Often these bills embody the election promises of the majority party, and usually receive nation-wide notice outside Parliament in the press and in public discussion. There is always a large amount of such legislation at every session, and since it is so important, and occupies most of the time of the House, it should be considered in its relation to the leadership of the Cabinet.

## THE HOUSE OF COMMONS AT WORK: CABINET LEADERSHIP

**Public Bills.** Public bills, concerning the welfare of the whole national community, are put forward with Cabinet sponsorship. The projection of legislation—such as the nationalization of the Bank of England in the autumn of 1945—has been foreshadowed in the electoral campaign, and has been announced as settled policy in the king's speech at the opening of the Parliament. Before a single word is printed, the minister, in whose department the matter lies, has consulted the experts in the civil service. After the measure begins to take shape, this minister puts the proposal to his colleagues in a Cabinet meeting, and all the ministers directly concerned offer suggestions and criticism. Finally, when full agreement has been reached, the measure is introduced into the House of Commons, usually by the appropriate minister. Sometimes the prime minister himself will conduct through the House a very important piece of legislation. Though most public bills are introduced in the Commons occasionally their introduction occurs in the Lords; and private bills may also originate there.

Occasionally there is a debate on the very day legislation is introduced; but ordinarily a date is set by the Cabinet (the Cabinet leadership having extensive powers to control the use of the large amount of time of any session which is reserved for public bills) for a debate on the second reading of the bill. The second reading debate is an outright contest between government and opposition on the subject of the general principles and broad features of the bill, conducted in large part by the leaders of the majority and the leaders of the opposition.

**Committee Consideration.** After passing the second reading, which guarantees House approval of the general intention and substance of the proposed legislation, the bill is assigned by the speaker to a committee for closer and more detailed consideration. The Speaker's functions, and the pattern of committee organization, will be described later in this chapter. Since the bill is discussed section by section or even sentence by sentence, the work of the committee invariably results in amendment or revision of the measure. The bill in its modified form is then reported back to the whole House and is reconsidered at this report stage for several hours or several days, according to its importance.

**Final Passage of a Bill.** Eventually a motion is made to read the bill a third time, in its amended and revised form, after the changes of the committee and those resulting from the discussion of the report, have been incorporated into the measure. At the third-reading debate only minor verbal changes are permitted, and on being passed the bill is sent to the House of Lords, where it receives consideration in stages similar to those it has already undergone in the Commons. If the bill originated in the Lords, its passage is completed in the Commons. If changes are made, they are considered by the House of Commons, with careful regard for the experience and knowledge of the Lords. After full agreement is reached the bill is finally sent to the king for signature, which is invariably given. It then becomes law, appearing in printed form in the statutes of that year. Finally it is put into active enforcement by the administrative departments and the courts.

Clearly, it would be impossible for Parliament to enact all laws necessary for the public welfare of a big industrial community—the statutes for each year are volumes of impressive dimensions—unless the procedures of making public bills were actively led and directed by the Cabinet. If the leaders, and the majority they command, did not take an active part in pushing business forward, very little could be accomplished. This is easily understood if it is remembered that the budget (the financial legislation which provides for the expenditures of large sums of money, and the taxes and borrowings to raise these funds) is one of the annual tasks of the Parliament, particularly of the House of Commons in which all financial legislation must originate.

One of the most important powers of the Cabinet has already been indicated in this life history of a public bill. The legislation is prepared by the Cabinet, and the ministers have the full, expert resources of the civil service in the administrative departments. They make use of economists, statisticians, administrative and technical specialists, and legal advisers available. Sometimes an intricate problem is made the subject of an extensive inquiry by a Royal Commission appointed for the purpose.

**Cabinet's Control of Debate.** At the second-reading debate, the members of the ministry lead the discussion, and explain the features of the bill. Because they can count on the loyal votes of their party majority, they may allot the time used for discussion by the use of the closure on debate. The control of debating time is achieved by several procedures: a positive limit on hours or days allowed (nicknamed the "guillotine"), the fixing of a timetable for the various sections of the bill (called "closure by compartments"), or the entrusting to the leaders and the Speaker the discretion to choose certain parts of the bill for discussion (called the "kangaroo closure" because it leaps from one important section to another, lightly omitting less controversial parts of the measure).

To state the whole process briefly, Parliament has an immense task every year, for it must pass a large amount of legislation bearing on financial, economic, social, and international problems. Since it is a large body of 640 members, it must be led and directed in this task in order to get it done. The Cabinet and the ministers, being members of either the House of Commons or the House of Lords, assume this task of leadership; they have at their disposal the expert personnel of the administrative departments to assist in framing measures, control of a large part of the time of the sessions which is reserved for public bills, and the discipline of the party majority to accelerate decisions. Ministers take the major share of the discussions at the second reading, conduct the bills through committee discussion, and defend the substance of the measure at the report stage.

**Commons' Control of Cabinet.** While the powers of the leadership are very great, so great that there has been criticism for some years of "Cabinet dictatorship," it must be remembered that the House still possesses sovereign powers. Questions can be used to express criticism of proposed policies; motions can be introduced to demand or forestall action; motions for adjournment can be used to precipitate general debates on projected legislation. The party majority is not a single block of obedient votes—though it may often give that appearance, as W. S. Gilbert in *Iolanthe* remarked many years ago:

> When in that House, M.P.'s divide,
>   If they've a brain and cerebellum, too;
> They've got to leave that brain outside,
>   And vote just as their leaders tell 'em to.

Actually, the government majority is made up of people holding various views. If the opposition can make effective criticism of policies, either legislative or administrative, a motion of want of confidence, or a substantial and significant change in a public bill, may recruit votes from disaffected members of the majority. The government may be defeated, and after a dissolution and an election, a new majority and new leadership may be entrusted with the task of developing different policies more in accord with public opinion. Naturally such a contest will not be brought about on minor matters; but when vital aspects of legislation are at stake, either the Cabinet or the House may act in a way which will lead to a dissolution and election.

## THE HOUSE OF COMMONS AT WORK: ITS ORGANIZATION

The way in which the House is organized to accomplish these tasks must be understood. During past centuries it has created a pattern of officers and committees, which serve to make orderly and efficient its transaction of business. There are sergeants-at-arms to prevent disorder (in feudal days, it was necessary to put a scarlet line down the aisle between the majority and the opposition to prevent the members from literally coming to swordspoints during the heat of debate); stewards and clerks to manage the affairs of legislative housekeeping; and quaint medieval survivals like the Gentleman Usher of the Black Rod.

**The Speaker.** The most important single officer is the speaker. Though he is elected, and persistently reelected, from one parliamentary constituency, he serves as an impartial and nonpartisan presiding officer—unlike the speaker of the United States House of Representatives who is a party leader as well as a presiding officer. Colonel Clifton Brown had to resign all hopes of a career in the Conservative party when he was elected speaker, August 1, 1945.[7] He was chosen by acclamation, as a mark of confidence by members of all parties. He will probably undertake for years the grave responsibilities of recognizing members wishing to speak, ruling motions out of order as dilatory or contrary to the rules (called Standing Orders), and assigning measures to committees for consideration. Tradition, firmly established since the early nineteenth century, has made the Speaker a trusted

[7] *London Times*, August 2, 1945.

arbiter of debate and conduct in the Commons. He will be rewarded for his service by a pension, and usually a peerage, when
he finally retires. Though he must give up all hope of being a
Cabinet minister, the dignity and prestige of the speakership are
ample compensations.

**Committees of the Commons.** The committees of the Commons
are less important than the committees of the American House of
Representatives. The reason is simple; the Commons, being
effectively led by the Ministry, transacts more business in the
full meetings of the House, and leaves less of importance to the
committees. Nevertheless, the committees contribute significant
services in the detailed consideration of legislation, and the work
of a Select Committee on Procedure, now sitting, seems likely to
increase the work of the Standing Committees in particular.[8]

The Standing Committees, as has been indicated, have much
to do with the consideration of public bills. These committees
have a large membership, usually forty to sixty members, chosen
by ballot of the House and reflecting proportionate party membership of the whole body. Meetings occur in the morning, and
the chief business is the preliminary discussion of public bills.
They are, in effect, small models of the whole House; their informal procedure gives opportunities for exploring thoroughly
all the aspects of a measure. If the legislation under consideration is an important part of the government program, a minister
or junior minister usually attends, and he may be the vehicle for
conveying Cabinet consent to modifications of the original proposals. There have been only four to six of these committees in
the past, though the number may be increased in the future.

**The Committee of the Whole.** Similar in function to the Standing Committees is the Committee of the Whole. This is simply
the House itself, sitting as a committee. The use of this device is
signalized by quaint traditional ceremonies. The motion is put
and carried that the House resolve itself into committee. This is
always done when the budget is under consideration and the
House resolves itself into a Committee on Supply to debate

[8] *London Times*, August 24, September 19, 1945.

appropriations, and into a Committee on Ways and Means to give consideration to taxes and borrowings. The speaker leaves the chair and the chairman of committees takes his place. The ceremonial mace, an impressive medieval symbol which lies on top of the table in front of the speaker's elevated chair, is taken by the sergeant-at-arms and placed underneath the table. The House debates the measure with informal short speeches, reaches a conclusion, and formulates a report. Then the motion is made to report back to the House. When it is carried, the speaker resumes the chair, the mace is restored to the top of the table, and the House, in its capacity as a sovereign legislative body, debates the report which it has made in its capacity as a committee. The practical advantages of this bit of play-acting are that as a committee, since they are not enacting laws, House members have the opportunity of accelerating consideration by informal procedures, and that the gains made in committee can be utilized in considering the report. Every legislative body, especially the American House of Representatives, makes use of this valuable legislative device.

**Select Committees.** The Standing Committees, and the Committees of the Whole, are always occupied with proposals for legislation. When the House is confronted by a complicated subject on which legislation seems necessary, a motion is often made to create a select committee (the present Select Committee on Procedure, which has been mentioned, is an example). Members of select committees are chosen usually by election, though the motion creating the committee may specify any appropriate method of choice of members. Such committees are small, rarely exceeding ten to fifteen members. Their procedure is judicial in character, using expert testimony, records, and memoranda. They often continue their sittings during a recess of Parliament, and may report their findings in the form of an analysis of the problem or a proposal for legislation, acceptable in general to the majority party. A similar result can be achieved by a royal commission, which has powers of the same character but whose members have been formally appointed by the king, actually by the

Cabinet on the basis of political experience, and expert knowledge of the problem under consideration.

The select committees on private bills perform similar functions, as has already been suggested, though they have a smaller
membership. It should be added that the private-bill committees
perform a very valuable service; they handle matters of local or
specialized importance, and save the time of the House for the
consideration of more significant questions of national policy.

### THE HOUSE OF LORDS: MEMBERSHIP AND FUNCTIONS

Though W. S. Gilbert remarked years ago that "noble statesmen do not itch, to interfere with matters which, they cannot
understand," the House of Lords continues to perform a useful
task in the process of legislation. The peers' usefulness is measured more by the influence they exert, however, than by the
power they may exercise. The powers of the House of Lords are
now strictly limited by the Parliament Act, passed in 1911, after
a severe contest between the two houses on questions raised by
the budget proposals of Mr. Lloyd George. The law permits the
House of Lords to prevent the passage of a law by as long a
time as two years—in effect, a two-year suspensive veto. This
veto has been used rarely. The Lords are able to achieve results
by the use of their influence, prestige, and experience, rather
than by employing their actual legal authority.

**Peers, Bishops, and Law Lords.** The membership of the House
of Lords is sufficiently distinguished, both for blood and for
brains, to make its recommendations carry considerable weight.
Some peers sit by right of birth, and ordinarily participate but
little in the work of the body. They do wield social prestige and
influence, however. The bishops, and the law Lords—judges in
the House of Lords sit as the highest appeal court—hold lifetime
places and represent ability and professional achievement. The
representative peers of Scotland and Ireland (the latter are dis-
appearing for there is no provision for their election by their
fellow peers) have some influence.

The most distinguished and often the most active members of the House of Lords are the recently created peers. Their honors are the rewards of distinguished service to the nation, or of business or political success, New Year's day and the king's birthday being the two occasions during the year when such honors are announced.

Actual attendance at meetings of the Lords is usually less than 100 out of a possible 700, and the result is careful and thoughtful consideration of legislation by an able and experienced group of men. While it cannot exert a decisive influence upon the general lines of policy, the House of Lords performs valuable services in improving the quality of measures, and usually a few peers are members of every Cabinet. The procedure of the House of Lords, over which the lord chancellor presides, is comparable to that of the House of Commons.

## PARLIAMENT IN WARTIME

In the preceding chapter the great extension of the use of administrative authority, particularly in the defense regulations, was described. At first glance this would seem to imply a corresponding reduction in the legislative authority of the House of Commons. Study of the parliamentary debates from the autumn of 1939 through 1944, however, shows that the activity of the House was as great as ever, and constantly reveals penetrating and critical discussion of the major acts of government policy. While any generalization is premature, it seems reasonable to predict that the function of the House of Commons may be changing as the result of the experiences of total war. What the debates reveal is less activity in the passage of detailed legislation, and more lively discussion of policy. The House of Lords undeniably declined in influence and prestige; but the Commons gained as it devoted its time to the broad objectives determinedly by the Cabinet.

It can be said without contradiction that there was no serious loss of responsibility for the formulation of programs of legislation and administration; the Parliament was as vigilant as ever in seeing that the Cabinet met the desires of the people. The voters, realizing that the importance of parliamentary debate was not dimished, continued to follow it with interest, and participated actively in by-elections.

## READINGS

The composition, and the working of Parliament has been the subject of so much excellent analysis that it is difficult to point to particular writings. The student can sample, with profit, some of the primary sources of information:

> *Parliamentary Debates,* called earlier *Hansard,* are the official reports of the proceedings of both houses. For the American student, the summary of these debates published daily in the London *Times* while Parliament is sitting, are more useful, since party designations are given.
>
> *Standing Orders of the House of Commons,* published every few years.

Three classic works repay reading:

> Bagehot, Walter, *The English Constitution,* New York, 1924.
>
> Dicey, A. V., *The Law of the Constitution,* 9th ed., London, 1939.
>
> Lowell, A. L., *The Government of England,* 2 vols., New York, 1921.

Some recent standard books are:

> Jennings, W. Ivor, *Parliament,* New York, 1940.
>
> Keith, A. B., *The Constitution of England from Queen Victoria to George VI,* London, 1940, Vol. I, chs. VI-X.

Two books critically analyzing the parliamentary system are informative and interesting:

> Laski, H. J., *Parliamentary Government in England,* New York, 1938.
>
> Muir, Ramsey, *How Britain Is Governed,* 3rd ed., Boston, 1935.

Footnote references and bibliographies in these books furnish many suggestions for further reading.

# CHAPTER 5

# POLITICAL PARTIES AND PARTY ORGANIZATION

IN THE last week of July 1945 English newspapers were able to release the results of the election which had been held on the fifth of that month. The delay in publication was due to the difficulties in determining the qualifications of the voters who had participated and in accurately counting votes in constituencies which had been contested by three or more parties. The general result of the election was quite decisive: the Labour party had received nearly twelve million votes and had secured a big majority of the seats in the House of Commons with over 390 members returned; the corresponding figures for the Conservative party were more than eight and one-half million votes and nearly 190 members; Liberals had polled two and one-half million votes and returned twelve members; various minor parties, divisions of the major parties, and independent candidates had received a little more than two million votes, and had secured about thirty-two seats.[1] This was the most substantial party victory since the election of 1906, and, because it meant that a Labour government would come into office, it was the subject of much discussion in England as well as in other countries which were interested in and concerned with what seemed to be a strong "swing to the left" in English politics and national leadership.

The simplest generalization about the election is probably the truest—the Labour party and its leaders won because the voters preferred them to the Conservative party, despite the picturesque and colorful campaigning of Mr. Churchill. All of us realize, if

[1] *London Times,* July 28, August 2, 9, 1945.

we focus our thoughts on the basic reasons for the Labour victory, that a partial answer may be found in the history and traditions of the parties. Further illumination comes from studying the organization and membership of these political associations. In any given election, the speeches of candidates and the election programs indicate the probable future policy of the leadership.

## The History of Party Alignments

**Ancestry of Parties.** In much the same way that Americans trace the ancestry of the present major parties back to the division between Federalists and Democratic-Republicans in the early days of the republic, so Englishmen find a fairly continuous line of descent for Conservatives and Liberals, beginning with the division between the Cavaliers and the Puritans in the civil war of the seventeenth century. The great question of royal authority versus parliamentary sovereignty divided the country into two camps which fought a civil war and continued the contest by means of political agitation after the Restoration. The names Tory and Whig, applied to much the same divergence of attitudes on the constitutional issue, arose in parliamentary debates in 1790, and served to identify the chief parties during most of the eighteenth century. While the Tory party had a wider membership than the Cavaliers, it showed a strong family resemblance to its political forebears, being willing to support the king, the court, and the church, and including in its ranks a large number of the country squires. The Whigs maintained the viewpoints of the Puritans, and represented in large part the new commercial and industrial community.

During the nineteenth century the extension of the suffrage after 1832 required the parties to enlarge the range of their political activities. Beginning with registration societies, which were needed to assist the new voters to establish voting rights under the complicated property qualifications which persisted throughout the century, both the Whig and Tory parties built up a national organization and enlisted the electorate in political activity. In the preceding century the contest between the two had been a parliamentary warfare, requiring discipline of the majority and the minority in the House of Commons; after 1832 the battlefield extended to the whole country, and the voice of the partisan rang through the land at election time.

**Conservatives and Liberals.** The Whigs claimed credit for parliamentary reform, but it was Sir Robert Peel who, in 1834, actually converted the Tories into the Conservative party, and put forward a cautious but constructive program of reform in the Tamworth Election Manifesto. Until the last quarter of the nineteenth century it was almost completely true for Gilbert's sentry outside the houses of Parliament to sing, "Every boy and every gal, that's born into the world alive, is either a little Liberal or else a little Conservative." With Mr. Disraeli the Conservative party began to appeal to young England. At the same time Mr. Gladstone elevated Liberalism into a dogma that assumed an almost religious intensity, so that one of his journalist critics said sarcastically: "I don't mind Mr. Gladstone always having an ace up his sleeve—what I do object to, is his saying that Almighty God put it there!"

**The Labour Party.** The two reform acts of 1867 and 1884 enfranchised nearly all of the working classes. Although Liberal Ministries introduced many reforms of living and working conditions, labor groups soon began to feel dissatisfied, particularly with legislation and court decisions which obstructed the organization of trade-unions and the use of collective bargaining in industrial relations. As a consequence of this dissatisfaction various socialist movements made their appearance, and it was they who became largely responsible for the establishment of the Labour party. Its political career began with the creation of a Labour Representation League organized by the Trades Union Council, which unsuccessfully presented candidates in the election of 1874. In 1906 various trade-union groups and socialist organizations united in the new Labour party, replacing the existing Labour Representation League of the Trades Union Council, and enjoyed a substantial success in the election of that year. Since that time the party has grown in membership and strength, actually obtained an uneasy control of the government in the 1920's and finally attained its present position of leadership following the 1945 election.

Generalizations about so complicated a subject as the history of political parties are always hazardous, because a simple statement is likely to be misleading. At the risk of inaccuracy, however, it may be said that during the twentieth century the Liberal party, as the advocate of change, has lost its position to Labour. Sir William Beveridge's attempt to revivify the party in 1945 failed at the polls; and the steady decline of Liberal membership and influence since World War I suggests that the future significant contest will be between Labour and Conservative. A number of former leaders of the Liberal party have left to join either the Conservatives or the Labour groups; and it is quite likely that the death of Mr. Lloyd George (Earl of Dwyfor) in the spring of 1945 presaged the end of the party he had led so skillfully.

### PARLIAMENTARY GOVERNMENT AND THE TWO-PARTY SYSTEM

Even in this brief summary one striking characteristic of English political history is manifest: for most of the time since the seventeenth century there have been only two major parties. It is not easy to explain this phenomenon, especially in view of the fact that in the Third Republic in France and in other European countries there were many parties, under somewhat similar conditions and comparable constitutional practices. Part of the explanation surely lies in history. During the existence of parliamentary government in England there has always been some predominant issue, or group of issues, upon which English voters have divided into two chief parties: Cavalier and Puritan opposed each other on the question of whether king or Parliament should be supreme; Whigs advocated electoral and social reform against the conservatism of Tories; Liberal reform programs were resisted by Conservatives. At the present time, socialist Labour must meet the opposition of capitalist Conservatives.

**Government vs. Opposition.** Minor circumstances have dramatized this conflict of viewpoints. The benches in the chamber of the House of Commons face each other, so that the majority of his majesty's government is confronted with the minority of his majesty's loyal opposition. The heckling of candidates in political meetings at street corners in towns and villages emphasizes the clash of party programs, and intensifies party loyalties. It should also be recalled that the traditional single-member constituencies have made it difficult for a minor party to secure adequate representation; the initial difficulties of the Labour party, and the present decline of the Liberals, are attributable to the misfortunes that a third candidate suffers in a three-cornered contest for one parliamentary seat.

The consistent practice of dissolution of the Parliament whenever a Cabinet loses its majority has also contributed powerfully to the maintenance of two major parties. Coalition governments, while frequent in English political history, are in the uncomfortable position of not being able to claim a clear mandate from the people. The persistent tendency is to settle an issue by taking it into an election campaign, where the supporters of the government and the adherents of the opposition argue the matter out in public meetings, on the air, and in the press. This practice of alignment into two groups has been so continuous and powerful that many shrewd and penetrating scholars of the late nineteenth and early twentieth centuries have argued that the two-party system is essential to the working of parliamentary government. The difficulties of conducting responsible government in France and Germany have been brought forward as additional proof of this generalization. Certainly it can be said with assurance that, whatever the underlying reasons, English practice steadily gravitates toward such a party alignment.

Part of the explanation for the two-party system may lie in the English temperament or character—if there is such a thing. The English, even as the Americans, are used to political groupings based upon tradition, inheritance of party loyalties, and willingness to compromise on minor issues in order to secure support for major policies. A scholar may look askance at descriptions of so vague a phenomenon as a national temperament. Nevertheless it does furnish at least a part of the explanation for the persistence of the two major parties (whatever their names or programs) in England and the United States. Whatever the explanation, the fact is unmistakable; and any satisfactory explanation must emphasize the influence of historical tradition and circumstance, while it includes political practice and national psychology. English parliamentary government seems to work most effectively when one major party acts as a critical opposition. The present drift of politics appears to be in the direction of putting the Labour and Conservative parties into these important roles.

## The Character of the Parties

It is fully as difficult to characterize English parties as it is adequately to summarize their history. Nevertheless it is necessary to form some conception of their platforms and their membership, if contemporary politics in Britain are to be understood at all. If the student will remember that the following generalizations conceal subtleties and distinctions which cannot be stated in brief—and probably cannot be stated at all, because they are buried so deeply in the minds and temperaments of party members—it is possible to learn a little of what might be called the nature of the principal parties.

**The Labour Party: Trade-unionists and Socialists.** The Labour party's program is one of economic and social reform, animated in considerable part by classic socialist doctrine. Mr. Attlee's Cabinet introduced legislation to nationalize the Bank of England before the end of 1945; present plans include nationalization of transport, coal mining, electric power production, and the manufacture of iron and steel. The party's origin is attributable in large part to the efforts of labor groups to maintain the status of trade-unions and their rights of collective bargaining. The party has always favored the extension of the educational system supported by the national government and the imposition of government regulation on big business enterprises, and has aggressively supported the social insurances throughout its history.

If this summary of party projects is carefully studied, it appears immediately that part of the plan is socialist in purpose, and part of it is merely economic and social reform. The ideas of English socialists have always displayed this mixture of purposes. The Fabian Society and its members—people like the Webbs, G. B. Shaw, G. D. H. Cole, and many others—have popularized the conception of gradual progress toward a socialist society, in which there would be no private ownership of productive property, either industrial plants or agricultural land. The announced program of the present Labour government is in complete accord with this traditional attitude.

It can be said, therefore, that the Labour party advocates a mixed program—and it certainly can be said that it has recruited a mixed membership. Many of its active members are, naturally, also members of trade-unions. The percentage of union membership in industry is quite high, ranging from 75 to 90 per cent of the workers in industry. Most trade-unions contribute funds to the political activities of the Labour party, and many of the leaders of the unions are also leaders of the party.

**Labour Party: Middle-class Supporters.** Nevertheless, though industrial workers cast many of the ballots counted for Labour M.P.'s, it would be a grave error to underestimate the influence of the middle- and upper-class members of the party. A few instances may be cited: Mr. Attlee is a solicitor by profession, that is to say, the equivalent of a successful practising attorney in the United States; Sir Stafford Cripps is a prominent barrister with a big professional income and influential business acquaintance; Mr. Hugh Dalton is a distinguished professor of economics. Such men represent the large number of solid citizens in business and the professions who support the reform proposals of the Labour party and who often hold quite advanced socialist views.

The Labour party membership, then, falls roughly into three

groups. The working-class membership, usually affiliated with the trade-unions, accounts for probably well over half the voting strength of the party, and furnishes a large proportion of the active party workers who attend meetings, help to canvass in election campaigns, and contribute funds in the form of a small fraction of their union dues. The use of union funds for political purposes is now regulated by the Trades Disputes Act of 1927, and it is necessary for each union member to "contract in," that is, sign an agreement with his union that part of the funds derived from dues may be used for this purpose, called a "political levy." Legislation to amend the Act of 1927 is now under consideration. A sizeable part of the membership of the party is the middle-class membership, sometimes organized in Socialist Leagues, or Social Democratic Associations, also contributing work, votes, and funds to the party. This membership includes professional people, part of the small-business community, agricultural workers and some small farmers. Associated with the Labour party in sympathies, but often willing to oppose parts of its program, is the Independent Labour Party, called the I.L.P. The views of its leadership are often more aggressively reformist than those of the general party membership, and it usually proposes its own candidates in a parliamentary campaign, and maintains a distinct organization in the House of Commons. The Labour party maintains a national headquarters and local committees in much the same way as do other English parties. These will be described when a typical parliamentary career is analyzed later in this chapter.

**Conservative Party: Members and Program.** The Conservative party—because of the history of the Irish question many of its members call it the Unionist or the Conservative and Unionist party—is the other major party, and furnishes at present most of the voting strength of the opposition in the present House of Commons. It has, as has been already explained, a much longer history than the Labour party, and in many ways is more difficult to characterize in terms of program and membership. The difficulties can be suggested by saying that Conservatism is as much an attitude, a tradition, or a cluster of long enduring social affiliations as it is a political party association.

The program of the Conservative party defies precise analysis. In the 1945 election the Conservative "Four-Year Plan" included maintenance of national control over transport and coalmining, extension of the social services, active government support for housing programs, and many other proposals which sounded very like the moderate socialist program of the Labour party. On the other hand, in past campaigns the Conservatives have actively supported plans for imperial tariff preference and for taxation and business subsidy schemes which appeared to be a very stiff-necked defense of capitalist enterprise. Perhaps the most accurate brief summary of the predominant attitude of the party would be that it is opposed to socialist planning, while it is ready to embrace quite extensive schemes for national regulation of important activities. One of Mr. Churchill's broadcasts, made before the end of World War II, may be taken as representative of these viewpoints. Speaking of the needs to be met in postwar Britain, he did not hesitate to use the word, "planning." He sketched projects for extending the social insurances, giving greater facilities for education, maintaining full employment, and rebuilding cities. While he warned against rash promises, he pledged himself and his party to far-reaching reforms.

The membership of the Conservative party can be separated into groups, although the groups are hard to distinguish. There are certainly many die-hard Tories, particularly in the country districts. The hunting, riding, and shooting county aristocracy made up of squires and large landowners is joined by a considerable number of smaller farmers and businessmen in small towns and cities, and all of them vote Conservative as much by instinct as by conviction. In the big industrial cities, members of the Federation of British Industries (an association comparable to the National Association of Manufacturers in the United States) and London's financial community (referred to as "the City") consistently support the cautious Conservative viewpoint. At the same time, as the program of the 1945 election showed, a

large fraction of the party subscribes to an enlightened Conservatism, and is ready to go far in reforms. For the last twenty years there has been a group of young M.P.'s, nicknamed the "Tory Socialists," who reflect the sentiment of an active reformist wing of the party. There are also many working-class people who vote for Conservative candidates because they believe in social reform but not in socialism.

A number of traditional institutions contribute strength to the Conservative attitude: the titled nobility, the established Church, the widespread affiliations of upper-class society. While the typical Tory is often pictured as a red-faced Colonel Blimp, equally representative would be an enlightened and liberal businessman, a scholarly university professor, or a public-spirited woman active in civic affairs.

**Liberal Party.** The Liberal party's situation has already been sketched in the short history of party development. It occupies an intermediate position, advocating reforms short of socialism, but unwilling to oppose change in the manner of some Conservatives. Its membership is much like that of the Conservative party; it has support from the upper classes, the middle classes, and the workers. Its weakness lies in the fact that it has insufficient support from any of these groups, and that it has difficulty in formulating a program distinct from that of the socialist Labour party and at the same time more decisive than the moderate reform program offered by progressive Conservatives. It has been losing members, votes, and leaders to the two major parties.

**Minor Parties.** Besides the Liberal party, there are a number of minor parties which show some strength in elections. Welsh Nationalists, Scottish Nationalists, and Ulster Nationalists represent provincial loyalties. The Communist party usually manages to return at least one M.P., and in 1945 elected two. The Common Wealth Party, organized in 1943 by Sir Richard Acland, and advocating a rather specialized kind of socialism, still maintains a little electoral strength. Fractions of two of the major parties, originating at the time of the National government of 1931, still persist: National Labour, and Liberal National. How long these separate wings of the parties can endure is problematical, now that the split in the parties has begun to heal, and fifteen exciting years have elapsed.

Finally, it must be noted that there are always a few Independents in every House of Commons: members who have deliberately refrained from affiliation with any party, and who have been able to achieve a personal victory in some constituency. As might be supposed, these men or women often have distinguished public careers, though it is unlikely that any of them could hold a ministerial post.

To summarize, the British political scene is at present dominated by two major parties: Labour and Conservative. One of these is sure to be in office, often with the support of some of the minor parties; the other, by the same token, is in opposition, aided by others of the minor parties. The minor parties continue to engage in political activity, in the hope that they will one day win major party status or succeed in inducing one of the major parties to carry out a part of their programs.

## THE PARTIES IN ACTION: THE CANDIDATE AND HIS ELECTION

All of the parties must maintain organization to achieve their purposes. This structure of the parties can be most vividly set forth in terms of an imaginary, but typical, political career.

An English election is won, not in the nation as a whole, but in the districts of the nation called parliamentary constituencies. The preceding chapter explained that a majority in the House of Commons—and with it the power to form a Cabinet and take over responsibility for policy—is the reflection of victories in a majority of the constituencies. Naturally, each of the parties is vitally concerned with the choice of candidates who stand a reasonably good chance of winning. In a "safe seat" where there is a long-established dominance for a party, almost any respectable and regularly affiliated candidate can win. In a "doubtful seat," personal merits and abilities may have a decisive effect.

**Local Party Committees.** Two party agencies participate in the choice of the person to contest a constituency. The local party committee, chosen informally by the party membership, is often able to select the candidate and place his name on the ballot. This is simple when the incumbent is ready to stand again, provided that he has a good record. However, the local committee may be confronted with a problem—the present M.P. intends to retire from politics, or he has been involved in some personal difficulty or political irregularity, and a new candidate must be found. Sometimes it is easy to find one within the party ranks in the locality. An active town or county councilor, a well-known citizen, a wealthy businessman who can contribute substantially to the expenses of the campaign—any one of these may be acceptable to the local party committee. These committees, it should be added, function in about the same way in each of the parties, but the membership varies from party to party. A Conservative local committee is likely to include several of the landed gentry, some local businessmen, a few workers; a Labour party committee is sure to include some of the local secretaries of trade-unions, a few professional or business people, and perhaps a few small farmers.

**The Central Office.** If the local committee finds itself in a difficulty, with no satisfactory candidate available or no agreement on one, it is likely to apply to the central organization of the party. Each of the national parties maintains in London what is called a central office. This is the national headquarters, roughly comparable to those of the Republican or Democratic National Committee in the United States. It differs from an American party headquarters in one important respect—because an election may occur almost any time, it is continuously active, not merely when there is a general election. The Labour party has several floors in a London building, called Transport House; the Conservative party is located in Bridge House, not far from the Houses of Parliament in Westminster. These party headquarters are what might be expected: a staff of secretaries, legal advisors, publicity agents, publication bureaus, committee headquarters, financial officers, and all the mechanism of a big nation-wide organization.

**Types of Candidates.** Suppose that the local committee of some party decides to apply to the national headquarters for suggestion of a candidate for the election considered likely to occur in the next few months. It writes, or sends a few of its members, to the central office. There the national secretary of the party has a nation-wide file of promising candidates: young men who have made distinguished careers in the debating societies of the universities, such as the Oxford Union or the Cambridge Union; retired business or professional men who have money enough to finance their own campaigns and who wish to enter upon a political career; trade-union secretaries who have made a reputation as able officials and whose friends might put up a little money for the campaign; journalists, authors, or scholars who have national reputations. These potential candidates have either approached the central office and asked for the opportunity to stand for Parliament, or national officers of the party, observing their abilities, have asked them if they would be willing to enter politics. The members of our local committee meet and interview several possible candidates, and finally decide to nominate and support one of them.

The well-established tradition that a member need not reside in the constituency he represents has made possible this wide recruitment of candidates. In the United States a member of the House or the Senate must, by the Constitution, live in the state he represents, but in England this is not the case. Very often a young man, just out of one of the universities with a distinguished record in his studies and in extracurricular activities, becomes acquainted with one of the party leaders. His family is ready, often eager, to have him make politics a career, and is willing to contribute to his campaign expenses. If he and his family have little money, but his abilities are clearly unusual, the national party organization, or his friends, may be willing to give financial assistance. As already stated, a business or professional man frequently will put up the money for a campaign because the prestige of a political career, and a genuine desire to serve the public, leads him into this new activity. In the Labour party—and occasionally in the Conservative or other parties—an effective performance in the leadership posts of the trade-unions makes a man a good candidate.

More should be said concerning the independent candidate. He (or she) possesses some of the qualifications described above, but is unwilling to affiliate with any one of the parties. In that case it is possible to contest any constituency, though the chances of success are diminished. But personal abilities and resources can overcome these obstacles, and an independent committee can be assembled in the constituency. Fourteen independent candidates won seats in Parliament in the 1945 election.

If our imaginary candidate won the election, he takes up his seat in the House of Commons. If he failed dismally, he may never have a chance to continue a political career. If he lost but made a creditable showing, he is regarded as more promising than ever; and he will probably have another opportunity, either at a by-election, or the next general election, to try again. Often his second chance may be in a more favorable constituency.

## The Parties in Action: The M.P.'s Parliamentary Career

Once in the House of Commons, our newly elected M.P. wants to get into the more important leadership functions of the party. This is equally possible whether his party won or lost the election; in the majority party the Ministry offers opportunities, in the opposition the "Shadow Cabinet" is the leadership group which will take office after some future victory. Even in the minor parties, or among the independents, the possibility of being chosen by a major party for a Ministerial post exists, as a reward for energy and ability demonstrated in the House and outside it.

Since the offside political career is so precarious, it is better to assume that our man is affiliated with one or the other of the major parties. It is likewise more useful to assume that he is a man. While it is true that recent Cabinets have included women, British politics is still predominantly a man's game. Finally, since it would be desirable to accelerate his progress for our convenience in observing it, let us assume that he comes into office as part of a nation-wide victory of his party, and that he is, consequently, a member of a government majority.

**Whips and M.P.'s.** The first obligation he must fulfill is easy: he must see the chief whip of his party, or the chief whip or one of the assistant whips will see him. All of these party officers hold government offices, and draw government salaries, and, though their duties are almost exclusively connected with the party organization in the House of Commons, they earn their pay in making the House efficient in the transaction of business. The chief whip holds the office of parliamentary secretary to the treasury, and the assistants hold office as junior lords of the treasury, and sometimes as financial officers of the royal household. The whips are also recognized as important in the general organization of the party, and spend a good deal of time in its Central Office. Corresponding to these government whips are the opposition whips, who are sustained in their arduous labors by the hope that their party will sometime achieve power, and then they will be rewarded by the salaries and perquisites which are now held by their opposite numbers.

The whips serve to keep the party majority in line. When an important division occurs—the House votes by "dividing," that is, the members march out into lobbies on each side of the chamber, choosing their lobby to indicate whether their vote is "yes" or "no" on the question—the whips serve as tellers, so that members are aware that their conduct is closely scrutinized and reported to the leaders of the party. The whips send around little notes to the members of their party, warning of the approach of significant divisions, underscored as many as three times to indicate the degree of obligation to appear and vote. This duty is one of their most essential tasks, for the necessary majority must be assured on all important government bills.

Our promising new member finds out quickly, however, that he has much more to do with these party officers than simple obedience to their instructions regarding voting. If he wants to speak on a question, he discovers that his chances are improved if the whips have been informed of his intention; if he wishes to introduce a motion, its progress is assisted by many arrangements which lie within the whips' control. Occasionally he is sought out by these same officers, and rebuked for indiscreet remarks in debate or impulsive statements to public meetings or the press.

Soon he is conscious of the fact that his merits are judged by these men, and that his occasional helpful remarks or suggestions attract the attention of party leaders. He sets himself, then, the task of impressing his fellow party-members in the House with his industry, ability, and good sense. He may even, if at all capable of it, strive for brilliance of expression and comment —though he is cautious in this respect, for although England always "expects every man to do his duty," she is likely to distrust him if he is too infernally clever about it. He learns fairly quickly, by studying the performance of his party leaders, that the best way to convince them and his colleages of his value, is to give the impression of slightly better-than-average abilities coupled with remarkable willingness to work hard at his job.

**The M.P.'s Work.** He also tends to develop a special field of knowledge as the best way of making himself useful to his party, to his country, and to himself. He may become, in an enlightened amateur way, an expert on government finance, putting in long hours of study and interviews of government officials; or he may build up a solid knowledge of local government problems, social insurance, or business regulation; or he may come to be a man exceptionally well-informed on the colonies, the dominions, or the vital aspects of foreign policy. If his gifts are truly unusual, he may set for himself the most difficult of all activities: gaining the reputation of being an effective all-round debater, able to say something sensible, lively, even witty, on most aspects of public affairs. If he makes a mark in the debates, serves intelligently on committees, votes faithfully on the right side of most important questions, his merits will attract the attention of the whips, and will be communicated to the leaders of the party. While this may seem at first glance a very high premium to set on speaking ability, it is only necessary to remember that the world of the twentieth century is, more than ever before, run by talk—the talk of business leaders in conferences, of labor leaders in industrial relations, of advertising men in developing promotion schemes, and so on.

**Junior Ministers.** Our young man does such things as these, and at the same time maintains satisfactory relationships with his home constituency so that he seems reasonably certain of re-election when the time comes round. He is soon—sometimes in his first term—regarded as "ministerial timber." He may have to survive a period when his party is in opposition, but he is invited to some of the conferences of the leaders, and feels confident that he is progressing in his political career. From then on his progress is fairly rapid—he becomes a junior minister such as one of the joint parliamentary secretaries of the Board of Trade, and acquires sound experience in meeting administrative problems. Then, provided he does not have the misfortune to suffer some conspicuous scandal (his domestic life must be above reproach) or is not forced by circumstances or his conscience into opposing his party's program on some major issue, he rises to one of the Cabinet ministries. Perhaps he may even become a prime minister.

## POLITICS AND PUBLIC LIFE

This picture of the mechanism of politics—the contemporary trends in British politics will be dealt with in a later chapter [2]—may properly be concluded with a few cautious generalizations. It has been suggested in this, and the preceding chapters, that the general tone of English public life is respectably high. Public interest in community affairs is lively and continuous, and the

[2] See Chapter 8.

quality of political leadership and administrative personnel is good. The pattern of politics contributes substantially to this situation.

In the first place, politics offers a career comparable to one in business or the professions. It recruits promising young people and energetic older people from the universities, the labor unions and working class organizations, the professions, and business. It offers advancement from the position of the M.P. to the greater prestige and salary of the Cabinet Minister. Like political activity in any country, it furnishes a chance to give real service to the nation, and it rewards that service more effectively than does the precarious career of politics in the United States. In addition to all this, the English community has been schooled by the developments of the nineteenth and twentieth centuries to the full realization that the public's business is of vital importance to the welfare and happiness of every private individual.

At the risk of offending the national sensibilities of the American student, it can be said that the average public performance of English leaders is somewhat higher in quality than that reached in the United States. Great statesmen are no more frequent in England than in America—but great statesmen are rare in every national community. The organization, the methods, and the membership of English parties give assurance that the average political career will display the characteristic British virtue of solid respectability—and as for the remarkable man his chances in England are as good as or better than in any other great state of the world.

### READINGS

As yet there is no satisfactory history of the parties. Some books, of the many special studies and general works on English government, may be cited:

Lowell, A. L., *The Government of England*, New York, 1921. vol. I, chs. xxiv-xx; vol. II, chs. xxxi-xxxvii.

Muir, Ramsey, *How Britain Is Governed*, 3rd ed., London, 1935.

Ostrogorski, M., *Democracy and the Organization of Political Parties*, rev. ed., 2 vols., New York, 1922. This is a classic work of scholarship.

Pollock, J. K., *Money and Politics Abroad*, New York, 1932. A very illuminating brief survey is given in the section on English parties, with emphasis on party financing.

A few specialized studies of the chief parties repay reading:

Brand, Carl F., *British Labour's Rise to Power*, Stanford University Press, 1941. A careful and objective history of the Labour party.

Feiling, K., *History of the Tory Party, 1640–1714*. London, 1924.

————, *The Second Tory Party, 1714–1832*. London, 1937.

Fyfe, H., *The British Liberal Party: an Historical Sketch*. London, 1928.

In addition to these, the biographies, and especially the autobiographies, of British statesmen shed much light on the nature of the English political career.

Finally, some source materials should be mentioned: the party manifestoes during the election campaigns, the official programs and publicity materials of the parties, the year books published by the major parties.

English newspapers and periodicals publish numerous articles analyzing the contemporary political situation. The names of a few are: *The London Times* (Conservative in outlook); the *Manchester Guardian* (Liberal); the *Daily Herald*, (Labour); the *Political Quarterly* (a scholar's journal); the *Contemporary Review;* the *Economist;* and many weeklies such as the *Spectator,* and the *New Statesman and Nation.*

## CHAPTER 6

# THE LAW AND THE COURTS

ONE of the most important daily tasks of any government is to provide for careful administration of the laws. In England, as in the United States, the average citizen constantly depends upon the courts, even though he may never be involved in litigation. His rights, in relation to those of other citizens, and his legal status in the community, depend upon continuous and equitable enforcement of law. Though administrative agencies may have a great deal to do with the conduct of his life, the defense of personal and property rights, and even of his general liberties, such as freedom of speech, depend upon effective action by the courts. Like all other English institutions, both the law and the courts are the product of a long historical development.

## THE DEVELOPMENT OF THE LAW

The extension of royal authority built up the system of the common law. In the twelfth century Henry I and Henry II made increasing use of the practice of sending out members of the *Curia Regis* to transact various aspects of the business of the realm in the counties. Often the council member was trained in the law and, besides handling various administrative matters, held court in the king's name, and tried cases. Since the king's courts offered orderly and impartial hearing of cases, brought to them under royal writs commanding the adjudication of disputes, the demands on these "itinerant justices" began to increase. But if the decision of any case was to be accepted in a particular locality, it had to be in accord with the feudal customs and long-standing traditions of the community. Consequently each justice acquired a knowledge of various local traditions. In order to avoid carrying in mind all the variations from one region to the next, the justices began to set down a system of law which would hold for many communities, and aided by the lawyers who accompanied them on their circuits, slowly built up the rules and precedents of the common law—"common" in the sense that it was a body of rules common to many districts. This development was made more extensive by the work of the lord chancellor and the royal courts at the nation's capital.

**Common Law and Equity.** Like any law rigidly based upon ancient custom and judicial precedent, the common law changed very slowly. Conditions changed more rapidly. At the end of the twelfth century and during the thirteenth, parliament lacked the power to make needed changes in the rules of the law. As a result subjects began to appeal to the king, as the fountain of justice, to redress injuries inflicted by the rigor of the common-law rules. Because such pleas were ordinarily heard by the lord chancellor, there was created another system of law, at first called "chancery," and later called "equity." For centuries these different rules were administered by different courts, but in the nineteenth century thoroughgoing reforms of the judiciary brought both sets of rules and pleadings under the jurisdiction of the regular law courts.

**Civil and Criminal Law.** The rules of law, both common law and equity, so far described, might be termed civil law, dealing as they did with the disputes between citizens regarding their personal and property rights. The development of the common law also created the rules of what is called criminal law, which is concerned with the administration of peace and order by the authority of the state. The distinction between the two kinds of law may be put simply by saying that civil law is the body of rules by which disputes between citizens are settled by the courts, criminal law defines the acts which are dangerous to the general public and punishable by the authority of the government. Quite frequently an act will be subject to both kinds of law; a motorist who injures a pedestrian has committed a crime and is punished by the state after being tried in the criminal courts; at the same time the pedestrian may sue him, under the rules of the civil law, for damages to redress the injury inflicted.

American as well as English law is based upon this historical development, for the English colonists brought this system of law to the Atlantic coast whence it later spread to almost all the states. In England, as in the United States, most of these ancient rules have now been enacted into statutes by legislative bodies, but the courts in both countries still make use of the precedents set up during centuries of experience in deciding cases.

## The Administration of Criminal Justice

There exists in England a hierarchy of courts to administer criminal law. The nature of the hierarchy may be described in terms of the history of cases.

**Justice of the Peace.** A minor crime or misdemeanour, a traffic violation or a petty theft, is heard first by a justice of the peace in a rural district, or by a stipendiary magistrate in a town or city. This procedure is comparable to the police court in an American city, or the court of the justice of the peace in a country town. Usually the case is heard in "petty sessions," with two or more Justices of the Peace on the bench, and the offender, if guilty, is sentenced. The "J.P.," as he is called, is appointed by the king, on the advice of the lord chancellor and the lord lieutenant of the country, but he is not skilled in the law, and places great reliance on his clerk, usually a trained solicitor, for information on points of law.

**Assize Courts.** The common-sense decision of the rural justice, advised by his clerk, is good enough for minor crimes, but for serious offences (called felonies) the offender is bound over for trial in the assize courts. These courts are held periodically in every county by judges of the High Court in London, traveling on circuit; and the full panoply of trial, with counsel and jury, is used for these cases. The pictures of these trials given in the English detective stories, familiar to nearly every American, is fairly accurate, though put in more dramatic terms than the average criminal case would justify.

If there has been an error in the trial, or new evidence appears, an appeal may be made by the defendant to the Court of Criminal Appeal which sits in London. In rare cases, a further appeal may be made to the House of Lords, the highest appeal court.

**The Police.** The apprehension of criminals, and the search for evidence, is carried on by the police force of the local government authority. The standards of police recruitment and training were raised during the nineteenth century by the supervision of the Ministry of Home Affairs, which has power to withhold grants of money made by the central government to the local government unless a satisfactory personnel is maintained. This explains the fact, so apparent to the American visitor in England, that all policemen, even in small country villages, look and sound much like the London "bobby." Local police authorities, confronted by a difficult investigation, may request aid from Scotland Yard, the central department of criminal investigation of the Metropolitan Police District of London.

The standard of law enforcement, both by the police and by the courts, is very high. This is due to a high quality of personnel, and to prompt and simple procedures. Equally important is the desire of the English citizen to have an orderly community, so that there is genuine public support for careful administration of criminal justice.

## THE ADMINISTRATION OF CIVIL JUSTICE

**County Court.** The County Court is the most readily accessible court for the British citizen who finds it necessary to resort to law for the collection of a claim or the adjustment of a small property conflict. The judge has been appointed by the Crown, and is skilled in the law. The court gives prompt and careful hearing of cases, but its jurisdiction is limited by the amount of money at stake in the litigation, usually from £100 to £200. Ap-

peals lie from this court to the Court of Appeals, and thence to
the House of·Lords on difficult points of law.

**High Court.** Where larger amounts are involved, it is necessary
to take the case to the High Court, which sits in London. This
court is organized in several divisions, for different types of cases.
The judges have been appointed by the Crown from the leaders
of the legal profession, and a very high standard is maintained.
Appeal is made to the Court of Appeals, and thence to the House
of Lords.

## The Legal Profession

The administration of law, both criminal and civil, depends
upon lawyers as much as it does on courts and judges. The legal
profession, much like the law itself, reflects traditional development. It is divided into two branches, barristers and solicitors.
The solicitor is trained as a legal adviser, having been "articled"
to a practising solicitor for a period of five years, and then having
been admitted to practice after passing examinations set by the
Law Society. The Law Society is an unofficial association, but
most members of the profession belong to it. With some regulation by laws and with some supervision by the judges, it establishes most of the rules governing the conduct of solicitors, and
sets the standards of the profession. A large number of solicitors
have had training in the law schools of universities before beginning their apprenticeships. They handle a great deal of legal
business for their clients, give advice on matters of law, and act
as business agents.

**Solicitors and Barristers.** Solicitors, however, do not argue cases
in the higher courts, for they have not been formally admitted to
the bar. If a client is involved in litigation, either civil or criminal,
his solicitor "briefs" a barrister for him. The barristers have usually had training in the law schools of the universities, and at the
same time have become members of the Inns of Court in
London, which maintain the standards of this part of the legal
profession. After studying law and passing examinations set by

"the benchers," the senior governing boards of the Inns, the youthful barrister begins by helping to prepare cases for a successful and established practitioner. Eventually he wins recognition and prestige and builds a practice of his own. When his reputation is great enough he may become a King's Counsel (K.C.) and can hope that eventually he will be appointed a judge. The judges are recruited from the barristers, and a judgeship is an appointment much sought after, for it means a secure and honored place and an important function to perform in the administration of justice. The High Court and Appeal Court judgeships are, of course, the greatest honors to be gained; but the County Court judgeships are highly regarded, and are filled by able and experienced men.

**The Bench.** The position of the judge with this experience and training contributes greatly to the excellent performance of English courts of law. Because of his secure tenure (only an address of the two houses of Parliament to the king will remove him from office), he is willing to assume active direction of the procedure of his court. He acts as a true presiding officer, often intervening in the examination of witnesses in order to see that the ends of justice are served. His distinction as a barrister before his appointment by the Crown, makes opposing counsel respectful of his action. The justices of the higher courts also serve as a council to advise the lord chancellor regarding the rules of procedure in the courts. The total result of all these arrangements ordinarily impresses the American lawyer visiting an English court, for the conduct of trials is remarkably simple and businesslike, and the procedures are swift and efficient.

With all these merits, English justice suffers from one very grave defect—it is costly. Litigation is expensive, and the costs are paid by the loser in the suit, so that there is real reluctance to go to court unless the case is important or the client is wealthy. The poor man is helped somewhat by legal-aid societies; and for some time there has existed a movement, which includes many progressive members of the legal profession, to reduce the costs of the administration of justice.

## The Rule of Law and the Rights of the Citizen

Behind the system of courts and law there exists a general presumption, which was aptly named "The Rule of Law" by a great legal scholar.[1] It refers to what might be called the spirit of the law and the general intention of the courts in enforcing it. Briefly stated, the rule of law means that the laws shall apply equally to all citizens, including officials of the government. By implication it also means that the rules of the law are uniform, publicly known, and applied equally to all cases.

**Habeas Corpus.** There are no general constitutional guarantees of citizen's rights as provided in the federal and state constitutions of the United States. The protection of liberty, freedom of speech and association, freedom of worship, and similar rights is achieved in England by particular laws. A good example is found in the Habeas Corpus acts, which have been on the statute books since 1679, with further elaboration in 1816. These require that any citizen, if arrested, can demand to be brought before a magistrate, and cause shown for his detention. The effect of the use of the writ of Habeas Corpus is to guarantee the citizen against false and improper arrest, but this liberty derives from the law, not from a constitutional guarantee such as those set forth in the first ten amendments to the U. S. Constitution.

**Suits against Officials.** One final aspect of the system of law must be briefly explained, partly because a similar situation exists in American law. While the British citizen can readily and easily bring suit against a government official, it is very difficult for him to sue the government itself. The reason is historical in nature: to bring such a suit in the regular courts would mean a proceeding against the king, and by the ancient tradition of the law, "the King can do no wrong." An injured citizen can petition the Crown through the secretary of state for home affairs, and, if the petition is granted a contractual claim or one of similar nature will be heard in the courts. If the award goes against the Crown, the Treasury pays the claim out of funds

[1] Dicey, A. V., *The Law of the Constitution,* ch. IV.

granted by Parliament for the purpose. Much the same presumptions in favor of the government exist in American law; it has long been held by the Supreme Court that the government cannot be sued by its citizens, in its own courts, unless it consents to the suit.

## The Courts and the Law in Wartime

The rights of the citizen were somewhat reduced by the necessities of the wartime emergency. Early in World War II the home secretary was empowered by the Defence Regulations to order the detention of any person who, in his opinion, might be dangerous to the security of the state,[2] and under this regulation a number of people were detained in prison. This was deemed necessary, but the action of the home secretary was subject to constant scrutiny and question in the House of Commons, and the number of persons detained in prison or under police surveillance was never very large.

While the power of the courts was curtailed by the extension of administrative powers of an emergency character, it was greatly increased in another way. Under various emergency acts, powers were conferred upon the courts to modify the ordinary provisions of the law to take account of emergency situations. A good example is the cases of war damage which affected tenant-landlord relationships. Courts were empowered to modify leases and contracts in such a way as to reduce the hardships which might arise from the bombing of property, the interruption of normal business relationships, and the like.[3] In addition to powers of this kind, provision was made for the establishment of war-zone courts, by which the services of the courts could be made available to the citizen, even under the disturbed conditions of defense areas and destruction by bombing

[2] Defence (General) Regulations, 18a, 18b, S. R. O. 1939, no. 1681, amended and extended in following years.
[3] Courts (Emergency Powers) Act, 1939, 2 and 3 Geo. 6, c. 67. Amended in subsequent years.

## The Courts and the Law: Summary

It is hardly possible in a chapter to more than sketch the machinery of the courts, and to suggest the nature of the administration of justice. In both criminal and civil justice, England has a long tradition which is familiar to every British citizen. The orderliness of the British community is attributable in large part to the historical influence of the developing system of law, but it is also due to careful administration by the courts, in which the high quality of the bench and the well-established standards of the legal profession play a large part. It is not surprising, therefore, that every Englishman regards his home as his castle, and that he rests assured that every right he possesses, and every action of government toward him, is controlled by the presumptions of the rule of law.

## Readings

The story of the development of the law, and the origin and growth of the system of courts, has been the subject of an extensive literature. Some works which give detailed information, and in every case many suggestions for further study, are listed below:

Ensor, R. C. K., *Courts and Judges*, Oxford, 1933. A brief discussion of the courts and the judges, still up-to-date in substance, though not in details.

Dicey, A. V., *The Law of the Constitution*, 8th ed. London, 1920. Chapters IV-XII give a classic analysis of the rule of law.

Jackson, R. M., *The Machinery of Justice in England*, New York, 1940.

Patterson, C. P., *The Administration of Justice in Great Britain*, Austin, Texas, 1936.

Robson, W. A., *Justice and Administrative Law*, London, 1928. A penetrating analysis of the work of administrative authorities and a comparison with judicial procedures.

# CHAPTER 7

# LOCAL GOVERNMENT

BOTH in England and in the United States the citizen's most important and immediate contact with government is the local administration of the area in which he lives. In both countries this is the authority which polices his conduct, regulates his health and living conditions, and provides the services of education, sanitation, lighting, and many others, on which he depends every day.

In addition, local government offers the best training in public affairs for the average citizen, and often for the future political leader. In both England and the United States there is a long tradition of self-government in local communities, the American town and county being in many ways a political descendant of the well-established institutions of British government, transplanted to the New World by the early settlers. In order that their present day operation may be fully understood, the history of these units of neighborhood government should be reviewed briefly.

## THE HISTORY OF LOCAL GOVERNMENT

The institutions of the Anglo-Saxon kingdoms furnished the pattern for the organization of local government in England. The shire, the predecessor of the modern county, was largely an autonomous community. The freemen assembled periodically to choose officers to carry on the business of the community, and it seems likely that there was a good deal of democratic determination of action, though the larger landholders naturally had a predominant influence. Besides the shire there was the hundred, a small district similarly governed, and there was also the borough, or town, in which the community had a considerable voice in managing its own affairs. The creation of an established church led to the appearance of the smallest of the units, the parish.

William the Conqueror imposed a moderate amount of central-government supervision upon these traditional communities, but the essential substance of local autonomy was maintained. Under the rule of the Tudors the responsibilities placed upon local authorities were greatly increased, and, though the supervision of the national government was simultaneously extended, the final result was to make local government more active and important in the life of every community. Reforms enacted during the course of the nineteenth century, beginning with the Municipal Corporation Act of 1835 and continuing through a series of statutes, slowly untangled the chaos of special areas and clarified the pattern of local government authorities. In 1929 and 1933 comprehensive legislation gave a fairly systematic pattern to the areas, powers, and functions of local authorities, and defined with some precision the financial aid given by the Treasury to local authorities.

## THE AREAS AND COMMUNITIES

An administrative map of England shows the country divided into sixty-two administrative counties, corresponding roughly to the ancient shires and bearing the ancient names: Devonshire, Lancashire, Derbyshire, and the like. Dotted about on this map are over eighty large cities, which are called county boroughs and combine the functions of both city and county. Within each of the administrative counties there exist boroughs (in America these would be called towns or municipalities), urban districts, and rural districts. In all of these districts there are parishes, which perform minor functions of government. For example, every English family lives in a parish, participates in the parish government, and depends upon it for minor government services. At the same time the parish of its residence is situated in an urban or rural district, the government of which concerns the family in many important ways: elementary education, streets, public utilities, and the like. This district is situated within one of the counties, and the authorities of the county council direct a further number of governmental activities: highways, secondary education, health, and police functions, which are county-wide in extent.

**Local Finance.** These services of the various local governments naturally have to be paid for, so the family pays "rates" (taxes in America) to the parish, the district, and the county in which its property lies. The local ratepayer, however, does not pay the full cost of local government; the national government contributes funds under a scheme of grants, called block grants, which flow into the treasuries of these local authorities. The block grants work under such a complicated scheme that the chancellor of the exchequer remarked in his budget speech in Parliament in the spring of 1946 that it required the training of an expert mathematician fully to understand the system. The English community has been committed for many years to the idea that when local governments receive aid for the maintenance of necessary services they are obligated to meet requirements of satisfactory performance in health, education, police, and other activities. These requirements are enforced by national and local officials, who inspect the operations and report on the quality of administration.

## CENTRAL SUPERVISION OF LOCAL GOVERNMENT

What has just been said suggests that there is a fair amount of supervision of local government by the national government. The work of inspection and supervision is carried on by a number of the ministries. The Ministry of Health possessed most of this power during the nineteenth century, and still retains, besides its duties with regard to health conditions, many of the responsibilities once vested in the Local Government Board, which was for a long time part of this ministry. The Board of Education requires satisfactory standards of schooling throughout the nation, and under the new Education Act of 1944 has increased authority. The Board of Trade has a great deal to do with municipally owned and managed utilities: water supply, gas and light, and similar services. The recently created Ministry of Town and Country Planning will take over significant functions with respect to housing, recreation areas, and other types of planning. The Treasury has always had wide powers over local borrowings. This incomplete list is proof that quite a large number of local activities are subject to inspection, advice, and financial and administrative supervision by the various ministries of the central government.

The general intention behind this system of central-government supervision and aid is maintenance of what was once termed a "national minimum" of services. The block grants from the Treasury are calculated, in considerable part, upon the needs of each local community: a poor community without much rateable property will receive more funds than a rich city which is better able to keep its performance at a satisfactory level. The regulations issued by the central ministries are designed to sustain a reasonably good standard in all areas.

## LOCAL COUNCILS AND PUBLIC PERSONNEL

**Councilors and Aldermen.** While national power is used to impose responsibility, it is not exercised to suppress local initiative in community affairs. The tradition of self-government is well-ingrained in every village, town, and county. The eligible voters in each area participate in the election of a council, which holds office for three years. In many parishes the business is carried on by a general meeting, which all voters may attend. In districts, towns, and cities the council election arouses considerable interest. The council, when elected, chooses a group of aldermen, partly from its own membership, partly from outside the council. The aldermen, a group one-third as large as the councilors, serve for a six-year term. They sit in the meetings of the council, serve on committees, and perform the same duties as their council colleagues, their longer term giving continuity to the work of the body as a whole. The mayor is elected by both groups, and serves for one year as a chairman and formal executive head of the government.

With the exception of those parishes which use parish meetings, all the areas are governed by these locally elected bodies. The general character of the membership is high; solid citizens with business and professional experience willingly serve their local communities. Politics in most communities is nonpartisan in character, though there is some activity by national party organizations.

**Committees.** One of the chief reasons that a responsible citizen is willing to assume these duties is the way in which the work of the councils is carried on. The real job of administering the affairs of the community is done in meetings of committees, of which there are a large number. Many of the committees are required by law, and are called statutory committees. Meetings are held frequently and, with health regulation, education, policing, town planning, and public works as the subject of discussion and action, are sufficiently important and interesting as to enlist the activity of their members. At the same time, the public officials in charge of the actual administration are well-qualified and carefully chosen, so that any committee may rely upon the skill and experience of the administrative staff. The committee on education has the advice and recommendations of the education officer to assist it in making decisions; the watch and ward committee deals with the chief of the police forces; the health committee relies upon the medical qualifications of the health officials.

**Expert Administrators.** The tradition of competence for salaried local administrative officers goes back to the reforms of the mid-nineteenth century, when statutory qualifications were set up by law to provide a satisfactory standard of performance. Since then, associations of local government officials, by encouraging training programs which lead to professional qualification, have done much to attract a good level of ability into the administrative staffs of the local authorities. Town clerks, medical officers, managers of municipal utilities, and the others, who hold office indefinitely, rise in their professions by promotion in the service of a large city or by moving from a small community to a larger one.

This combination of an expert trained staff with the elected, unpaid councilors and aldermen has imparted to English local government the same benefits which the national government derives from the association of ministers and permanent officials. The needs and desires of the community are expressed by its representatives chosen in elections; the accomplishment of technical tasks is assured by the training and experience of the administrative officials. A similar development in city government has been taking place in the United States during the course of the twentieth century. The city-manager type of government which has been adopted in many American cities, and the county-manager or county executive in a few American counties, is an effort to secure the same combination of public responsibility and administrative competence which has been built up in English localities during the nineteenth and twentieth centuries.

There has been no intention in this description to suggest that the English have devised an ideal pattern for the conduct of local affairs. The most cursory reading of journals and periodicals devoted to this subject or of the national newspapers would immediately reveal serious problems and severe criticisms of the ways in which situations are met by local authorities. Nevertheless, the usual performance in villages, cities, and counties has been good. Public interest has been well-sustained, and public administration has been careful and honest.

## LOCAL GOVERNMENT IN WARTIME

The war placed as great a strain upon the various communities as it did upon the national government. The immediate effect was to impose a staggering number of duties upon every local authority. Civil defense had to be organized, fire precautions had to be increased, and essential public utilities had to be maintained under emergency conditions. At the same time the national government greatly extended its control over the work of the local governments, but increased the financial aid given by the national treasury. Twelve regions were defined; and regional commissioners were entrusted with large powers of coordination and supervision of the activities of the local authorities within the regions. In vitally important activities, like fire-fighting and air-raid defense, the authority of the central government was widely exercised.

**Wartime Coordination and Postwar Possibilities.** While the story of the war is still incomplete, the general observation can be made that the local governments, with some national aid, were entirely adequate to meet the problems created by bombing, evacuation of city populations, and preparation for invasion. The good quality of local administrative officials, and the acute public concern were sufficient to meet the many problems which arose. It is not unlikely that many of the changes introduced during the war will persist. Successful coordination of local services may be as valuable in peacetime as it was in the face of air war. The movement of population into the centers of war industry may well require an alteration of the boundaries of the traditional local areas. Extension of the social services, by policies such as those embodied in the Education Act of 1944, may lead to new duties and new financial aids to the various local government bodies, particularly under Labour leadership.

While it is too soon to predict future developments, it is reasonable to assume that the range of activity of local government and the relationships between areas will change materially from what they were under the provisions of the acts of 1929 and 1933. And it is equally reasonable to assume that traditional local self-government, having been justified by the vigor and energy displayed by towns, counties, and parishes throughout World War II, will continue. Self-government has a long past running back to the ancient customs of the Anglo-Saxon kingdoms, and a creditable record of performance in the nineteenth and twentieth centuries. Even if new conditions impose new requirements, the active public interest of the English town or county will continue to demand that a considerable range of activity be left to the autonomy of the local community.

## READINGS

The subject of local government, being somewhat specialized, is covered by a truly immense literature. It is possible to mention only a few books, which will serve to give further suggestions to the student:

Anderson, William, ed. *Local Government in Europe,* New York, 1939. Chapter I, written by R. K. Gooch, gives an excellent brief description of English local government, and a valuable bibliography of the subject.

Finer, H., *English Local Government,* New York, 1934.

Clarke, J. J., *Outlines of Local Government of the United Kingdom,* 13th. ed., London, 1938.

The periodical *Public Administration,* published in London, is devoted to local government problems in large part. *The National Municipal Review,* published in New York, frequently contains good discussions of English local-government problems.

CHAPTER 8

# PROSPECTS FOR BRITAIN AND THE EMPIRE-COMMONWEALTH

As a European nation, England plays an important role in world affairs; as Great Britain, the leader of the Empire and the Commonwealth, her influence internationally is far greater. The total population of the Empire-Commonwealth is approximately 558 million, and the total area some 13 million square miles. These peoples and territories are scattered over the whole earth, and include nearly one quarter of the world's population and nearly one quarter of its area. When it is remembered that these territories contain a large share of the most important industrial raw materials, and that their locations are of great strategic value, the significance of the Empire-Commonwealth in world affairs is easily recognizable.

No discussion of Britain, therefore, can omit description of the Empire and the Commonwealth, although it is hardly possible in a brief account to more than suggest the complexity of the relationships between the various communities of this great association which have been built up during the course of centuries. Nevertheless, the significance of the subject requires analysis of its most important aspects, however difficult it may be to state them concisely.

## THE HISTORY AND THE PATTERN OF THE EMPIRE-COMMONWEALTH

The founding of the Empire began in the seventeenth century. Early in that century the first English settlements were made on the Atlantic seaboard of North America. At the same time the East India and African Companies began to carry English trading operations down the coast of Africa and on into India. It must be remembered that the expansion of national power by settling colonies and by establishing trading posts was a commonplace of all the national states of the time; the British competed with the French and the Dutch in both activities. By the end of the seventeenth century a British Empire had made extensive claims and during the first part of the eighteenth century had achieved a dominant place in the world.

**Origins of Self-government and Trusteeship.** The successful revolt of the American colonies at the end of the eighteenth century was accompanied by a change of viewpoint in England toward colonial empire. The doctrines of laissez faire, so effectively expounded by Adam Smith, combined with the industrial and commercial expansion of the industrial revolution, led to the abandonment of mercantilist policies in England. A quite widespread conviction arose that the normal history of empire should show progressive advance toward independence on the part of all colonies. This change of opinion occurred, paradoxically, while more territories were being acquired. In India, and in the many island possessions, it was impossible for England to withdraw immediately from her earlier conquests, for investments, obligations to the native population, and the creation of a system of imperial administration had involved the nation too deeply. In the early part of the nineteenth century the progress toward complete self-government on the part of Canada, Australia, and New Zealand was begun—on the assumption that these communities would show a life history like that of the American colonies. The Durham Report of 1839 proposed self-government for Canada, and similar developments appeared in other territories which had been settled by Englishmen.

In the latter part of the nineteenth century England participated in the imperialist activities of the other European national states. Further acquisitions of territory were made in Africa; concessions and trading ports were secured in China. The idea that all subject territories should eventually achieve self-governing powers persisted, however, and was embodied in the policies which English historians of the Empire have called the "principle of trusteeship." After the end of the Boer War in 1902, South Africa acquired a status comparable to that of Canada; and in the imperial conferences before and after World War I the principles governing dominion status were gradually established. At the same time reforms were undertaken in India, in 1911 and 1919, which began to confer some real powers of self-government upon the Indian communities. Similar projects for native self-rule appeared in other parts of the Empire. The final result of this long and complicated history was the creation of what may properly be called the Empire-Commonwealth.

**Types of Territories: Colonies, Protectorates, Dominions.** Because the status of the various territories is the product of a long development in each community, it is extremely difficult to generalize about the present pattern of relationships between the home government and the colonies and dominions, and between the different parts of the whole association. But the different areas can be classified in three broad categories. The territories which are administered in large part by British authority, centering in the office of the Secretary of State for Colonies, are the colonies and the protectorates like Tanganyika and Nigeria in Africa, the Malay States in the Indonesian area, Gibraltar and Malta in the Mediterranean, the small islands in the southern Atlantic such as the Falklands, or the many island groups in the Pacific, the Fiji Islands or the Gilbert Islands. Though the legal status of colonies differs from that of protectorates, both have a similar relationship to the Colonial Office. The second classification would comprise India and Burma, great communities which have considerable powers of self-government under the reforms of the twentieth century, but in which British influence and authority are powerful. The importance of these two territories is reflected by the fact that there exists in the home government the secretaryship of state for India and Burma, bearing important responsibilities for policy concerning the government of both.

The third category can be described as the British Commonwealth of Nations, and includes the self-governing communities
of Canada, Australia, New Zealand, South Africa, Newfound-
land (after a brief loss of powers of self-government due to her
own acknowledged financial problems), and the Irish Free State,
now called Eire. Over this last-named group the British government has no significant powers; but the association between these
communities is close and enduring, expressed in political, diplomatic, and economic ties. If the difficulties between the native
states, and the Hindus and Moslems, can be overcome, it is
quite likely that India and Burma may achieve independence
during the course of the next few years, though they may retain some association with the Commonwealth.

This rough classification of the territories is useful in showing that their relationships to the home government are diverse.
The phrase, "the British Empire," often creates the mistaken impression that all the areas colored red upon the map of the world
are possessions of the home government. Actually the colonies
and protectorates, while sometimes subject to completely British
administration, often possess, as in the case of Ceylon and
Malta, very considerable powers for governing their own affairs.
In the third category of this loose classification are the completely
independent dominions—the neutrality of Ireland during World
War II demonstrates the independence of these communities.
India, while still lacking the full powers of a dominion, controls
much of the work of local and provincial government through
elected councils, and much of the tariff and financial policies
of all her provinces and states. Recently Prime Minister Attlee
announced in the House of Commons that India will become
completely independent in 1948.

A short summary cannot possibly convey the diversity and
complexity of the constituent parts of the Empire-Commonwealth. What has been said will serve to show that slow growth
through hundreds of years, combined with a fairly steady intention to pursue a policy of trusteeship and grant more powers
of self-government to the many communities, has developed

a pattern in which stability has been achieved by permitting a wide range of different relationships with the home government.

**Imperial Ties and Economic Relations.** The ties which unite these parts of the Empire and the Commonwealth are not easy to define. The Crown serves as a symbol of unity, and the administrative powers of the ministries of Colonies, and of the Dominions, sometimes impose requirements of uniform action. The substantial British investment in economic enterprises in these scattered territories, and the facilities of finance and trade offered by the English business community, are of value to England and to all the parts of the Empire-Commonwealth. It should not be supposed, however, that trade and finance are monopolized by the home community—about 40 per cent of England's exports go to territories lying within the Empire-Commonwealth, and less than 30 per cent of English imports come from those sources. The Ottawa Agreements, negotiated in 1932, arranged for some degree of imperial preference in tariff policies, but a large share of the trade of every one of these communities is carried on with countries outside the Empire-Commonwealth.

Probably the most influential bonds of association in this widespread community are intangible. The dominions have inherited laws and customs which form a basis of sympathetic association with the home government and the other self-governing communities; the practice of trusteeship, however fluctuating, has bred confidence in the colonial territories and the protectorates. Despite the frictions engendered by rising national feeling in India, Burma, or the islands of the South Pacific, the possibilities of maintaining association appear to be favorable.

## BRITAIN'S POSTWAR PROBLEMS

The situation of Britain and the Empire-Commonwealth during the period of transition following World War II will surely be difficult. The most serious problems arise from the economic position of the English community. The industrial development of the nineteenth century, in which English industry and commerce enjoyed the advantage of a long lead in the development of large-scale industry, now produces a serious, and even dangerous, economic and social crisis.

**Population and Exports.** The expansion of English industry and commerce during the nineteenth century was accompanied by a four-fold increase of population—the present population of the United Kingdom is over forty-five million, and the population of the whole of the British Isles is very nearly fifty million. So large a number of people can not find employment and food unless a large foreign trade is maintained. Every year before World War II there was a constant inflow of payments of interest and dividends on overseas investment, but that important part of the British trade balance will nearly disappear in the postwar years, since most of these investments were sold to meet the needs of supply for the conduct of the war. Therefore present purchases of food and raw materials must be financed by exports of manufactured goods. The best estimate that British economists and government agencies can make for the future shows a need for a 50 per cent increase in exports, in order to maintain the economic community of the British Isles as a going concern, with a standard of living comparable to what has formerly existed.[1]

**Socialist Planning.** Faced with this situation, the Labour government is proposing quite far-reaching schemes for government regulation and direction of a number of basic industries, extension of the social insurances, and reorganization of the great export industries under government leadership. Broadly speaking, the existing leadership is proposing to experiment with socialist planning to meet the needs of the English community in the coming years. Conservative opposition to the government's proposals has concentrated so far on criticism of these projects, rather than on the expression of fundamental objections which would arise from a defense of capitalism. In the election of 1945

[1] For a good general discussion of this economic problem, see George Soule, *America's Stake in Britain's Future*, New York, 1945.

the Conservative leadership put forward a "Four-Year Plan" which resembled, in many of its suggestions, the program of the Labour party.

While any prediction about the future course of government is hazardous, it is worth while to explore briefly the implications of the present situation. Satisfaction of England's needs for the next few years clearly depends upon the stimulation of exports. To meet this necessity the leaders of both parties are proposing government aid and regulation to maintain a high per cent of employment, an active and productive industry, and a level of income for the people which will make possible increased education, better housing, and wider social insurance. The debate between the two major parties seems likely to revolve about ways and means of achieving these goals, rather than any doctrinaire defense of either socialism or capitalism.

## RECENT PARTY HISTORY

**Conservative-Liberal Coalition.** Some illumination of these future possibilities is furnished by the history of English politics for the last two decades. World War I was conducted by a coalition of the Conservative and Liberal parties. The problems of reconstruction following that war were first met by a coalition led by the wartime Liberal Prime Minister, Mr. Lloyd George, following the so-called "khaki election" of 1918. Conservatives finally withdrew from the support of this government, won the general election of 1922, and formed a cabinet under the leadership of Mr. Bonar Law. In this election the Liberal party split into two groups, one under the leadership of Mr. Lloyd George, the other under Mr. Asquith. The Labour party, with a parliamentary membership of 142, became the most coherent and effective opposition group. The Prime Minister's health failed at the end of the first nine months, and he was succeeded by Mr. Stanley Baldwin. Mr. Baldwin's views on the tariff question— he favored a form of moderate protection—necessitated, in his opinion, a new election to secure a mandate from the electorate.

The Cabinet had suffered loss of public support during its term of office, and the election held in 1923, resulted in the end of the Conservative majority in the House of Commons. The Liberal and Labour parties, acting in coalition, placed the first Labour ministry, led by Ramsay MacDonald, in office.

**The First Labour Cabinet.** The difficulties of this first Labour ministry sprang in large part from the fact that it did not control a true majority. The Conservatives had the largest membership in the House of Commons, with 258 seats; the Labour party held 191 seats, and the Liberals, 159. Though the ministry was able to carry through some domestic reforms, and enjoyed some real successes in foreign policy, the association between Liberals and Labour was precarious, and in the autumn of 1924 a parliamentary defeat made an election necessary. That election was bitterly contested, and confused by accusations of Communist conspiracy, but it resulted in a victory for the Conservative party. The standing of the major parties in the House of Commons was then as follows: Conservatives, 412; Labour, 151; Liberals, 40.

**Conservatives Again.** Mr. Baldwin formed a Conservative Cabinet, and this government remained in office for a full five-year term, the maximum permitted under the Parliament Act of 1911. It is hard to explain why the government lost popularity, for its policies were moderate and reasonably successful—after it survived the dramatic interlude of a general strike called by the Trades Union Council in 1926 in an effort to force action on labor questions and particularly on the question of the organization of the coal industry. The period from 1924 to 1929 was one of great difficulty, and the economic problems which confronted the government were serious. When the election took place in the spring of 1929, however, the dissatisfaction of the people was revealed, for Labour polled 8,400,000 votes and secured 280 seats, Conservatives polled 8,800,000 votes, winning 260 seats, Liberals polled 5,300,000 votes and won 59 seats. Though the Labour membership was larger than in 1923, this distribution resulted in another Labour Ministry which had to depend upon

Liberal support to obtain the necessary parliamentary majority.

**The National Government.** Mr. Ramsay MacDonald once more headed a Labour government, but again was unable to introduce the full program of his party. The economic and financial situation of England, confronted with the problems produced by a world economic depression, became steadily worse. In August 1931, with the gold reserve of the Bank of England rapidly diminishing, consultations between the major-party leaders took place, King George V participating, and an emergency national coalition cabinet was formed, headed by Mr. MacDonald and including Mr. Baldwin and Sir Herbert Samuel, one of the leaders of the Liberal party. Both the Liberal and Labour party membership split on the question of supporting this national government, and, while a parliamentary majority might have been mobilized to support it, the decision was made to hold an election. Again the campaign was bitterly contested, but the new leadership won a decisive majority, largely made up of Conservatives. The internal divisions in the Labour and Liberal parties appeared in the Parliament which assembled after the election: the government majority was made up of 472 Conservatives, 35 Liberal Nationals and 33 Liberals, 13 National Labour, and 8 Independents and Nationals; the opposition consisted of 52 Labour and 4 Independent Liberals.

This Cabinet remained in power for a full parliamentary term, and strove, with mixed success, to meet the urgent problems of economic reconstruction and the dangers of foreign policy. The association between the various groups within the majority was always uneasy, and in the summer of 1935, when Mr. MacDonald retired from active participation in the Cabinet, Mr. Baldwin succeeded to the leadership.

**The Second National Government.** In November 1935 a national election was held, with the predominant issue centering around foreign policy. It was a favorable moment for the leadership to go to the country, for the government seemed clearly committed to some system of international collective security, in the face of the aggressive foreign policies of Italian fascism and German nazism. The result was to return the National government, but it practically ceased to be a coalition, as the figures of its parliamentary majority were: Conservatives, 387; Liberal National, 33; National Labour, 8; National, 3; Independent, 4. The opposition consisted of Labour, 154; Independent Labour (a more aggressive wing of the Labour Party), 4; Liberal, 21; Communist, 1.

**Cabinets in World War II.** The problems of foreign policy became increasingly grave, and the government's prestige was seriously damaged by the widespread public criticism of the Hoare-Laval plan for dealing with the Italo-Ethiopian conflict, followed by the difficulties of the application of sanctions to Italy. Mr. Baldwin's conduct during the constitutional crisis which ended in the abdication of Edward VIII restored his popularity considerably. He retired from politics in 1937 after the coronation of George VI, and was succeeded by Mr. Neville Chamberlain, who had to wrestle with the diplomatic crises which finally culminated in the outbreak of World War II in September 1939. But Mr. Chamberlain was unequal to the task of organizing public opinion for the conduct of the war. After the successful German campaign in Norway and the rapid penetration of France in the spring of 1940, Mr. Churchill succeeded to the prime minister's post and began his long and successful career as one of Britain's great war leaders. Parliament extended its own life by successive yearly acts beginning in 1941. Finally, after the end of war in Europe, it was possible to hold an election, with the result that has been described in Chapter 5. The victory of the Labour party should not be interpreted as expressing ingratitude toward Mr. Churchill's brilliant leadership during the war, but as an expression of public opinion on the desired general direction of postwar policies of reconstruction and reform.

A perspective of the movement of British opinion, culminating in the present Labour leadership, may be achieved by noticing the popular vote, and the parliamentary representation, given to the chief party and opinion groups during the last three elections. While it would be unwise to assume that the trends which appear in the voting represent a steady and continuuous movement of public opinion, it is possible to base some interpretation upon the figures given.

VOTING IN RECENT BRITISH GENERAL ELECTIONS [2]
(Figures for popular vote in millions; parliamentary seats in actual numbers).

| PARTY | 1931 | | 1935 | | 1945 | |
|---|---|---|---|---|---|---|
| | Pop. | Parl. | Pop. | Parl. | Pop. | Parl. |
| CONSERVATIVE | 11.75 | 472 | 10.49 | 387 | 8.66 | 189 |
| National | .05 | 2 | .10 | 3 | .14 | 2 |
| Liberal National | .63 | 35 | .87 | 33 | .76 | 13 |
| Total | 12.77 | 522 | 11.80 | 431 | 9.56 | 204 |
| LIBERAL | 1.51 | 37 | 1.38 | 21 | 2.23 | 12 |
| LABOUR | 6.65 | 52 | 8.33 | 154 | 11.98 | 393 |
| Independent Labour | | | .14 | 4 | .05 | 3 |
| Common Wealth | .... | ... | .... | ... | .11 | 1 |
| Communist | .07 | ... | .03 | 1 | .10 | 2 |
| Total | 6.72 | 52 | 8.50 | 159 | 12.24 | 399 |
| MINOR PARTIES AND INDEPENDENTS | .26 | 4 | .34 | 4 | 1.03 | 25 |

The figures given in the table indicate the major groupings of opinion on public policy during the past fifteen years. It must be remembered, of course, that these are records of votes cast in the elections, and that many cross-currents of thought occur in the intervals between. It should also be noted that the figures show the defects of single-member constituencies; the fluctuation in the proportion between electoral vote and parliamentary representation is particularly striking in the case of the Liberal party.

**Growth of Labour Strength.** In the table the various party groups are combined to show general affinities of viewpoint. The first group shows orthodox conservative opinion on policy; in 1931 these parties formed the main voting strength of the gov-

[2] Sources for the above table: 1945, London *Times*, July 28, Aug. 2, 9, 1945; 1931 and 1935, W. Mallory, ed. *Political Handbook of the World*, New York, 1932 and 1936.

ernment coalition. The steady voting strength of the Conservative party shows clearly in its popular vote; the strength of this combination of parties declined during the whole period, but even in 1945 it represented not much less than half the total vote cast. The support for moderate socialist policy and social and economic reform is revealed in the third group in the table, and it is worth notice that even in the adverse circumstances of 1931, when a national crisis seemed to call for a unification of opinion, the popular vote for Labour and allied groups was about a third of the total. This fraction increased to the majority of the ballots cast in 1945. The Liberal party, occupying a center position, suffers from that circumstance as the table indicates. While it is probably true that the leaders of the Labour party were surprised to find themselves in command of a genuine parliamentary majority in 1945, the growth of the party is unmistakable during the course of these three campaigns.

**The Labour Victory.** The Labour victory, then, is clearly not a sudden overturn of opinion; it is the result of continuous agitation and recruitment of membership and support during the whole period since World War I. The vote won by the Labour party, while constituting a solid majority in both the country and the House of Commons, is not overwhelming. Recent debates on the program of legislation indicate that both the government and the opposition realize that Britain's situation calls for reform and reconstruction, and the strength of the Conservative party and its allies will serve to make criticism of proposals effective. If the circumstances of the campaign are recalled, the choice made by over twelve milion voters was to endorse a program of active change offered by the Labour party, as compared to the somewhat similar but less decisive program offered by the Conservatives.

### Socialist Planning and Democratic Government

Naturally the performance of the Labour government in Britain is a matter of deep concern to the people of England; but it is a matter of great interest to other nations as well. It is likely to be an experiment in combining social planning with democratic, responsible government. The long tradition of individual liberty, freedom of expression of opinion, and participation in self-government, which has existed in England, will not readily yield to the requirements of economic and social controls, unless those controls can be made responsive and responsible. In the short time which Mr. Attlee's Cabinet has had so far to introduce measures, there is every indication that programs of legislation will be moderate in extent. Certainly they have so far been thoroughly debated.

**Planned Reconstruction.** Two other circumstances, arising from the recent history of England, are also significant in this connection. In the first place, the British community has had the experience of extensive government direction of economic activities in order to maintain the effort of a great war, with the ever-present threat of invasion from 1940 to 1943. In the second place, the pressure of the financial and commercial problems which England faces in the process of postwar reconstruction makes the need of united action very urgent still. The present leadership, therefore, can rely on a wider consensus of support for decisive policies than the size of its popular majority would show. The necessities of housing, of rebuilding industrial plants, of educating an active and alert population to engage in efficient production for export, of safeguarding the welfare of the community through extension of the social insurances—these requirements brought about considerable similarity in the programs offered by the major parties in the 1945 election.

**Planners and Experts.** There are two features of English government, as it has been described in the preceding chapters, which will interest students watching the course of events. First, the administrative staff of the national government is of top-notch quality. It has developed, during the course of the nineteenth and twentieth centuries, a true feeling of impartiality in carrying out its duties. Perhaps a Labour leadership will impose a greater strain on the civil service than the alternation of Liberal and Conservative leadership produced, but it seems likely that the expert administrators will serve the Attlee Cabinet as loyally as they worked for Mr. Churchill. This means that the new government will have competent expert advice on all its programs and careful and efficient administration of its policies.

Secondly, the electorate is actively interested in public questions, and the political parties have maintained discussion of public policy at a fairly high level. The drama of debate in the House of Commons, and in the country, is lively and vital enough to enlist the interest of most voters. In addition, there has been for many years a great deal of nonpartisan study and discussion of public questions by civic groups and workers' institutes and in adult education. Comment on these facts, by the way, should not be taken as praise for the British character; they are the products of the situation of England and the Empire-Commonwealth. The same generalization could be applied at present to the American voting community; interest in public policy is rising as the necessities of public action become more visible. In England this situation has existed for a longer time. Since the middle of the nineteenth century the political, social, and economic problems of the United Kingdom and the associated communities of the Empire and the Commonwealth have claimed the attention of its citizens.

**Conservatives and Planning.** One prediction may be made with some confidence. Should Mr. Attlee lose his present majority, and a general election result in the return of the Conservative party to power, the broad outlines of policy will remain much the same. The extension of the social insurances, the introduction of some government planning into the export industries, the development of public housing and town and country planning, in fact, a wide range of policies now undertaken by the Labour government, were all proposed by Mr. Churchill's coalition government as desirable postwar projects. A change of leadership would not interrupt, though it might modify, these proposals. They have been made necessary by circumstances; they are not the product of socialist doctrine alone. The foreign policy and the imperial policies which have been put forward by Mr. Bevin bear a strong resemblance to those of his predecessors; similarly, the successors of the present leadership will continue many policies which are now being put into action.

The next few years in England, then, are of interest to many people besides the English. Cabinet government, which has been developed by centuries of practice, is to be put to new uses. It possesses great merits of responsiveness to public opinion, promptness and decisiveness of action, and competence in administrative performance. It has been able to rouse the interest of its citizens, so that the participation of the electorate in party activity, in local government, and in public discussion, has been lively and sustained. At the same time, a long tradition of the rights of the individual, under a rule of law, serves to restrain any leadership from embarking upon extreme policies.

The problems faced by this government are of great complexity and danger. The resources of British national and imperial organization must be used to the full extent, if the difficulties of the postwar years are to be met and solved.

### READINGS

The British Empire-Commonwealth is the subject of a vast literature. The few books mentioned contain further suggestions for reading.

Keith, A. B., *The Governments of the British Empire*, New York, 1936.

———, *The Dominions as Sovereign States*, London, 1938. These two books are works of authoritative scholarship.

Simnett, W. E., *The British Colonial Empire*, New York, 1940. An interesting, brief, but useful account of the colonies.

Viton, A., *Great Britain: An Empire in Transition*, New York, 1940. An interesting discussion of the place of the Empire in the World, with a good bibliography.

*The Round Table*, published quarterly in London, is devoted to the affairs of the Empire-Commonwealth.

On contemporary British politics notice the list of newspapers and periodicals given at the end of Chapter 5 above.

# FRANCE

# CHAPTER 9

# THE CONSTITUTIONAL HERITAGE
# OF THE THIRD REPUBLIC

THE development of French government can be surveyed in
the same manner as English constitutional history. The purpose
in so doing is the same—to understand the significant characteristics of contemporary French political institutions by explaining
their historical development. Viewed in this way, the story
centers on two fairly continuous lines of development: (1) the
creation of the agencies of effective national administration, and
(2) the establishment of popular control of government policy
through the use of parliamentary institutions similar to those
which grew up in England.

## THE GROWTH OF CENTRAL AUTHORITY AND
## NATIONAL ADMINISTRTRATION

National power originated in France almost as early as in
England. The same institution—royal authority—was the means
by which an effective national organization was created in feudal
France. Skillful kings, aided by clever and often unscrupulous
ministers, constructed a powerful central government by advantageous marriages, diplomacy, and the occasional use of
military force. The story, quite as romantic and interesting as
Dumas' tales of the three musketeers, must be reduced here to
notice of the fact that by the close of the seventeenth century
an absolute monarchy had been established. The machinery of
administration was still feudal in many of its outward appearances, but the real power was in the hands of the Bourbon kings
and their ministers.

**Royal Absolutism.** The growth of royal authority in France was not accompanied, as it was in English constitutional development, by a parallel growth of representative institutions. Absolute monarchy was coupled with aristocratic privilege; and during the eighteenth century the power of the king was the subject of criticism by French philosophers, who worked out an intellectual and rational case for the civil and legal rights of the citizen, and for the vesting of political sovereignty in the people as a whole. (It is only necessary to mention the names of Montesquieu, Voltaire, and Rousseau, to recall that the doctrines of popular sovereignty were carefully thought out and given eloquent statement in eighteenth-century France.)

**The Great Revolution.** The accumulating grievances of the middle and lower classes, combined with the fiery statements of revolutionary programs by intellectual leaders, led to the Great Revolution of 1789. This political upheaval was so extensive in its effects that the patterns of administration were altered as much as were the institutions of royal absolutism, and the first steps were taken to create the highly centralized system of administration which has since characterized French government.

Because the republican reformers wished to abolish all the aristocratic features of the old regime, the ancient provinces were replaced by administrative districts called *départements;* and the new national democratic government, anxious to extend the program of the revolution to all France, exercised fairly considerable powers of supervision over these local districts, even though popularly elected councils were created in each of them. In the same way, plans were laid to replace local feudal customs by national laws. It was assumed by the leaders of the revolution that the law would be uniformly administered throughout the land.

The new revolutionary government of France was quickly involved in foreign wars, and at the same time great confusion was produced within France by the pace of change. The result was that power passed rapidly from the national assemblies to a Committee of Public Safety, and thence to a small body called the Directory. It was finally seized by Napoleon Bonaparte, who made himself emperor in 1804, having exercised the powers of an effective dictator since the end of 1799.

Napoleon I was a great administrator and organizer as well as a great military commander. Probably his success in organizing France was due to those same qualities which won his victories—industry, ability to concentrate attention on essential problems, and personal magnetism which won the respect and loyalty of the men who worked with him. Another significant factor in the construction of the administrative patterns of the First Empire was the fact—which now seems paradoxical—that Napoleon was regarded by the people as "the son of the Revolution," the leader who would put into effect the program of 1789. He did do much to realize the goals of equality and fraternity, by systematically organizing national services with opportunities for all classes to participate, and he completed the transition of France from a feudal monarchy into a patriotic national state, but he was hardly a democratic leader.

**Napoleonic Centralization.** Two of the reforms of the Empire left a permanent imprint on French political institutions. The first was the centralization of administration. The new *départements* were supervised, if not fully governed, by prefects appointed by the central government. The national government extended its control over highways and public works, education, financial policies, and police administration. The people, after suffering from the disorders of the revolution, welcomed the systematic performances of the new officials, which guaranteed uniform conditions in all parts of the country. The new state services were open—just as Napoleon's officer corps had been—to all qualified citizens, and great care was exercised to establish *"la carrière ouverte aux talents,"* equal opportunity for every able person to enter the service of the state. The result was competent and efficient administration of the public affairs of the whole national community, though liberty—in the sense of representation of the people and popular influence upon policy —was not achieved.

**The Napoleonic Codes.** At the same time that the state services were improved, the administration of law, and the laws themselves, were made the subject of thorough reorganization. A board of jurists, in whose deliberations the Emperor himself often participated, drew up the Napoleonic codes, which still impart the form and much of the substance of French law. Diverse local customs, varying enactments of the Revolutionary period, and ancient feudal practices were consolidated into comprehensive codes of law, of which the most important was the Civil Code, modeled largely upon Roman law. The Civil Code covered a wide range of property, family, and contractual relationships, and its establishment had the result of making such laws uniform for all of France. In this way the new government was able to give every citizen an assurance of a system of civil rights which could be successfully invoked in any locality. The standards for the courts and the judges were improved at the same time; law and the administration of law acquired certainty, orderliness, and system. After the confusion of revolutionary change, the people seemed ready to sacrifice political liberty for the benefits which derived from a well-organized and efficient government.

**Survival of Napoleonic System.** The importance of the Napoleonic organization of France can hardly be exaggerated. This centralized administration and ordered symmetry of the codes of law survived all the succeeding changes of the nineteenth century. Centralization derived, of course, from the power of the absolute monarchy which had flourished during the eighteenth century. Under the Bourbons, particularly in the time of Louis XIV, a well-knit national state had been built up by determined kings aided by skillful ministers. The centralization of the First Empire persisted in the Third Republic. While French leaders and French students of government have often complained of the system, its merits were sufficient to maintain it until the defeat of 1940. It is quite likely to reappear because the French people have become fully accustomed to its precision and uniformity.

## REPRESENTATIVE PARLIAMENTS AND POPULAR SOVEREIGNTY

Probably the best introduction to the vicissitudes of popular representation and responsible government can be obtained by recalling the chronology of the governments in France during the nineteenth century. Assuming that the century begins with the Great Revolution, a table of dates shows:

| | |
|---|---|
| 1789 | The Estates General becomes a National Assembly, "the rights of man" are declared. |
| 1790–95 | The Revolutionary constitutions, the abolition of the monarchy, the involvement of the Republic in foreign wars. |
| 1795–1804 | The rising reputation of Napoleon, the Directory, Napoleon's seizure of power, and the proclamation of the First Empire. |
| 1814–15 | The Congress of Vienna at the close of the Napoleonic wars, the restoration of the Bourbon monarchy in a constitutional parliamentary form. |
| 1830 | The Revolution of July, the establishment of the constitutional monarchy of Louis Philippe, called the July Monarchy. |
| 1848–51 | Revolution, the establishment of the Second Republic. |
| 1852 | Coup d'état of Louis Napoleon, the proclamation of the Second Empire, after a plebiscite which showed popular approval. |
| 1870–75 | The defeat of France by Prussia, the election of a National Assembly, the episode of the revolutionary Commune of Paris, the adoption of the constitutional laws which established the Third Republic. |

The most obvious fact in this chronology is the repeated change of the form of government, each time accompanied by revolutionary action. The Great Revolution declared the program of the "rights of man," including the right of representation in a legislative assembly. The Napoleonic Empire ended popular responsibility, but under a constitutional monarchy elections were restored. Napoleon III, though he made adroit use of plebiscites, again denied the citizens any real participation in government. The Third Republic provided the forms of parliamentary responsibility. The table of dates reveals, moreover, that constitutional parliamentary government never lasted longer than twenty years until after 1875, and that periods of personal or autocratic rule were equally short.

Nevertheless, the idea of popular government, once declared in 1789, persistently reappeared. Though the French people have been willing at times to yield to the appeal of a dictator, a "man on horseback," the driving force of the democratic ideals formulated by the eighteenth-century philosophers has always been strong enough to bring about the election of constitutional assemblies which, in turn, have provided for parliaments and responsible ministries.

**The Third Republic.** The sequence of events which led to the establishment of the Third Republic began with the defeat of the Second Empire by Prussia in the autumn of 1870. Napoleon III, with one of his armies, surrendered at the battle of Sedan. The remaining effective army was quickly encircled at Metz. The collapse of the Empire necessitated the creation of an emergency government. A provisional government was organized in Paris after the news of Sedan, and proclaimed a republic. Its leaders, notably Léon Gambetta, maintained resistance against the Prussians during a siege of Paris.

In January 1871 leaders of the provisional government arranged an armistice with the enemy. Elections for a National Assembly, authorized to determine the final conditions of peace, were announced for February 8. Whether the National Assembly had power to frame a constitution for a new government—though it was called an *Assemblée Nationale Constituante*—was not clear in the minds of the voters who balloted for candidates. Since the Republicans were associated with the idea of continuing the war, conservative groups (chosen by an electorate who wanted to be sure of peace) commanded a majority when the body finally assembled in Bordeaux. While the negotiations for the peace were in progress, an insurrection in Paris created the revolutionary government of the Paris Commune. This socialist government had a brief life from the middle of

March till the end of May. The National Assembly, which had moved from Bordeaux to Versailles at the very time that the Commune made its appearance, proceeded to the consideration of two laws of constitutional significance while progress continued in the arrangement of the peace. The Rivet Law which made the president of the republic responsible to the National Assembly was finally passed in August 1871; the Broglie Constitution which forbade the president to address the Assembly except at the request of the Council of Ministers, was passed on March 13, 1873. These laws expressed the discontent which many members of the National Assembly felt with the dominating leadership of Adolphe Thiers, a strong leader who had been designated "Chief of the Executive Power of the French Republic" in February 1871.

Whether the Assembly was fully empowered to frame a constitution became an academic question, as events forced it to assume this responsibility during these troubled years. The conservative majority hoped to create a constitutional monarchy, but there was division of opinion concerning the designation of a monarch. Conflicting claims were finally reconciled when it was agreed that the Count de Chambord, the heir of the Bourbons, should be king, with the succession going to the Count de Paris, grandson of Louis Philippe. The Count de Chambord, however, refused to accept the tricolor as the flag of France and insisted upon the emblem of the Bourbon monarchy. These circumstances explain the paradox that a monarchist majority finally accepted a presidency. Marshal MacMahon, whose conservative views were widely known, had been elected president in May 1873, while Orléan and Bourbon supporters were still seeking a compromise. The following November the presidential term was fixed at seven years. Monarchists anticipated that by the end of the MacMahon presidency the question of the kingship could be permanently settled.

The law which determined the "septenate" (the seven-year presidential term) also created a committee of thirty members to draft constitutional laws. In 1875 a series of laws, defining the executive power and providing for the election of senators and deputies, were passed between February and November. These constitutional laws, reflecting the debates of the preceding four years, served as the constitution of the Third Republic. The National Assembly dissolved, and in 1876 elections were held for the Senate and Chamber of Deputies, which together may be called the parliament. These arrangements, despite their makeshift character, lasted longer than any of the more elaborate constitutions adopted in France during the nineteenth century.

**Merits of the Constitution.** The durability of the constitution of the Third Republic is probably attributable to the simplicity of these fundamental constitutional laws. The essential elements of parliamentary government were established. The president served as a formal head of the state, and was chosen by the Chamber and the Senate sitting together as a national assembly. The senators, indirectly elected for long terms—including, at first, prominent public men appointed to life senatorships—provided a restraining conservative influence upon government policy. The deputies, elected by direct universal manhood suffrage, continued the tradition of popular sovereignty. Ministries were responsible to the Parliament, and in practice the Chamber exercised decisive powers over the life of any cabinet. One further token of the acceptance of the constitutional laws may be mentioned. During the life of the Republic there were only three amendments, and none of them affected the essential substance of the original laws.

This complicated story is frequently described as a series of paradoxes. A National Assembly which was not specifically authorized to draw up a constitution nevertheless proceeded to make the constitutional provisions which lasted until 1940. The National Assembly contained a large Monarchist majority, but it established the Third Republic. The Count de Chambord might have been king of France, but would not sit upon a throne over which waved the tricolor. The constitution which finally went into effect was not a constitution, but three laws making minimum provisions for the organization of the government.

The complications arose from the cleavages of opinion which divided the French people. The Monarchists, the Republicans, and the Socialist Revolutionaries who set up the Paris Commune, all represented viewpoints which were able to win support in varying degrees. The eventual result was inevitably a compromise. While many Frenchmen were dissatisfied, the Third Republic proved itself to be an adequate government. Beginning in compromise, it provided the machinery by which reconciliation of differing programs could be achieved.

## CONTRASTS WITH ENGLISH CONSTITUTIONAL DEVELOPMENT

Thought it is hardly permissible to make direct comparison between the histories of two such different communities, the constitutional history of France may be clarified by pointing to some striking differences between it and that of England.

**English and French Chronology.** In the first place, there is an obvious difference in the timing of the two stories. French experience, compared to the slow process of establishing responsible parliamentary government in England, is compressed into approximately a century. The growth of national power and the corresponding development of parliamentary sovereignty in England stretched over seven centuries, from the twelfth to the nineteenth. There was no similar accumulation of experience with representative assemblies in France during the centuries. While the old regime did not survive unchanged until the Revolution, it should be pointed out that the Estates General, when once more called into existence to meet the financial problems confronting the government in 1789, had not met since the early part of the seventeenth century. It is hardly an exaggeration, therefore, to say that French parliamentary history is telescoped into a single century and that the French people had not acquired the requisite experience to manage the difficult and intricate working of constitutional representative government.

**French Philosophy—English Practice.** A second contrast with the English story is equally striking. Parliamentary institutions in France were the product of a series of revolutionary changes. The Revolution of 1789 was in many ways more violent than the seventeenth-century struggle between Puritans and Cavaliers in England, and was followed by revolutions of 1830 and 1848 and the revolutionary character of the events accompanying the establishment of the Third Republic, 1871–75. Republican and representative institutions were born of conflicts in France, and each left a residue of political sentiments in the memory of the people. In England, parliamentary supremacy once established remained a stable way of organizing political sentiment. The English constitution was the product of gradual adjustment, even though the Reform Bill of 1832 followed agitation which exhibited some revolutionary symptoms. In France, the token of the persisting ideals behind political disturbances appears in the continuance of attitudes supporting the various forms of government which held power during the nineteenth century. A shadowy remnant of the aristocracy of the old regime still remains, stubbornly defending the idea of monarchy. There are Bonapartists who look back wistfully to the glories of the First and Second Empires. Ardent republicans of all sorts argue with much passion that the ideals of the French Revolution are as yet unrealized.

This troubled development may be summed up by saying that the French political community still harbors many groups which are irreconcilable, whatever the existing form of government. When a political crisis arises, the effect is often not merely a demand for change of leadership, but an attack upon the existing constitution. During the course of the twentieth century, the Third Republic was often exposed to such agitations.

**French Revolutions—English Reforms.** A third contrast with English development is suggested by this revolutionary history in France. In one sense the Revolution of 1789 came too late. The political events which led to constitutional representative government in France occurred during the period of other great changes in European history. By the time the old regime was displaced politically in France, the Industrial Revolution was beginning in Europe. As a result, successive republican governments in France had to grapple with the tremendous social changes which were brought about by the expanding trade and increased productive power of a new European economy.

**Industrial Change and Socialism.** The growth of the factory system in industry and accompanying new techniques in agriculture led to important shifts in the social structure. All governments were forced to concern themselves with the welfare of a new urban working class. Factory legislation, health regulations, education, and other social programs made their appearance. In addition, revolutionary socialist doctrines were formulated in all European countries during the course of the nineteenth century; Karl Marx and Friedrich Engels published the Communist Manifesto in 1848. Socialist parties, with large working-class memberships, were organized in Germany, France, England, and Italy, and exerted real influence in politics.

In England, the rise of a politically conscious working class was reflected in agitation for the electoral reforms of 1832, and in the programs of the Labour party which began its career in the last quarter of the nineteenth century. The Liberal party was able to introduce its program of reforms during the course of the century, and the Conservative party participated in the changes made necessary by the new conditions. Change was accomplished by constitutional methods and parliamentary government responded to the demands of the electorate.

**French Social Conflicts.** In France, the life of representative institutions was interrupted by conflicts that often reached the dimensions of civil war. The temper of reforming groups was accordingly more intransigent, and manifestations like the Commune in Paris in 1871 exhibited revolutionary social objectives. The Third Republic was forced immediately to deal with social conflicts of great importance. French politics have always been disturbed by the social attitudes expressed on the Left and on the Right. This need not be taken to imply that if representative institutions had been firmly entrenched in popular confidence before the nineteenth century all social conflict might have been avoided. But it is true that parliamentary government in France, established as it was during the course of the nineteenth century, was subjected to severe strain.

A fourth contrast with England will finally illuminate the character of French constitutional development. French democracy was based in considerable part upon the declared philosophy and programs worked out by French political theorists of the eighteenth century. In France, political theory preceded practical political changes; in England philosophy followed political change. This bald statement is hardly defensible as an historical generalization; nevertheless, it contains substantial truth. The Revolution of 1789 was based largely on the political philosophy enunciated by Montesquieu and Rousseau. Montesquieu had opportunities to observe English government in action, and was a close student of the writings of John Locke. His description of democratic practice, though incorrect in many important details, had a considerable influence upon the constitutions of France and the United States. Rousseau formulated a democratic program, declaring the rights of man, and demanding that government should express the will of the community.

**The "Unfinished Revolution."** Revolutionary change in France was therefore designed to realize the benefits of democratic political philosophy. Doctrines and programs had a real influence on the establishment of republican institutions as they were created during the nineteenth century. It is important to remember that the earliest constitutions of revolutionary France embodied an elaborate "Declaration of the Rights of Man." The English, while they undoubtedly believed in the liberties of the citizen, embodied the safeguards for his freedom in the ordinary practice of the law and courts.[1] When principles are declared, devotion is evoked among the people. It is not surprising that French politics show more doctrinal fervor than is found in Anglo-Saxon nations. A shrewd English observer of recent French politics has pointed out that the French citizen is still

[1] See A. V. Dicey, *The Law of the Constitution*, chs. IV and V for a classic discussion of this point.

powerfully influenced by the ideas and purposes of the "Unfinished Revolution." [2]

## SUMMARY: FRENCH ADAPTION OF PARLIAMENTARY GOVERNMENT

The result of nineteenth-century changes in France was the creation of constitutional parliamentary government, modeled in large part on English practice. Since conditions were not the same in the two countries, there were certain distinctive features embedded in the French political system.

**Representation and Centralization.** Representative institutions were combined with a much higher degree of centralized administration than in England, since local communities had never had the same vitality of self-government. While the Revolution developed the principles of popular sovereignty, its program was also designed to nationalize the government of the whole community. The elaborate administrative mechanism, centering in the national capital, made national affairs—and national influence in local affairs—an important factor in politics. The action of political parties accordingly conformed to the administrative authority of the central government. This produced a situation in which the citizen's interest was absorbed in the action of the ministers and the government departments; by the same token, political leadership was constantly subject to a variety of local influences.

**Multiple Parties.** Since the development of the constitutions was often the product of civil strife, greater diversity of political attitudes appeared in the French electorate. Parliamentary action was achieved by coalitions among many parties, and the multiple-party situation arose from the existence of various groups adhering to traditions declared by both republican and imperial leadership. Party sentiment ranged from an extreme conservative Right, to a revolutionary socialist or communist Left. There were never less than five parties organized in the electorate, and these

[2] W. L. Middleton, *The French Political System*, ch. 1.

divided into as many as nine or eleven in the Chamber of Deputies. This made the operation of responsible cabinet government very difficult. There were observers of the French political scene who believed that this would always be a hazard to the Third Republic.

**Social Reform.** A third factor, which has already been suggested, increased the instability of politics: the promises of social change which were implicit in the program of the first revolution were never fully realized. During the course of the nineteenth century the Industrial Revolution gathered momentum, and by the opening of the twentieth century there was extensive large-scale industry in France. Working-class demands for improvement of working conditions were met by the reluctance of the business community to embark upon reforms. Added to this was the natural conservatism of the agricultural community, with an unusually large proportion of small farmers. Social and economic issues complicated the party situation, and created further divisions in the electorate.

The result of this constitutional heritage, in which was combined revolutionary changes, political doctrines of contradictory implications, and the constant pressure of social and economic issues, made it difficult to adopt successfully the institutions of constitutional government and Cabinet responsibility which had been effective in meeting similar problems in England. French politics under the Third Republic were chronically unstable, as the following chapters will show.

## READINGS

The constitutional history of France has been the subject of as much research and writing as that of England. The literature of the Revolution of 1789 is immense. A few suggestions may be offered which elaborate the story.

Bodley, J. E. C., *France*, 2 vols., New York, 1898. The careful observation of an English student of French affairs, still useful to read.

Brogan, D. W., *France Under the Republic: The Development of Modern France, 1870–1939,* New York, 1940. A brilliant history of the Third Republic.

Dickenson, G. Lowes, *Revolution and Reaction in Modern France,* New York, 1898. A fine analysis of the ideas and the achievements of the revolutionary movements.

Guérard, Albert, *The France of Tomorrow,* Cambridge, 1942; ——, *France, a Short History,* New York, 1946. Two penetrating and profound books by a distinguished scholar.

CHAPTER 10

# ADMINISTRATION UNDER THE
# THIRD REPUBLIC

THE administrative side of French government has been remarkably stable and enduring, despite constitutional changes and fluctuations of party leadership. Because it is likely that the new French republic will maintain the familiar pattern, a description of the organization and operation of the various agencies of the Third Republic should be studied. The French citizen, even during German occupation and the reconstruction after liberation, depended upon administrative agencies and permanent officials for regulation of a large share of the activities of his daily life. The ministries of the national government, the staff of civil servants, the supervision of local government activities, and the judicial functions of both regular and administrative courts form the substance of the old (and the new) political organization in France.

## THE MINISTERS AND THE PRESIDENT

The ministers, who headed the departments of the national government in Paris, were quite comparable to Cabinet ministers in England. Like the English Cabinet minister, *Monsieur le Ministre* held his place by virtue of his participation in the leadership group of the coalition of parties which controlled a majority in the Chamber of Deputies, the popularly elected lower house of the national Parliament. He was, therefore, an amateur in the actual business of administration, though his past experiences in the changing Cabinets may have professionalized his amateur status. Since the activities of all modern states must be much the same under the conditions of the twentieth century, the list of departments headed by ministers was much like that in England, though it was likely to be longer.

**Departments and Ministers.** Important activities like finance, interior (home affairs and local government), foreign affairs, national education, war, navy, agriculture, commerce, and labor, were invariably represented in the Cabinet by ministers. Frequently the minister was aided by one or two undersecretaries who were, in effect, assistant ministers. There were, therefore, twelve to fifteen ministers and nearly as many undersecretaries in the typical Cabinet of the Third Republic; the Popular Front ministry headed by Léon Blum in 1936–37 included twenty-one ministers and fourteen undersecretaries. This longer list reflected the extended range of activities of this particular government, which was carrying out a program of reforms and therefore included a ministry of national economy, and undersecretaries for sports and leisure and for child welfare.

**Formation of a Ministry.** The selection of a Ministry, which will be described more fully in the following chapter on politics, was formally announced by the president of France, upon the advice and suggestion of the parliamentary leaders of the group of parties which controlled a majority in the Chamber of Deputies. The announcement of a Ministry was always preceded by much consultation among the leaders of the many parties in the Chamber, and the necessities of compromise and adjustment among these political groups affected the size of the Cabinet. Quite frequently, in the years following 1936, influential political leaders were included in the list of ministers, being designated as ministers of state without portfolio and therefore participating in the formulation of government policy without the responsibilities of directing the affairs of a particular department. This practice is occasionally followed in England, but the exigencies of the political situation in France made it a commonplace.

**The President.** The president of the Republic, though his office has been the subject of many sarcastic epigrams by political leaders and students of government, was of real use in the process of forming a ministry. The president was elected for a term of seven years by a majority of the Senate and the Chamber of Deputies, sitting together as a National Assembly. Since party allegiances were diverse and many, he was almost always a man who was acceptable to many groups, thought not actively supported by any. He was not likely to be a strong leader in public affairs, but invariably he had long political experience in the Chamber and the Senate, and also in some ministries. His knowledge of the political scene, and the confidence inspired by his political experience and moderate partisanship, contributed substantially to the compromises among party groups at the times when a new slate of ministers had to be selected. In addition he occupied the position of formal executive head of the French state —presiding over the meetings of the Council of Ministers, receiving ambassadors from foreign countries, and appearing at important state functions. His office—originating as it did, from a compromise between Republican and Monarchist sentiment in the National Assembly which finally drew up the fundamental laws of the Third Republic—combined some of the formal features of the English monarchy with some of the aspects of political leadership which have developed in the American presidency. It is important to remember, however, that in prestige the office fell far short of that of either the king of England or the president of the United States, not being hedged with the divinity which surrounds the Crown, nor being invested with the authority of the people's choice. French presidents, in consequence, were almost always mild and inoffensive men like Doumer or Lebrun. Active and aggressive leaders, like Millerand, resigned the office, often as the result of political pressure springing from public disapproval of their positive exercise of political leadership.

**France and England Compared.** In summary, the French government exhibited a form of parliamentary government recognizably similar to that of England. A Cabinet, made up of experienced parliamentary leaders, assumed responsibility for the general formulation of policy, and proposed and defended that policy in the Chamber of Deputies and the Senate.[1] The ministers and undersecretaries at the same time undertook the general direction of the various departments of the central government. Selection of this leadership group was arrived at by consultation among the parties, assisted by the experienced and disinterested advice of the president of the Republic. The president performed the formal duties of the head of the state, and also influenced the definition of general policy. But political support of the leaders depended upon a coalition of parties, because a majority of the Chamber was necessary to enact any legislation required by the announced policies. Consequently Cabinets resigned frequently and were succeeded by new ones. The new Ministry, however, was rarely greatly changed in membership from the preceding one, and policies were gradually modified in response to the demands of a legislative majority which likewise had changed only partially from a preceding coalition. French government therefore exhibited the contradictory aspect of instability of Ministries combined with stability of fundamental policy.

**The Precarious Ministerial Career.** The changing membership of Cabinets had also the effect of giving a somewhat different experience to individual ministers, than resulted from a typical career in English politics. The chances were that the average minister had already had some experience of the responsibilities of office. While he remained an amateur, like his British counterpart, it was nevertheless true that he acquired a good deal of actual contact with the duties of directing a department of the central government quite early in his career, and had occasional opportunities thereafter to repeat this acquaintance with administrative and leadership activities. The relation of amateur and expert, which has been earlier described in the English administrative pattern, existed in a somewhat modified form in the

[1] For a scholarly study of the character and qualifications of these Cabinet members, see two articles by John G. Heinberg in the *American Political Science Review*, vol. XXV, May 1931, pp. 389–96, and vol. XXXIII, April 1939, pp. 267–79.

French Third Republic. The political head of one of the ministries possessed in some small degree the qualifications of the expert. On the other hand, he was disabled by the uncertain tenure of his office—sometimes as short as a few weeks or even a few days—so that his dependence on the permanent officials was even greater that it might have been had he been in the more secure position of an English Cabinet minister, who can count on the support of a disciplined majority in the Commons.

In any case, it was clear that since *Monsieur le Ministre* could scarcely count on an opportunity to familiarize himself thoroughly with departmental routine, he was forced to place reliance upon the loyalty, efficiency, and practical experience of his staff of permanent officials. The qualities of that staff, since it furnished expert advice and gave decisions on minor matters, had an important effect upon the actual day-to-day performance of governmental action.

## The Civil Service: "Les Fonctionnaires"

The French people at times make fun of government officials, complaining of bureaucratic red tape which complicates so much of the government's work. The French word for these details is contemptuous, *"paperasserie,"* conveying the impression of masses of paper and paper work. Even though a sneer is implied, the French realize that, for a great deal of practical action, the officials are the real rulers of France. Ministers may come and go, but the civil servants go on till retirement, and while that may not be forever, it is a good long time.

**Selection of Civil Servants.** The method of selection of civil servants was based upon competitive examinations. As in England, the examinations for those categories which led to important and responsible positions placed a high premium upon a general university education, rather than upon particular qualifications for a specific job. The tests were administered by the individual ministries rather than by a personnel authority like the English or American Civil Service Commissions. Applicants were numerous, and competition was consequently severe. The French word *"concours,"* meaning a race, was the official (and appropriate) designation of these examinations. It should be added that a number of the tests were somewhat specialized in nature: prospective engineers for the Ministry of Public Works usually were graduates of the technical schools; most of the candidates for the Foreign Office had graduated from *"L'École Libre des Sciences Politiques."*

**Promotion of Civil Servants.** Once inducted into the staff of a particular ministry, the civil servant began a long apprenticeship, rising slowly by promotion, based upon either merit records or further examinations or some combination of both, to a responsible job. As in every government service, there was considerable tension over the questions of pay and advancement, and under the Third Republic associations of government employes were formed, called *syndicats,* which brought pressure to bear upon the directors of the various bureaus and agitated for legislation to improve the situation of the public officials. These activities were stimulated throughout the period following World War I by the fact that the levels of pay were very low. In fact, a considerable number of the public officials really needed a private income in order to maintain even the unpretentious standard of living expected of the public servant.

**Prestige of the Civil Service.** Offsetting the disadvantages of a relatively low salary scale and the slow rate of advancement were some substantial inducements. Tenure was protected by regulations governing dismissal and suspension, and a right of appeal to the highest administrative tribunal made these guarantees effective. Provisions for pensions and retirement, while not generous, were sufficient to give a modest security. Finally, the social prestige of the public servant was fairly high. From Napoleon's time the importance of the place was recognized, and during the nineteenth and twentieth centuries this regard for the work of the responsible official was maintained. The American student, more used to a monetary measurement of success, should remember that in Europe, especially on the Continent, the social prestige attached to state service makes it attractive to a man possessing ability and educational qualifications.

Both French and foreign observers agree that, in general, the public officials under the Third Republic were of good caliber, and that many of them worked with distinction.[2] The industry and honesty of the civil servant could be relied upon by the average citizen, and, since the frequent changes of Ministry would otherwise have produced a great deal of uncertainty in public policy, the permanent staff fulfilled an important function.

## CENTRAL SUPERVISION OF LOCAL GOVERNMENT

Under the Third Republic the citizen was particularly dependent upon the work of officials because of the degree of supervision exercised by the national state over local community affairs. As the history of France shows, the tradition of centralized direction of local government originated in the old regime; it was strengthened and elaborated in the First Republic, and organized systematically by Napoleon. The American and British citizen, accustomed to a haphazard organization of relatively autonomous local communities, is hardly prepared to understand the symmetrical pattern of public business in the districts and communities of France.

**Local Government Areas.** The ancient provinces, like Normandy or Burgundy, ceased to be units of governments at the time of the Revolution, and were replaced by the *départements,* which became districts in which the actual work of administration was carried on. There were ninety *départements,* each about double the size of a typical American county. These districts were divided fairly symmetrically into *arrondissements,* subdistricts created to facilitate the work of administration. The *communes,* ranging in size from small country villages to large towns

---

[2] W. R. Sharp, *The French Civil Service; Bureaucracy in Transition,* New York, 1931. This is one of the most careful scholarly surveys of the nature of the service.

and cities, constituted the lowest rank of the administrative hierarchy.

**Local Government Executives.** In the *département* and the *arrondissement* a prefect and a subprefect, respectively, appointed by the minister of the interior, bore the chief responsibility for the executive and administrative functions of government. In the commune the mayor, chosen by the locally elected council, performed similar duties, but he was subject to a substantial degree of direction and supervision by the prefect and the subprefect. In each of these districts a council was elected by the citizens; but, by the very nature of the system, its powers over the practical conduct of administration were limited. As might be expected, the prefect was chiefly concerned with matters pertaining to police, education, health, and the like; but he inevitably exercised a number of informal and extralegal political duties connected with representing the national government in his locality. The prefecture was the center of a wide range of political and administrative activities.

This centralized control of local affairs was accepted without serious objection by the average Frenchman. It was traditional, and therefore seemed natural and appropriate, and it possessed the solid merits of imparting uniformity and consistency to local governments. The system was, of course, accompanied by the defects of delay in having to secure confirmation from Paris for all sorts of community projects. It also frequently invited the pressure of local politics upon matters of national policy. While the French system might seem dictatorial to an Anglo-Saxon because of frequent interference in matters of local concern, it could be depended upon to efficiently administer the business of the community and the larger district.

### JUDICIAL ADMINISTRATION: ORDINARY AND ADMINISTRATIVE COURTS

The system of courts in the Third Republic was as highly organized as the administrative divisions. The Court of Justice of the Peace existed in every *canton,* a subdivision of the *arrondisse-ment,* and handled the type of litigation, both civil and criminal, which is dealt with by the corresponding court in England and America. More important cases originated in the Courts of First Instance in each *arrondissement*—the Poincaré reforms in the twentieth century grouped some of these districts for greater efficiency in handling judicial business—and then appeals were possible to the appropriate courts set up in larger districts.

**Legal and Judicial Careers.** The general character of the legal profession was similar to that of England. The distinction between the trial lawyer and the legal adviser was not quite so clearly defined, but since 1908 admission to the bar has required a period of apprenticeship for every legal aspirant, followed by an investigation of his qualifications and character by the leader of the local bar. In this manner a young man might become an *avoué* or a *notaire,* and carry on a private practice much like that of an American attorney-at-law. If a young man who had completed legal training in a university wished to embark upon a judicial career, he took a competitive examination which, if successfully passed, led either to an appointment as an assistant prosecutor in the ordinary courts or to membership on the staff of one of the administrative courts which will be described on the following page.

There existed, therefore, three distinct types of legal career: (1) the practice of law after admission to the bar, (2) the judicial hierarchy of the ordinary courts, and (3) the work of a councilor or judge in the administrative courts. While it was difficult to transfer from one field to another after reasonable advancement, each offered satisfactory opportunities to a man of intelligence and industry.

Promotion in either the ordinary or administrative courts was recommended by boards of judges designated by the minister of justice. Occasionally political pressure influenced these recommendations, since every minister was exposed to party and personal demands. Nevertheless, advancement was usually the result of meritorious service, and the French people had genuine confidence in the professional qualifications and personal integrity of judges and other officials of their courts.

**Court Procedure.** French court procedure differed from English and American court procedure in two ways. In courts above that of the justice of the peace there was usually a group of justices. This practice of "collegiality" is ordinarily found only in appeal courts in Anglo-Saxon countries. The second difference springs from the first: there was less use of the jury in French trials. The bench of judges could weigh evidence on matters of fact, and could serve also as a group of experts to apply the rules of law to the circumstances. For important criminal trials a jury was always impaneled, but most proceedings were controlled entirely by the judges. Since the judiciary was a career, quite carefully administered, the interests of the citizen were sufficiently safeguarded in actual practice.

**Administrative Courts and Law.** Enough has been said of the character of French administration to suggest that the citizen, being frequently subjected to the authority of appointed administrative officials, needed some method of appealing from their decisions if he had a legitimate grievance. Therefore, in addition to the hierarchy of regular courts, there existed a system of administrative courts.

Anglo-Saxon common law embodies the maxim that "the king can do no wrong," and consequently an English or American citizen cannot institute a suit against the state without the state's consent. He may, however, sue the individual official who has exceeded or abused his authority. The Frenchman, on the other hand, could readily initiate a complaint against government action in the administrative courts and confidently expect a full investigation of any injury done him by state action.

The lowest administrative court was called the Council of the Prefecture. Its members were appointed by the central government, and were either trained in the law or were experienced officials. Many of the councilors were selected by competitive examinations, as has been explained earlier in the discussion of the legal profession. In 1926, *départements* were grouped into larger districts, and the administrative courts (for these councils should really be regarded as courts) handled cases for the wider area. The jurisdiction of each was defined by law, and covered minor complaints concerning taxation, public works, elections, and similar matters. More important litigation, and appeals from the decisions of the lower administrative courts, could be brought before a national tribunal, the Council of State. The members of the Council of State were distinguished jurists and administrative officials. This system of administrative courts made it possible for the French citizen to obtain a careful hearing whenever administrative action had an injurious effect upon his business or his property.

The administrative law which defined the relationships of citizens and officials was partly enacted by the national parliament, and was partly built up by the decisions of the Council of State. Precedents and judicial interpretations gave it the character of "judge-made" law, and in this respect it differed from the ordinary law which was more fully expressed in codes. While the original intention of the system was to protect the official against the protest of the citizen, its development during the nineteenth century clarified the mutual relationships of public official and private citizen. These rules, and the prestige of the tribunals which interpreted and enforced them, were clearly valuable in the highly centralized government of the Third Republic.

## ADMINISTRATION IN A NEW FRENCH GOVERNMENT

The foregoing brief sketch of the administrative system of the Third Republic has been presented in the past tense, and the student is fully entitled to ask whether it is worth while to learn about a pattern which may not continue in existence. To such a query, only a tentative answer may be made at present: when considering future possibilities, it is well to keep in mind that the accumulated weight of custom and tradition is powerful in every community, and that during the nineteenth century these forces have been especially significant in France. The Third Republic succeeded, not without criticism naturally, in giving to the French a systematic and orderly administration of public affairs from 1871 to 1940. The centralized administration of local affairs was criticized, especially by the advocates of "regionalism," for being too much subject to excessive administrative delays and for failing to evoke genuine local initiative. The pressure of local interests upon national affairs, invited by the centralization of the government, also seemed to many observers an undesirable feature which in some ways corrupted the activity of political parties. It is quite possible that the experience under the Vichy government, and the necessities of emergency action under a provisional government since liberation, may make changes in these traditional patterns. Nevertheless, it is undeniable that under the Third Republic the French developed a government that worked sufficiently well to provide a reasonably satisfactory condition of affairs. Habitual methods of getting practical problems solved may well re-establish many of these procedures and institutions, or at least produce new institutions which bear a strong ancestral resemblance to the ones which served France, under various types of political leadership, for the greater part of three generations.

## READINGS

Ensor, R. C. K., *Courts and Judges in France, Germany and England,* London, 1933. A brief but valuable description and analysis of the ordinary courts.

Sait, E. M., *Government and Politics of France,* Yonkers-on-Hudson, 1926. Though published more than twenty years ago, this is a penetrating analysis of the action of French government.

Sharp, W. R., *The Government of the French Republic,* New York, 1938.

———, *The French Civil Service, Bureaucracy in Transition,* New York, 1931. These two books by one of the foremost American students of French government furnish an excellent condensed description.

Valeur, R., "French Government and Politics," in R. L. Buell, ed., *Governments in Europe,* revised edition, New York, 1938.

In view of the present situation in France, this limited list is sufficient for the student's purpose. Professor Sharp's books give excellent bibliographies. The new government of France will undoubtedly be the subject of much more extensive publication in the future.

# CHAPTER 11

# POLITICAL PARTIES AND PARLIA-
# MENTARY PRACTICE UNDER
# THE THIRD REPUBLIC

WHEN studying parliamentary institutions, the student is usually introduced first to the subject of elections and legislative activities, since politics and parties are then more easily understood. But the action of the Senate and the Chamber of Deputies under the Third French Republic was largely determined by the existence of a multiple-party system. There were always many parties in contrast to the two or three leading parties in Anglo-Saxon countries. Therefore a full appreciation of the character of the French political scene must begin with the parties and then proceed to the work of the legislative assemblies.

## THE MULTIPLE-PARTY SYSTEM

The American student often observes the behavior of parties in France with a feeling of rising exasperation. The puzzles presented by the simultaneous action of eleven or more parties in a legislature seem designed solely to confuse the foreigner! Taking the picture as it is, time can be spent profitably in seeking some explanation of the appearance and continuance of a group of parties.

**Constitutional History and Party Development.** As was suggested in the chapter on constitutional development, the most satisfactory explanation lies in French constitutional history. The story presents a series of constitutions, with each successive change of government depositing a residue, so to speak, of traditions and loyalties. Monarchists, Bonapartists, Republicans of various kinds, liberals, and socialists—all look back on episodes in the development of political institutions and cling to the doctrines formulated by their fathers or grandfathers. Coupled with this history is another influence readily comprehensible to an American, the persistence of attitudes of mind in various parts of the territory of France. The ancient provinces of Brittany and Normandy harbor a traditional conservatism, made up of the natural caution of a thrifty farming population combined with the restraining influences of devout Catholicism. The "Midi," the France south of the Loire river, has been the setting for active republicanism and moderate socialism—the trumpet notes of the *Marseillaise* are a token of revolutionary tradition. In the industrial suburbs of Paris, called the "red belt," and the working populations of the industrial cities of the North lies the strength of labor unionism and working-class socialism, and the more extreme programs of the Communist party. The financial and business communities of the great industrial areas in the northeast, where much of French heavy industry is located, furnish leadership and funds for moderate conservative groups.

**French Temperament and Parties.** In the chapter on English political parties some reference was made to the possible effect of national temperament on political party organization.[1] Many acute observers of the French political scene have pointed to the French temperament as a reason for the multiplicity of parties. Certainly many French citizens, despite the Anglo-Saxon's impression of their excitability, have a harder, clearer, and sharper view of parties, programs, and leaders than have many Englishmen or Americans. The typical voter prefers to have his ballot express precisely his views on public policy; and if no existing political association embodies these opinions, he is quite willing to start organizing a new party which will. It is perhaps wise to repeat the qualifications made before on the subject of national characteristics. Frenchmen differ from each other as much as they differ from Americans, and generalizations regarding a na-

[1] See Chapter 5. p. 69–70.

tional spirit or mentality are always deceptive. The fact remains, however, that numerous parties existed during the life of the Third Republic; and after all, it was a nation of Frenchmen who made the history of France.

What has just been said is not meant to suggest that any one of these factors fully explains the existence of many parties. French governmental history, with its series of revolutionary constitutions, may only mean that there is some persistent characteristic which produces many constitutions and many parties. Perhaps a better statement is: the story of the constitutional development, the influence of local conditions, and the political temperament of the people, combine to produce the multiplicity of parties. Other subtler influences may have an effect as well.

**Parties and Parliament.** Given this kaleidoscope of parties, it is not surprising that French parliamentary practice has been adapted to fit the situation. One peculiarity of Cabinet government in France is worthy of notice in this connection. Unlike the House of Commons in England, the French Chamber of Deputies was dissolved but once in the history of the Third Republic. That occasion, famous enough to receive the name of the "Sixteenth of May," took place in 1877 during the term of the first president, Marshal MacMahon. He exercised his constitutional right to dissolve the chamber. His own conservative views influenced his action, and when the electorate returned the group of parties supporting the Ministry then in office, he eventually resigned. Since then, the right of dissolution has never been exercised, with the result that adjustment and coalition among parties has been the traditional means of forming a majority in support of a Ministry. Once these procedures were well established in practice, they exerted a steady influence in the direction of maintaining many parties. The absence of elections turning upon hotly debated particular issues, as in England, did not require the citizens to align themselves into two groups. Since multiplicity of parties has been a consistent feature of French politics it must always be taken into account as giving a special character to the operation of Cabinet government in the Third

Republic, and it may well persist in any future government in France.

## THE ELECTORATE AND THE PARTIES

French parties ranged from a Communist Left to a Conservative, if not Monarchist, Right. Eleven or more parliamentary groups were represented in the Chamber of Deputies. The table of postwar elections given in the following chapter illustrates the situation which existed under the Third Republic.[2] However clear and sharp the French voter's mind might be, he would suffer a nervous breakdown if he tried conscientiously to discriminate between such delicate gradations of political doctrine. It was only natural, therefore, that certain parliamentary groups associated with others at the time of a Chamber election, which occurred every four years. This produced a distinction between what have been called electoral parties and parliamentary groups.[3]

**Electoral and Parliamentary Parties.** A striking example of an electoral association of parties was the Democratic Alliance, which presented candidates in many electoral districts (usually with the same boundaries as the arrondissements), maintained committee organizations for campaigning, but did not function at all as a parliamentary group in the Chamber. Deputies elected by its support affiliated with various Republican and other parties of the center and with the moderate right. The opposite phenomenon was also observable. Frequently there appeared in the Chamber a "splinter" group, separated from either the Radical Socialist or Socialist party. Such a parliamentary group lacked an electoral party organization. Communists, Socialists, Radical Socialists, and Popular Democrats were successful in maintaining a higher degree of discipline in their membership, and ordinarily functioned in both capacities—as electoral parties

[2] Chapter 12, p. 167.
[3] W. L. Middleton, *The French Political System*, New York, 1933, ch. IV.

conducting campaigns in the country, and as parliamentary groups engaged in parliamentary maneuvering.

**Elections.** The normal procedure of elections for the 615 deputies in the Chamber was adapted to this political situation. To determine the representation of an electoral district, elections on two successive Sundays were invariably necessary, very like the two successive ballotings in the Democratic primaries in a number of the southern states in the United States. On the first ballot a number of parties presented candidates, and the result was usually indecisive. The following Sunday the two leading contenders and their supporters continued the electoral battle, the less successful candidates by then having withdrawn and pledged their support to one or the other of the candidates who had polled the largest votes. The voter cast his ballot for the candidate of the party whose program was closest to that he had originally supported.

Voting qualifications were much the same as those required by law in England and the United States. Local officials drew up a list of qualified electors, and verification of this list was by challenge and inquiry after it was published. Participation was high; ordinarily three-fourths to nearly nine-tenths of the male citizens exercised the suffrage.

While this electoral process may seem confusing to the foreigner, in practice the French voter found that he could make fairly simple and significant choices. The committee of the party of which he was a member agreed to support a candidate. The activities of the campaign were conducted in public meetings, café conversations, and local newspapers. At the first general election he cast his vote strictly in accord with party loyalties and convictions. If his candidate polled a sufficiently large vote to remain in the running the following Sunday, he maintained his loyal support. If not, consultation and discussion gave him sufficient information to choose one of the two leading competitors.

**Candidates.** As a result of this general party situation, the typical candidate for deputy was a man who had built up a considerable reputation in his own electoral district. National party organization was not strong enough to induce local committees to accept recommendations from central party headquarters. This contrasts sharply with the strength of the Central office of an English party, which frequently proposes candidates to local party leaders. The potential deputy had a record of membership in local government councils, frequently had been a mayor of a town or village, or in other ways had built up a personal as well as a political following in his own community.

The general quality of the candidates was quite good; most of them were solid citizens. The conduct of elections, while not so strictly regulated as in England, was responsible and respectable. The usual methods of campaigning were employed: newspaper advertising, wall posters, public meetings, and, in addition, a great deal of discussion in small neighborhood groups. Expenditure of money was rarely excessive, even though legal regulation of political campaign funds was not elaborate.

**Senators.** A little should be said about the choice of senators. The constitutional laws had clearly established the Senate as a checking and restraining influence upon the action of the popularly elected Chamber. Senators were chosen by electoral councils, made up of members of local government councils, deputies, and delegates chosen from the communes, the small villages receiving excessive representation. Since the Senator's term was for nine years, and the body was renewed one-third at a time every three years, the political temper of the Senate was often quite different from that of the Chamber, whose members' term lasted only four years. Its membership was usually distinguished, but since it was once removed from the source of popular sovereignty its authority and hence its influence upon policy was less decisive, though not inconsiderable.

## Lawmaking and Policy Formulation in Parliament

**Forming a Cabinet.** As in English Cabinet government, one of the most important tasks of the legislative body was to organize a majority coalition willing to support a group of leaders, the

Ministry. In the preceding chapter the difficulties of arranging a coalition of the various party groups have been suggested. The president of the Republic conferred with the leaders of the chief parties in the Chamber. A premier accepted the task of finding leaders who would act with him, and finally the names of the Ministry could be announced. At times a painful period of suspense occurred, while the terms of association were being arranged; and not infrequently a Ministry would resign within a few weeks, or even a few days, while a stable coalition was in the process of formation.

Once the Ministry was assured of a true majority in the Chamber—the Senate rarely felt strong enough to exercise powers of life or death over the Cabinet—it assumed powers comparable to those of a Cabinet in England. All major projects of legislation were introduced with ministerial sponsorship, and refusal of the Chamber to pass them, or the introduction of substantial and vital amendments, precipitated a resignation and a new alignment of parties behind a new or modified leadership. At the same time every minister was subject to questions on his conduct of the affairs of his particular department. The *interpellation*, a question addressed to a minister followed by a debate upon the answer given, was frequently used. This practice is quite different from that of the question hour in the English House of Commons, where the minister's answer is not debated. Since the Cabinet's majority was always somewhat unstable and unreliable, frequent changes of Ministry occurred as a consequence of debates upon legislation or administrative policy.

**Committees.** The committees of the Chamber exercised much greater influence upon the legislative process than the committees do in the English House of Commons. Chosen by ballot, with allotment of members in proportions to the shades of opinion in the Chamber, each committee gave thorough consideration to projects of legislation; and the chairman and the reporter of the committee frequently took as important a part in the general debates as the minister. The list of committees approximately paralleled the ministries. For example, the committee on finance carefully scrutinized the budget proposed by the finance minister, and in the days of the Popular Front (1936) succeeded in forcing the modification of budgetary policy, after general debate in the Chamber.

These variations from English parliamentary procedure are all explicable as products of the multiple-party situation. Frequent opportunity for debate in the Chamber, committee action affording careful consideration of policy, reconsideration under similar procedures in the more decorous and restrained atmosphere of the Senate, allowed for the continuous arrangement of compromises between differing parties and viewpoints, and for the necessary changes of leadership, as conditions in France and Europe shifted.

**Merits and Defects.** The defects of the system are apparent from this brief description. It was always hard to organize leadership, and it was hard for any leadership to take decisive action. Sometimes France was actually left leaderless in times of crisis; or an existing leadership found itself powerless to embark upon a new or aggressive policy. The merits of the system were, oddly enough, an aspect of its faults. It furnished responsive government, for the necessity of continuous adjustment of programs reflected fairly faithfully the shifts of public opinion, and also prevented hasty action which might prove injurious, either to groups or to the nation as a whole. Stability of policy was provided even though the personnel of Ministries changed. There was rarely a sweeping change; instead, there was a continuous "dance of the portfolios," in which ordinarily a number of ministers reappeared in successive Cabinets, not infrequently in their former positions.

**Political Careers.** In one way the French Cabinet system produced the same effect attained in England. The Chamber and the Senate offered opportunities for a political career, and served as a training school for leaders. The deputy was elected because he had performed public duties in his home district, and had acquired some acquaintance with the problems of government. In the Chamber he had an opportunity to participate in debates on public policy, and in his committee assignments he learned a great deal about the intricacies of administration of public affairs. Changes of ministry and realignment of party groups gave him chances to hold an undersecretaryship if he showed promise; and eventually he became, in the French phrase, *ministrable*. Minor ministries led to more important posts, and finally—if his career continued successful—to the premiership. In his later years he might well be elected to the Senate, where his acquired experience and knowledge could still be valuable to his country, though he might be excluded from decisive participation in more active political life with its frequent dramatic crises.

### SUMMARY: THE FRENCH PATTERN OF POLITICS

While many Frenchmen were dissatisfied with the Third Republic, its continuance through the trying years of the late nineteenth century, its management of France during World War I, and its whole life of over sixty years—a long life for a French constitution—suggests that many of its characteristics may reappear in France.

In any nation political traditions and customs tend to persist—as indeed, they have already persisted in France—so that many of the attitudes and programs maintained by the parties are likely to continue under a new constitution. At the same time, the lack of decisive leadership is a fault which may lead to experiment in new methods.

The next chapter will be devoted to political trends and problems of reconstruction as they have been manifest since the defeat of the Third Republic in World War II.

### READINGS

A great deal has been written about the character of the French parliamentary system. The following suggestions in every case furnish bibliographies which give further guidance, and most of the references given at the end of the two preceding chapters are informative on this subject.

Guérard, Albert, *The France of Tomorrow*, Cambridge, 1942.

Middleton, W. L., *The French Political System*, New York, 1933. A penetrating analysis of parties and Parliament by a shrewd English journalist.

Siegfried, André, *France, A Study in Nationality*, New Haven, 1930. A brilliant essay by a distinguished French scholar on political psychology and behavior.

Soltau, R. H., *French Parties and Politics*, rev. ed., New York, 1930. A brief, but thorough and careful, account of the history and conduct of the parties.

Werth, Alexander, *France in Ferment*, New York, 1934.

——, *Which Way France?*, New York, 1937.

——, *The Twilight of France*, New York, 1942. These books by the Paris correspondent of the Manchester *Guardian* give an excellent account of the political movements in France before, during, and after the Popular Front election of 1936.

This list could easily be greatly extended, but these suggestions are all valuable for the student.

# CHAPTER 12

# THE FOURTH REPUBLIC AND
# ITS PROBLEMS

IN 1940 the Third Republic suffered a crushing military defeat. For the next four years France was governed by German occupation authorities, though the Vichy government, headed by Marshal Pétain, was allowed a little freedom of action. In October 1944 the provisional government of France was recognized by the United States, Great Britain, and the Soviet Union, and the process of creating a new government was begun. It is impossible to tell the complete story of this troubled period, because the record is still not fully known. The chief events, however, can be set forth, and the development of a Fourth Republic can be indicated.

## THE FALL OF FRANCE

On September 3, 1939, Premier Daladier announced in a national broadcast that France, fulfilling her treaty pledges, was entering the war because the Hitler government had attacked Poland. Mobilization of the army had already begun, and the government proceeded to organize for war by a series of emergency decrees. There followed the period which was called "the phony war," during which the Maginot Line was garrisoned, and industry was organized for the war effort. Preparations were made for civilian defense; and rationing schemes, price controls, and financial plans were undertaken to meet the demands of war. The Ministry was reorganized to widen its political support, and the Chamber voted to give the Cabinet powers of issuing decrees.

In March 1940 the successes of the German campaign in Norway led to criticism of the Daladier Cabinet; and Paul Reynaud, following Daladier's resignation, organized a new Ministry with a wider representation of parties. Political disunity was apparent, however, and the Chamber failed to give the new leadership the support of an absolute majority, many deputies abstaining from voting.

**The Blitzkrieg.** In May the German blitzkrieg began in Belgium and Holland, and the German armies crossed the French frontier before the end of the month. General Weygand replaced General Gamelin as commander of the French armies, but the military situation was quickly revealed as hopeless. On June 10 Italy entered the war against France. Four days later the German armies entered Paris, which had been declared an open city to spare it the effects of an attack. The government was removed to Bordeaux, and Reynaud appealed to President Roosevelt for American aid in supplying military equipment, especially airplanes. While the reply to this appeal assured all possible help, it was clearly not enough to alter the desperate situation. On June 16 the British government proposed a plan for a Franco-British union, in the hope that the French leadership could be induced to continue the war. But by this time there was a profound division in the Ministry. Reynaud resigned, and General Pétain headed a new Cabinet which asked the Germans for an armistice. On June 22 and 25 armistice agreements were signed with Germany and Italy respectively, and by July 10 a partial membership of the Chamber and the Senate, sitting as a National Assembly, voted to abrogate the constitution of the Third Republic, and adopted a few basic laws which conferred wide powers to organize a new government upon Marshal Pétain.

Any complete explanation of why the Third Republic fell is as yet impossible. Among many conflicting views which have been expressed concerning these events, a few substantial causes can be discerned. First of all, it is well to remember that France was a victim—immediately after Poland, Belgium, and Holland

—of a new type of mechanized warfare, the blitzkrieg. The Allied nations were unable to win a victory over the German armies until they had adopted and improved this new technique. Defensive preparations were shown to be inadequate against new weapons and new methods of using old ones.

The French high command has been criticized for rigidity of mind and lack of imagination in being unable, or unwilling, correctly to foresee future possibilities and to develop new techniques to meet the dangers. There is probably considerable truth in this criticism, but it does not apply to France alone. British and American military leadership was also slow to act. The Germans, forced by the necessities of their situation, were more ready to make use of invention and discovery.

Finally, political leadership in the Third Republic has been accused of weakness and corruption. Many of the stories of unworthy intrigue among parliamentary leaders probably have some foundation, but the evidence is not yet conclusive. One undisputed conclusion may be taken as significant: it has always been difficult to organize decisive leadership within the parliamentary framework and under the political practice of the Third Republic. It was especially difficult in 1939 and 1940 because there were deep divisions in French opinion, stemming from controversies which had arisen over the Popular Front program of 1936. Confronted by the grim necessities of war, the methods of coalition and compromise did not deliver sufficiently prompt and effective action.

For the student, the fact that France fell is the most important consideration, for it made necessary an emergency government to deal with the situation after the defeat.[1]

## GERMAN OCCUPATION AND THE VICHY GOVERNMENT

The armistice agreement with Germany divided France into two zones. The northern part, including the whole of the western

[1] See the list of references at the end of this chapter for discussions of the fall of France.

coast down to the Spanish border, was occupied and administered by German military authorities. The remainder was left under the rule of the Vichy government, of which Marshal Pétain was the chief, with Pierre Laval as an influential member of his Cabinet. Though this area was called "unoccupied France," it was soon clear that the Marshal's government was subject to German control in all significant policies. The political temper of the Vichy Cabinet combined ultraconservative viewpoints with acceptance of the idea of a permanent domination of Europe by Germany.

**The Vichy Government.** It is hardly necessary to give more than brief mention to the organization and policies of the Pétain government, since after V-E Day its work was almost completely swept away. There was a great concentration of power in the hands of Marshal Pétain as the chief of the French state, though his ministers probably exercised all real authority. Constitutional acts proclaimed that legislative assemblies would be created, but no meetings were ever called. The system of courts remained much as it had previously existed, but extensive changes were made in local administration. The powers of the central government were increased by diminishing the degree of local initiative and representation possessed by the larger towns and cities. The *départements* were grouped into regions, and regional prefects coordinated the work of the *département* prefects. The civil rights of citizens were greatly reduced; freedom of expression and of political organization, and the civil rights of Jews and of Freemasons, were substantially modified.

In brief, the program of Pétain and his colleagues resembled the organization of a totalitarian state. Since the Vichy government lasted only from July 1940 to the summer of 1944, it may be regarded as an interlude in the life of the nation. Eventually many of its leaders were convicted of treason, and a number were executed. It is unlikely that its existence will leave any permanent impress upon French political institutions, though its brief existence revealed the desires of many ultraconservative elements.

## THE RESISTANCE MOVEMENT AND THE
### PROVISIONAL GOVERNMENT

Shortly after the armistice had been announced, General de Gaulle called on Frenchmen to continue resistance against Germany from the French empire and from England. This was the beginning of the "Free French" movement, which in succeeding months recruited members from French territory and established a committee to direct activities and furnish leadership. After the relationship between various French groups and the British and American governments had been adjusted following the invasion of North Africa, a French Committee of National Liberation was set up in Algiers. In September 1943 a Consultative Assembly was established, and the membership of the Committee and of the Assembly was widened to include representatives of all the important former parliamentary parties and the various resistance groups. This constituted, in effect, an emergency government for France.

**D-Day.** In August 1944 the government moved from Algiers to Paris, following the victories of British and American armies, heroically assisted by the French Forces of the Interior, to use the name accorded to the armed forces of the Resistance. The Consultative Assembly was once more enlarged in membership, and for some months the provisional government, under the leadership of General de Gaulle, administered the complicated domestic and imperial affairs of France, and conducted foreign policy. Election of a Constituent Assembly had been promised, and on October 21, 1945, members of this assembly were elected. At the same time French voters cast ballots in a referendum, voicing a strong majority in favor of giving the Assembly power to draft a constitution for a new government, and simultaneously placing limits on the power of the Assembly to govern the country until the new constitution could be put to work.

The Assembly began drafting the constitution in committees created for the purpose. It also carried on the task of governing

France, though the association between the three major parties was not always harmonious. The draft of the new constitution, which reflected the influence of the Socialists and Communists in large part, was adopted on April 19, 1946, by an Assembly vote of 309 against 249. A national referendum was announced to obtain a popular verdict on its provisions. There was lively debate in the Assembly, and active discussion throughout the country.[2]

**The 1946 Constitution.** The most important features of the constitutional proposals of 1946 should be briefly stated, since they embodied French ideas on the reconstruction of republican institutions. One of the striking features of the draft, differing from the fundamental laws of the Third Republic, was the careful recital of the rights of the citizen. The civil and political equality of men and women was declared, a new departure in France, though proposals for woman suffrage had been discussed many times since 1900. Besides listing the classic political and civil rights which had been a part of French tradition since the Declaration of the Rights of Man in the early revolutionary constitutions, this document went on to enumerate a number of social and economic rights. Guarantees were given for the furnishing of educational opportunities, for the organization of labor unions, the use of collective bargaining procedures, and for the establishment of a broad system of social insurances.

The framework of government provided that the chief powers of legislation and determination of policy should be vested in a unicameral legislative assembly. This concentration of power in a single representative chamber was partially modified by the creation of a Council of the French Union, elected by the councils of *départements* in metropolitan France and in the territories overseas, which was to exercise advisory powers over proposed legislation. Powers of advice were also to be exercised by an economic council, its membership to be determined later by law.

[2] The Assembly vote on the draft is reported in the *New York Times,* April 20, 1946; and an English text of the constitution is given in the *New York Times,* April 23, 1946.

The problem of strengthening leadership was met by altering the relations of the Ministry and the Chamber, for the election of the president, and the powers of his office, were left much as before. Instability of Ministries, the chronic weakness of the Third Republic, was to be remedied by positive use of the power of dissolution. The Chamber could dissolve on its own motion, if passed by a two-thirds majority; the president was empowered to dissolve it by decree, provided more than two ministerial crises occurred during the second half of the life of the legislature. Restrictions were placed upon the use of the interpellation and the vote of want of confidence, to avoid the easy means of forcing the resignation of Ministries which had been available under the procedures of the old Chamber of Deputies.

Encouragement was given to the development of greater local initiative in communes and *départements* by provisions for wider elections of representative councils and increase of their powers. This would imply a corresponding decrease of central supervision, and could easily lead to a substantial change in the power exercised by the central government.

**Principles of the Constitution.** Two general intentions may be found in this first draft: first, the establishment of social and political rights for all citizens, regardless of sex; secondly, the provision for more decisive political leadership, drawn from a single representative assembly. This latter purpose, it should be added, was strongly urged by the Socialists and Communists, who believed that many French voters were ready to support decisive changes, and therefore hoped to carry out programs of socialization of industry by means of more direct popular representation.

Debate in the Constituent Assembly, and discussion in the country before the referendum on the constitution which was held May 5, 1946, centered principally on the question of the unicameral legislature, with moderate groups opposing the proposal against the support of the parties on the Left. While unicameralism versus bicameralism was formally the issue, the underlying questions involved a broad range of social and economic possibilities. The constitution was defeated by a substantial majority, approximately 10,000,000 votes to 8,900,000. This made necessary the election of a second Constituent Assembly, which took place June 2, 1946.

**The Second Assembly and Constitution of 1946.** The responsibilities of the second Assembly were the same as those of the first. It supported Ministries and guided the policies of the Provisional government. At the same time, in its committees, it drafted a second constitution, which was presented to the voters on October 13, 1946. The referendum resulted in the adoption of the draft by approximately 9,000,000 votes to 7,000,000. Nearly 30 per cent of the electorate refrained from voting, however, so the decision lacked finality. General de Gaulle's opposition, expressed in press statements and speeches, probably contributed much to this unsatisfactory result.

The legislative Assembly elected in November 1946 is likely to propose amendments to the second constitution. The differences between it and the first 1946 constitution are worth notice. The most striking contrast between it and the earlier draft lies in the composition of the Parliament, which is to have two chambers. The Assembly, like that provided in the first constitution, is to be elected by direct popular vote, the electoral methods to be prescribed by law. There is provision for a Council of the French Republic, elected indirectly, partly by local councils, and partly by the Assembly. This upper house is to have a six-year term, and its members are to be chosen one-half at a time every three years. The Council's legislative powers are limited. It may examine and revise legislation within two months. The Assembly may then accept this advice, or reject it. Rejection requires a public, recorded ballot, and an absolute majority. If the Council fails to report a bill back within the two months, it becomes law without further action. The Council of the French Republic, therefore, possesses only a two months' suspensive veto; but it is able to force a second careful consideration of legislation. Two bodies provided for in the first constitution—the Council of the French Union, a deliberative assembly for the French empire, and the Economic Council—are retained.

There is also some substantial difference between the two drafts with regard to the powers of the president of the Republic. The choice of a premier must be confirmed by an absolute majority of the Assembly under the new provisions; and dissolution of the Assembly occurs by its own decision, with the advice of the president of the Assembly if crises arise after the first eighteen months of its legislative life. These curtailments of the president's powers of leadership and decision probably had much to do with General de Gaulle's opposition to the second constitution.

Amendment of the second constitution is possible without a referendum if majorities of three-fifths of both houses, three months after the first proposal of an amendment, can be secured. The first constitution invariably required popular referendum.

Finally, the second constitution reduces substantially the number of specific guarantees made in the bill of rights. A preamble was substituted for the elaborate provisions of the first constitution. General declarations promise the maintenance of the traditional political and civil rights of 1789, and principles calling for economic and social guarantees are enunciated.

Until amendments modify it, this second constitution will serve as the basis for the government of France. A few predictions can be made now with confidence. The maintenance of democratic, republican government is clearly assured. The prospect of social and economic reforms, with some programs of nationalization of banking and large industries already accomplished, seems likely to be realized. Future policy will naturally depend upon the strength of parties as they continue to put forward programs to meet the problems of reconstruction.

## Parties and Political Alignments

It has never been easy to interpret the French political spectrum. Since liberation several of the old parties have reappeared, and new ones have been organized. During the years of German occupation, underground movements existed, and when political freedom was recovered they quickly developed into parties. The necessities of resistance brought about new associations among Frenchmen, with the result that the new parties have large voting memberships, and may eclipse the old in popular influence.

The first opportunities for French voters to declare their sympathies at the ballot box occurred April 29 and May 13, 1945, when communal councils were elected. On September 23 and 30 of the same year cantonal elections were held. These two elections, each requiring second ballotings to determine final choices, did not clearly show political alignments. Local personalities and issues were considerable factors, and more than twenty parties put forward lists of candidates. Nevertheless, these elections had a considerable value, for active campaigning stimulated interest in public affairs and gave leaders opportunities to meet the voters, after a political blackout which had lasted for more than four years.

In October 1945, in June and November 1946 national elections were held for the Constituent Assembly, which was to frame a constitution and conduct the government of France. Interest was keen in all contests, 80 per cent or more of the voters participating on each occasion. A form of proportional representation was used in these elections, with voters declaring for lists of candidates. Though alliances between parties made it difficult to measure the strength of all groups precisely, the figures reveal trends of opinion. The table given on the following page summarizes the official figures of the popular vote and parliamentary membership received by groups of parties.

A few interpretative comments can be made on the alignments revealed in the elections. The most striking single aspect is the strength of the three leading parties in both elections. While the traditional multiple-party situation appears in the total number of groups, the Popular Republicans (MRP), the Communists, and the Socialists (SFIO and allied groups of the Left) maintained substantial strength in the popular vote and in Assembly membership. This might mean that the French

NATIONAL CONSTITUENT ASSEMBLY ELECTIONS, 1945 AND 1946 [3]

| PARTIES | POPULAR VOTE | | | | | | SEATS | | |
|---|---|---|---|---|---|---|---|---|---|
| | 1945 | | June 1946 | | Nov. 1946 | | 1945 | June 1946 | Nov. 1946 |
| | Millions | Per cent | Millions | Per cent | Millions | Per cent | | | |
| *Left:* | | | | | | | | | |
| International communist | 0.01 | 0.07⎫ | 0.04 | 0.25⎫ | ... | 0.3⎫ | 154 | 148 | 168 |
| Communist & URR | 5.00 | 26.1⎭ | 5.14 | 25.98⎭ | 5.2 | 28.2⎭ | | | |
| SFIO; SFIO–UDSR; SFIO–MLN | 4.49 | 23.4 | 4.19 | 25.14 | 4.2 | 17.9 | 136 | 120 | 107 |
| Rad. Soc.; UDSR; Jeune Rep.; other left | 2.02 | 10.6 | 2.30 | 11.6 | 1.97 | 11.1 | 41 | 40 | 45 |
| *Center:* | | | | | | | | | |
| MRP | 4.58 | 23.9 | 5.59 | 28.22 | 5.03 | 26. | 145 | 162 | 160 |
| *Right:* | | | | | | | | | |
| Entente Rep.; All. Dem.; Fed. Rep.; Parti Paysanne; P.R.L.; other right | 2.89 | 15.2 | 2.53 | 12.77 | 3.14 | 16. | 43 | 43 | 82 |
| *Others Unaffiliated:* | | | | | | | | | |
| Algerian groups and independents | 0.11 | 0.6 | 0.01 | 0.06 | 0.09 | 0.5 | 8 | 17 | 12 |

Abbreviations used above:

All. dem.—*Alliance démocratique* (moderate Right or Center)

Entente rep.—*Entente républicaine* (moderate Right or Center)

Fed. rep.—*Fédération républicaine* (moderate Right)

Jeune rep.—*Jeune République* (reformist republican)

MLN—*Mouvement de libération nationale* (northern resistance groups, reformist)

MRP—*Mouvement Républicain Populaire* (Catholic moderate reformist)

P.R.L.—*Parti Républicain de la Liberté* (rightist and conservative)

Rad. Soc.—*Radical Socialiste* (moderate socialist and reformist)

SFIO—*Section Française de l'Internationale Ouvrière* (socialist)

UDSR—*Union démocratique et socialiste de résistance* (reformist groups of the resistance)

URR—*Union des républicains et résistance* (Leftist groups of the resistance movement in the south)

party kaleidoscope is to be simplified by the predominance of three primary colors, and that the delicate shadings of opinion will be diminished to fringes of the traditional Right, Center, and Left. The high percentages of popular participation in the three

[3] The data for the table is taken from *Le Monde*, Paris, October 25, 1945, June 4 and 6, November 11 and 12, 1946.

elections indicate that the voters are fully aware that their ballots may have a positive effect upon government policy.

**Opinions and Policies.** It is hard to state any general drift of opinion on the basis of these elections. Policies of nationalization of the banks and credit institutions were developed, and government controls or nationalization in some of the large industries were partially accomplished during the period covered by the three elections. The new constitution was drafted and offered to the people, and its provisions suggested that the governmental practice of the Third Republic was to be modified in order to achieve more positive leadership. Its bill of rights, by setting forth economic and social guarantees, promised a policy of active reform. The referendum on the document was unfavorable, but the tendencies just mentioned are likely to remain influential.

Cabinets have reflected the opinions revealed by the popular votes. General de Gaulle announced a Cabinet of commissioners for the provisional government of France on August 30, 1944, just four days after his dramatic entrance into Paris. After the first election, October 21, 1945, the full strength of Socialist and Communist opinion was definitely shown. A few weeks of discussion in the Assembly led to de Gaulle's resignation, and Felix Gouin, leader of the Socialist party and formerly president of the consultative assembly, was elected president, November 8, 1945. A tri-party cabinet, representing the major political groupings, conducted the affairs of the government.

In the second national election, May 5, 1946, the MRP increased its popular vote and assembly membership, as the table shows. Georges Bidault, who had been a leader in the resistance movement and had made substantial achievements as minister of foreign affairs in preceding Cabinets, was elected president of the provisional government by a large vote in the new Constituent Assembly. Under his leadership the cooperation of the three major parties has continued. The strength of the MRP indicated that French opinion, while it was ready to support the active program of domestic reform already in progress, was not prepared for extensive schemes of socialization. The MRP, though it is reformist in temper, favors moderate measures that accord with the caution of its members.

The future government of France still awaits precise definition in amendments to the new constitution, which may be proposed by the Assembly elected in November 1946. Maintaining the traditions of democracy, the French must now meet the difficult problems of domestic reconstruction, and conduct of foreign policy in the postwar world.

### READINGS

The fall of the Third Republic has already been made the subject of an extensive literature. A few illuminating accounts are:

Armstrong, H. F., *Chronology of Failure*, New York, 1940.

Géraud, André (Pertinax), *The Gravediggers of France*, New York, 1944.

Marchal, L., *Vichy: Two Years of Deception*, New York, 1943.

Simone, André, *J'Accuse: The Men Who Betrayed France*, New York, 1940.

The development of the provisional government of France and the framing of a new constitution are too recent for analysis in books. Discussion in English is accessible in the following publications:

The New York *Times*

*The Times*, London

*Foreign Affairs*, New York

*Foreign Policy Reports*, Foreign Policy Association, New York

*The World Today*, Royal Institute of International Affairs, London

*The Contemporary Review*, London

Two books, discussing French political tradition with the purpose of analyzing contemporary changes, may be mentioned:

Fernand-Laurent, J. C., *Gallic Charter: Foundations of Tomorrow's France*, Boston, 1944.

Munro, Katharine, *France Yesterday and Today*, London, 1945.

For those who read French, *Le Monde*, the Paris daily newspaper which has succeeded to the authoritative position of *Le Temps*, is a useful source of information.

# THE SOVIET UNION

# CHAPTER 13

# THE BOLSHEVIK REVOLUTION AND THE USSR

THIRTY years ago a revolutionary leadership established in Russia a new form of government. The political and economic program of the Bolshevik party in 1917 was based upon the ideas of Karl Marx and the many socialist thinkers who followed him. It was modified by Lenin, and the other leaders of the revolution. The Communist party has been continuously in power since its capture of authority in November 1917, and for three decades has striven to create the institutions which would embody the ideal society envisaged by Marx and Lenin.

The Soviet Union must be regarded not only as a new form of government in Russia, but in many respects as a new form of government among the nations of the world. As such, it has inevitably become the subject of discussion and controversy. Its economic resources and political power make its policies almost as significant for Americans, Englishmen, and the peoples of every other nation, as for Russians. This has only intensified the discussion and embittered the controversy. This is of course not unusual, since all revolutionary governments, and it is no exaggeration to say that the revolution in Russia is still in progress, generate such controversy.

The difficulties imposed by limited information, and the difficulties arising from disputes over ideologies, are increased by the fact that communism is an international movement. Its victory in Russia affected the history of other nations in Europe and Asia. The fascist state in Italy, the Nazi dictatorship in Germany, for example, were partly the results of resistance to the spread of revolutionary socialist doctrine. The story of the Soviet state must be told in terms of the ideas it represents; their significance spreads beyond the Russian boundaries.

## THE COMMUNIST PROGRAM AND THE BOLSHEVIK PARTY

Karl Marx and Friedrich Engels published *The Communist Manifesto* in 1848. The fundamental doctrines of what they called "scientific" socialism, to distinguish it from earlier "utopian" socialism, were set forth in this brief pamphlet. After nearly twenty years of laborious research in the British Museum in London, Marx in 1867 published his first volume of *Capital,* a formulation of the economic theories which would support the plan of action proposed in *The Communist Manifesto.* Lenin, while he was engaged in organizing the revolution of 1917, found time to write *The State and Revolution,* in which he refined and sharpened the political implications of Marxian economic theory. Many other writers have elaborated these doctrines and defended them against criticism during the years since 1848.

This combination of social theory and fighting creed can hardly be compressed into a brief summary. Three central ideas, however, give it explosive force: (1) the labor theory of value, (2) a philosophy of history, and (3) a theory of the nature of the state.

**The Labor Theory of Value.** The labor theory of value, reduced to its barest essentials, asserts that the exchange value of commodities arises from the labor embodied in them. From this the moral implication logically follows that the laborer, having created the worth of goods, is entitled to receive their value in full. All income should come from work, Marx argued, and, since he believed that both interest and profits arose from ownership, they seemed to be simply appropriation of "surplus value," and therefore socially unjustifiable.

**The Philosophy of History.** The Marxian philosophy of history, called "dialectical materialism" by its supporters, explains the changes which occur in social organization by identifying the class struggle as the most important, if not the sole, cause.

Changes in the system of production from handicraft methods to factory techniques brought into existence the laboring class and the capitalist class of the nineteenth and twentieth centuries, and created the conflict between them. Just as serfs in a feudal society finally revolted and destroyed the privileged position of the landowning aristocracy, so will laborers revolt in modern industrial society and "expropriate the expropriators."

**The Nature of the State.** The theory of the state is closely related to the economic determinism expressed in the philosophy of history. The state, in any society, is regarded by Marxians as the instrument of the dominant class. In feudal society it was the tool of the landed gentry; in the nineteenth and twentieth centuries it was, and is, dominated and controlled by the owners of productive property. Lenin, interpreting Marx and Engels, argued that only by a revolutionary seizure of power, and the establishment of the "dictatorship of the proletariat," could the laboring masses hope to establish a classless society in which they would receive the just reward for their effort. Violence would be required because owners would use the power of the state to defend property rights.

*The Communist Manifesto,* as its name implies, was more than a declaration of these theories, it was a call to action. Socialist parties were organized in the European nations, and engaged in political agitation. Many modifications and revisions were imposed upon the original doctrines. Fabian socialists in England, participating in the organization of the Labour party, relied upon reform and gradual change to achieve the desired goals. German Social Democrats organized the trade-unions and directed political activity toward political and economic reforms.

**Bolsheviks and Mensheviks.** In Russia, however, the Czarist government suppressed political agitation. The Social Democratic party was forced to adopt the secret methods of political conspiracy, and to hold its party congresses in other countries. In an international socialist congress which assembled in Brussels and continued its meeting in London in 1903, the representatives of the party split into two groups over the question of political tactics. The larger group, called by the Russian word *Bolsheviki*, which means majority, favored organizing a revolution to carry out the socialist program. The minority (Mensheviki) believed that peaceful agitation would be the better strategy.

**Other Parties.** Besides Bolsheviks and Mensheviks, other political groups formed in Russia. The Socialist Revolutionaries, who strictly were not among the followers of Karl Marx, were concerned chiefly with agrarian reform and the improvement of the social conditions of the peasants. The Constitutional Democrats, called Cadets, proposed a constitutional parliamentary government. Though the repressive measures and the secret police of the Czar's government made all political agitation dangerous and difficult, these four organizations managed to build up some following among the Russian people.

## Czarist Russia and World War I

The difficulties of building a national state in Russia, complicated by a long history of invasions by Asiatic peoples, finally were resolved by the establishment of the autocratic rule of the Czars. Absolute rule by means of a bureaucracy, in which the aristocracy had a claim on most of the key positions, was firmly established well before the nineteenth century.

**Early Reforms.** Beginning with proposals for reform in 1808, which were accomplished in part when a State Council was created, and the ministries were reorganized, some changes were achieved. Alexander II emancipated the serfs in 1861; and within the next ten years local government councils (zemstvos) were reorganized, judicial administration was improved, and a few other political changes were made. These changes, with their very limited effect upon the absolute power of the Czar and his officials, have been called the "Great Reforms."

Despite the serious disturbances caused by the Nihilist movement, the Russian state seemed to be immune to the political agitation and revolutionary sentiment in nineteenth-century Europe. In 1905, after the defeat inflicted by Japan, demonstrations by peasants and laborers occurred, and agitation was conducted by the political groups already described. Nicholas II was forced to grant some fundamenta. civil and political liberties and to agree to a fairly extensive franchise for election of members to a representative assembly, called the Duma, possessing some measure of legislative power. The membership of the first two Dumas included representatives of Cadet, Social Revolutionary, Menshevik and even Bolshevik parties. The demands of these reform and radical groups led to an early dissolution of both assemblies. Modification of the electoral laws reduced or excluded the membership holding unorthodox political views, so that the third and fourth Dumas were much more willing to accept the existing situation.

**World War I.** The political structure of the Russian state could not survive the strain of World War I. The national legislature was unrepresentative, the administrative bureaucracy was too highly centralized and insufficiently trained, and the army command was unimaginative. The fighting front was the scene of crushing defeats; the home front was disorganized and distressed. The palace intrigues conducted by Gregory Rasputin, who had great influence over the Czarina because he was able to improve the fragile health of the heir to the throne, further confused the policies of the government. Russian armies fought with great bravery, but by the spring of 1917 soldiers and people alike had lost confidence in the government.

**Provisional Government.** During 1916 and 1917 moderate liberal and progressive members of the Duma had criticized the government's errors, and had built up a following in the Duma and among the people. In March 1917 a provisional government was formed, with the support of the Duma.[1] Members of the Duma, with members of the Union of Zemstvos (a council made up of representatives of local government councils), and of the Petrograd Soviet of Soldiers' and Workmen's Deputies (a revolutionary council organized in Petrograd), were its leaders. This

[1] This is sometimes called the "February Revolution," the date being figured according to the old Russian calendar in use at the time.

emergency government induced the Czar to abdicate, and called elections for a constituent assembly which was to draw up a constitution for a new Russian state. Until the constitution could be drafted and put into operation, the provisional government assumed authority.

### The Bolshevik Revolution

The provisional government, under the leadership of Alexander Kerensky, attempted to continue the war and to introduce the reforms needed to solve agrarian and industrial problems. But the Russian people were utterly discouraged with the war, and the accumulated grievances of centuries made them dissatisfied with the promise of gradual changes in agriculture and in industrial working conditions. Politically, the new leaders suffered the serious handicap of being unable to claim that they truly represented public sentiment. Both the Duma, and the Union of Zemstvos, were only partially representative of the people. The promised constituent assembly could not be elected until November. Several efforts were made to create representative assemblies: the Moscow State Conference, called in August, included delegates from a wide variety of organizations; the Democratic Conference, assembled in September, was made up of local government representatives.

**"Dual Power."** Meanwhile, the Bolshevik leaders had achieved a more influential position in the Petrograd Soviet. Lenin had returned to Russia in April, aided in his journey across Germany and Poland by the German government. During the summer he was finally able to convince the leading Bolsheviks that a thoroughgoing socialist revolution could be accomplished, and soviets of workers and soldiers were organized in many cities and villages. Bolshevik agitation had a large share in the creation of these extra-legal councils. The resulting situation may be shortly described in Trotsky's phrase, "dual power." There were two governments in Russia: (1) the provisional government, depending on the Duma and various improvised legal representative assemblies for support, pursuing policies of moderate reform, and advocating the continuance of the war; (2) the Petrograd Soviet, claiming to represent the masses of the people through its connection with other soviets, proposing a program of revolutionary change, and promising to arrange an immediate peace. The elections to the constituent assembly gave a majority to the moderate reform groups, but by that time Lenin had convinced his associates that they were ready to seize power.

After the Bolshevik leaders took charge, they forcefully dispersed the newly elected assembly. Negotiations were begun with Germany to arrange peace, and in March 1918 humiliating and costly terms were accepted at Brest-Litovsk. A sweeping program of nationalization of land and basic industries was proclaimed. Control of production by factory committees of workers replaced the former managers and owners. The dictatorship of the proletariat seemed to be swiftly establishing the new classless society.

## War Communism and the Soviet Constitution

Lenin's confident and aggressive action was based in part on an expectation which failed to materialize. He had assumed that "the Revolution" would rapidly spread to other European countries. It would be easy, he expected, to carry out his program in a Russia surrounded by friendly socialist states. Instead civil war broke out in various parts of the country, under the leadership of men like General Denikin and Admiral Kolchak who wished to return to the old institutions or to support the moderate program of the provisional government. The Allied governments, deeply disturbed by the Russian withdrawal from the war, pursued diplomatic and economic policies which were often hostile toward the new Soviet government.

**Civil War.** The years from 1917 to 1920 were dangerous and difficult for the new leadership. The Red army had to be organized, and furnished with supplies to carry on a civil war. The new state was isolated from other nations by a diplomatic *cordon sanitaire*. The Bolshevik domestic policy has been called

"War Communism." The state appropriated and managed all important economic activities, and established a system of grain collections from the peasants, who had seized their lands from their former landlords. These actions were dictated by both the communist program and the necessities of re-establishing activity in the disorganized condition of the Russian economy. In addition, a rigorous policing of dissenting opinion was organized, and many conspirators against the regime (and innocent opponents of its program) were executed. Some degree of public confirmation of the action of the revolutionary leadership was secured by calling congresses of peasants' and workers' soviets, in which a partial representation of a few of the reform parties was reflected.

**Soviet Constitutions.** The Fifth Congress of Soviets ratified a constitution for the new state on July 10, 1918. The draft which was adopted at that time was the product of discussion in earlier congresses of the same year, and had been framed by an executive committee approved by the assembled deputies. Its provisions created the machinery of government which continued in operation until the 1936 constitution was drawn up and approved by the Seventh and Eighth Congresses of Soviets.

The Russian constitution of 1918 created a Federated Soviet Socialist Republic (RSFSR). In 1923 a Union of Soviet Socialist Republics (USSR) extended the plan to national groups and regions in Asia and the Caucasus. The suffrage was restricted to workers and peasants. Owners, officials, members of the priesthood, and other groups associated with the former regime, were disqualified from voting. The method of representation was one of indirect election: local soviets (the Russian word for council) in villages and cities chose representatives to regional councils; these in turn chose delegates to provincial and republic soviets, from which the members of the national legislative bodies were chosen. Urban districts were given a higher proportion of these councils than were the country regions, because the strength of the Communist party was greater in the industrial cities. All the soviets acted as governing bodies for their respective areas, whether a village, city, or one of the republics.

**Governing Bodies.** The Union Congress of Soviets chose a large executive committee, divided into a Soviet of the Union and a Soviet of Nationalities. From this committee a smaller body, the Presidium, was elected. The Presidium acted as an advisory body to the Council of Commissars. When the Union Congress of Soviets was not in session, the Presidium had power to pass laws which later had to be confirmed by the Congress. The Council of Commissars was made up of the heads of the various executive departments. Each commissar, like a Cabinet minister in a parliamentary government, directed the activities of a government department; the Council of Commissars determined the general lines of policy.

The relationship of the republics to the union may be briefly stated by saying that the USSR was a federal government in which there was a high degree of centralized power. Each of the member republics and regions possessed a substantial authority over local government and cultural affairs; but the Council of Commissars administered foreign affairs, defense, and the great industries such as transportation, coal mining, and heavy manufacturing.

**The Communist Party.** The comparisons with parliamentary government which have just been used are subject to a vital qualification: the Communist party was able to maintain an effective party dictatorship through the indirect election of members of the various soviets. The members of the Presidium of the Union and of the Council of Commissars were among the leaders of the party. The many local organizations, scattered through the country and concentrated in the large cities, exerted a powerful influence on the affairs of every community. The executive committee of the party, with support from occasional party congresses, defined the general line of government policy. Though the party membership included but a small fraction of the whole citizen body, it was able to secure a monopoly of power.

While it must be recognized that the Bolsheviks were a minority who imposed their will by force, it is important to remember that their policies were accepted by a large part of the Russian people. The new government had ended the war; the peasants had seized the land; the workers felt they had some share in the management of industry; the promise of a new society had been popularized by effective slogans. While it is impossible to measure the proportion of support the new leadership was able to win outside the narrow limits of party membership, it can be said safely that many peasants and workers who did not understand the Communist program nevertheless consented to its policies. Political dissent was ruthlessly suppressed by a secret police which was organized during the years of civil war. This was nothing new for the government of the Czars had also denied opposition groups the opportunity to express themselves. The Russian people were hardly ready to use representative institutions; many of them were quite ready to agree to policies which were imposed with little chance for discussion.

### CONTINUANCE OF THE REVOLUTION

When revolution failed to appear in Germany and other European states, the Bolshevik leaders organized the Third International, an association of socialist parties throughout the world. The Comintern, as it came to be called, was inevitably dominated by the Communist party in Russia. In the last quarter of the nineteenth century socialist groups had been associated in a similar organization, the Second International. The Comintern claimed succession as the leader of revolutionary movements, but the Second International continued to exist advocating a moderate Menshevist program.

The Comintern continued to declare a program of world revolution till its seventh congress in 1935. At that time the rise of fascism in Italy and nazism in Germany led to the adoption of a policy of cooperation with moderate socialist and democratic parties in a "United Front" against fascist parties and the aggressive action of Italian and German dictatorships. In 1943, after the Soviet Union was engaged in World War II on the side of the democracies, the Comintern was dissolved by the proclamation of its presidium.

The official abandonment of the hope of world revolution accompanied a change in the Communist domestic program in Russia. After Lenin's death in 1924, Stalin succeeded to the leadership. His official position as secretary of the party made this possible; Trotsky and other more picturesque revolutionaries could not count upon control of party organization. In 1929 the first Five-Year Plan was announced; and thereafter the policy of "building Socialism in Russia" engaged the efforts of the government. Since there seemed little likelihood of the establishment of a world of socialist states, the communist state in Russia urgently needed industrial and military strength to meet the possibility of economic isolation, or diplomatic and military aggression. The series of five-year plans were designed to meet these needs, and they required years of sacrifice and effort from the Russian people. Party dictatorship in a revolutionary situation seems likely to continue for some time. In fulfillment of the plans, capital equipment must be increased, labor must be trained, and the collective organization of agriculture must be completed.

## Contrasts with French Constitutional Development

Though thirty years have elapsed since the November Revolution, it is still impossible to assess its full significance. The contrasts made in Chapter 9 between British and French constitutional developments may be referred to here in order to clarify the nature of the changes which took place in Russia.

Like the French Revolution, the Bolshevik Revolution was belated. A doctrine requiring aggressive action had been formulated, and political agitation had spread this fighting faith. At the same time, political absolutism in both France and Russia had long been able to suppress criticism and prevent reforms.

After the first explosion in 1917, a revolutionary situation persisted for several years until the new forms of organization had achieved stability. Both these stories contrast sharply with the process of gradual adjustment which took place during the centuries of English constitutional history.

In one respect the changes in Russia were much more decisive than those in France. The Bolsheviks initiated a far more extensive social and economic program than did the French Republicans. The French Revolution of 1789 swept away the political organization of the old regime, the Bolshevik Revolution in 1917 created not merely a new government but a new society. A citizen body with little experience in political activity could hardly take an active part in solving problems of such staggering dimensions. Dictatorship made its appearance in the history of both countries.

All revolutionary governments arouse suspicion and distrust in other nations, and neither French nor Russian leaders were able to avoid difficulties in their relationship to other governments. Each movement was regarded, with good reason, as a potential risk to the existing pattern of affairs within communities and between the states of the world.

The combination of revolutionary program with new forms of social and political organization makes it difficult to evaluate the policies and purposes of the Soviet Union. Even though the Bolsheviks were to forswear all propaganda, the social experiment which they have set on foot cannot fail to profoundly influence men's thoughts everywhere.

## READINGS

A few of the many books dealing with the Bolshevik Revolution are:

Batsell, W. R., *Soviet Rule in Russia,* New York, 1929.

Bunyan, J., and H. H. Fisher, *The Bolshevik Revolution, 1917–1918,* Stanford University Press, 1934.

Chamberlin, W. H., *History of the Russian Revolution,* 2 vols., New York, 1935.

Harper, S. N., *The Russia I Believe In,* University of Chicago Press, 1945.

Pares, Sir Bernard, *A Short History of Russia,* New York, 1943.

Schuman, F. L., *Soviet Politics, At Home and Abroad,* chs. I-V, New York, 1946.

Treviranus, G. R., *Revolutions in Russia,* New York, 1944.

Trotsky, L., transl. by Max Eastman., *The History of the Russian Revolution,* 3 vols., New York, 1937.

CHAPTER 14

# THE COMMUNIST PARTY IN THE
# SOVIET UNION

SINCE the Communist party possesses a monopoly of political power, it is appropriate to begin the discussion of Russian government with a description of party organization. The most striking single fact is worth stating immediately. The total membership of the party, rising from a few hundreds of thousands in 1917, has fluctuated between two and one half and five and three quarter millions; the membership of the party, combined with its allied youth organizations has rarely exceeded a maximum of fifteen to twenty millions. The total population of the USSR is certainly more than 170 millions, and the qualified voting population is more than ninety millions.[1] Briefly, these figures mean that a small fraction of the citizens hold the reins of political authority, in spite of the wide franchise granted by the 1936 constitution. How is it possible for so small a group to exercise so much power?

## THE RECRUITMENT OF MEMBERS

Before 1917, when the repressive measures of the Czar's government were in full force, the Bolsheviks had to be very careful in admitting new members to their revolutionary brotherhood. Lenin convinced his associates that a small, highly disciplined organization could be the "vanguard" of the movement to sweep

[1] Figures on party membership, and on total population, must be approximate, since official figures have been almost unobtainable since World War II. The magnitudes given are substantially correct. See John N. Hazard, "Soviet Domestic Policy in the Postwar World," in *The American Political Science Review*, February 1946, XL, pp. 80–89.

away the existing social structure and replace it with the new classless society. In the opinion of the leaders this strategy is still needed. From 1917 to the early 1920's new members were admitted, provided they had the sponsorship of members in good standing. At present most of the recruitment for the party comes from its affiliated youth organizations. A promising boy or girl, frequently recommended by a teacher in the schools, may join the *Octobrists* when only eight or nine years old. The child participates in some of the contests, athletic and literary, conducted by the organization, and learns something of the accepted doctrines. From this he progresses to the *Young Pioneers*, whose age range is from ten to sixteen, and takes part in a broader program. If he seems loyal and industrious, he enters the *Komsomol* with other young people sixteen to twenty-three years old.

The young people in the *Komsomol* carry on a wide range of activities. Meetings are devoted to the discussion of the Communist program, and the economic situation of the nation and their home community. They frequently attend the meetings of the village or city soviet, and they help to carry on propaganda campaigns among the citizens. A determined effort is made to enlist their efforts in a great many civic affairs. The *Komsomol* publishes its own newspaper. They are all, of course, closely bound by the program and doctrines of the party, but within that range they are invited to develop suggestions and make proposals. During their *Komsomol* membership these young people are observed by the members of the primary organ (local group) of the Communist party of their locality, and a large proportion of them "graduate" into full party membership. All these youth groups have regional and territorial committees and conferences, and maintain national headquarters which are closely connected with Communist leadership. A career in public affairs may begin with these youthful affiliations. There is a good deal of fun, some excitement and drama, and an enormous amount of serious work for the young people who are members of these organizations. When they become full-fledged Communists they have been imbued with the official doctrines, have often become acquainted with party leaders, and have gained experience in many kinds of work for the program.

Besides these training organizations there are other associations which lead to connection with the Communist party. Trade-unions, cooperative societies, and agricultural collectives have continuous contact with party workers, and active participation in groups of this kind occasionally leads to Communist membership.

Clearly the power and influence of the small Communist minority in Russia springs in large part from the character of its membership. Careful selection and training guarantees loyalty and industry in all the members. A small number of people can exercise a dominant influence, provided they are, in terms of the desired objectives, the "right" people.

### ORGANIZATION AND DISCIPLINE

Once in the party, the man or woman who is a member finds that responsibilities and obligations are heavy. He must attend all meetings in his region; he must faithfully contribute dues; he must maintain a high standard of personal conduct. He must be careful to know, and defend, and explain the official viewpoint of the Communist leadership. Most members have a job in industry or agriculture, so the tasks imposed by the party take up many hours outside the regular working day. The motivation for assuming this burden is readily understandable: Communists have opportunities opened to them in the many state services, in the trade-unions, and in cooperative societies. Besides the chances for responsible and better-paid positions, there is political influence and social prestige as an inducement.

**Party Organization.** The organization of the party is a vast network which covers all of the republics of the union. Primary organs (formerly called cells) in industries and cities, in villages and factories, are knit together by district committees. Districts are coordinated by provincial and republic committees, and at the top of the hierarchy is the Central Committee.[2] This body works through three agencies: a Secretariat, an organization bureau (*Orgburo*), and a political bureau (*Politburo*). The *Politburo* exercises the vital function of formulating the official party doctrine, and once this is declared all Communists must support and defend it.

**Party Meetings.** "Intraparty democracy" is provided through the conferences of the localities, districts, and regions. All-Union Congresses of the party are called at irregular intervals, in theory at least every three years or every year, though the rule has not been strictly observed. Congresses are mass meetings of more than 2000 delegates and are dominated by the personal force and long experience of the leaders, though deliberation on policies and election of the Central Committee may open opportunities for discussion.

**Party Discipline.** The conduct and viewpoints of members are subject to the discipline of periodic purges. Local primary organs create committees, usually with one or two members added from regional or provincial committees, which in public meetings examine members closely on their conduct and their loyalty to the official doctrine and hear the opinions of fellow members. In addition, the state secret police, since 1934 a part of the Ministry of Internal Affairs,[3] has power to arrest and punish members for actions disloyal to the party. Occasionally, as in 1935, 1937, and 1938, the purges take the form of the sensational treason trials of influential leaders. Penalties for deviation from the party line or for lapses in conduct becoming a Communist, run all the way from removal from party office, or expulsion from membership, imposed by purge committees, to execution or imprisonment for serious counterrevolutionary activities, imposed by the Supreme Court of the Union.

[2] For a description of the personnel of this committee, see F. L. Schuman, *Soviet Politics, At Home and Abroad,* New York, 1946, pp. 351–58.

[3] The Supreme Soviet some months ago announced that the Commissariats would henceforth be called Ministries. (*New York Times,* March 16, 1946.) This Ministry and its police are called the NKVD.

Uniformity of viewpoint and diligent performance are achieved by these means. Not only are the "right" people carefully selected and trained, but continuous investigation and supervision insures conformity to the party's program. Morale and loyalty in this governing group serve to maintain it in political power.

The widespread network of committees, and the tightly organized command in the Central Committee, assure united action. At the same time they establish Communist membership and influence in all the soviets of the villages and the cities. Communists also occupy positions of authority in the state services, in the large-scale industries, and in the consumers' and producers' cooperatives. A career in the party is frequently one of the means of securing advancement in any one of a wide range of economic or professional activities.

## The Party and the People

If the approximate figures given at the first of this chapter are recalled, it is clear that most Russian citizens are neither members of the party nor directly affiliated with it in other ways. Article 126 of the 1936 constitution recognizes the "Communist Party of the Soviet Union (Bolsheviks)" as "the vanguard of the working people in their struggle to develop the socialist system." Communists have a virtual monopoly of political activity, though many other public associations such as the trade-unions, exist. In addition, the state controls the press by censorship and by ownership of such great national publications as *Izvestia* and *Pravda*. The radio, the theatre, and the motion picture are likewise owned and managed by the government. In possession of the power of the state, the Communist leadership manages these powerful agencies of public opinion. Significant limitations on these controls of publicity and propaganda do exist. The many wall newspapers published in factories and villages and the journals of the trade-unions and cooperative associations offer some opportunity for variety of opinions. In these associations, however, the presence of Communists in important positions insures a general conformity to the accepted socialist viewpoints, though there is a considerable diversity of expression possible within the limits of fundamental doctrine.

The school system naturally reflects the dominant conception of the socialist society. Great efforts have been made to extend the general educational system, and to reduce the percentage of illiteracy; in fact, this stands as one of the most substantial social services performed by the Soviet government. The teachers' associations, and the central publication of books and teaching materials, impart to the whole system a dominant socialist tone. Since 1917 the government has been trying to establish in the minds of the new generations the ideals of the new society; at the close of thirty years there are not many Russians living who remember with distinctness any other way of life. The heroic performance of the whole people in resisting the German armies during the war, while subject to the qualification that nearly every national community is willing to defend its homeland, is powerful evidence that the average citizen gives sincere support to the Communist leadership, and feels that he has some real share in the society of which he is a member.

## THE VOCATION OF LEADERSHIP

Returning to the question raised at the first of this chapter (how can the small group of Communist party members exercise this monopoly of power?), the answer has been indicated by this brief sketch of the membership, the organization and discipline, and the range of activity of the governing brotherhood. If these features of the party are reconsidered as stages in a career, the influence exerted by them is more readily understood.

**A Party Career.** An intelligent and active boy or girl is likely to be brought to the notice of the youth organizations at any time after the age of nine years. While this is too tender an age for full comprehension of the materialist dialectic of history, an enthusiasm for the slogans of the program can be instilled.

During adolescence there are organized activities which have real
vitality and significance: attendance at meetings of the *Komsomol,* assistance with various party functions, connection with
government activities in the community. The same response that
Boy and Girl Scout scrap-metal collections evoked in the United
States during the war is elicited from the budding Soviet citizen.
Ahead of the young man or woman lies the prospect of membership in the party and opportunities for an important place in the
new socialist society. While party connection is not an absolute
qualification for these chances for advancement, it contributes
significantly. The relatives of the young *Komsomol* member
naturally are interested in his progress, and their attitude toward
the Communist party reflects the concern of kinship. Full membership in the party, when it is finally achieved, brings power
and prestige. It may also carry with it a concrete reward in income, since it has a relationship to the pay and responsibilities of
a job in industry, agriculture, or the state services.

The younger Communists of today are the product of this
careful training, and they are ready to accept the rigorous discipline defined by the national *Politburo* and enforced by committees in each locality. A mixture of compulsion and enthusiasm
maintains conformity of behavior, and sustains belief in the
"vanguard of the revolution."

**Communists and Ordinary Citizens.** The nonparty citizen is
subject to the influence of the press, the radio, and the motion
picture. He is a member of a trade-union, an agricultural collective, or a professional association, and Communists exert influence in all these groups. Furthermore, every citizen knows
that the investigations of the state police are not limited to the
party members. Prosecution and punishment is applied to anyone
judged guilty of actions ranging from opposition to sabotage. The
secrecy of the procedures used invest them with the compulsions
of mystery and fear.

Since Communist doctrines and methods are the subject of
controversy even among members and sympathizers, it is not
easy to measure the full strength of the party's dominant posi-

tion. The brief description, which has just been given, is restricted to its most essential features. In a country containing many different national populations, there is a great diversity of practice from one community to another.

It is important to keep in mind a fact already referred to more than once in preceding pages—a revolution is still in progress, and each of the five-year plans is regarded as a battle for industrialization. Economic and social changes of corresponding magnitude have stretched over generations or centuries in England and the United States. This need not imply that the pace of change is justified, or even that it might not be accomplished by less intense propaganda and compulsion. The circumstances of the seizure of power in 1917, combined with the desire of the leaders to achieve their declared objectives in the shortest possible time, has led irresistibly to the dominant position of a disciplined minority.

**Limited Freedom of Opinion.** While all this regimentation is maintained, there is some opportunity for the expression of divergent opinion. One of the principles of the party is expressed in the phrase, "democratic centralism." At the time that a policy is under discussion, local and provincial committees express their particular views. National committees and conferences discuss the matter with considerable freedom, though it is not permissible to question fundamental socialist doctrines. The drafting of the new constitution of 1936 is an example of this process. The *Politburo* finally declares "the party line," and after that all members are bound to subscribe to it. The range of discussion is limited, but it has been invited on a number of occasions.

"Democratic centralism" within the party is supplemented by the meetings and publications of the affiliated organizations as, for example, the cooperative societies mentioned earlier in this chapter. The columns of *Izvestia* are open to letters and statements of "socialist self-criticism." The term itself suggests that fundamental policies cannot be questioned, but the remarks made are sometimes quite sharply critical of persons or practices. Naturally, every critic is inhibited by the fear of transgressing some limit rigorously prescribed by Communist doctrine, and enforced by the power of the state police.

A final comment should be made. Although Stalin's leadership is glorified in many ways, the dictatorship is of the party, not of a person. Lenin was succeeded by Stalin without destruction of the loyalty of the membership, though Trotsky's eventual banishment shows that there was a sharp contest for authority. Party dictatorship is unmistakable, but it is vested in the organization. Whether the passage of time may modify the rigors of party discipline is problematical, but the 1936 constitution may open the way to a greater freedom of opinion.

## READINGS

The party's position, like the 1917 Revolution, has been the subject of many books. A few of them are:

Chamberlin, W. H., *Russia's Iron Age,* Boston, 1935, chs. ii, vii, viii. A critical survey by a well-informed journalist.

Duranty, Walter, *The Kremlin and the People,* New York, 1941. Written by the former correspondent of the New York *Times.*

Harper, S. N., *Civic Training in Soviet Russia,* University of Chicago Press, 1929, and

———, *Making Bolsheviks,* University of Chicago Press, 1931. These two books by the late Professor Harper are still valuable accounts of the party's activities.

Popov, Nikolai N., *Outline History of the Communist Party of the Soviet Union,* 2 vols., New York, International Publishers, 1934.

Webb, Sidney and Beatrice, *Soviet Communism,* 2d ed., New York, 1938. Vol. I, chs. v and vi. A sympathetic, but careful and detailed account.

See also the books cited at the end of the following chapter.

# CHAPTER 15

# THE GOVERNMENT OF THE SOVIET UNION

COMPLETE and exact information about the Soviet government is not easily obtainable. The Communist leadership, while it permits a certain amount of discussion and criticism in Russia, is very sensitive to comment from the world outside. Reports of the Russian political situation and their interpretations are colored by the viewpoints of the reporter and the reader. As a result description of the operation of the Soviet government is difficult. However, the federal relationship of the republics, the work of deliberative bodies, the character of administrative agencies, courts, and local government can be described in general terms, but the student will notice that details of practical operation are not given as fully as in the description of English government. By referring to the text of the 1936 constitution, and making use of current reporting of its operation, an account of the chief aspects of Russian government can be made.

## FEDERAL RELATIONSHIPS OF REPUBLICS AND REGIONS

Like the United States, the Soviet Union is a federation of diverse communities. The central government, however, possesses a much more extensive range of powers than the American federal system; and the constituent republics and regions, otherwise comparable to American states, are not entirely equal to each other in constitutional status or political authority. With the addition of territories gained during World War II, there are sixteen republics. The Russian Federated Socialist Republic is much larger than the other fifteen, and includes some fifteen autonomous republics, six autonomous regions, and ten national districts. Autonomous republics, regions, and national districts exist within the area of several other republics. Communities other than the republics of the union do not send as many delegates to the Council of Nationalities, and in other ways are not fully equal in political status to the republics, but they have considerable powers in administration of local affairs.

**Powers of the Union Government.** As has been said, the powers of the Union are more extensive, under the terms of the constitution, than the powers of the United States federal government. Foreign trade, transportation, a number of heavy industries, and other comparable activities are the responsibility of, and are fully administered by, the government of the Union. A second category of powers is shared concurrently by both the Union and the republics; these include the management of a number of consumer-goods industries and public health. A third class of powers covers cultural and social affairs, education, and local government, and lies almost entirely within the jurisdiction of the republics. In 1944 each republic was empowered by the Supreme Soviet of the Union to create its own ministries of foreign affairs and defense. (The Ukraine and White Russia are members of the United Nations, and send delegates to the UN Assembly.) This indicates the possibility, which exists in every federal state, of shifts of authority within the federal structure. As yet there is little indication of any real decentralization of power in the conduct of foreign relations.

**The Powers of the Republics.** Any student of the government of the United States has observed how the distribution of powers in a federal system constantly fluctuates with changing conditions. Experience and practice, over long periods of time, modify the relationship between the states and the nation. A similar condition prevails in the Russian government; and added to them is the force of the dominant party, which makes it difficult to analyze with confidence the place of the republics in the union. Based on the limited available information, a general statement of division of authority between the republics and the Union is all that can be offered.

Economic and political matters of general concern are administered by the central government. These powers of administration, coupled with authority of the Supreme Soviet to annul the acts of republics whenever they are contrary to national laws or administrative rules, give Russian federalism a high degree of centralization. At the same time, the powers of the republics, autonomous regions, and national districts over cultural affairs and social policy are extensive. Shifts of jurisdiction have occurred in these relationships, and are likely to appear again in the future.

## Representative Councils

The 1936 constitution made an important change in the method of electing members of the Supreme Soviet of the USSR. Direct election from districts was substituted for the indirect elections which had been used under the 1923 constitution, in which voters chose members of local soviets, and these soviets in turn chose the members of the higher councils. Under the 1936 constitution the Supreme Soviet is divided into two chambers. The Soviet of the Union is composed of over 500 members, elected each from a district of approximately 300,000 population. The Soviet of Nationalities is designed to represent the various communities: republics elect twenty-five delegates each, autonomous republics eleven, autonomous regions five, and national districts one.

**Nominations and Elections.** This new method meant that the Soviet citizen cast his ballot for a candidate who would directly represent his district in the Soviet of the Union. In one district in Georgia this candidate, in 1937, was Josef Stalin. Stalin had been embarrassed by the fact that many district nominating conferences had put forward his name, and finally chose the district where his mother lived—a nice use of filial sentiment. His position in the national election, therefore, could be compared to that of Mr. Churchill or Mr. Attlee in the English election of 1945—that of a national party leader elected from one district in the country. Every voter in every district was fully aware of the fact that a vote for the Communist candidate of his district was at the same time an endorsement of Stalin and the ministers who acted with him.

While this comparison with England may be suggested, it must be remembered that the election of members of the Supreme Soviet differs decisively from English, French, or American electoral procedure.

Various organizations may propose candidates, and did so in December 1937. A subsequent conference, guided by local Communists, finally agreed upon one candidate among the nominees put forward in that year. The result was that voters, and over 90 per cent of the eligible citizens participated, found only one name (approved by the party) for each office on the ballot. The discussion of nominees by organizations, and subsequent meetings to agree upon one candidacy, did give opportunities for some expression of public opinion, but, until more careful study of these procedures has been made, it is hard to say how much or how little the voter's preference means.

A soviet of one chamber is elected by similar procedures in each of the republics and regions. Similar councils also exist in cities, local districts, and villages. Terms of office range from four years for the Supreme Soviet of the Union and of the republics to two years in the local districts. Elections were postponed during the war, as was the case in England and France, so that as yet there has been little opportunity for observation of the system in action.

**Procedure in the Soviets.** The procedure of these bodies is much the same in all jurisdictions. After assembling, the two chambers of the Supreme Soviet elect a Presidium, a nucleus of their own membership which sits between sessions and has power to make decisions on policy, though these acts must be later confirmed by the whole body. The ministers (formerly called Commissars) are chosen by the two chambers in a similar manner, and according to the constitution are responsible to the Supreme Soviet. This implies ministerial responsibility like that of the English Cabinet, but practice has not as yet conformed to the implication. While there is debate on the reports of the ministers and on the proposals of the council of ministers, the powers of forcing resignation of the ministers by an adverse vote, or the corresponding power of the ministers to dissolve the Supreme Soviet have not appeared.

In the republics there are corresponding presidia and councils of ministers, and similar procedures. The same pattern is found in the localities; the city or village soviet chooses an executive committee which assumes responsibility for administering affairs and proposing laws and ordinances. In rural villages it is not unusual to find a general meeting of all the citizens participating in electing the Soviet and in suggesting broad lines of policy.

All of these soviets make laws on subjects which lie within the range of their power. The proposal of legislation is usually made by the councils of ministers, or by executive committees. After consideration and debate, these proposals become law by majority vote. In the Supreme Soviet, majorities in both the Soviet of the Union and the Soviet of Nationalities are required for the enactment of laws. Since there is considerable use of decrees and ordinances by executive agencies, the volume of legislation passed by the various soviets is less than that of corresponding legislative assemblies in the United States or England.

The influence of the Communist party membership and the power of its leaders control the behavior of all these representative assemblies. No organized and recognized opposition exists to bring criticism to bear upon legislative proposals or administrative acts. Unanimity of action, however, does not preclude a considerable amount of discussion; every member of all these soviets is expected to report to his constituents the general character of the work of the body to which they elected him. While socialist democracy and "democratic centralism" may often baffle the observer, it would be unwise to conclude that public opinion is without influence upon the course of national and local policy.

### National Administration

The ministers act together as a council, and each heads a national government department. The ministries are divided into two classes, all-Union and Union-republic, depending upon whether the powers are exercised by officials of the Union, or jointly administered by officers of the Union ministry acting with those of a corresponding ministry in each of the several republics and regions. The names of these departments show the wide range of state authority: finance, internal affairs, justice, public health, food industry, textile industry, and others of a similar type are Union-republic ministries; the all-Union ministries include foreign trade, navy, coal industry, heavy machine building, armaments, electrical industry, and other comparable activities.

**Ministers and Civil Servants.** Each of these ministries maintains a large expert staff, as do a number of boards, such as the State Planning Commission (Gosplan). The recruitment and training of the civil service has confronted the government with difficult problems. The list of ministries given in the preceding paragraph indicates that the scope of state activity is very wide, including the management of large-scale industrial enterprises as well as the usual functions of government. This assumption of authority occurred suddenly, immediately after the Bolshevik revolution, and during the course of a civil war. Former officials, owners, managers, and technicians were regarded with suspicion, and their services were used with reluctance for fear that they might engage in counterrevolutionary activities. At the same time, the educational system of the old Russia was inadequate and could not furnish the trained personnel required. In the years since 1917 the new educational system has been used to train officials, technicians, and administrators. State scholarships, awarded after competitive examination, have brought promising students into institutions of specialized training. Nevertheless, the constant complaints of "bureaucracy" which are voiced by the leaders indicate that the problem of staffing the state services with competent personnel is still far from solved. The demand for party loyalty has complicated the problem; party membership has an influence upon appointments and promotions, though it cannot be said that a "spoils system" exists. Studies of the problem of selecting managers in state industry show how hard it is to maintain a satisfactory standard of training and experience in the great industries.[1] Staffing the more orthodox government services, such as finance or public health, is equally difficult. Progress is easier as the educational system is extended, but it is still slow and painful.

**Courts and Judges.** The organization of the courts, and the administration of justice, are regarded quite differently than in England and the United States. Though the 1936 constitution declares (Article 112) that judges are independent and subject only to the law, it also vests supervision of the execution of the laws in the procurator, or prosecutor, of the union. The courts are really considered a part of the administrative machinery of the government.

The hierarchy of courts is provided for in the constitution and in the judiciary law passed two years later. In every local district there is a People's Court, the judge and two lay assessors being elected by the voters of the district. The function of the two assessors is to give common-sense advice to the judge, since juries are not used in the Russian courts. The People's Courts have jurisdiction over a considerable range of minor criminal acts and over civil disputes between citizens. For more serious crimes and disputes, courts are established in the provinces and territories. The judges in these higher courts are chosen by the soviets of the appropriate area. Each republic has a Supreme Court, with jurisdiction over more important cases. The judges and assessors of the Supreme Courts of the republic are chosen by its soviet. The Supreme Court of the Union is the highest tribunal of the government. Its panel of more than forty judges, and half as many assessors, is chosen by the Supreme Soviet. The high pro-

[1] Gregory Bienstock, Solomon N. Schwartz, and Aaron Yugow, *Management in Russian Industry and Agriculture*, New York, 1944.

portion of judges emphasizes the appellate jurisdiction of the Supreme Court. In all these courts no case is tried with less than one judge and two assessors to hear the evidence and the arguments. This principle of the "judicial college" is comparable to the use of a bench of judges in the courts of the Third French Republic.

A large proportion of the cases is brought to the courts by the procurators, using procedures comparable to indictment or complaint under American or English law. The chief procurator of the Union is appointed by the Supreme Soviet, and he is empowered to appoint the procurators of the republics and regions. They, in turn, make similar appointments for districts and cities. The function of prosecuting, therefore, is more highly centralized and consequently more subject to the influence of the government of the Union than is the judiciary.

**The Codes of Law.** The laws administered by these courts have been collected into comprehensive codes. Each code is devoted to a general subject, such as housing, marriage and family relationships, crime. The citizen involved in a judicial proceeding goes to a college of advocates to get assistance in the presentation of his case. The personnel of these colleges of advocates are comparable to members of the legal profession in England or the United States.

The Soviet codes of law differ substantially from those of capitalist countries, since private property exists in Russia only within the strict limits of personal belongings. A very large proportion of English, American, and French litigation involves questions of property rights and private relationships. The distinction between criminal and civil law is much less clear in the Russian courts, for most business enterprises are state-managed. Judicial proceedings are therefore analogous to the criminal proceedings in western law, in which the community interest is directly represented by the public prosecutor.

The general result of the purpose of the law, and the organization of the procurators' offices, is to make the judiciary part of the administrative organization of the government. By American and English standards, this impairs the independence of the judiciary. In addition, the powers of the secret police to arrest, investigate, and punish for actions regarded as dangerous to the state further reduce the safeguards which an English or American citizen would expect from the judiciary in his country. Against these considerations some other factors should be weighed. Though the law and the courts may appear to be a weapon of the state, the judges and prosecutors bear a heavy official responsibility; and the presence of lay assessors in every trial brings the influence of unofficial opinion into the proceedings. Property and wealth have little effect upon trials, though official and political influence could be significant.

The administration of justice is a joint responsibility of the republics and the Union; Justice is one of the Union-republic ministries. While the general principles of the codes apply to all of the Soviet Union, the republics of the Caucasus, for example, maintain their own traditions and social customs, and conduct court proceedings in their area in their own languages.

## Administration of Local Affairs

Local government has been mentioned in other connections in the earlier part of this chapter and in Chapter 14. The chief responsibility for organization of local government rests upon the republics and regions, and, in deference to the sentiments of national minorities, much variation is permitted. The fundamental pattern of villages, districts, and provinces is present in all of them; and the vesting of authority in a soviet for each locality is also typical. These soviets are elected by the citizens of the area, and their committees and committee members carry on the actual work of local administration.[2] They are aided in these duties by the party and its affiliated youth organizations in the locality. In large cities and districts a presidium, comparable to the Presidium

[2] A good brief account by Bertram W. Maxwell, covering recent developments, of local government, appears in a volume edited by William Anderson, *Local Government in Europe*, New York, 1945.

of the Supreme Soviet, is elected at the first meeting of the local soviet. This presidium serves as a directing and coordinating committee. The functions of local governments are quite closely comparable to those of an English or American town, except that the range of public ownership is usually much wider, including all types of public utilities, housing developments, health and hospital facilities, and other social services. Finance for the local government is derived from a variety of taxes and surcharges, and from the earnings of public enterprises.

**Central Supervision.** Before the outbreak of World War II there appeared to be a tendency toward freeing local authorities from many of the financial and supervisory controls imposed by the larger districts and the republics. At the same time, the dominance of the local Communist party organization sounded the prevailing note for the activities of all communities. In many ways, the general picture of central supervision of local governments is not unlike that in France shortly after 1789. The theory of both the Bolshevik and the French revolution set a high value on the initiative of citizens and communities; the practice of both was to ensure the continuance of the revolutionary program by the imposition of central control. Accounts by competent observers give a picture of lively community life, and it is possible that a greater degree of local autonomy may develop in the Soviet system.

## THE CITIZEN'S RIGHTS AND DUTIES

One of the most extensive chapters of the 1936 constitution (Articles 118–33) recites the rights of the citizen. Besides declaring rights of political equality, freedom of conscience and worship, freedom of expression and assembly, it goes on to guarantee a number of social and economic rights such as education, employment, equality of races and sexes, support in old age or illness, and medical services. The same chapter enumerates duties: to abide by the constitution, to maintain labor discipline, to perform public obligations and military service.

There seems little doubt that the obligations to perform duties are fully enforced, but there is little unanimity among observers of Russian affairs as to the actual realization of the defined rights of a citizen. It is pertinent to repeat once more that the intensive effort of the five-year plans has maintained a revolutionary situation in the USSR, and that under revolutionary conditions the actual substance of rights always diminish in any country.

Some assessment of the citizen's relationship to his government can be made, throwing a little light on his status. The equality of men and women has been established in work, in public affairs, and in party activities. The treatment of minority racial and national groups, in strong contrast to the policies of "Russification" under the Czars, has been remarkably successful, and that success has been due in large part to the freedom allowed for cultural, social, and educational customs and traditions. Freedom of religion, though subject to some question, seems to have been restored since the adoption of the constitution; at least, the Orthodox Church has been recognized.

**Participation in Public Affairs.** The citizen's participation in public affairs, while limited by the dominant position of the Communist party, is much greater than under the Czarist regime. Freedom of expression and political organization are, for instance, not comparable to either English or American conditions; but participation in local government activity, in elections, and in a wide range of organizations such as the trade-unions and the cooperative societies, is active and lively. Economic programs offer continuity of employment at the same time that they require discipline; the social services of education, medical care, and cultural activities have been steadily extended and improved. Since government activity permeates nearly all the activities of daily life, the average citizen expends a great deal of interest and energy upon public affairs.

**The State and the Citizen.** It is easy to see that the socialist state has a large share in the life of the average citizen. His job is likely to be in a state-directed industry, or on a collective farm organized by the state. In either organization he votes for a committee which represents the workers, and exercises some power of determining the program of production, and general working conditions. In his factory he is a member of a trade-union which is affiliated with a regional and a national organization. A cooperative society, in either the factory, city, or agricultural village, supplies him with a considerable share of his household purchases. His house or apartment is likely to be part of a public housing development, built and administered by the city soviet. His children are educated in the state schools; if they show promise in their studies, they may win scholarships to state technical schools or universities. Though he himself may not be a Communist, his children may be affiliated with the youth organizations of the party.

The radio, the newspapers, the publications of his trade-union or collective farm, even the motion pictures, concerts, and art museums, express the propaganda of the socialist community. He is constantly aware that the secret police of the state is on the alert to investigate and punish actions which are contrary to the economic and political policies of the government.

This chapter has described the organization and work of political and constitutional agencies, and suggested the relationship of the citizen to the state, but any summary of the attitude of the Russian people as a whole toward their government and its policies must be inconclusive. During World War II the people loyally defended the Union against invaders; but there were many patriotic motivations involved besides devotion to the government. Nevertheless, the average Russian probably has a sufficient sense of participation in a great national enterprise to make him willing to accept the discipline which the Communist program imposes.

## Readings

A few recent books dealing with the Soviet Union's government and its constituent republics, each of which offers extensive suggestion for further reading, are:

Chamberlin, W. H., *The Russian Enigma, An Interpretation*, New York, 1943.

Dallin, David J., *The Real Soviet Russia*, Yale University Press, 1944. Severely critical, but informative.

Florinsky, M. T., *Towards an Understanding of the USSR*, New York, 1939.

Gibberd, Kathleen, *Soviet Russia, An Introduction*, rev. ed., London and New York, 1946.

Harper, S. N., *The Government of the Soviet Union*, New York, 1938.

Mandell, William, *A Guide to the Soviet Union*, New York, 1946.

Maxwell, B. W., *The Soviet State*, Topeka, Kansas, 1934.

Pares, Sir Bernard, *Russia*, New York, 1943.

Schuman, F. L., *Soviet Politics, At Home and Abroad*, New York, 1946.

Webb, Sidney and Beatrice, *Soviet Communism: A New Civilization?* 2 vols., New York, 1938.

The text of the 1936 constitution is given in Schuman and Webb, cited above, and also in:

Rappard, W. E., and others, *Source Book on European Governments*, New York, 1937.

Strong, Anna L., *The New Soviet Constitution: A Study in Socialist Democracy*, New York, 1937.

National Council of American-Soviet Friendship, *Constitution of Union of Soviet Socialist Republics*, New York, 1941.

Embassy of the Soviet Union, Washington, D. C., *Fundamental Law as Amended*, December, 1945.

A few periodical publications which are of value in studying current Russian political and economic developments are:

*The American Slavic and East European Review*, published for a committee of American scholars, George Banta Publishing Company, Menasha, Wisconsin.

*Bulletins* of American Russian Chamber of Commerce, 245 Fifth Avenue, New York.

*American Review on the Soviet Union*, published quarterly by The American Russian Institute, 58 Park Avenue, New York.

*Russian Review*, published semi-annually, 215 West 23rd Street, New York.

*The Slavonic and East European Review,* London, published by
the School of Slavonic and East European Studies, University
of London.

*Soviet Russia Today,* published monthly, 114 East 32nd Street,
New York.

*USSR Information Bulletin,* published by the Embassy of the
USSR, Washington, D. C.

In addition to the publications named above, the journals mentioned
at the end of Chapter 1 frequently publish articles bearing on the
government of the USSR.

# CHAPTER 16

# SOVIET ECONOMIC PLANNING
# AND SOCIAL POLICY

THE economic program of the Soviet Union is fully as important to its citizens as the political and constitutional structure. When the Supreme Soviet adopted the fourth five-year plan in March 1946, it meant the resumption of efforts to establish the socialist economy—"to build socialism in one country." It meant also that there would be no respite for the Russian people who had borne the struggles and privations of World War II after the stringent living conditions which had accompanied the first three five-year plans.

## PROGRESS TOWARD PLANNING

The history of economic planning which lies behind the announcement of a fourth five-year plan began when the Bolsheviks first seized power in 1917. At that time the Russian economy was disorganized by the strains World War I had imposed on it, and the policy adopted by the leadership has been called "War Communism." What happened was that the new government issued decrees nationalizing industry, land, and natural resources. The management of industrial enterprises was taken over by workers' committees in factories and mines, while the peasants were permitted and often encouraged to seize their holdings from their landlords. The state assumed general powers of direction over the whole economy, and strove to increase the production of goods and services. By these means it was possible to supply the army during the civil war, but Lenin soon found that production was declining, especially in agriculture. The peasants were discontented because industrial goods were not available, while the state grain collections were rigorously enforced in order to bring sufficient food to the city populations. Under these conditions, the peasants began to restrict their production to the point where it met their own subsistence needs, and refused to expend effort on growing a surplus which would be taken from them by the state collections. In industry and transport the lack of skilled workmen and technical experts led to confusion and interruptions of production.

**The NEP.** Perceiving the implications of this situation, Lenin had the imagination and courage to abandon temporarily the socialist program which had dominated the thoughts of the leaders. In the spring of 1921 the New Economic Policy was announced, which Lenin characterized at the time as a step backward from the socialist economy in order to make possible two steps forward in the future. The NEP, as it was called, permitted private trading and small-scale manufacture by individual enterprisers. Instead of being based upon the needs of the society, and therefore claiming a large share of the peasant's total production, grain collections were fixed at a definite amount, and the producer was allowed to sell any surplus in a legal market. Similar rules were applied to the small handicraft industries; and hiring of labor in small shops and on farms was permitted.

The response to this policy was increased production, since usual and familiar profit incentives were offered. NEP-men, as these dealers and producers were called, appeared in light manufacture, retail trade, and agriculture. Large-scale industry, such as steel, coal, iron, and oil production, remained under state direction. Construction programs, including tractor factories and electric power developments, were also undertaken by the government. Finance, banking and currency remained under state control. Described briefly, the NEP was a mixture of socialist and capitalist economy. Consumers' goods were manufactured and sold by private traders and manufacturers; and peasants were encouraged to produce a surplus for market. The scarcity of food, textiles, and similar commodities was relieved; but planning by the government was maintained and extended for large-scale industries and capital construction.

**The "Socialist Offensive."** Lenin died in 1924 before this temporary expedient had run its course. One of the issues in the struggle for leadership, which finally enabled Stalin to succeed Lenin as head of the Communist party, was the question of how long the policy should be continued. Successful peasant farmers were getting control of more land and hiring labor to operate larger holdings; private traders were entrenching their position; light manufacture was assuming a capitalist character. If the Communist program was to be accomplished, the "socialist offensive" must be resumed. In addition, the leaders were constantly haunted by the fear that the capitalist nations might adopt hostile policies toward the Soviet Union, and were therefore anxious to build up industry to the point where the Russian economy would be self-sufficient.

In 1928 the first five-year plan was announced, after preparatory studies had been made and an organization had been created to administer it. The change from the NEP was frequently ruthless; and peasants and dealers were forced to accept the new situation. The state once more took charge of the Russian economy, and embarked upon a vast program of socialization and industrialization. Special emphasis was placed on the development of hydroelectric power and the construction of large industrial plants.

## THE GOSPLAN AND THE FIVE-YEAR PLANS

Central planning of the total economy of so large and diverse a community, possessing such varied resources, is a truly staggering undertaking. It is a bigger task than the organization and supervision of the economy of the United States during World War II. If the student recalls the problems of rationing, war production, price control, and the large number of emergency agencies which struggled with the problems imposed by total war, he can form some conception of what planning requires in Russia.

**Development of the Gosplan.** The first requirement for general planning is the collection of data and the study of conditions. During the period of War Communism a commission worked out a plan for industry based on a rapid development of electric power. Lenin secured its adoption by the congress of soviets in 1920. The following year the Gosplan (the State Planning Commission) was established, and began the work which it has carried on ever since; the fixing of control figures for all types of production. The end of the NEP was signalized by the announcement of the first five-year plan.

**The Gosplan's Experts.** The Gosplan is a commission appointed by the Council of Ministers, but occupying a somewhat independent position. Though the dominance of the Communist program determines the general policy embodied in the plans, the expert economists and engineers who are members of the Gosplan exercise a considerable amount of discretion and initiative in drafting an economic blueprint for the nation. A large staff of technicians from all fields collects data and prepares reports, and a branch office exists in each one of the republics.

**Production Schedules.** The staffs of the Gosplan and its branch offices make surveys of natural resources, and collect data on all aspects of production. Statistics are assembled showing quantities and rates of output, working conditions, cost levels, and requirements for capital equipment. On the basis of this information, tentative schedules are drawn up for the next five-year period. These schedules are then sent to the ministries in charge of various industries, and eventually reach every plant, factory, mine, or collective farm. Each unit carefully studies the figures, and a report is made on the possibilities of achieving the planned objectives. The revised estimates for every industry are then coordinated and subjected to further analysis. Finally the control figures are announced, with scheduled yearly or monthly rates of production. The job of actually achieving the projected results is entrusted to the various ministries, working through subordinate republic and regional organizations. The Gosplan, while it does not administer the plan, continues to collect data on every enterprise, and reports frequently on progress. At the same time, it uses this information to outline the next five-year plan. Leeway is allowed for unforeseen developments, and revision of the figures takes place when they prove unworkable.

This brief sketch of the procedures hardly suggests the immensity of the undertaking. All sorts of problems arise. The coal output of a mine in the Don basin has been increased on a predetermined schedule, but the railway cars to move the tonnage do not put in their appearance at the appropriate times. The collectivization of agriculture proceeded so rapidly in 1930, that Stalin published a letter in the press, "Dizzy with Success," in order to slow up the pace of change and diminish the grievances of the peasants. These are isolated examples among many, mentioned to convey a sense of the intricacies involved in central planning and administration.

## MANAGEMENT AND LABOR IN INDUSTRY

The Gosplan is an economic general staff which determines the objectives; the achievement of the objectives is entrusted to management and labor in industry and agriculture. Coal-mining, to choose an example, is one of the all-Union ministries. The minister is responsible for the industry throughout the whole Union. Republic and territorial organizations in areas where the mines are located exercise supervisory controls under the direction of the minister. In a particular mine a manager, appointed by the minister, is responsible for running the plant. He must deal constantly with a committee, chosen by the workers. He must also be able to get along successfully with the trade-union of the coal workers, which has local, territorial, and national organization.

**Managers and Trade-unions.** While Russian trade-unions cannot be compared to unions in capitalist countries, it can be pointed out that the labor discipline enforced by the Soviet government puts the members of its unions in a position comparable to that of public employees in the United States and deprives them of the right to strike. The presumptions behind the socialist program are that the workers participate fully in all the gains made under state ownership of the means of production, and that there is no conflict of interest between management and labor. Actually, the determination of rates of pay, working conditions, and methods of production is the subject of a great deal of discussion between the management staff, the committees of workers, and the trade-unions. For example, when production schedules for the five-year plans are considered all interested parties have a chance to make suggestions. Many of the managers and trade-union officials are Communist party members, so the influence of the party pervades all the large-scale industries.

The organization just sketched applies to large-scale industrial enterprises such as coal and oil production, tractor manufacture, and railway transport. The day-to-day running of plants is carried on under the direction of the ministry with its divisions for allied industries. The general plans, formulated by the Gosplan and its branches in the republics, define the objectives to be attained. A commission of state control, first organized as the division of workers' and peasants' inspection of the Communist party, and now elevated to the status of a government agency comparable to the Gosplan, continually assesses progress toward the fulfillment of the plans.

**Financial Planning.** The control of finance, credit, and currency is a powerful weapon of the state. Saving is one of the most important economic activities in an industrial economy. Its importance, aside from the familiar maxims urging the citizen to lay aside a fund for some eventual and inevitable rainy day, is concealed from many people in capitalist countries. In America, the many little savings of individuals, and the big reserves of large business enterprises, are collected into funds by the banks and investment houses and eventually materialize into the machinery, plants, and raw material reserves of industry. In the Russian socialist economy this function of accumulation of funds for the construction of hydroelectric developments, or tractor factories, or steel plants, is planned and directed by the state. When a worker buys a state bond, his saving is a personal act. On the other hand, the accumulation of capital is often involuntary and concealed, being in the form of taxes or state credits. The Ministry of Finance raises large sums by taxation, especially by the turnover tax upon purchases of many kinds, and a big proportion of the state funds is invested in industrial development. The state bank controls credit, and puts balances at the disposal of ministries and their constituent plants which are used to buy materials and meet payrolls. Various special banks are the custodians of investment funds derived from the profits of industries.

**The State Bank.** The state bank's accounting procedures, which have been improved during the past ten years, serve as a constant check on the performance of particular plants. At the same time, the control of credit can be used to direct the flow of funds. When a tractor factory is granted a balance against which it may draw to pay workers and purchase materials, the effect of this policy is to divert labor and resources to the creation of capital goods—in this instance, tractors. Under conditions of practically full employment, which have obtained during the period of the five-year plans, this means that there is less labor available for the production of textiles, food products, or other consumer goods. With constant emphasis on the construction of industrial plant, the average citizen has been saving involuntarily—doing without consumer goods while his government built electric power plants or increased steel production.

**Handicraft Associations.** Small-scale industry such as bread baking, clothing manufacture and repair, and other activities of a handicraft type, are conducted by small workshops organized into associations of producers' cooperatives. These enterprises are an intermediate type, between the socialized large-scale industries and the individual small businesses. The small producer owns his equipment and tools and often employs a few workers, some of whom are apprentices. The cooperative association, of which each shop owner is a member, sets wage rates and rules for working conditions, and often conducts marketing operations and the purchase of materials and equipment. Retail trade is carried on by cooperative associations, and also by large state stores. The influence of the state and the party is just as powerful in these cooperatives as it is in large industry, for much the same reason—the membership of the association includes many Communists, and state inspection and regulation is imposed for purposes of general planning.

## Collective Agriculture

The decision to introduce collective organization into agriculture was based on considerations of social policy and economic needs. Since a class of successful farmers had begun to appear under the NEP, the Communist leadership desired to forestall the growth of individual enterprise in agriculture. At the same time, the need to increase agricultural production called for the introduction of new methods of farming. The ambitious program of collectivization of agriculture, begun at the time the first five-year plan was put into operation, was designed to consolidate small holdings into large fields so that tractors and machine techniques could be used. The state tractor factories were prepared to deliver the machinery. Experiments with large state farms, each of the type called a *sovkhoz*, had indicated that large-scale agriculture managed on the model of big industry, was not successful.

**Agricultural Collectives.** The collective farm, called a *kolkhoz*, was decided upon as the most desirable form of organization to meet both the social and technical aspects of the agricultural problem. Peasants who became members of a *kolkhoz* pooled their holdings of land, and a large part of their livestock. They worked the large fields in brigades, organized and directed by an executive committee elected by the membership.

At central points the government set up machine-tractor stations where the collectives could arrange for the use of tractors and machinery and receive improved types of seeds and livestock, technical advice, and other services. These inducements, it was hoped, would attract peasants into the *kolkhoz;* but it was necessary to use severe compulsions, in a campaign to "liquidate the *kulaks*" (the wealthier peasants). These *kulaks* were heavily taxed, and the state police imposed penalties of imprisonment or banishment to Siberia on many of them. After a few years more than 80 per cent of all farming was carried on in collectives.

This revolution in agriculture had the effect of bringing the peasant into the general program of planned economic activity. Not only was farming made into a large-scale, mechanized enterprise, but the machine-tractor stations also served as headquarters in the rural districts for the propaganda and educational programs of the party and the state. Schools were established in the villages, and a broad social program of medical care, recreation, and social insurances was introduced into the agricultural communities. Some satisfactions of individual initiative are still permitted to the peasant. The most common type of *kolkhoz*, called the *artel*, leaves him his house, garden, and some livestock which he may regard as personal possessions, and gives him some opportunity to market any surplus produce left after meeting the charges for the services of the tractor station and the taxes and collections imposed by the government.

## FOREIGN TRADE AND SELF-SUFFICIENCY

Because of its experiences in arranging commercial relations with capitalist countries during the civil war, and because of the settled conviction that "socialism could be built in one country" during the period of the five-year plans, the Communist leadership has steadily striven to insulate Russia from the fluctuations of the world economy by managing all the relationships of foreign trade. The leaders have constantly prepared for the possibility that hostile commercial policies, economic depressions, or wars, might force the Russian socialist economy to depend almost entirely on its own resources.

Besides these motives, there was the practical necessity of stabilizing currency rates with other countries in order to purchase generators for hydroelectric plants or machine tools for the new factories. Exports of raw materials, such as manganese ore, lumber, and grain, were made in great quantities for the purpose of building up credit balances which could be used to finance the purchase of capital equipment.

**State Foreign Trade Monopoly.** This combination of policy and needs led to a complete state monopoly of foreign trade. The Ministry of Foreign Trade conducts all trading operations with foreign countries, and any individual trading in foreign currencies or commodities is subject to severe penalties. It is impossible to make this control completely effective, and a certain amount of black-market trading has always gone on, particularly in border areas.

The general purpose behind the foreign-trade monopoly is to make purchases on the most advantageous possible terms, and also to maintain price and wage relationships unchanged within Russia. If these conditions are maintained, the program of rapid industrialization can be carried on even though it means heavy sacrifice on the part of the citizens in doing without consumer goods which might be bought abroad. Fixed prices can be administered within the country, and rationing schemes enforced whenever necessary. If the long-run objective of industrial self-sufficiency can be attained rapidly by building up plant and capital equipment, the socialist community is safe, in the opinion of its leaders, from the commercial and diplomatic risks which would otherwise endanger its security in a capitalist world. The performance of the Russian economy in World War II, particularly the dramatic transfer of whole factories to the industrial districts of the Urals, gives some justification for these policies of self-sufficiency.

While the monopoly of foreign trade is understandable in these terms, it carries some risks which the Communist leaders have tended to ignore. It has exposed the Soviet Union to accusations of dumping commodities on world markets, and at all times it makes the Russian market difficult for exporters and importers of other countries. Adherence to the policy over a period of years indicates, however, that it is firmly established as an accompaniment to the general program of a socialist planned economy.

## THE ECONOMIC LIFE OF THE CITIZEN

This brief sketch of the Russian planned economy can be made more real by illustrating it in terms of the life of the average person. The city resident, and the proportion of urban population is now approaching half of the total, is usually a worker in industry or retail and wholesale trade, either in an office or as a skilled or unskilled artisan. In many cases, of course, he may be employed as an official; or he may be a handicraft worker or enterpriser in a producers' cooperative. All of these jobs are comparable to similar employment in England or the United States. Despite the equalitarian presumptions of the socialist society, levels of income vary widely. Responsible and skilled people, from trained craftsmen to technicians and administrators, are paid a higher level of compensation than unskilled labor. The Stakhanov movement has been used to stimulate the efficiency of labor, and piece rates of pay offer rewards to higher productive power. Labor turnover figures, so far as they are available, indicate that the Russian worker seeks more advantageous employment and better living conditions as persistently as the employee of capitalist enterprise in other lands.

He lives, frequently, in a house or apartment that has been constructed by the city as part of a public housing development. His household purchases are made in the state stores, or in a cooperative which often is maintained in the industry in which he works. During the past two decades he and his family frequently have found that it is not easy to buy what they want; basic commodities like bread and meat have been rationed for months at a time.

**Social Services.** Most of the services he requires are furnished by the state. Education, medical care, hospitalization, and various social insurances, if not made available by the state are part of the activities of the trade-union in which he almost invariably maintains membership. His wife and family are frequently employed as well. For his wife maternity leaves and benefits are available; nursery schools, school meals for older children and various comparable services are organized by the state and in the industries.

The natural desire to improve the job and increase income is met by educational programs for adults which offer training of various kinds. Chances for promotion within the hierarchy of each industry are reasonably good. As previously noted, membership in the union or the cooperative society, and participation in political activities connected with the Communist party, have an effect upon social status.

Recreation is organized, in large part, by the state and by the trade-unions. Theatres, concerts, parks, and museums are state activities, maintained at quite a high level. Vacation tours, and resorts maintained by the state or the trade-unions, offer opportunities for travel and holidays.

**The Professions.** The professional man is a member of an association and frequently is an employee in some organized state service. The doctor, for example, usually has a post in a clinic or a hospital, though he has some opportunities for private practice. Engineers and laboratory technicians are employees of the great industries, or occasionally hold posts in the scientific institutes and universities maintained by the government. Artists and writers obtain access to the public through the state-managed theatres and publishing houses. The Communist party line imposes limitations on artistic performance, but within the framework of socialist doctrine there has been considerable range for creative expression.

**The Peasant.** The peasant's situation, since the drive for collectivization, is now comparable to that of the city dweller in many respects. While the member of the *kolkhoz* often feels that he is the owner of his house and garden, a large part of his working days is spent in the common fields of the collective farm as a member of a brigade of workers, directed by the executive committee and the manager. He has lost the independence of the small farmer, but he benefits from the improved methods of production, and the social services which have been introduced into the rural communities. Like the industrial worker, he has some opportunities for training and advancement. The machine-tractor stations are centers for agricultural education as well as technical services; and a promising boy or girl may be given the chance to pursue higher studies and qualify for technical or administrative responsibilities.

Country life has certainly lost much of its former character, but the extension of the social services and recreation activities has given it other attractions. The school, the clinic, the motion picture, and the radio are being brought to the rural communities. The Communist party has conducted active propaganda at the same time that the policy of agricultural collectivization has been carried on, for the party has been weakest in the country ever since the time of the Bolshevik revolution. The total effect of all these social and political changes has been, therefore, to make the peasants much more conscious of the government's program during the course of the past fifteen years.

**Standards of Living and Work.** For the vast proportion of its members, the ultimate test of a society is its living standard and the freedom of activity it allows. Restrictions on information and controversy over its meaning make generalization about Russian conditions extremely difficult. The emphasis on industrialization which was characteristic of the first two five-year plans, and only slightly relaxed in the third, has certainly imposed tension and hardship on the people of the Soviet Union. There have been serious shortages of food and other consumer goods. At the same time there has been a constant tightening of labor discipline. Living standards and working conditions in one country are not easily compared with those in another, for the statistical bases are frequently different, but it seems likely that, while the conditions have been improving in Russia, they still fall short of standards in other industrialized countries.

There is a psychological compensation, however, for the rigors imposed by the task of "building socialism in one country." The new industrial plants, the housing developments, the opportunities for education, give the Soviet citizen a sense of pride in the collective achievement of his community. The leadership constantly promises that the benefits of higher production will be reflected in the income of the worker and the peasant. While propaganda and compulsion undoubtedly have much to do with public acceptance of the socialist program, a feeling of participation in achievements contributes a substantial part to the stability of the government and the dominance of the Communist party.

## READINGS

Most of the books listed at the end of the two preceding chapters deal with the economic system. In addition, a few others are:

Baykov, Alexander, *The Development of the Soviet Economic System,* New York, 1946.

Bergson, Abram, *The Structure of Soviet Wages: A Study in Socialist Economics,* Harvard University Press, 1944.

Bienstock, Gregory, Solomon Schwartz and Aaron Yugov, *Management in Russian Industry and Agriculture,* New York, 1945.

Hoover, C. B., *The Economic Life of Soviet Russia,* New York, 1931.

Hubbard, L. E., *Soviet Labor and Industry,* New York, 1943.

———, *The Economics of Soviet Agriculture,* New York, 1939.

———, *Soviet Trade and Distribution,* New York, 1938, and other books.

Yugov, Aaron, *Russia's Economic Front for War and Peace,* New York, 1942.

For current developments, see the list of periodicals listed at the end of the preceding chapter.

# ITALY

# CHAPTER 17

# THE FASCIST REVOLUTION

ITALIANS who are more than forty years old have a youthful recollection of a parliamentary government and constitutional monarchy. Italian men over fifty years of age were eligible to cast ballots for a chamber of deputies, and can remember that many parties put forward candidates and conducted political campaigns in 1919 and 1921. Younger citizens have lived in an Italy dominated by Mussolini and the Fascist party, and have been taught a Fascist interpretation of the history of their country in school and by youth organizations.

The story of Mussolini's capture of power in October 1922 and the historical development which made it possible are the first prerequisites for an understanding of the present Italian political situation.

## THE UNIFICATION OF ITALY

Less than a hundred years ago the Italian peninsula was divided politically into several small states and petty kingdoms. The tradition of the medieval city states, the great temporal authority of the Popes, and the power of the old Austrian Empire had prevented the establishment of a national government. Differences in economic activity and social structure, particularly between northern and southern communities, emphasized political disunity. Liberal and national movements in Europe had stimulated men like Mazzini and Cavour to work for the idea of national unity. The *Resorgimento* is the name given to the period during which this idea grew into a movement.

**Mazzini and Cavour.** Mazzini, forced to spend much of his life in exile from Italy, expressed his idealistic hopes in his writings.

Cavour, as prime minister of the northern state of Piedmont, was able to secure the adoption there of a liberal constitution, called the *Statuto,* with the aid of the king, Charles Albert. An attempt to free northern Italy from Austrian rule failed in 1848, but the succeeding king, Victor Emmanuel II, refused to revoke the *Statuto* even though he was strongly pressed to do so by the Austrian government. This steadfastness of purpose attracted sympathy throughout all Italy, and within the next ten years the diplomatic skill of Cavour, now foreign minister, secured foreign support for the liberation of Italy. The wars which were fought to achieve independence were made romantic by the exploits of Garibaldi and "The Thousand." In 1860 Victor Emmanuel was proclaimed king of Italy, and the *Statuto* was adopted by plebiscites held in various Italian states. Italy was not yet fully united. The Austro-Prussian War in 1866 and the Franco-Prussian War in 1870 made it possible to bring the remaining provinces of Venice and the Papal states in central Italy into the newly created nation.

These are the bare facts of the story. However shrewd Cavour's diplomacy had been and however heroic was the performance of Garibaldi and his volunteers, a large share of the final success was due to the aid of France and Prussia. The role of Italy in European affairs was destined to be subordinate to that of the other powers of Europe during the latter part of the nineteenth century. Newly created Italian national feeling suffered some disappointments, and the frustrated desire to assert the strength of the new nation was one of the sentiments which an aggressive leader could turn to advantage later.

**Parliamentary Institutions under the *Statuto*.** More important than the psychological effects of national unification was the nature of the parliamentary government which was established. Cavour, and other leaders, were admirers of English government; the *Statuto* provided an adaptation of English parliamentary practice to the political situation of Piedmont.

Victor Emmanuel II, though he had exercised some powers of popular leadership in unifying Italy, readily accepted the position of a constitutional monarch. He was willing to appoint ministers who were leaders of a parliamentary majority, and in the manner of an English king, to abide by the policies they put forward. The national parliament was modeled on the legislative bodies of England and France, and was designed to represent popular sentiment.

**Deputies and Voters.** The Chamber of Deputies was elected from districts. It increased in size, as successive territories were added to the kingdom, from 204 members in Piedmont to 535 at the close of World War I. The life of the Chamber was fixed at five years, but the use of dissolutions limited the average term to about three years during the period from 1849 to 1915. Premiers often dissolved the Chamber for reasons of political strategy, choosing favorable moments to wage an electoral campaign, and unhesitatingly making use of local officials and government influence to increase and consolidate their parliamentary majority.

The voters who chose deputies were at first a very small proportion of the citizens, by virtue of property-holding and tax-paying qualifications. Literacy was accepted as an alternative qualification in 1882, and in 1912 and 1919 the suffrage was finally extended to all male citizens. Since the percentage of illiteracy was high—ranging from 11 to 25 per cent in the north to over 60 per cent in the provinces south of Rome—this extension of the franchise brought in many voters who were seriously disabled in their understanding of public affairs.

It is important to notice that the extension of the franchise was not made in response to popular pressure, such as that which brought about the Reform Bills of 1832 and 1867 in England. It was rather a campaign device employed by parliamentary leaders to increase their influence, and its ultimate effect was to grant an unwanted privilege to a large number of uninformed and uninterested citizens. Over a third of the electorate abstained from voting in 1909, and nearly a half in 1913 and 1919.

Elections were held in single-member districts until 1882. Larger districts returning five members were used for the following nine years, and after a resumption of the single-member district, a system of proportional representation was adopted for the elections of 1919 and 1921. The average voter, hardly ready to express any convinced opinion on questions of national policy and much influenced by local loyalty and provincial patriotism, was unable to make effective use of his ballot.

**The Senate.** The Senate, under the Piedmontese *Statuto,* was designed to act as a restraining influence upon the popularly elected Chamber. Its members were appointed by the king, on the advice of the premier, from twenty-one categories, including administrative officials, army officers, distinguished scholars and scientists, and persons who paid high direct taxes. Senators held office for life, and the body steadily increased in size, since there was no constitutional limit upon its membership. In 1921 there were 391 Senators; Mussolini packed the Senate by increasing it to 440 in 1925. Despite a fairly high proportion of men of experience and distinction, the Senate exerted little influence upon the course of national policy. Ministries were always able to influence its attitudes by appointing new members with the proper point of view.

**Courts and Local Government.** Judicial organization was similar to that which existed in the Third French Republic. Beginning with praetors (comparable to English and French justices of the peace) in localities, a symmetrical system of courts was provided. District Courts, and Tribunals of First Instance in larger districts heard cases. Appeal Courts reviewed the decisions of these lower courts, and five Courts of Cassation served as the highest courts of appeal. The law administered in all these courts was strongly influenced by the tradition of the Roman law, and like the French law was systematically codified. Judges were chosen after a training which prepared them for the bench, and were assured permanence of tenure. While Italian justice was not as unified in administration as French, it was well organized and adequately applied by competent personnel.

Local government was highly centralized. The central government appointed prefects who exercised large powers over the administration of affairs within the provinces, assisted and advised by locally elected councils. The provinces were divided into smaller districts, with similar functions and organization. The most genuine expression of local sentiment was found in the towns and villages, called communes. These were governed by a locally elected council, headed by a mayor (*sindaco*). The work of running local affairs was directed by committees of the councils, but all these local authorities were subject to supervision by the prefects, very much as were the communes in France.

**Church and State.** The relationship of the Roman Catholic Church to the new state created a difficult problem. The final establishment of the capital at Rome was made possible when the Franco-Prussian War necessitated the withdrawal of French troops who had afforded protection to the temporal authority of the Pope. The Law of the Papal Guarantees, which had been designed to compensate the Church for its loss of political authority, led instead to a controversy between Church and State. The Pope declared himself to be "the prisoner of the Vatican," and called upon devout members of the Church to refrain from participation in the new government. It was not until 1904 that the Pope's prohibition on voting in elections for deputies was lifted; and while it is likely that Catholics had taken some part in politics before that time, this ban on political activity reduced the chances of developing a party organization which would fully reflect public opinion.

**Political Parties and Parliamentary Leaders.** It has been said, wittily but cruelly, that "Italy found herself endowed with a constitution imitated from Britain imported in a bad French translation." [1] In Piedmont the outstanding leadership of Cavour had made possible the union (*conubio*) of all parties in the struggle to establish a constitutional monarchy and extend its influence to the whole peninsula through national unification. Once the process was finally completed in 1870, divergent political views, often intensified by local and sectional interests, led to the creation of a number of political parties. These parties aligned

[1] Quoted by Margot Hentze, *Pre-Fascist Italy*, London, 1939, p. 21.

themselves into a right and a left in the manner of continental European politics.

Liberals, Republicans, Italian Democrats, Democrats, and Social Democrats maintained the liberal constitutional viewpoints which had contributed to the creation of a united Italy. Socialists, Reformist Socialists, and Unitary Socialists represented the growth of socialist doctrines, and made their appearance during the nineteenth century. Communists, and socialists of a more revolutionary temper than the other socialist parties, began to exert some influence during the twentieth century, and increased their activity after the Bolshevik revolution occurred in Russia in 1917. All of these party groups secured representation in the Chamber, and their leaders engaged in the intricate maneuvers of forming coalition Ministries.

**Social and Economic Changes.** While the new government was being established and put into operation, it was confronted with the social problems arising from the industrial revolution. In this respect the political development of Italy may be compared with. the history of the Third French Republic.[2] Large-scale industry appeared in the northern provinces; labor and management relations assumed new forms. Divergence of economic interest between the industrial North and the agricultural South became a perennial problem of Italian politics. The need for enlightened consideration of the new social problems became steadily more urgent, but neither the electorate nor the leaders seemed able to take the necessary steps to secure effective action by the government.

National feeling had been brought into existence by the *Resorgimento,* and by the wars for national unity. A true consciousness of the character of democratic government, and a willingness on the part of the citizens to concern themselves actively with public affairs, was not produced at the same time. Italy had been created, but the Italians were not ready to undertake the responsibilities which parliamentary democracy required.

[2] See Chapter 9 above, pp. 129–133.

## THE DEFECTS OF PARLIAMENTARY GOVERNMENT

The persistence of provincial loyalty was enhanced by the power of the central government over local affairs. The average member of the Chamber of Deputies regarded himself as a delegate from his locality, obliged to obtain as much financial benefit and administrative favor as possible for his constituents. This made him susceptible to parliamentary maneuvers, and led him to organize pressure upon whatever Ministry was in power in order to induce it to make concessions or dispense funds in return for his vote.

**Multiple Parties.** The long-run effect of a multiple-party situation was much the same in Italy as in France. Coalition Ministries were always in office, but rarely in possession of real power. Parliamentary maneuvering, conducted by such masters of strategy as Giovanni Giolitti, absorbed the attention of leaders and deputies. Instability of Ministries made conduct of national policy indecisive. While the system developed some great statesmen, the risk was always present that a national crisis might find the country unable to mobilize effective leadership.

**Popular Distrust.** *Transformismo* (the Italian term applied to this grouping and regrouping of ministers and parties) affected the attitude of the citizens, at the same time that it weakened the action of the government. Italians lost confidence in their parties and political leaders. Pressing issues, such as "the problem of the South" with its agrarian unrest and chronic economic depression, failed to receive the close attention and careful action required. Fluctuations of domestic and foreign policy, based upon party alignments in the Chamber of Deputies, discouraged the voter who wanted his government to declare and explain its policies. Don Sturzo, a Catholic priest who organized the Popular party (*Popolari*) in the years following World War I, characterized this situation in the phrase, "the crisis in the political class."[3] One of the symptoms of the citizen's discouragement is revealed in the low percentage of voting in the parliamentary

[3] Luigi Sturzo, *Italy and Fascismo*, London, 1926, ch. III.

election. Hardly more than 60 per cent—and often less—of the eligible voters actually exercised their franchise.

Under the *Statuto* the government of Italy, even though it had a respectable record of achievement, failed to recruit leaders who declared positive policies or who could evoke wide popular support. The strain imposed by a great war was likely to lead to political revolution.

## WORLD WAR I AND ITS AFTERMATH

When the Austro-Hungarian Empire issued an ultimatum to Serbia in July 1914, Italy was a member of the Triple Alliance. The clauses of the treaty, to which Italy, Austria, and Germany were parties, imposed obligations on each to consult with the others on diplomatic policies, and to give aid in the event of a defensive war. Antonio Salandra, the prime minister, perceived that Austrian action did not oblige Italy to enter the war on the side of the Central Powers. Since the Libyan War with Turkey (1911) had revealed serious deficiencies in Italy's military organization, and since public opinion was clearly not willing to give assistance to the Austrian Empire, long a traditional enemy of Italian national unification, Salandra's Cabinet declared a policy of neutrality and nonintervention.

As the war spread to other states of Europe, it became increasingly difficult for Italy to remain neutral. Sympathy for the Allies developed in Italy, and diplomatic promises made by England and France in the secret Treaty of London finally led to Italy's declarations of war against Austria, Germany, Turkey, and Bulgaria during May 1915. The Italian war record was a mixture of crushing defeats and heroic resistance. The war effort seriously disorganized the home economy; and the military campaigns took a heavy toll in casualties.

**Discontent with the Peace.** The settlement which followed was a profound disappointment to Italian national aspirations. While some territorial gains were granted, popular acclaim for the poet D'Annunzio's romantic seizure of Fiume was a token of dissatisfaction with the peace terms. The nation felt that its leaders had failed to present its case at Paris, and that the sacrifices made during the war had been disregarded.

Even more disturbing was the social and economic distress which became manifest during 1919 and 1920. The dislocation of finance, industrial production, transport, and agriculture produced real hardship in the form of unemployment, labor disputes, inflation of prices, and shortage of goods.

Faced with this crisis the government was unable to formulate effective policies and win popular support for them. Strikes in the industries of the North exhibited the alarming form of occupation of factories by the workers. The Bolshevik revolution in Russia had deeply influenced the Socialist parties; and conservative groups feared that a communist revolution might occur. Italian socialism, divided into extreme (Maximalist) and moderate (Minimalist) wings, was not able to conduct a revolution, but the social disturbances of the winter of 1919–20 encouraged both revolutionary and counterrevolutionary sentiment.

Had the government and its leaders been able, during the years since 1870, to convince the people that the Chamber and the Ministry afforded means of proposing needed measures and winning public support, the crisis might have been surmounted by constitutional measures. As matters stood, many Italians began to look for a leadership which could solve the problems by creating a new government. Benito Mussolini and his Fascists were already advocating revolutionary action.

## THE FASCIST PARTY AND THE MARCH ON ROME

To the visitor in Italy after 1922, fascism seemed to be mostly Mussolini. He began his political career as a revolutionary socialist, and endured some hardships for the cause. By 1912 he had risen to the editorship of the leading socialist newspaper, *l'Avanti!* Before Italy's entrance into World War I, he had been expelled from the party for organizing workers' groups to support intervention in the war on the side of the Allies. He founded a newspaper, the *Popolo d'Italia,* in Milan in September 1914, after a brief service in the army. In 1919, declaring a vague program of nationalism and reform he began recruiting ex-soldiers, small shopkeepers, and some laborers into groups called *Fasci di Combattimento.* The symbol of the bundle of sticks *(Fasces)* recalled the grandeur of the Roman Empire. In 1915 he had had experience with similar groups which had agitated for Italian intervention in the war. For nearly two years the movement was only a loose association of these local groups but, in a meeting at Rome in November 1921, the National Fascist Party was established and a more regular discipline imposed upon the local squads.

As a party engaged in the normal activities of campaigning and electing candidates to parliament, the movement was a failure. Making use of an alliance with the Nationalist party and propagandizing actively, the Fascists were able to elect only 35 deputies to the chamber in the election of 1921, compared to 122 Socialists and 106 of the new Popular party. Beyond aggressive and obstructive tactics in the chamber, the performance of Mussolini and his Fascist colleagues was not impressive in parliamentary action.

Illegal activities were more successful. By the use of violence and intimidation, Fascists captured local governments or frightened local authorities into accepting their policies. Taking advantage of the fear of Bolshevist revolution, they broke up Socialist meetings and obstructed trade-union activities. Though it may never be completely proved, there is little doubt that they received funds from large corporations who wished to destroy the socialist movement; and it is certain that their activities were permitted and even encouraged by the police in many cities.

**Black Shirts and Propaganda.** The pageantry of the movement became more conspicuous during 1921: the black shirts of the party militia, the parades, and the lively tune "Giovinezza" were in evidence throughout Italy. While a program of specific proposals was not declared, a philosophy of action and nationalism was propagandized. Though the economic and social situation

improved, the Ministries headed by Bonomi and Facta were
unable to arrive at decisive policies which would receive parliamentary or popular support. The Fascists were ready to embark
upon an unconstitutional seizure of the power of the state; and
many Italians, weary of the hardships and confusion of the war
and the postwar years, were ready to give consent to such a move.

In October the "March on Rome" was proclaimed, and some
thousands of Fascists, not including Mussolini, assembled in
Civitavecchia, a little north of Rome. Fascist demonstrations
occurred in other cities at the same time. Prime minister Facta,
a good-tempered and well-meaning man, was obstructed from
taking effective army or police action by the lack of a solid
majority in the chamber, and by the refusal of the king to
sign the order for a state of siege and to sanction the use of the
army. Salandra asked Mussolini if he would serve under him in
a Ministry; and the proposal was refused. On October 29, a
week after some 50,000 Fascist militia entered Rome, the king
sent a telegram to Mussolini in Milan, where he had been pru-
dently awaiting the turn of events, inviting him to form a ministry. Accepting the offer, Mussolini announced with his customary
flair for drama, "Tomorrow Italy will have not a ministry but a
government."

**Mussolini's First Ministry.** The Ministry included himself and
four other Fascists, several members of other parties, and two
technical experts without party affiliation. Unlike previous prime
ministers, Mussolini dominated the Cabinet's deliberations and
declared its policies. Appearing before the Chamber, he lectured
it for its inconclusive debates and demanded approval of the
Cabinet's program. After receiving one or two votes of confidence, his first major legislative proposal was a revision of the
electoral laws. The law provided that the party which polled
the largest popular vote, provided it was at least one-fourth of
the total vote cast, should receive two-thirds of the seats in the
Chamber. The remaining one-third of the seats would be distributed among the other contending parties in proportion to the
votes each received. The Chamber approved the law, and after

a dissolution in January 1924, the elections were held the following April for a new parliament. Active campaigning for the national Fascist list of candidates, including illegal acts of the party militia, brought a result which was a surprise even to the Fascists. The national list received nearly two-thirds of the popular vote.

**Parliamentary Crisis.** When the Chamber assembled the minority groups freely exercised the usual parliamentary rights of criticism, even though the solid fascist majority assured the new government complete control of policy. Once more Mussolini insisted upon full powers for his government, and was criticised by the Socialist deputy, Matteotti. In June 1924, Matteotti was murdered, in circumstances which indicated that government police officials had connived in the crime. Popular indignation mounted against the regime, and the membership of the Cabinet was modified in an effort to disarm criticism and rally support. At this point the opposition groups withdrew from the Chamber, and met as a separate body of protest in a hall which they engaged on the Aventine hill. After a period of uncertainty, Mussolini assessed the ineffectiveness of the opposition. He became confident that the Fascist leadership could override unfavorable public sentiment, and, disregarding the protests of the dissenting minority, he began to entrench fascism in power. Censorship was imposed upon the press; local fascist groups engaged in violence and intimidation; political opposition was suppressed.

**Dictatorship.** Fully in command of political power, and having successfully survived the risks of loss of support which attended the Matteotti murder, the new government proceeded to establish the fascist state and confer dictatorial powers upon the party and its leader, in a series of laws enacted in 1925 and the years following.

### READINGS

The record of parliamentary government in Italy is analyzed in the following:

Hentze, Margot, *Pre-Fascist Italy*, London, 1939.

Spencer, H. R., *Government and Politics of Italy*, Yonkers-on-Hudson, 1932.

Salamone, A. W., *Italian Democracy in the Making*, University of Pennsylvania Press, 1945.

Sturzo, Luigi, *Italy and Fascismo*, London, 1926.

The story of the fascist revolution has been the subject of many books. Besides Spencer and Sturzo, listed above, others are:

Borgese, G. A., *Goliath: The March of Fascism*, New York, 1938.

Rossi, Angelo, *The Rise of Italian Fascism*, London, 1938.

Salvemini, G., *The Fascist Dictatorship in Italy*, New York, 1926.

Schneider, H. W., *Making the Fascist State*, New York, 1928.

All the books listed above give bibliographies which can serve as guides to further reading.

# CHAPTER 18

# THE FASCIST CORPORATIVE STATE

IN July 1943 the Fascist Grand Council assembled in Rome, demanded Mussolini's resignation, and asked the king to appoint a prime minister. Allied armies, British and American, had oc-- cupied Sicily and were preparing to invade the Italian mainland. Marshal Pietro Badoglio was designated by the king, and selected a Cabinet of civilian officials and military officers. Within a month this government agreed to an armistice with the United Nations. In October Italy declared war on Germany. Thereupon the United States, Great Britain, and the Soviet Union accepted Italy as a cobelligerent in the war. More than a year of hard fighting against German armies finally ended in May 1945. Shortly before the end of the war Mussolini was captured and shot by partisans in Milan.

The ignominious end of Il Duce and his government gave to the twenty years of fasicism the character of an episode—a nightmare. Since fascism is part of the recent history of Italy, however, the student should be familiar with its institutions and practice.

## The Dominance of the Fascist Party

Developing from a loose association of local squads, the party finally achieved a disciplined hierarchy. Commanding authority was placed in the leader and in the Grand Council. In every province there was a secretary and a council, which supervised the activities of local groups and their secretaries. Loyalty to the person of the leader, and to the fluctuating policies of the party, was enforced by the organization. Given the status of an auxiliary branch of the regular military establishment in 1924, the party militia occupied the position of a private army under the direction of the party leaders, and its force was used to suppress opposition.

This Fascist militia originated in the early days of the party, when it was expected that the capture of power might have to be achieved by force, even to the extent of outright civil war. While the party was "capturing" local governments and breaking up meetings organized by trade-unions and socialist organizations, the members of these Fascist squads terrorized local officials, inflicted brutal beatings on individuals who opposed the movement and administered castor oil to leaders and members of opposition groups. The victims of the attacks frequently died, or were permanently disabled. After the seizure of power, the use of violence diminished somewhat, but the wrecking of shops and homes, the attacks upon persons and groups, the beatings and the occasional murders continued as an organized technique of maintaining power.

**Recruitment of Membership.** Regular party membership was limited. After the early revolutionary days, recruitment was conducted by a series of training organizations. The Wolf Cubs and the *Balilla* took in little boys of six to nine years of age, and the *Avanguardista* continued the training for youths from fourteen to eighteen. These training organizations included girls in separate divisions, for the Fascist party was a men's organization and women held places only in auxiliary associations. Discipline was strictly enforced by the leaders. Policies were declared by the Grand Council, though there were provincial and occasional national meetings. The influence of the party was spread among the citizens by many affiliated organizations. Fascist syndicates were organized among laborers, and professional associations of lawyers, doctors, journalists, and teachers extended the influence of the party among Italians who were not members.

Pageantry and propaganda were skillfully used. Marching parades, athletic contests, uniforms and banners were all combined with speeches of the leaders and propaganda in the press to maintain enthusiasm for the greater Italy under fascism. The

threat of violence, the operations of the secret police (O.V.R.A.),
and the sentences imposed by the Special Tribunal for the Defence of the State continued to be forces in regimenting opinion.

To describe fully the methods of espionage, the secret trials,
and the large number of sentences of imprisonment or banishment to the Lipari Islands is still impossible. Many distinguished
Italian journalists, political leaders, and labor union officials were
convicted and punished by these procedures. The stories told
by people who escaped from Lipari are full of horror. Any protest against the regime had to be organized in secret, and every
member of an anti-Fascist group knew that he was endangering
his own life and liberty, and that of his friends and family, when
he engaged in such activities.

Fascist monopoly of political activity depended in large part
upon its control of the wide powers exercised by the government.
After 1934 a government undersecretary controlled the press,
and after 1937 he expanded his activities to justify the new title
of minister of popular culture. The Ministry of Education imposed fascist doctrine on the teaching and the textbooks in the
schools. Even the universities, long seats of free learning, were
dominated by the party program, though many scholars refused
to yield and left Italy. Films and radio were also carefully controlled.

Organized opposition was quickly suppressed whenever it appeared. The final effect was the establishment of a one-party
state, with fascist leaders completely in command of political
activity.

## The Fascist Government

In the first few years after the march on Rome, the powers
of the state were concentrated in the hands of Il Duce. As head
of the government, he and his Ministry possessed the power of
issuing decree laws, subject only to the compliant advice of the
Grand Council of the party. This was an advisory body, made up
of party leaders and high officials. It is still impossible to de-

termine whether its advice was completely in accord with the
desires of the party chiefs, many of whom were among its members, or whether it exerted some real influence upon the course
of policy. In any case, there were no outward evidences of any
divergence of views between the head of the government and his
Ministry and the Grand Council until military defeat was apparent in 1943.

**New Electoral Laws.** The Chamber of Deputies, as has already been explained, contained a solid Fascist majority of carefully selected members in 1924. Further modification of the
electoral law in 1928, which entrusted to the Grand Council the
task of nominating all the candidates for the Chamber in a
single national list, converted it into a docile cheering section.
In 1938, the Chamber of Deputies was replaced by the Chamber
of Fasces and Corporations, the members being delegates from
various economic and political organizations. This was a large
body, and worked chiefly through its committees. The Senate,
which continued to exist, remained a body of appointed members as it had been under the *Statuto*. Because of its composition,
it was chiefly an honorary assembly, and exerted little influence
on government policy.

This concentration of power was enhanced by Mussolini's
practice of taking over two or more important ministries himself.
Indeed, at times he came close to being both the head of the
Ministry and the Ministry as well.

**Centralized Administration.** Besides the concentration of authority, there was also a great centralization of power. Italian
local government, which had formerly been supervised by prefects in the provinces, was brought under more complete national control by the appointment in every town and village of
a *podesta*, responsible to the prefect and to the minister of the
interior. Correlated with the tightly organized hierarchy of the
party, this meant that the whole country was effectively ruled
by the Fascist government in Rome.

The civil service and the courts were staffed with loyal Fascists
since officials who would not give full loyalty to the party lost

their positions. The same policy, it should be added, was applied to teachers in the schools. There is insufficient information for an accurate assessment of the qualifications of administrative officials, but the evidence indicates that a party spoils system seriously impaired the quality of government personnel.

**The Accord with the Catholic Church, 1929.** The political strength of the Fascist movement benefited from the agreement with the Catholic Church which Mussolini was able to conclude in 1929. This Lateran Accord provided for a financial indemnity to the Church, in settlement of its claims which had been pressed since 1871. Vatican City was recognized as an independent sovereign state, and the Pope's authority within the small area was fully guaranteed. At the same time the Vatican agreed that it would remain aloof from the usual questions of national and international foreign policy, confining its activities to the religious and moral sphere. The moot question of education was settled by a compromise which provided for religious education in schools, but left the control of the regular curriculum in the hands of the civil authorities. The vexing question of Church and State, which had long been a problem of Italian politics, was settled in a way which contributed substantially to Mussolini's power and prestige.

## The Corporative State and Social Policy

The essential purpose of fascist economic policy was to organize the economic activities of the community under the guidance and direction of the state. Fascism was to end the class conflict; and the authority of the government was to reconcile the interests of all economic groups. The claims of the whole society, expressed by the Fascist party and realized in the action of the state, would enlist the willing cooperation of labor and capital, industry and agriculture, in a national harmony which would make the nation strong and prosperous. This, at least, was the theory, but it included no specific proposals for reconciling the interests of different social groups.

**Labor Sydicates.** Laborers were organized in Fascist syndicates, which replaced the former trade-unions. Pressure by the government and the party broke up the socialist and Catholic unions, but the new syndicates never succeeded in enlisting all the labor force of the nation. An elaborate hierarchy of local and provincial syndicates centered in the national confederations of syndicates existing in each industry or groups of industries. By these means labor was organized in industrial groupings, and was consistently denied the opportunity of building a national organization which would express its general interests. The influence of the party permeated all of these organizations, for most of the key positions were held by Fascists.

It must be remembered that most laborers were forced by intimidation and violence to enter the new Fascist syndicates. The free trade-unions were disbanded by the power of the state, their leaders were beaten, or bribed to cooperate, and the strength of the labor movement in Italy was broken. The new labor syndicates never received representation in the councils of the corporations at all commensurate with their membership. The whole system was weighted heavily in favor of large financial and corporate interests.

**Employers' Confederations.** Employers were grouped in corresponding syndicates and confederations. The Charter of Labor, promulgated in 1927, envisaged a system of collective labor contracts between employers' and laborers' syndicates, which would regulate wages and working conditions in all industries.

The function of the state was to act as an arbitrator and guide in the relationships of the parallel organizations of capital and labor. A series of corporations, giving representation to the employer and employee syndicates and confederations, was set up by the state. These corporations were all represented in the National Council of Corporations, and the government maintained a Ministry of Corporations which directed and supervised all corporate activity. In addition, the state established a system of labor courts, which heard and decided disputes between capital and labor under the terms of the collective labor contracts.

This corporative organization may be indicated by a tabulation, as follows:

| Labor | The State | Capital |
|---|---|---|
| Employees' syndicates grouped into federations and confederations, in industries, agriculture, commerce, and banking. | The Ministry of Corporations<br>The Council of Corporations, containing representatives<br>Twenty-two Corporate representatives of labor and capital<br>The labor courts | Employers' syndicates grouped into federations and confederations, paralleling corresponding workers groups |

This tabular statement can be elaborated by naming some of the twenty-two corporations, which were designed to cover a whole cycle of productive enterprise: Grains, covering all operations from growing of wheat to milling of flour and baking of bread; Textile products, from growing of silk to manufacturing of all types of yarns and textiles; Metallurgy and machinery, from mining and smelting of metals to the manufacture of metal products; Tourist and hotel trade, covering all aspects of the conduct of these enterprises.

To illustrate further, workers in the textile industry through their syndicates and confederations, dealt with the syndicates and corporations of employers in the same industry. Each set of organizations was represented by delegates in the Corporation of Textile Products. So far as possible, disputes between labor and employee organizations were reconciled and adjusted in the corporations, where government and party influence was exerted by the Ministry of Corporations. At the same time, it was possible for the state to approach industries through this machinery and ask for policies which would contribute to the national strength and economic welfare. Particular industrial disputes were subject to arbitration in the labor courts.

**State Guidance of the Economy.** Theoretically, the guiding hand of the state was thus imposed on the whole range of the nation's economic activity, and at the same time the rights of private ownership and individual initiative were preserved. It was the function of the state to arbitrate between groups, and at the same time to safeguard the public interest by directing the policies of industry toward the real needs of the community. Strikes and interruption of production were prohibited, on the assumption that adjudication by the state would provide means for protecting the equities of all individuals and groups.

In actual practice, labor was consistently underrepresented in the corporations. And, while the labor courts frequently gave decisions in favor of labor's claims, the real economic effect of many rulings was simply to diminish slightly the amount of wage reductions. It is extremely difficult to assess with accuracy the changes in wage levels and standards of living. Money wages were lowered consistently throughout the whole period of Fascist rule. Living costs tended upward as the result of policies of economic self-sufficiency, so that the laborers' standard of living was steadily depressed. Since the labor syndicates were dominated by party influences, and the corporative system allowed no effective protest on the part of labor organizations, workers were unable to do more than complain of the hardships.

Probably the most significant aspect of the corporative system was the powerful influence of the state in economic affairs. Financial and foreign trade policies were directed toward the objective of national self-sufficiency. In many respects what was achieved in Italy was a war economy in peacetime. This result was greatly intensified by the response to sanctions imposed by the League of Nations during the period of the Italo-Ethiopian War, 1935–1936. Policies for increasing grain production and for developing essential industries were carried out through the mechanism of the corporations.

The objective of national self-sufficiency imposed hardships on the whole Italian community. The "Battle of the Wheat" increased the cost of bread and spaghetti for all Italian consumers, because it limited the importation of wheat from abroad. Grains of all kinds could be purchased more cheaply on the world market than they could be produced in Italy. The diversion of labor and capital from the production of dairy products, wines, and olive oil, to the production of cereals was a wasteful and costly use of Italy's resources. This was true of a large part of the Fascist economic program, and the general effect was to distort the whole economy in order to maintain an artificial self-sufficiency.

**Welfare Activities.** Besides these economic controls, the Fascist state encouraged various welfare policies. *Dopolavoro,* an organization of laborers sponsored by the party and the state, carried on a variety of leisure-time activities for workers, and made vacation trips and recreation available on moderate terms for working men and their families. It also administered a number of social services, such as unemployment benefits, health and accident insurance, and similar programs. While the scale of these benefits was not generous, the workers felt that the Fascist state did have a real concern for their welfare.

## ITALY AND FASCISMO

Now that the Axis has been defeated and Italy is striving to re-establish democratic principles and practice, it may be possible during the next few years to analyze the record of the Fascist government more comprehensively. Although at present there is a lack of exact and detailed information, some of the most important aspects of Fascism can be weighed.

The fact of political dictatorship has long been obvious. The party maintained a monopoly of political activity, and through its youth organizations recruited the small disciplined membership which could successfully dominate the state and its people. Violence and intimidation were used unhesitatingly; pageantry and propaganda mobilized popular acquiescence; power was concentrated in the hands of Mussolini and a small group of leaders; and centralized administration made this power effective in all parts of Italy. The seizure of power in 1922 was accomplished by a mixture of force and propaganda, and Socialist and Popular parties were unable to organize successful opposition. Once the state was in the hands of the fascists, its full power was utilized to make dictatorship effective and permanent.

The weakness of parliamentary government in Italy opened the way for the establishment of some sort of revolutionary leadership in the years of social and economic distress which followed World War I. In some ways it seems surprising that socialist groups, encouraged by the success of the Bolsheviks in Russia, were unable to win power. Part of the explanation lies in their own divisions into Maximalist and Minimalist wings, part lies in the fact that the fascist glorification of nationalism, denied to all socialists by the international character of their program, was better suited to the temper of the Italian people after the disappointments of the peace settlements.

Undoubtedly the fear of Bolshevist or socialist revolution brought funds to the Fascists from large industrial enterprises, and enlisted the support of a considerable part of the middle class. Later developments in corporative organization seriously hindered the free play of capitalist enterprise, and the record of wage levels and living standards shows that the laboring classes suffered hardships under fascist rule. Social policy, while it had some small achievements to its credit, was not liberal or generous. The lot of the average citizen was undoubtedly hard.

Mussolini's preoccupation with colonial empire, and with an aggressive foreign policy, was the most dangerous factor in the Italian situation during the years of fascism, as the final defeat of the German armies on Italian soil in 1945 was abundantly to demonstrate. While the excitement of a few victories in Ethiopia, and a few diplomatic triumphs in Europe was probably a source of satisfaction to a number of Italians, the eventual risks of war and the economic hardships of self-sufficiency more than outweighed the doubtful prestige gained in these adventures.

The period of Fascist rule brought hardship and suffering to most Italians. There followed the humiliation of German occupation, and the whole sorry adventure concluded in defeat by Allied armies. Liberty of thought and expression had been sacrificed, political and intellectual leaders had been forced into exile or imprisonment, many people had been beaten, abused or murdered, living standards had declined, and propaganda had distorted the thinking of the new generation. The boasts of national discipline, the promises of a new Roman empire, the glorification of national feeling—all this culminated in domination by Nazi armies. The Italian community now faces grave problems as it tries to reconstruct its political life and economic activities.

## Readings

Much has been written about the Fascist government. The books listed below have been chosen because most of them are brief and compact descriptions, and each makes some assessment of the results of the Fascist experiment. Each offers bibliographies which furnish suggestions for further reading.

Ascoli, Max, and Arthur Feiler, *Fascism for Whom?*, New York, 1938.

Ebenstein, William, *Fascist Italy*, New York, 1939.

Finer, Herman, *Mussolini's Italy*, London, 1935.

Florinsky, M. T., *Fascism and National Socialism*, New York, 1936.

Matthews, H. L., *The Fruits of Fascism*, New York, 1943.

Schmidt, C. T., *The Plough and the Sword; Labor, Land, and Property in Fascist Italy*, New York, 1938.

———, *The Corporative State in Action; Italy under Fascism*, New York, 1939.

Schneider, H. W., *The Fascist Government of Italy*, New York, 1936.

———, and Shepard B. Clough, *Making Fascists*, University of Chicago Press, 1929.

Steiner, H. A., *Government in Fascist Italy*, New York, 1938, and a chapter on local government in Italy in *Local Government in Europe*, edited by W. Anderson, New York, 1939.

Welk, W. G., *Fascist Economic Policy; An Analysis of Italy's Economic Experiment*, Harvard University Press, 1938.

# CHAPTER 19

# ALLIED OCCUPATION AND POLITICAL
# RECONSTRUCTION IN ITALY

THE circumstances leading up to Italy's entrance into World
War II should be briefly recalled. The Italo-Ethiopian War and
the imposition of sanctions by the League of Nations led to
diplomatic association with Germany, whose aggressive foreign
policies had also brought about a break with the League. In
1936 a diplomatic accord between the two nations was announced, which eventually acquired the name now familiar to
everyone, the Rome-Berlin Axis. This later became the Anti-
Comintern Pact, which Japan joined. Italian and German intervention in the Spanish civil war followed; and Mussolini co-
operated with Hitler in the Munich conservations of 1938.

When England and France declared war on Germany in
September 1939, following the German invasion of Poland, Italy
was bound by a military alliance to enter on the side of Germany. Mussolini waited, partly because the strains of military
and economic action in Ethiopia and Spain still impaired Italian
strength, and partly because his policies had always been guided
by the desire to play a sure thing rather than to take chances.
By June 10, 1940, evidence of the success of the German campaign in France seemed conclusive, and the Italian declaration
of war was made against France and England. This secured the
advantages of an Italian-French armistice agreement, and the
prestige of participating in the "New Order" in Europe.

The final collapse of the Axis has already been referred to in
preceding chapters. Allied Military Government (AMG) was
set up in Italy wherever Allied forces went. Four months after
the Sicily landings, the armistice with the Badoglio government

having been signed, an Allied Control Commission was established to enforce the armistice terms. In the summer of 1945, the word "control" was dropped from the title, in accordance with the general intention of assisting Italy to establish the type of government which was consistent with the general aims of the Allies. The policy followed by all these authorities has been directed toward the encouragement of democratic government, the termination of fascist influence in politics and in local government, and the restoration of economic activity. The most urgent immediate needs were the establishment of civil order after the confusion of the military operations, and the organization of relief for a distressed civilian population.

## ALLIED OCCUPATION AND CONTROL

Teams of American and British civil affairs officers went into Sicily with the invading troops, and often preceded combat units in taking over towns. The first duty of these military government units was to establish order, organize necessary services, and thus give aid to the continued progress of military operations. Once these initial responsibilities were fulfilled, the units took up the more difficult tasks of organizing civil government and restoring economic activity. These stages were repeated on the mainland of Italy, and continued until the final surrender of the German armies in northern Italy.

The tasks of the Allied Commission and the Allied Military Government, important and significant as they were, need only be briefly summarized here.[1] Subcommissions took over the supervision of a number of vital tasks: public health, displaced persons, monuments and fine arts, courts and the law, transport, public safety, local government, and performance of other economic and political functions. A continuous effort was made to

[1] For a brief and authoritative, but vivid and interesting account, see *Review of Allied Military Government and of the Allied Commission in Italy, July 10, 1942 to May 2, 1945*, Public Relations Branch, Allied Commission.

encourage Italian initiative in conducting all these essential services. The Grand Council of the Fascist Party deposed Mussolini in April 1943; and the king and his prime minister, Marshal Badoglio, moved to Brindisi. The Allied Commission thereafter followed the practice of handing over territory to this government of Italy as rapidly as possible.

A year later the political support of the Badoglio Cabinet was enlarged by the cooperation of various parties, and it was possible to entrust larger territories to the administration of this Italian government. In June 1944 Rome was occupied by Allied armies. King Victor Emmanuel transferred the royal authority to his son, Prince Humbert, as lieutenant general of the realm. Marshal Badoglio resigned and Ivanoe Bonomi was named premier, heading a coalition Cabinet composed of representatives of the chief political groups which had been active in a Committee of National Liberation. Election of a national assembly was promised at the earliest practicable date.

Despite the unifying demands of participation in the war as a cobelligerent, the relationships between the various Italian parties were difficult. Divergence of views arose on the monarchy, on programs of social and economic reform, and on the purge of former fascist officials. Bonomi resigned in November 1944, but was able to reconstitute his Ministry at the invitation of Humbert, the lieutenant general. This Cabinet remained in power till the collapse of the German resistance in northern Italy. The parties which had been associated in a Committee of National Liberation of North Italy then demanded a new leadership, and a Cabinet headed by Feruccio Parri took office. The Bonomi and Parri Cabinets were unable to claim the support of a popularly elected legislative assembly, and were faced with great difficulties in reconciling the position of the various parties.

## POLITICAL TRENDS AND RECONSTRUCTION PROBLEMS

The question of the continuance of the monarchy became one of the most prominent political issues. As a result, one more

Cabinet change occurred before the first national elections were
held: the Parri Cabinet resigned at the end of November 1945,
and was succeeded by a Ministry headed by Alcide de Gasperi,
the leader of the Christian Democrats, a moderate reformist
party much like the Popular party which had been led by Don
Luigi Sturzo in 1919. This Cabinet, despite the increasing agitation over the monarchy and one or two dramatic episodes staged
by young followers of Mussolini, was able to remain in office till
the national elections were held on June 2, 1946.

**Referendum on the Monarchy.** A referendum on the continuance of the monarchy was combined with the elections to the
national assembly. The vote on the monarchy was decisively
but not overwhelmingly in favor of the establishment of a republic, approximately 12.7 million votes for, to 10.7 millions
against, a republic. Humbert, who had succeeded to the kingship
after his father's formal abdication on May 9, 1946, waited till
June 13 before finally leaving Italy. A few riots occurred be-

NATIONAL ASSEMBLY ELECTION, JUNE 2, 1946.[2]

| Party | Popular vote (thousands) | Seats |
|---|---|---|
| *Left* | | |
| Communist.......................... | 4343 | 104 |
| Socialist............................ | 4745 | 115 |
| *Center* | | |
| Action Party........................ | 334 | 7 |
| Christian Democrat.................. | 8083 | 207 |
| Republican.......................... | 998 | 23 |
| *Right* | | |
| Uomo Qualunque (Common Man)....... | 1210 | 30 |
| National Democratic Union........... | 1559 | 41 |
| National Freedom Bloc............... | 636 | 16 |
| *Scattering affiliations* | | |
| Small parties and independents........... | 1045 | 13 |
| Totals.............................. | 22,953 | 556 |

[2] Data taken from *The World Today,* Royal Institute of International
Affairs, London, July 1946, II, p. 311; see also pp. 305–13.

tween monarchist and republican groups before the issue was finally settled by the Court of Cassation's announcement of the final vote on the referendum.

The elections for the national assembly, which was to frame a constitution for the new republic and also serve as a national legislature, showed the predominant strength of a few large parties. This result had been foreshadowed in the municipal elections of March 10, 1946. The parties which had taken an active part in the movements for national liberation had won majorities in many communes. The results of the elections for the assembly are shown in the table on page 252.

This summary shows the principal political alignments. The classification of parties into right, center, and left viewpoints is somewhat confused by the importance of the issue of the monarchy, which put certain groups into positions they may not continue to maintain now that the decision is made in favor of a republic. In addition, the disputed territories of Venezia Giulia and Bolzano did not hold elections for the thirteen seats and four seats assigned to each respectively, which would have brought the total number of seats in the assembly up to 573.

Election districts were large, ranging from seven seats in Caserta to thirty-six in the district of Milan. Each party put forward a list of candidates in a district, and there was a national pool of surplus votes cast in each constituency, which in this election accounted for eighty of the seats won. This was not a precise system of proportional representation; but, as the figures show, each party received approximately the share of the assembly which its popular vote justified. It seems likely that this system of election will be continued.

**Tasks of the Assembly.** The life of the assembly was limited to eight months. During that time it had to draw up a constitution, and also designate and support a government. This latter task was not easy. The assembly met on June 25, 1946, and in the course of the first four days by a large majority elected provisional president of the Italian Republic, Enrico de Nicola, a former Liberal leader of the old Chamber of Deputies. Alcide

de Gasperi, leader of the Christian Democrats, was able to form
a Cabinet which combined with his own the three other large
parties, Socialists, Communists, and the Republican groups. This
was, in effect, a continuance of the leadership in power at the
time the elections were held, for de Gasperi had been designated
premier to succeed Parri in December 1945.

The de Gasperi Cabinet received an overwhelming vote of
confidence from the assembly on July 25, 1946. At the same
time resolutions were carried instructing the prime minister, who
was temporarily acting as minister for foreign affairs, to strive to
secure a just peace for Italy. After that time, much of de Gasperi's
time was spent at Paris, where he presented the Italian case to
the peace conference.

**Problems of the Future.** Any discussion of the Italian political
scene must be tentative. The conspicuous problems, which will
continue to be vital to the life of the provisional republic, can
be easily discerned. Settlement of peace terms, in which the disputed territories of Trieste and Venezia Giulia are prominent,
will have a powerful effect upon Italian public opinion. Some
disturbing parallels with the situation in 1919 exist in 1946. If
the final terms of a peace settlement are definitely unfavorable,
the life of the provisional republic and the prospects for a democratic constitution may be endangered. The present alignment
of parties indicates a preponderant sentiment in favor of representative constitutional government, but national sentiment
might lead to a revival of dictatorial leadership.

Equally important are the questions of economic reconstruction and social reform. The corporative state under Fascist
leadership had raised extravagant hopes of a better life for
Italians, and a new government will be forced to assume the
task of positive leadership in organizing economic activity. This
is a problem, or rather a series of problems, of great difficulty.
The solutions will depend on Italy's relationships with the rest
of the world, as well as on the course of domestic policy. The
present membership of the assembly presages the continuance of
moderate reformist leadership, which will be prepared to under-

take active policies of reform, and is ready to maintain democratic institutions. If effective association can be maintained between the chief parties, which apparently have a better hold upon the loyalty of the citizens than did the parties during 1919 and 1920, it should be possible to meet the problems of reconstruction and maintain the prestige of representative government.

## READINGS

Three recently published books are valuable to the reader seeking understanding of the contemporary situation in Italy:

McCartney, M. H. H., *The Rebuilding of Italy,* New York, 1946.
Sforza, Count Carlo, *The Real Italians,* New York, 1942.
Sturzo, Luigi, *Italy and the Coming World,* New York, 1945.

Current authoritative reporting is available in English in the following:

The New York *Times*
*The Times,* London
*Foreign Affairs,* New York
*Foreign Policy Reports,* Foreign Policy Association, New York.
*The World Today,* Royal Institute of International Affairs, London.
*The Contemporary Review,* London

In addition to the foregoing, the journals listed at the end of Chapter 1 frequently publish articles on Italian government and politics.

# GERMANY

# CHAPTER 20

# THE WEIMAR REPUBLIC AND
# THE NAZI REVOLUTION

On JUNE 4, 1941, the former Kaiser, Wilhelm II, died at Doorn in Holland. He had been living in exile since 1918, when the imperial government collapsed on the eve of Germany's submission to the Allies. At the time of his death he was eighty-two years old. In the last year of his life he had seen the armies of the Third Reich occupy Holland, and his death preceded by little more than two weeks the beginning of Hitler's invasion of Russia. Wilhelm's life reflects the political changes which occurred in his country during the twentieth century— he was emperor of the first of three successive governments of the German people, observed the second from exile, and died at the time the third reached the peak of its power in Europe. Germans in their middle forties can recall the days when he was Kaiser Wilhelm II, and any German over twenty has some recollection of the Second Reich, the Weimar Republic.

## The Unification of Germany

Until the middle of the nineteenth century, Germany, like Italy, was more a "geographical expression" than a nation. The patchwork of medieval free cities and petty kingdoms, further confused by the persistence of the idea and some of the institutions of the Holy Roman Empire, prevented the process of national unification which took place much earlier in France and in England. The Napoleonic wars imposed a brief, but alien, organization upon the many German states. The settlement of Europe at Vienna in 1815 approved the establishment of a German Confederation which provided a minimum basis of association among the cities and principalities.

**Dominance of Prussia.** One of the German states, Prussia, achieved a considerable place in the affairs of Europe during the eighteenth century under the leadership of able and vigorous monarchs, assisted by capable ministers. Her military strength and economic development made her a likely candidate for dominant influence in the process of unification during the nineteenth century. A customs union, the *Zollverein*, was organized among the northern states in 1834, and the membership of other states was invited. This initial economic tie demonstrated the advantages of associated action. In 1848 liberal sentiment was expressed in revolutionary action in a number of the German states, and the Frankfurt Congress of that year proposed a democratic constitution for a united Germany. The refusal of the king of Prussia to accept a crown limited by constitutional rules defeated this movement, with the result that it remained for Bismarck, after he became president of the Council of Ministers in Prussia in 1862, to achieve the unification of Germany by "blood and iron."

The story of Bismarck's diplomacy need not be told in detail here. The Austro-Prussian War in 1866 led to the establishment of the North German Federation. The Franco-Prussian War, four years later, aroused national feeling and enhanced the prestige of Prussia. In 1871 the First Reich[1] was proclaimed at Versailles, during the conference which settled the terms of peace with France, and Wilhelm I, grandfather of the late Wilhelm II, was made the first Kaiser.

**Centralized Federalism.** The new state was a federation, faintly comparable to the United States, but differing sharply in the large powers assigned to the central government, and in the limited influence of the Reichstag, the lower house of the legisla-

---

[1] Strictly stated it was the Second Reich, the first being the medieval empire. For convenience in this chapter it is referred to as the First Reich, the Weimar Republic is referred to as the Second Reich, and the Nazi State as the Third Reich.

ture. The emperor continued to be king of Prussia also, and this increased his influence. The real powers of determining policy gravitated into the hands of the chancellor who headed the Cabinet, since the legislative body lacked prestige. The broad powers of the federal or imperial government, coupled with the predominant economic and political power of Prussia, gave an autocratic character to the First Reich.

In 1890, two years after Wilhelm II succeeded to the throne, Bismarck resigned—the inability of the two to act in concert being aptly characterized by Tenniel's cartoon in *Punch,* "Dropping the Pilot." The aggressive economic and diplomatic policies pursued by Germany from 1888 to 1914 led to her involvement in World War I. Defeat was followed by political revolution, and the Second Reich, a republican federation, was established in 1919.

**Germany and Italy Compared.** The similarities between Italian and German unification invite comment. Both were instances of delayed national unification, compared to other European states. National feeling was stimulated in both communities, but neither Germans nor Italians had experience in the management of representative institutions. The effects of the industrial revolution complicated the situation faced by their new governments during the last quarter of the nineteenth century and the first decade of the twentieth. In 1918 the Germans lost the war, and in 1919 the Italians felt that they had lost the peace. Political revolution followed in both countries.

The differences are as striking as the similarities. Constitutional democracy accompanied unification in Italy, though it failed to operate successfully. Liberalism in Germany yielded to the militaristic nationalism mobilized by Bismarck. Coalition governments in Italy failed to develop decisive policies to meet domestic problems or to make a place for Italy in the diplomatic affairs of Europe. Autocratic government in Germany was admired throughout the world for the efficiency of its civil service, its paternal direction of an expanding economy, and its advantageous manipulation of diplomatic relations. Because of the

identification of imperial Germany with the humiliating defeat
of World War I, a new democratic government should have succeeded. But a people accustomed to paternalistic autocracy could
not match the successes of the First Reich.

## The Weimar Republic

The Second Reich never escaped its legacy as the inheritor
of defeat. Loss of territories, the war-guilt clause, and the continuing burden of reparations were unwillingly accepted by it
under the terms of the Versailles Treaty. The Empire's record of
efficient and decisive government had not prepared the Germans to be loyal to representative institutions, which necessitated
endless discussion and compromise.

**The Weimar Constitution.** The constitution, framed and
adopted by the liberal democrats, social democrats, and parties
of the center, provided an elaborate mechanism of representative and responsible government. A great deal of earnest purpose
and expert knowledge was applied to the framing of its provisions. The president was elected by the people, to avoid the
weakness of the presidential office in the French Third Republic; the lower house of the Reichstag was chosen by a complex system of proportional representation, which accorded to
each political party a share of the seats almost precisely in accord
with its popular vote; an Economic Council, representing the
chief industries, agricultural interests, and the financial community, was empowered to offer advice on legislation affecting
economic activity. Cabinet responsibility to the Reichstag was
required, and provisions for referenda on policy were designed
to afford opportunity for the electorate's verdict on national
policy. In the event of an emergency, special powers were available under Article 48 by which the president, with the countersignature of the chancellor, could issue decrees having the force
of law. The Reichstag had power to revoke them within six
months, but presidential decrees became very nearly the regular
method of government after 1930.

The Weimar Republic was an expression of the ideals of liberals and reformers in Germany. It reflected the hopes of the time of its framing, that the world had been made safe for democracy. It made use of the modern devices of constitutional government: proportional representation, direct legislation by initiative and referendum, the advice of a council representing economic groups. It declared the responsibility of the Cabinet to the representative legislature, and still provided for strong leadership by giving real authority to the popularly chosen president. The federal pattern limited the powers of the states, particularly it curtailed the influence of Prussia. When it was first adopted, Germans had high hopes that stability and prosperity could be achieved under reformist leadership, and that their country might soon have a respected place in the councils of European states. Remembering the spirit of this constitution, and the quality of the leadership which took power, no one can easily explain why these hopes failed to materialize.

**Failure of the Weimar Republic.** An important part of the difficulties arose in the field of foreign policy. Gustav Stresemann, as chancellor and as foreign minister, defined the policy of "fulfillment" which guided the Reich's relations with other states from 1923 to 1929. This required observance of the terms of the Versailles Treaty, in the expectation that eventually Germany would be recognized as a peaceful partner in world affairs. Examples of it are the Dawes Plan for reparations and the signing of the Locarno guarantees of the frontiers of Germany and her western neighbors. Germany was admitted to the League of Nations, and adjustment of her relationships with other powers seemed to be progressing favorably. German national feeling, however, suffered from the continuance of the war-guilt clauses, and from the losses of territory, particularly the corridor which separated East Prussia from the rest of Germany. Reparations, even when finally determined by the Young Plan in 1929, had the appearance of a long-term mortgage upon the German economy. Demands for equality of armament, either by the disarmament of other states or the raising of restrictions on the republic's armament, were fruitless. Hitler was able to tell excited crowds that Germany was "enslaved," and have an increasing proportion of the people believe him.

**Multiple Parties and Coalition Ministries.** The system of proportional representation, as was intended, gave expression to the many varieties of public sentiment, and made it possible for numerous parties to achieve representation in the Reichstag. The result was not unlike the situation in France and in pre-fascist Italy—there was a succession of coalition ministries, unable to agree upon decisive policies. When the world depression wrecked some of the most important German banks, and the decline of industrial activity produced unemployment figures exceeding six millions, Chancellor Bruening was forced to resort to the use of emergency powers in order to carry on the policies of retrenchment and deflation his Cabinet deemed necessary. The various parties tended to become class and interest groups, and the conflict of views between them was irreconcilable. It is not exaggerating the situation to say that democratic procedures were suspended after 1930, under the stress of domestic problems and adverse relationships with other states.

**Effects of Inflation.** The inflation which followed the end of World War I had inflicted a severe shock upon the social structure. Many middle-class families lost all or a large part of their savings, and suffered serious losses of income. A great many of the solid citizens lost confidence in the government and its policies. Fears of social revolution were added to the discouragement which accompanied loss of economic security and opportunity. Trade-unions, associated with the Social Democratic party, tried to defend the standard of living of the workers. Big corporations, fearing the possibility of a communist or socialist revolution, looked about for political movements which would support the existing order.

**Reichstag Elections.** The voting record in the Reichstag elections gives some measurement of the effect of this political and social unrest, for the system of proportional representation accurately mirrored the strength of various parties. It is unneces-

sary to give the election figures in detail; a general d
will suffice. In May 1928, a cluster of moderate parties,
the Social Democrats, the Catholic Christian Socia
Bavarian Peoples' parties, and a few liberal and democra
ties received approximately 70 per cent of the popular vo.., and
a corresponding share of the seats in the Reichstag. In the election of 1932, after a steady decline of strength in the intervening elections, this proportion had dropped to only 39 per cent.
During the same period the Communist party rose from less
than 12 to a little more than 15 per cent; and the National
Socialists (Nazis) rose from 4 to 37 per cent. This meant that
extreme points of view, both of the Left and the Right, increased
their voting strength at the expense of the moderate groups of
the center. A larger and larger number of Germans were ready
for revolutionary action. The only question was: what kind of
revolution, brown or red?

## THE NAZI REVOLUTION

As early as 1919 Adolf Hitler became member No. 7 of the
executive committee of an insignificant political party in Munich,
the *Deutsche Arbeiterpartei* (German Labor Party). He dis-
covered in himself a rewarding talent—he had tried many activities without success before—the ability to stir the emotions of a
crowd. At first the crowds were small, but before the end of the
year he was attracting thousands of people to mass meetings
conducted by the party, now named the *Nationalsozialistische
Deutsche Arbeiterpartei* (National Socialist German Labor
Party, NSDAP, nicknamed Nazi). The twenty-five points of the
program, many of which contradicted others, were formulated
by Hitler and Gottfried Feder early in 1920. The story thence-
forward was one of continuous agitation, increasing membership,
and the organization of a party militia to protect the meetings and
to engage in various forms of violence.

**The Munich *Putsch*.** In November 1923, in conjunction with
General Ludendorff and various dissatisfied veterans' groups,

Hitler attempted to capture the city of Munich by violence, with the intention of eventually seizing the state of Bavaria and then of rebelling against the government of the Reich. The failure of this effort was a mixture of tragedy and comedy, and early the following year Hitler was tried and sentenced to prison. The effect of the trial and the sentence, ironically enough, was to further the Nazi movement. The trial gave him an opportunity to attract the attention of Germans in all parts of the country, and to declare his intention of gaining power by legal means. The imprisonment, humanely administered in the fortress of Landsberg am Lech, gave him a needed interval of peace and quiet which he devoted to the writing of *Mein Kampf* (My Battle). This extraordinary autobiography, partly a discussion of political strategy and propaganda, partly a defense of the twenty-five points, (and all reading very much like a psychiatrist's case history of a hopeless patient), became a best-seller even before political pressure was applied to its sale.

**Nazi Electoral Success.** Released from prison after nine months, Hitler resumed his activities. As the situation in Germany grew worse, the Nazi membership increased, and it became the second largest party in the Reichstag after 1929. In 1930 the party began to achieve substantial electoral successes. The intrigues which finally led to Hitler's appointment as chancellor can be quickly summarized. President von Hindenburg, after refusing to grant further emergency powers to Bruening, placed in office two successive Cabinets headed respectively by Franz von Papen and General von Schleicher. Neither of these "monocle" Cabinets could claim popular support, nor was either able to deal with a Reichstag made unruly by the noisy tactics of the Nazis. Meanwhile Hitler had been able to assure German business leaders that he would defend the state against communist or socialist revolution, and a basis of cooperation was arranged with the conservative Nationalist party led by Dr. Alfred Hugenberg. On January 30, 1933, President von Hindenburg invited Hitler to become chancellor, though in earlier interviews he had stubbornly refused to deal with this upstart leader.

The reasons for von Hindenburg's action are still obscure. Hitler was asked in August 1932 to accept the vice chancellorship in von Papen's Cabinet. He refused and, according to the story told by several observers, made a very unfavorable impression on the president. The following January, however, the difficulties encountered by presidential Cabinets which lacked popular and parliamentary support had been fully demonstrated. It is probable that the men around von Hindenburg induced him to accept Hitler on the presumption that Hitler and his mass following could be used to strengthen the government, without concessions to declared Nazi policy.

**Hitler's First Cabinet.** Hitler's first Cabinet, much like Mussolini's first Ministry, had few members of his own party. Goering and Frick were given important posts, and the rest of the Cabinet were orthodox conservatives, Nationalists, or men without definite party affiliation. The power of the government was immediately used to disband the Communist party and suppress its political activities. The Reichstag was dissolved February 1, 1933. The night of February 27, the Reichstag building was burned. The government accused the Communists of the act, a wave of fear swept over Germany, and decrees were issued to "protect the nation from the Communist menace." On March 5 elections for the new Reichstag resulted in a meager Nazi and Nationalist majority, 52 per cent of the popular vote and Reichstag seats. The Nazis received 44 per cent of the total popular vote, the Catholic Center parties 14, the Social Democrats 18.3, and the Communists 12.3. The election was not a free election, though it was conducted in an orderly manner in many districts. The power of the government was used to restrict the agitation of the moderate parties, while intimidation by the Nazi party militia was in no way obstructed in many parts of Germany.

The Reichstag assembled on March 21 in the Garrison Church in Potsdam, with the 81 Communist members excluded. Two days later Hitler introduced an Enabling Act which gave decree powers to the Cabinet. Only the Social Democrats voted against it. Equipped with these decisive powers, Hitler was able to achieve his "legal" revolution. Henceforth, the Führer's words could be given the force of law. Under the leadership of his mystical intuition, Germany entered the Third Reich.

## READINGS

Analysis of the record of the Weimar Republic, and of party alignments under it, may be found in the following books:

Brecht, Arnold, *Prelude to Silence: The End of the German Republic*, New York, 1944.

Ermarth, Fritz, *The New Germany: National Socialist Government in Theory and Practice*, Washington, D. C. 1936, ch. 1.

Halperin, S. W., *Germany Tried Democracy*, New York, 1946.

Kosok, Paul, *Modern Germany*, University of Chicago Press, 1933.

Kraus, Herbert, *The Crisis of German Democracy*, Princeton University Press, 1932.

Schuman, F. L., *Germany Since 1918*, New York, 1937.

Of the many accounts of the nazi revolution, the following books may be suggested:

Heiden, Konrad, tr. from the German, *History of National Socialism*, London, 1934.

———, tr. by Ralph Manheim, *Der Fuehrer*, Boston, 1943.

Hitler, Adolf, *Mein Kampf*, ed. by John Chamberlain and others, New York, 1941.

Hoover, C. B., *Germany Enters the Third Reich*, New York, 1933.

Rauschning, Herman, *The Revolution of Nihilism*, New York, 1939.

Roberts, S. H., *The House That Hitler Built*, New York, 1938.

Schuman, F. L., *Nazi Dictatorship*, 2d ed. rev., New York, 1936, chs. I-VI.

# CHAPTER 21

# THE NAZI TOTALITARIAN STATE

THE Nazi state lasted for more than twelve years, and at the peak of its power controlled Europe from the Atlantic coast to the banks of the Volga at Stalingrad. No German living will easily forget the regimentation of thought and action imposed on him during those years, and some may still recall the triumphs with pride. The student needs to understand its chief features, for it might be said that while nazism lasted only half as long as fascism, it was more than twice as thorough.

## THE PARTY AND THE PEOPLE

Once the Nazi party was in power, its recruitment of members was comparable to the methods used by the fascists in Italy. Youth organizations inducted boys and young men into the discipline, and inculcated the doctrines. Auxiliary organizations for girls and young women carried on similar activities. Adults qualified for membership if their ancestry, and their loyalty to the Führer, proved acceptable. Purges, the most sensational being the "Blood Purge" of 1934, assured unquestioning obedience to the leadership.

**Party Organizations.** The party spread to all of Germany, and was systematically organized with characteristic German thoroughness. Cells, the smallest party unit, included four or five blocks in the cities, and small communities in the country. From these cells a hierarchy rose through community groups and provincial organizations to the forty-odd party districts. The leader of each district was appointed by Hitler, and the enforcement of the leadership principle brought the whole organization under the direction of a central party Cabinet. This Cabinet was not unlike an army high command, with appropriate divisions for finance, propaganda, women's auxiliaries, and other activities. The two divisions of the militia, storm troops and elite guards, were under the command of high party leaders and owed ultimate allegiance to Hitler. These troops appeared quite early in the Nazi history and functioned as a private army under the Führer's direction. The constant threat of force which they conveyed to the nation made them comparable to the fascist militia. Their shirts were brown while those of the fascists were black, but their behavior was much the same and their enthusiasm for their duties just as keen.

**Party Methods.** Full party membership was held by some six million people during the heyday of Hitler's power. The way of extending the influence of the ruling *élite* to the rest of the population combined propaganda, pageantry, economic pressures and inducements, education, and terror. Again the parallel with Italy is obvious. Other political parties in Germany were disbanded within four months after Hitler assumed the chancellorship. The distorted genius of Goebbels made the Ministry of Propaganda and Public Enlightenment a means of regimenting the press, the motion pictures, the radio, the theatre, and even night clubs and music halls. Pageantry and parades were used with great skill to whip up a frenzy of devotion—the rotogravure sections of newspapers during the years following 1930 are worth study to recall to the student the ingenuities of lighting, banners, and massed demonstrations which took place at the annual Nuremberg Congress, or at occasional meetings in the Tempelhof airdrome in Berlin. The climax of one of these meetings was carefully arranged: the crowd assembled, bands played, and lights flooded the platform crowded with Nazi symbols, the Führer entered with his trusted aides, guarded by his faithful uniformed troops. Then followed a few speeches, ending with Hitler's feverish harangue, interrupted by thunderous "Sieg heils!" The American student can recognize the familiar techniques of the football rally; only the speech would have baffled him, for it lasted literally for hours.

**Racial Doctrines.** To this political pageantry was added the myth of race. Jews were persecuted in ways which reached horrible excesses during World War II. They were denied the privileges of membership in the German *Volk* (people, folk, or race). Many Jews lost their property by confiscation; and infinitesimal traces of Jewish blood, inherited from great-grandfathers or more remote relatives, disqualified professional men and civil servants from their occupations and their place in society. To the hardships of loss of livelihood were added the horrors of the concentration camps. Still, the opportunity to leave Germany was denied to this oppressed minority.

Terror was employed with calculated brutality to intimidate the whole citizen body. The secret police, the Gestapo, after 1934 under the direction of Heinrich Himler, used methods of espionage, secret arrest, concentration camps, and punishments of extraordinary cruelty. Political activity was monopolized, education and communication completely controlled. By these methods, now notorious, the Nazi leaders galvanized their following, and worked their will upon the German nation.

## THE NAZI GOVERNMENT

The structure of the government exhibited the two characteristics of concentration of authority and centralization of power which have been described in the fascist government of Italy. The Enabling Act of 1933 conferred full decree powers upon the Cabinet. These powers were never relinquished, though they were finally destroyed by defeat. The Cabinet, in which Hitler held a dominant place, exercised powers of legislation and administration. The Reichstag, summoned occasionally to hear pronouncements of policy, never debated but always applauded.

**End of Federalism.** The federal division of powers between the nation and the states was abolished in 1934, and each state was placed under a national administrator (*statthalter*). Through a chain of command, the same control was exerted over the provinces of Prussia and all local districts and municipalities.

**Coordination of the Civil Service.** This extension of government authority increased the range of activities of the civil service. Germans had long been accustomed to efficient and methodical performance by government officials. Nazi policy toward government personnel was ingenious. The administrative services were purged of nonsympathizers in the first two years after the seizure of power. The Civil Service Acts of 1935 and 1937, while requiring "Aryan" ancestry and loyalty to the Nazi program from every civil official, also maintained a fairly rigorous standard of training and experience for responsible positions. The temper of the administrative staff undoubtedly changed, but the quality of performance was quite well maintained. Since many experienced officials had families to support and pension rights to safeguard, they were forced to accept the situation and give at least formal support to Hitler. Consequently, the service was disrupted less than might have been expected.

**Coordination of Courts and Law.** The courts and the judiciary were subjected to as rigorous a discipline as the administrative staff. The system of courts rising from district tribunals to the supreme courts of the states was left undisturbed, and the handling of civil cases was not much modified. But criminal trials were substantially altered, in accord with the doctrine that the "tradition and instinct of the *Volk*" should control the principles of law. Judges were summarily removed if they did not conform to this mystical standard. In addition, a hierarchy of People's Courts, using summary procedures, was created to deal with treasonable acts against the new regime. The traditional civil rights, which the Weimar constitution had made certain and secure, practically disappeared.

**Use of Plebiscites.** Plebiscites were frequently used, not only to elect the members of the Reichstag by balloting for one national list, but also to give the affirmation of the whole citizen body to general lines of policy such as Germany's withdrawal from the League of Nations and the Disarmament Conference. These occasions were strategically chosen, propaganda was organized on a tremendous scale, and questions were framed to elicit an affirmative vote. Such mass expressions of unanimity, in which the percentages of approval reached extraordinary figures exceeding 98 and 99 per cent, were hailed as acts of the *Volk* endorsing the policies of the leadership. While the claim was constantly made by Hitler and Goebbels that this was true democracy as contrasted with the plutocracy of other states, it was in truth an expression of control by emotion and hysteria.

**Coordination of Schools.** The mobilization of the educational system to produce support for the government in the minds of children and young people was one of the powerful instrumentalities used by the state. Textbooks were rewritten to foster a conception of history, politics, and economics which would accord with Nazi doctrine. Teachers were subjected to Nazi discipline by a professional association, and their race and loyalty were made the subject of careful investigation. Ceremonies placed emphasis upon the swastika and other symbols of the regime.

The schools were used as a reservoir for the recruitment of the Hitler youth. Service in the army, and in the labor battalions on farms and in public works, took a year or more of every young person's life, and offered means of indoctrinating him with the creed of the "New Germany." Even the universities, as was the case in Italy, were subjected to the discipline of totalitarianism. Science was declared to have a racial character; slogans proclaimed that people thought with their blood. Scholars in the fields of anthropology, economics, literature, history, even physical science and mathematics, often resisted the process of intellectual coordination, and lost their positions or were placed in concentration camps.

## THE STATE OF ESTATES

The organization of the economic life of the community was comparable to the corporative state in Italy, though it was much more elaborate and more efficient in controlling industry, labor, and agriculture. Employers were associated in the Reich Economic Chamber, and grouped in divisions of industry, power, banking, insurance, trade, and handicrafts. Chambers of commerce and industry in every district and province made possible the transmission of policy to every individual enterprise. Each of the divisions maintained a hierarchy which supervised a group of related industries.

**The Labor Front.** The free trade-unions were suppressed, and their funds were seized. In their place a Labor Front organized the workers and their employers (as leaders of the workers) into industrial and territorial associations corresponding to the divisions of the Economic Chamber. Relationships of management and labor were institutionalized with remarkable thoroughness, and courts of "trusted men" performed functions analagous to those of labor courts of the Italian corporative state. The commanding position of the government's agencies, such as the Ministries of Economics, Labor, and Public Works, assured accomplishment of the state's objectives by employers' and employees' organizations.

**Welfare Policies.** A welfare policy was conducted for workers through a nation-wide organization called Strength through Joy (*Kraft durch Freude*). Its purposes were quite closely comparable to those of the Italian *Dopolavoro*. Educational and recreational programs, permeated with Nazi and "Aryan" doctrine, were sponsored in plants and localities. Holiday trips and vacations were provided by nationally organized facilities; and a considerable part of the social insurances was administered by the workers' organizations. In any case, membership was one of the conditions of eligibility for benefits.

**The Food Estate.** Agriculture was brought into the Reich Food Estate. The most significant aspect of the Estate's activities was the control of the marketing and processing of agricultural products. Various types of producers' and credit cooperatives, which had existed for a long time before the Nazi capture of power, were brought within the jurisdiction of the general agricultural organization. The power of the Ministry of Agriculture was as great in this field as the authority of the ministries in industry and finance. Determined efforts were made to make Germany self-sufficient in food crops, though this ran contrary to the long history of industrial development. The Land Law of 1933 was designed to guarantee the continuance of ownership of farms by peasant families, and contributed to each farmer's acceptance of extensive government control. While this afforded a measure of protection against loss of land through debt, at the same time it resulted in tying the farmer to his land.

**Finance and Investment.** Great ingenuity was exhibited in the management of currency and finance. Banks, investment houses, and the stock market were controlled in order to provide a flow of investment funds to finance the enterprises of the expanding economy. Foreign trade was closely regulated by elaborate exchange controls, blocked balances, and various types of currency. The ultimate effect of the complicated financial policies was to insulate the German economy from the currents of world trade, and to make it possible to control wage levels and price levels regardless of changes on international markets. The general purpose was to make the nation self-sufficient, so that it could survive isolation in the event of war. It was also possible to repatriate debts owed abroad on advantageous terms. A drive for increased foreign trade was carried on, particularly in southeastern Europe, and currency and exchange manipulation contributed powerfully to the extension of trading influences in neighboring states.

Trade policy, like foreign policy, was aggressive. The economy of the state of estates was mobilized for war, even in times of peace. Domestically, the results were successful. Activity expanded, employment increased, and hope replaced pessimism regarding future opportunities. People saw chances for jobs, and felt at the same time that welfare policies would give assurance of security to the laborer and the farmer.

One remark should be made concerning the stimulation of economic activity. Hitler had the good fortune to come to power on a rising market. In 1933 the world depression had reached nearly its lowest point. After 1934 the world's foreign trade began to recover, and economic activity revived in every country.

Recovery in Germany would probably have been better balanced, and the living standard of the people would have risen more, without the unorthodox methods used by the Nazi leadership. Germans, and many people outside Germany, gave Hitler credit for performing miracles, when what actually occurred was largely the consequence of a reviving economic activity throughout the world.

## GERMANY UNDER THE THIRD REICH

Viewed in retrospect, it seems surprising that Hitler and the Nazi party were able to remain in power as long as they did. Without attempting a final judgment, the student may wish to consider some aspects of the people's attitudes toward the new government. In the first place, the third Reich gave satisfaction to national aspirations. World War I had ended in a crushing and humiliating defeat, and the years following seemed to make Germany's situation worse rather than better. Reparations appeared to be the cause of economic depression; diplomatic defeats entailed loss of prestige; resentment of German minorities outside the Reich's boundaries were manipulated by Hitler to stimulate demands for revision of the peace treaties. The nation was apparently caught in a cycle of inaction that produced despair, and despair that produced inaction. Until 1939 Hitler delivered a series of bloodless diplomatic victories by aggressive foreign policies. State control of the economy was accompanied by increased economic activity and increased opportunities for employment. Germany seemed to be winning her proper place in Europe.

Secondly, the state of estates, however much it might impose regimentation upon enterprise, gave to many people the feeling of participation in a tremendous collective effort. Germany was building things: networks of highways, great public edifices, the fortifications of the Siegfried Line. Laborers could get jobs, university graduates obtained professional opportunities, farmers were guaranteed possession of their land.

To the stimulation of national feeling and the satisfaction of economic activity was added the excitement induced by skillful use of propaganda. The dismal years after defeat were succeeded by times of feverish activity. Life had been dull; suddenly it became exciting.

The price paid by the German people in lowered living standards, shortages of commodities, and regimentation of conduct through terror was ignored by many. The war sacrifices to come were only dimly discerned, if not entirely disregarded, as the Rhineland was reoccupied by German troops, and Austria was brought into Greater Germany. Despite the apparent successes, however, it must be remembered that underground movements continued to oppose the Nazi policies.

The task of re-establishing democratic government in Germany will undoubtedly be difficult. Propaganda has prostituted critical intelligence, and human integrity has been betrayed. The young have been educated in Nazi schools, the parties representing liberal viewpoints have been suppressed, the newspapers and the radio have been controlled. Opposing these influences, the revelation of the horrors of the concentration camps and the memory of complete defeat will aid occupation authorities in obliterating the totalitarian discipline which has been imposed on the German people for years.

## Readings

The Nazi state has been discussed in many books. The following all give suggestions for further reading:

Ebenstein, William, *The Nazi State,* New York, 1943.

Loewenstein, Karl, *Hitler's Germany,* new ed., New York, 1940.

Morstein Marx, Fritz, *Government in the Third Reich,* rev. ed., New York, 1937.

Pollock, J. K., *The Government of Greater Germany,* New York, 1940.

The following books analyze the economic organization and policies of the nazi state:

Brady, R. A., *The Spirit and Structure of German Fascism,* New York, 1937.

Neumann, F. S., *Behemoth: The Structure and Practice of National Socialism,* New York, 1942.

Reveille, Thomas (pseud.), *The Spoil of Europe: The Nazi Technique in Political and Economic Conquest,* New York, 1941.

In addition to the foregoing, most of the books listed at the end of Chapter 20 discuss the organization of the nazi government and its economic policies.

# CHAPTER 22

# ALLIED OCCUPATION AND
# POLITICAL CHANGE

THE problems faced by Allied occupation in Germany have been much more complex than those which arose in Italy.[1] There it was possible to hand over an increasingly large area to the administration of an Italian government; and the efforts of occupying authorities were early directed toward bringing into being a representative democratic national authority which could assume the responsibilities of Italy's place in the world.

In Germany there were not even the rudiments of an acceptable national government. What unity now exists was achieved by the Allies through their own central agencies, not by building up German authority. In addition, it was inevitable that Soviet Russia and France should both participate; the integrated Anglo-American administration which had been an incident of the combined command in Italy was not available as a method of controlling Germany. Hence there are four separate zones, each with its own office of military government. Agreement is reached among the four only at the top level, where the commanding generals meet in the Allied Control Council for Germany. The actual administration of policy is carried on by four separate organizations.

The intentions of the four powers have not always been reconcilable. The French have favored separatist policies; the purposes of the Russian government are not yet clear. In July and August 1946, American and British military government offices took active steps to coordinate the activities in their respective zones, continuing earlier policies of cooperation.

[1] Sources of information for the chapter are given in the Readings.

These circumstances make it difficult to describe the present German situation. At the time of writing, the work of the Allied Control Council is still in progress. Information is still not readily available. Consequently only a general analysis of the most important aspects of policy can be made.

## THE POTSDAM AGREEMENT AND ALLIED OCCUPATION

The German surrender took place on May 8, 1945, by which time each army, in conducting military operations, had set up some form of military government in the areas it occupied. Less than a month later a joint statement was issued by the American, British, French, and Russian governments, declaring that there would be four zones of occupation and agencies for coordinating policy. Further consultations during July resulted in the Potsdam Declaration, which was published August 2, 1945. On the basis of previous agreements, the Allied Control Council had been set up with headquarters in Berlin and on August 30 it formally announced its assumption of authority for all of Germany. The members of the Council are the four Allied commanding generals, and they act in accordance with instructions sent them by their home governments. Each of the powers has assembled a large secretariat, organized in divisions, such as legal, education, and internal affairs. Procedures have been set up for regular consultations of corresponding divisions from the several headquarters, with the purpose of reconciling the viewpoints of the four occupying powers. The decisions of the Council are based upon the principles of the Potsdam Declaration which are outlined below, the instructions of home governments, and the solutions worked out by the divisions in day-to-day consultation.

**Objectives of Occupation.** The first task of the occupation authorities was to disarm all German military forces, detain those in automatic arrest categories, demobilize in an orderly manner the surrendered personnel in Allied hands, and take all necessary precautions to prevent a renewal of armed conflict. This included not only the destruction of ammunition dumps and other supplies of war, but the disbanding of semi-military organizations which might be a menace in the future.

**Political Aims.** The political responsibilities imposed on the Council, and on each governor in his respective zone, were long-term problems which are still in process of solution. The Nazi party and all its auxiliary organizations must be disbanded, and its members removed from positions of authority. Laws which expressed the policy of the former nazi government were to be stricken from the statute book, and courts and administrative authorities were to modify their practice accordingly. Communities were to become self-governing as quickly as possible, and education was to be reorganized to eliminate the indoctrination which had been carried on under Hitler. Early establishment of a central German government was not permitted, but the Control Council was instructed to work out means of coordinating activity between the four zones to secure as much uniformity of policy as possible.

**Economic Policy.** The guiding principles for economic policy impose upon the control authorities a twofold responsibility which will be hard to perform. Economic activity must be re-established, so that employment and production can be resumed. At the same time the centralization of German industry in cartels and large enterprises is to be reduced as much as possible, and the industries which contribute to war potential are to be curtailed. If the high degree of industrialization of Germany is recalled, the student will realize that these two objectives are not readily reconcilable.

**Legal and Administrative Changes.** The *Gazette* of the Allied Control Council shows that considerable achievements have already been made in clearing away the Nazi legal system. Laws discriminating against minorities with respect to civil rights, taxation, eligibility for government positions, and property rights have been revoked. Instructions have been issued governing the conduct of administrative officials under the supervision of occupying authorities, which will guarantee equal treatment to all groups. To prevent the reappearance of Nazi principles, investigations have been made to determine the affiliations and political attitudes of Germans performing judicial and administrative tasks. A police training school, for example, was established quite early in the British zone to recruit police officers who could be trusted to carry out the general purposes outlined in the Potsdam Declaration.

Provision has been made to establish schools as rapidly as possible, and to provide textbooks and teaching staffs which will inculcate democratic attitudes toward public affairs. Permission has been granted for the organization of political parties and for holding political meetings. Newspapers have been licensed to appear, and have been subject to a minimum of restrictions with regard to editorial policy and the publication of news.

The laws controlling the organization of trade-unions and professional associations have been drastically modified to eliminate the practices of the former Labor Front. Works councils have been made genuinely elective, so that workers in industry may have the opportunity to develop truly representative labor organizations.

Early in the autumn of 1945 efforts were made to enlist German initiative in the conduct of local government affairs. Nominated advisory councils were set up in local government districts, and elections for community councils were promised for the earliest possible date. During 1946 the promises were fulfilled, and a large number of communal elections took place.

The general picture is one of slow, but steady, progress in the difficult task of eliminating nazi laws and practice and stimulating local initiative.

## PARTIES AND PUBLIC OPINION

One of the general statements in the Potsdam Declaration announces that the general intention of the Allied powers is to give the German people opportunity to reconstruct their lives on a democratic and peaceful basis. In due course, it is expected, they should be able "to take their place among the free and peaceful

peoples of the world." To accomplish this end, political leadership must arise, and popular sentiment needs to find expression
through organized political parties. As yet, progress in this direction has been slow and hesitating.[2] The German people are,
naturally enough, much more concerned with the pressing personal problems of finding employment, housing, and the every-
day necessities of life than with political activity or the discussion
of public affairs. In addition, the range of political activity has
necessarily been restricted by military government authorities,
and the amount of actual power exercised by German leadership
cannot be large at first. Observers report apathy, if not actual dis-
taste, for political action—Germans have had too much politics,
of a kind, in their lives since 1933.

Communal elections, newspapers, and public meetings indicate that some political parties are achieving organization and
creating popular interest. The Social Democrats, the Christian
Democrats (the groups referred to as the parties of the center in
Chapter 20), the Communists, a Social Unity party composed
of both socialists and communists, as well as various minor groups
have made their appearance. Lacking the opportunity to conduct
national elections, with Germany divided into four zones, these
parties have confined their activities to local affairs. In the absence of voting figures for the nation as a whole, it is impossible
to assess the relative strength of party organizations.

### THE PROBLEMS OF THE FUTURE

The foregoing description of the work of the Allied Control
Council suggests most of the obstacles that lie in the way of
creating a new Germany after the defeat of Hitler's government.
The persistent problems can be discerned and stated briefly.

Some degree of coordinated action has been achieved through
the Council, and particularly between the American and British

[2] A careful account of the status of parties is given by Robert G.
Neumann, "The New Political Parties of Germany," in *American Political Science Review*, August 1946, XL, 749–59.

zones. The existence of four zones and the absence of a central German government are attributable to the reluctance of each of the powers to relinquish its hold on the situation, combined with the inability to come to a common agreement. The final solution of this problem will have to await the terms of a peace treaty, which will determine, with a greater degree of certainty and finality than the Potsdam Declaration, the relationship of Germany to the Allied Powers and the United Nations.

On March 10, 1947, the Council of Foreign Ministers, representing Great Britain, the United States, the Soviet Union, France, and ultimately China, assembled in Moscow to discuss the final treaty with Germany. From the outset it was clear that agreement on boundaries, reparations, and the final form of the German government would be difficult to achieve.

The re-establishment of full economic activity is also dependent on the eventual terms of a treaty. Until requirements for reparations are defined, and the peaceful range of industrial development is determined, uncertainties of employment and living conditions will take up the major portion of every German's attention. The interruption of economic relationships which follows inevitably from the boundaries of the occupation zones hampers the development of normal business conditions.

Psychological factors are at present extremely difficult to analyze. It is hardly possible to say whether the discouragement of defeat outweighs the hopes of the future. A generation of young people have been subjected to twelve years of intense propaganda in the schools, in youth organizations, and in all the relationships of normal life. The people who remember the Weimar Republic are all middle-aged or elderly, and have been exhausted by the political, economic and physical ordeals of nazi revolution, regimentation, and defeat. The history of the Germans shows evidence of great recuperative powers. If recovery can be directed with skill and fairness, the twentieth century may yet see their characteristic energy, inventiveness, and organizing talent put to use in ways which will contribute to their welfare and that of the world.

## Readings

The student may well be interested in the principal official sources of information concerning the progress of occupation policy.

*The Official Gazette* of the Control Council for Germany, issued monthly by the Allied Secretariat, first appeared October 29, 1945. It contains the laws, proclamations, and ordinances which govern Germany at present.

Reports prepared by the divisions and sections of the four occupying authorities which set forth actual conditions and problems of administration, have been only partially released. The U. S. Office for Military Government has released some of the information bulletins prepared by its sections.

British Military Government Authorities publish a *Military Government Gazette,* which within the British zone, is comparable to the Control Council's gazette mentioned above. In addition, the *British Zone Review* has been published fortnightly since September 29, 1945. In content and format it has much the appearance of a biweekly periodical, with reporting on conditions, official statements, comment by journalists, and a number of photographs.

These will be for some time the best and most authoritative accounts. The newspapers and journals listed at the end of Chapter 19 will also be of value, because interpretative articles will appear in them from time to time.

A few recent books analyze the nature of the present situation, and some are listed here:

Bach, Julian, *America's Germany,* New York, 1946.

Knauth, Percy, *Germany in Defeat,* New York, 1946.

Koch-Weser, Erich, *Hitler and Beyond,* New York, 1945.

Minshall, T. H., *Future Germany,* New York, 1945.

Morgenthau, Henry, Jr., *Germany Is Our Problem,* New York, 1945.

Pollock, J. K., and others, *Change and Crisis in European Governments,* New York, 1947.

Richter, Werner, *Re-educating Germany,* University of Chicago Press, 1945.

# JAPAN

# CHAPTER 23

# THE HISTORICAL BACKGROUND OF JAPANESE CONSTITUTIONAL GOVERNMENT

FOR the student, one of the most troublesome factors of Japan's political structure has been the contradiction between the apparent and the real. Upon first approaching the subject, he observes that during her modern history Japan has utilized governmental institutions not strikingly dissimilar to those of western nations. Thus he finds a cabinet composed of the appointed heads of administrative ministries, an elected legislative body, an independent court system, and so forth. But upon more careful observation, he also finds that these institutions have not operated in the accustomed western manner. Rather their behavior has been peculiarly Japanese.

**The Influence of Premodern History.** This situation is the consequence, in part at least, of the way in which Japan emerged from her feudal past. For more than two hundred years, from approximately the mid-seventeenth century to the mid-nineteenth century, Japan experienced self-imposed isolation. Almost completely cut off from the rest of the world, denied the influence of outside knowledge and experience, her own institutions reached a high stage of national development. Then suddenly the doors were thrust open to the foreign world. Eagerly Japan sought the benefits of western science and industry. With remarkable speed she applied new learning and within a generation emerged as a modern state, an important member of the world community. As part of this adoption of western experience to her own needs, her leaders erected a new structure of government, formalized in a

written constitution promulgated in 1889. It is this structure of
government which strikes a familiar chord to the western student. Its substance, however, the manner in which it operates,
is very different, for this substance, the true heart of the system,
has followed centuries-old Japanese patterns of thought. The
adoption of new institutions amounted very largely to the establishment of a façade of western prototypes behind which characteristically Japanese practices continued to operate. The student of Japanese government, accordingly, must have a look,
however brief, at the premodern history of Japan to appreciate
the fabric of political thought and experience which was carried
forward and which has persisted to the present. Otherwise he
will seriously misunderstand the constitutional system under
which Japan operated for three quarters of a century prior to
her overwhelming defeat by the Allied powers, and he will even
more seriously fail in his evaluation of the revised constitutional
system which is being developed during Allied occupation of the
country.

## THE FEUDAL MILITARY DICTATORSHIP

When Commodore Perry of the United States Navy succeeded in 1854 in opening Japan to the outside world, the country was dominated by a highly organized military dictatorship,
a system of government which had evolved over more than six
centuries, and which permeated every phase of Japanese life.
Power rested in the hands of hereditary feudal lords, or *daimyo,*
who derived their wealth, in the agricultural society which pre-
vailed, from the rice produced on their large land holdings. In
order to protect themselves the feudal lords retained professional
warriors, or *samurai.* It was these samurai who lived according to
a rigid ethical code and who wielded the famous double swords.
Below the daimyo and the samurai, the mass of the common people toiled on the land to produce the all-important rice. Artisans,
located chiefly in towns clustered about the towering castles of
the lords, served the simple requirements of the people, but also

developed remarkable skills in the production of lacquer and metal wears, ceramics, fine textiles, and other art goods. Supreme over the feudal lords and their warriors ruled the military dictator, or *shogun,* the holder of the most extensive lands and the possessor of the greatest military strength. To the shogun the lords and warriors owed obedience and homage. Although permitted a degree of autonomy within their own lands, they were controlled by the greater authority of the military administration supervised by the shogun.

The Tokugawa Shogunate. This military rule of Japan reached its greatest perfection under the Tokugawa shoguns. Ieyasu Tokugawa, the first ruler of the clan, gained control of the country after a series of civil wars terminating in the early seventeenth century. His successors held that control until 1867, shortly after the emergence of the country from its long isolation. The early Tokugawa rulers were preoccupied with the task of perfecting a form of government which would perpetuate their dominance. The success of their efforts was attested by the length of their rule and that of their successors, two and a half centuries. From their capital at Edo, the site of present-day Tokyo, they evolved a pattern of rigid regulations and controls, binding the other feudal lords and their warriors as well as the entire social and economic fabric of the nation. Approximately one-fourth of the country, including a large proportion of the richest lands and all principal cities and seaports, passed into the hands of the Tokugawa clan. Feudal lords of doubtful loyalty were assigned lands removed from Edo, separated from each other by Tokugawa holdings or those of faithful lords. As a further guarantee, the lords were required to reside for part of each year in the capital, and to leave their families in Edo as hostages for the remainder of the time. Marriages between the families of the lords were closely supervised lest alliances against the Tokugawa rule be arranged. The Tokugawas likewise established military control over strategic highways and passes and supervised travel between the lands of different lords by means of a rigid passport system. Throughout the nation, the shogunate maintained political police, trained in the fine arts of espionage, reporting on the activities of lords and their subordinates.

Not only the lords, but all of society was regulated to an amazing degree. Rigid social regulations were imposed upon the people, distinguishing the privileged military caste from the rest of the population. Each caste was instructed in detail what behavior it could follow, what clothes it could wear, and even whom it could marry. Severe punishments were meted out for infringements of these regulations.

**Exclusion Policy.** Perhaps the most significant of all controls employed by the Tokugawa regime to assure its position was that of national exclusion. During the late sixteenth century Japan had developed extensive contacts with the western world as well as with China. Japanese trade had expanded along the Asiatic continent as far as Indonesia, and a Japanese diplomatic mission visited the Pope at Rome. European traders reached Japan, establishing themselves in a favored position with some of the feudal lords. Christian missionaries, who followed the traders, achieved considerable success in introducing Catholicism into the country. But for political reasons the Tokugawa rulers turned the nation away from these foreign influences. They feared that certain lords might employ the foreign trading connections and the alien religion to build up their strength against the central authorities, and they feared also the introduction of new ideas inherent in Christian doctrines. Consequently they prohibited all overseas contacts, with the exception of a mere trickle of trade through the port of Nagasaki, and suppressed and almost completely eliminated Christianity by violent and ruthless persecution.

**Military Administration.** Under this highly organized regime, the actual operation of the government was in the hands of an aristocratic military bureaucracy, or *bakufu* (literally military camp), which was responsible to the shogun. Having emerged from a period of civil warfare, the government constituted in effect an extension of the wartime military command into a period of peace, and Edo became the administrative as well as the military capital of the country. Important political decisions were made by a council of the highest officials. Subordinate councilors supervised the work of numerous executive and judicial officers, located in the capital and principal cities, and at the headquarters of the feudal lords. Within their own domains these lords followed the example of Tokugawa procedures, so that a high degree of legal and administrative uniformity was achieved throughout the whole country.

During this long period of Japanese history the military dictator, the shogun, was the real ruler of the country. In theory, however, the emperor remained the supreme, august sovereign of the nation. But the emperor reigned only; he did not rule.

**The Position of the Emperor.** Earlier in the history of Japan, for several centuries following the first emergence of organized government at about the time of Christ, the imperial family did rule the primitive agricultural nation. It was during this period that the myths concerning the divine origins of the Japanese islands and their rulers evolved into a systematic justification of the authority of the imperial line. But in the seventh century, following the introduction of Chinese culture and the resulting advance of Japanese society, a series of strong civil dictators seized political power, which they held until the first shogunate was established in the twelfth century. The interesting feature of this long experience is that the acceptance of the divine authority of the emperor was so strongly implanted that neither the civil nor military dictators replaced him. As a matter of fact, the early myths were further elaborated to enhance the imperial position. The imperial dynasty was never deposed. The emperor remained the symbol of national sovereignty, while the real powers of government passed into other hands, frequently as the result of the use of force. In theory, the holder of political authority possessed it only by imperial sanction. Actually, he was the one with the power to seize and retain it. The emperor's role was reduced to mere performance of certain ceremonial and religious functions and to presiding over the imperial court, which remained in the ancient capital of Kyoto. On numerous occasions, moreover, the emperor was a minor, controlled by a regent appointed by the civil or military dictator. Thus there was firmly established the principle of indirect rule, by which the real governors of Japan operated behind the emperor, the spiritual and ceremonial head of the nation.[1]

## HERITAGES FROM THE FEUDAL PAST

As already indicated in the introductory paragraphs of this chapter, Japan's feudal past has had a profound conditioning effect upon contemporary political, economic, and social institutions. Before 1600 Chinese influences, and to a considerably lesser degree those from western Europe, produced marked changes in Japanese development, but the isolation which was forced upon the country for the next two and a half centuries by the Tokugawas enabled Japanese culture to undergo a process of continuous refinement and perfection, insulated as it was from alien ideas and institutions. The Tokugawa period was one of intense internal growth and consolidation. Many of the unique features of contemporary Japanese life, such as the glorification of the warrior spirit, the emphasis upon loyalty, and the subordination of women, reached their ultimate perfection during this period of exclusion. Consequently, by the time the exclusion policy was terminated and Japan again came into contact with the outside world, the pattern of Japanese thought was so deeply ingrained that all subsequent developments were molded and fashioned according to firmly established principles and practices.

**National Unification.** One of the principal inheritances was that of two and a half centuries of national unification and development. By the time Commodore Perry arrived, Japan had experienced a long period of internal peace and security under centralized authority. Unlike China, which to this day has been unable to attain national unification, Japan came upon the modern scene with a closely knit, highly organized and well-

[1] For a description of premodern Japan, see G. B. Sansom, *Japan; A Short Cultural History.*

disciplined society. She already possessed an internal structure, nationwide in scope, upon which to build the instruments of modern administrative and technological techniques.

Significantly, however, this nationalization was achieved and maintained by repression, not by consent. From the past the Japanese inherited not only a glorification of the martial spirit, but a tradition of government by force by a military machine. Closely associated with this tradition, moreover, was the extensive use in politics of violence, treachery, and intrigue.

**Subordination of the Individual.** The most deeply implanted of the political heritages, perhaps, was the subordination of the individual to the group and to the state. The Japanese failed to develop the western notion that the individual possessed certain inalienable rights which could not be abridged by the state, and that all men were by nature equal. In their experience the individual existed primarily as a member of a family, of a clan, and ultimately of the greatest of all families, the whole Japanese nation. As an inferior being he was expected to accept the dictates of the head of the family, and of the head of the nation, the father and superior of all, the emperor of Japan. The highest of all virtues was loyalty, the loyalty he owed to his family and to the emperor, who was the personification of the nation.

In western Europe and in the United States the rights of the individual are protected by the acceptance of the principle of government by law. No such restraint upon political authority developed in Japan. Rather, as a subordinate member of society, the individual did not look to laws as defenses guarding his individual rights but as lists of his duties as a member of the national community, duties determined by an official class which itself was superior to the law. It can readily be seen how this principle accorded with the domination of the government by a relatively small, exclusive ruling oligarchy.

**Interference of State with Private Affairs.** Japanese political theory likewise sanctioned the interference of the state into all affairs of the community and the nation. It already has been indicated that the shogunate ordered political, social, and economic life to an amazing degree. Unlike the West, Japan did not develop a *laissez-faire* theory of economics. The state could and did concern itself in the greatest detail with matters of production, distribution, and consumption.

To the student an interesting feature of Japan's long isolation is that her people were completely cut off from eighteenth- and nineteenth-century political developments in America and Europe. The political concepts and doctrines which played such an important part in the development of popular government in the United States and in the countries of western Europe were unknown to the Japanese.[2]

## THE RESTORATION

At the time Commodore Perry reached Japan, strong internal forces threatened the continuation of the Tokugawa regime. Certain of the feudal lords and their enterprising samurai chafed under the repressive measures of the shogunate. Moreover, they beheld western encroachments upon neighboring China and feared that the same fate would befall their own country unless she modernize her government and defenses. They drew the support of a few members of the emperor's court, and of a wealthy and rising merchant class that likewise resented the restrictions of the feudal system which relegated them to the bottom of the social scale. In 1867 these elements forced the shogun to yield his authority and to restore formal control of the nation to the emperor.

**National Progress.** The Restoration, as this political change is known, heralded a period of remarkable progress. The new leaders, who were an exceedingly intelligent and able group of men, eagerly sought knowledge from abroad in order to catch up with the material advances of the western world. They sent observers and students to Europe and America to learn the latest methods of industry, trade, education, and national defense. Foreign ex-

[2] Chapter 1 of R. K. Reischauer, *Japan, Government, Politics* contains a brief but excellent interpretation of Japanese political thought.

perts were brought to Japan to assist in the construction of arsenals, dockyards, factories, railroads, and in the planning of a modern educational system. Feudalism was abolished. The lords exchanged their lands for government bonds, and the samurai gave up their cherished swords and their special privileges.[3]

## HISTORICAL SETTING OF THE CONSTITUTION

The modern governmental system of Japan, which remained in operation until the adoption of a new constitution following unconditional surrender to the Allied powers, dated from the Restoration period. It took its formal shape in terms of numerous laws and imperial rescripts and ordinances, centering in the promulgation of a written constitution by the emperor in 1889.

**The Nature of the Restoration.** In attempting to understand the structure and operation of the modern government of Japan it is helpful to keep in mind the conditions which prompted its establishment. Although the Restoration brought about new organs of administration and set loose forces which produced remarkable changes in the pattern of Japanese life, it was not a political or social revolution caused by the organized protests of the mass of the people. On the contrary, it represented a shift of authority from one ruling oligarchy to another. It has been noted that the leadership for the Restoration was derived from certain lords and samurai, associated with rich city merchants, plus a few members of the imperial court. These statesmen and their supporters were not interested in promoting popular government; it is quite certain that the thought never occurred to them. What they desired was the creation of a strong, autocratic central government which could sweep away the restrictive features of the feudal system, institute broad economic and military reforms to prepare Japan to face the increasing threat of western inter-

[3] This period in Japanese history is referred to as the Meiji period, deriving its name from the emperor whose authority was restored. For an outstanding interpretation of this period, see E. H. Norman, *Japan's Emergence as a Modern State.*

ference, and act quickly against the possibility of internal social unrest. Moreover, they sought to erect a system which would ensure the continuation of their own control of political affairs.

**The Role of the Emperor.** The most significant and effective device at the disposal of the Restoration leaders to ensure their control was the Shinto dogma of absolute loyalty to the divine emperor. By restoring the emperor as a source and center of all political authority, they possessed an extremely potent means of commanding acceptance of the new regime by diverse elements. Thus the Restoration leaders revived the ancient Shinto doctrine that the emperor descended in direct line from the Sun Goddess and that he himself was a living god who rightly claimed the unquestioned devotion of all his subjects. It naturally followed that the emperor's ministers and officials were to be regarded not as public servants but rather as executors of his supreme, divine authority. These leaders sedulously employed the new school system, the newspapers, and other means to impress the ancient legends and dogmas upon the minds of the people. The Shinto faith became a state religion, with state support of the priesthood and shrines, many newly erected or refinished. Characteristically, the constitution of 1889 was presented as a gift of the emperor to his people.

The Restoration leaders perpetuated and reinforced the traditional practice of indirect rule. By emphasizing the theoretical authority of the emperor, while at the same time providing organs through which they alone could "advise" him in the use of this authority, they effectively guaranteed their own dominant position. When they studied the governments of foreign nations, these statesmen observed in Prussia a system which most perfectly satisfied their own requirements. Here they found concentration of authority in the hands of the Kaiser, but provision for the exercise of that authority by a small ruling oligarchy through advisory organs of government. As a result the Japanese constitutional system embodied many features of its Prussian model.[4]

[4] H. S. Quigley, *Japanese Government and Politics*, pp. 40–44.

Following this summary of the historical setting, a description of the structure of Japanese government which evolved in the years immediately following the Restoration may be described.

## THE EMPEROR

The emperor was the supreme head of the nation, the source of all political authority, and the personification of the national will. The constitution identified the emperor with the state and proclaimed that the imperial dynasty reigned unbroken through ages eternal. The constitution further declared that the emperor was sacred and inviolable, thus buttressing his political position with added religious sanction. For purposes of description the functions and powers of the emperor may be grouped into six categories.

**Symbol of the Nation.** Great emphasis was placed upon the emperor as the symbol of the nation. According to the constitution the emperor was the head of the empire, combining in himself all the rights of sovereignty. Much attention was devoted to the emperor's ceremonial duties: religious duties which he performed as high priest of the Shinto faith, military duties as commander in chief of the armed forces, political duties as head of the state, and family duties as head of the imperial family and of the larger family including all Japanese people.

**Head of the Imperial House.** The emperor exercised control over all members of the imperial family, just as the eldest male exercises control of each Japanese family. Imperial family affairs were regulated by the Imperial House Law, which was promulgated in 1889 at the same time as the constitution, and which could be amended only by the emperor with the advice of the Imperial Family Council and the Privy Council, thus placing it beyond the reach of the elected representatives of the people. The Imperial House Law provided for succession by the nearest male descendent of the imperial line. A regency could exercise power in the name of the emperor during his minority or when he was incapacitated.

**Supreme Commander of the Army and the Navy.** Absolute control of the armed forces of Japan was vested in the emperor. Since this authority was derived from his personal prerogative as military head and not as political head of the state, the supreme direction of the army and the navy was subject solely to commands which he issued upon the advice of military officers rather than of political officers of the government. The consequence of this arrangement was the separation of the command of the military forces from the administration of other government matters, resulting in a situation frequently called "dual government," in which the Japanese army and navy acted with a considerable degree of independence, even in political matters and in foreign affairs.

**Executive Powers.** The executive powers of the emperor included the appointment of officials, determination of the organization of administrative branches of the government, reception of foreign envoys, conclusion of treaties, issuance of ordinances and rescripts, declaration of a state of martial law, conference of titles of nobility and other honors, and issuance of pardons and commuting sentences.

**Legislative Powers.** The imperial legislative powers included the convocation, opening, closing, and prorogation of the Diet, the dissolution of the Lower House, and the sanction and promulgation of laws. At times when the Diet was not in session the emperor could issue emergency ordinances which had the effect of law, but which had to receive the approval of the Diet at its next session to remain in force. Since the constitution was a gift of the emperor to the people, it could be amended only upon the initiative of the Throne, although the approval of the Diet was required. Until the promulgation of the new constitution of 1946, no constitutional amendments were proposed under the document of 1889.

**Judicial Powers.** The judicial functions of the courts were exercised in the name of the emperor. All the important judges were appointed by the emperor and could be removed for cause by him.

## THE ADVISORY ORGANS

An enumeration of the emperor's prerogatives demonstrates that they included all the attributes of sovereignty. It should be remembered, however, that although the will of the emperor was the will of the state, the emperor performed only upon the advice of others. All acts of the government were accomplished in his name, but he was no more than the symbol of authority. He did not participate in the formulation of policy, although policy was carried out in his name. His powers as head of the imperial house were exercised only upon the advice of the imperial household minister and other officials of the court; decrees, ordinances, and orders were issued and legislation was promulgated only over the countersignatures of the ministers of the administrative departments concerned; and the disposition of the army and navy was determined upon the counsel of the military supreme command. With such a system of government the observer must look behind the emperor to locate the instruments of political power which actually determined national affairs.

**Imperial Household.** The lord keeper of the privy seal was the highest imperial adviser and outranked all other court officials. He was responsible for the imperial and state seals which had to be attached to all laws and ordinances before they became valid. His close personal contact with the emperor gave him considerable influence in political affairs, and he usually was consulted upon the selection of a new prime minister.

The imperial household minister supervised all matters relating to the imperial family, such as the management of imperial estates, the granting of awards and decorations, amnesties, contributions to charities, the keeping of imperial records, the performance of ceremonies and rituals, and other affairs relating to the emperor and his household. The Imperial Household Department, which was beyond the control of the Cabinet, was responsible only to the emperor. Although the advice of the minister was sought on household matters, he frequently was consulted as well on other questions of state. A large measure of the influence of these officials was due to the fact that appointments for an imperial audience were made through them. Holders of these important posts were selected by the emperor upon the advice of the prime minister. Dismissals could be made in the same manner, but it was customary for these officials to serve for life or until they wished to resign.

**Privy Council.** The Privy Council was created originally by an imperial ordinance to act as the supreme advisory body during the deliberations upon the constitution. Its existence was recognized subsequently in the constitutional provision that the emperor could consult the Privy Council for advice. This body was composed of twenty-six members, who were appointed for life by the emperor upon the advice of the prime minister and the Council itself. Cabinet ministers were *ex officio* members of the Council and were entitled to vote. Certain matters had to be submitted to the Privy Council for its consideration, including changes in the Imperial House Law, laws and ordinances supplementary to the constitution, amendments to the constitution, emergency imperial ordinances issued while the Diet was not in session, ordinances bearing penal provisions, proclamations of a state of martial law, changes in the Privy Council itself, and treaties. In practice the Privy Council deliberated upon all matters of great political significance to the nation, and its influence was strong. Rarely was the Cabinet able to take action which had been opposed by the Privy Council.

**Military Advisers.** The chief military advisers of the emperor were the Board of Field Marshals and Fleet Admirals, the Supreme War Council, and the ministers of war and the navy. By virtue of the separation of his military and political powers, described above, the emperor consulted these military advisers rather than the civilian Cabinet members on all matters pertaining to the administration of the two services. The Board of Field Marshals and Fleet Admirals was the highest advisory body on military matters, but since its membership for the most part was limited to high ranking imperial princes it had little real power. The Supreme War Council included the members of the

Board, the chief of the military and naval general staffs, the ministers of war and the navy, and other generals and admirals appointed by the emperor upon the recommendation of the Council, making a total membership usually of twelve in which the army and navy were about equally represented. In time of war the Supreme War Council was reconstituted as the Imperial Headquarters, which was presided over by the emperor.

The two chiefs of staff were the most influential among the military advisers. In addition to their authority concerning military and naval operations and strategy, they controlled many details of the recruitment, training, discipline, internal organization, and disposition of the armed forces. If these matters were handled by the ministers of war and the navy, as they are in most countries, the Cabinet might have exercised control over them. By placing them outside of the administrative powers of these ministers, such control was avoided. Members of the Supreme War Council had the right of direct access to the emperor, which meant that on all matters pertaining to strictly military functions their authority was independent of other organs of government.

Further independence of the civilian branches of the government was derived from the broad powers of the ministers of war and the navy. Their right of direct access to the emperor placed them beyond the reach of their civilian colleagues in the Cabinet. Moreover, an imperial ordinance limited the appointment of these ministers to generals and admirals on the active list. No officer could accept appointment in a Cabinet without the approval of the Supreme War Council. By refusing to grant this approval the Council could dictate to the rest of the government. To take a specific example: In 1937 General Ugaki was designated by the emperor to form a Cabinet. But Ugaki was not in the good graces of the high command because at an earlier date he had been responsible for a reduction in the size of the army, and because it was feared that he was too favorable to the political parties. No officer was permitted to accept the War portfolio under his leadership and he accordingly was forced to abandon his attempt to form a Cabinet. In other instances the supreme command forced the resignation of an entire Cabinet by withdrawing a minister of war.[5]

**The Cabinet.** The Cabinet played an important part in policy formulation and was the principal executive organ of the govment. Its existence was recognized in the constitutional provisions that the respective ministers should give their advice to the emperor and be responsible for it, and that all laws, ordinances, and imperial rescripts relating to affairs of state required the countersignature of a minister of state. The Cabinet was composed of the prime minister and about twelve associates, each of whom headed a separate ministry. It also was common practice to include several ministers without portfolio. The prime minister was appointed by the emperor after consultation with the lord keeper of the privy seal, the imperial household minister, the president of the Privy Council, and other dignitaries. The prime minister selected his own colleagues after consultation with these and other officials and requested that they be appointed by the emperor.

**The Diet.** Under the constitution of 1889 the legislature of Japan, the Diet, was a bicameral body consisting of the House of Peers, and the House of Representatives. The House of Peers was composed of imperial princes and marquises, elected representatives of the lesser nobility, of the highest taxpayers, and of the Imperial Academy who served for seven years, and 125 persons appointed for life by the emperor on the basis of distinguished service to the nation. The total membership varied, but was usually more than 400. The House of Representatives was composed of 466 members, elected by universal male suffrage from multimember districts for four-year terms.

The Diet met annually in December for a term of three months. Extraordinary sessions were held upon the call of the emperor as the necessity arose. The emperor could prorogue the Diet for periods of fifteen days or less. He could dissolve the

[5] The relationship of the military advisers to the Cabinet and emperor is described in C. Yanaga, "The Military and the Government in Japan," *American Political Science Review*, June 1941, XXXV, 528–539.

House of Representatives, but in such cases an election had to be held and a new House convoked within five months.

The Diet possessed certain definite powers. Legislative proposals could be initiated in either house, and all laws had to receive a majority vote in both houses. Emergency orders which had been issued since the last session had to be approved if they were to remain in force. Amendments to the constitution, although initiated only by the emperor, had to be submitted to the Diet for approval. The national budget also required the approval of both houses, and the Diet voted national taxes and exercised a degree of supervision over financial accounts. Members of the Diet could interpellate Cabinet ministers, requesting an explanation of their activities.

A number of significant restrictions were imposed upon the powers of the Diet. Should either house fail to approve the budget submitted by the Cabinet the one for the preceding year remained in force. Moreover, the Diet had no authority over items in the budget listed as fixed expenditures, such as the salaries of officials, expenses of the Imperial Household, ordinary expenses of the various administrative agencies and the army and navy, expenses arising from international treaties, and expenditures that arose from the effect of law and from the legal obligations of the government. The Diet had no control over administrative fees or other revenue such as the receipts of the post office and the government railways. The Diet, in other words, did not hold the purse strings of the government.

## LOCAL GOVERNMENTS AND THE COURTS

It has been pointed out that one of the principal purposes of the Restoration leaders was to provide an efficient, centralized regime. As a part of this effort they established new organs of local administration. In this respect their motives were similar to those of the statesmen of Napoleonic France, and the plan which they followed bears a similarity to that developed there. The country as a whole was divided into some forty prefectures, which were not units of local self-government but administrative subdivisions of the national government. Prefectures, cities, towns, and villages were placed under the close supervision of the Ministry of Home Affairs, performing functions delegated to them from above by laws and ordinances. The governors and subordinate officials of the prefectures were appointed and super-vised by the Home Ministry and they in turn exercised broad powers of review over the officials of the lower units of local ad-ministration. Local assemblies, elected by popular vote, possessed very limited authority. Two of the principal responsibilities of local government, police and education, were removed from local control and placed under direct supervision of the national gov-ernment. The police of the entire country were under the juris-diction of the minister of home affairs, who thus exerted a di-rect control over every individual in the empire. Likewise the schools, in which Japanese children were indoctrinated with intense pride of race and nation, were instrumentalities of the national government, under the operation of the Ministry of Education. It was principally through these two ministries, Home Affairs and Education, that the national government was able to maintain a high degree of control over all of the people and to organize them into a united, compact nation.

**The Judicial System.** The judicial system, which operated in the name of the emperor, also was national in structure and jurisdiction. The judicial organization, which was modeled chiefly upon the French pattern, was divided into regular and administrative courts. The regular courts consisted of four levels, headed by a single Supreme Court, but there was but a single Court of Administrative Litigation. Although the judicial system was European in form, it was Japanese in substance, so that western institutions operated according to long-established Japa-nese customs, producing seeming peculiarities and contradictions. By and large the quality of the judicial system was satisfactory. Judges and procurators were admitted as probationers by exami-nation following graduation from Tokyo Imperial Law School and advanced under civil service regulations.

## GEOGRAPHICAL FACTORS

To conclude this discussion of the establishment of new instruments of government by the Restoration leaders, it might be well to draw attention to the fact that the geographical features of the Japanese archipelago contributed to the creation of a highly unified, centralized state. The islands are small, compact, and densely populated, covering a total area a little less than that of California. In earlier times the broken mountainous terrain was conducive to the establishment of autonomous feudal units, but the compactness of the country and the relative ease of communication, particularly after the construction of a modern railway network, made possible a high degree of political unity and centralization.

Japan, moreover, was unified by the marked homogeneity of her people. The mixing of Asiatic and Indonesian strains to form the present Japanese type occurred before recorded time. Only a few thousand *ainu,* or aborigines, remain to remind the Japanese of the distant past. Social rather than racial factors are responsible for the existence of the small *eta,* or outcast, class.[6]

## READINGS

*Bibliographies*
> Borton, H., S. Elisséeff, and E. O. Reischauer, *A Selected List of Books and Articles on Japan, in English, French, and German,* Washington, American Council of Learned Societies, 1940.
> Pritchard, E. H., ed., *Bulletin of Far Eastern Bibliography,* vols. 1–5, 1936–40, Washington, American Council of Learned Societies; continued in *The Far Eastern Quarterly.* This bibliography is a ready guide to current books and articles on Japan.

*Historical Development*
> Brinkley, Frank, *A History of the Japanese People From the Earliest Times to the End of the Meiji Era,* New York, 1915.

[6] G. T. Trewartha, *Japan, A Physical, Cultural, and Regional Geography.*

This comprehensive political history is valuable as well for its 150 illustrations.

Latourette, Kenneth Scott, *The Development of Japan,* 4th ed. rev., New York, 1938. This book provides a short and readable account of the history of Japan.

McLaren, Walter Wallace, *A Political History of Japan During the Meiji Period, 1867–1912,* London, 1916. This is a standard history of the Restoration period.

Norman, E. Herbert, *Japan's Emergence as a Modern State,* Institute of Pacific Relations, New York, 1940. This extremely valuable book by an outstanding scholar relates the political, economic, and social developments of the Meiji period to contemporary problems.

Sansom, George Bailey, *Japan; A Short Cultural History,* rev. ed., New York, 1943. This is the best general history of pre-Restoration Japan.

*The Constitutional System*

Colegrove, Kenneth W., "The Japanese Privy Council," "The Japanese Emperor," "Powers and Functions of the Japanese Diet," "The Japanese Foreign Office," "The Japanese Cabinet," *American Political Science Review,* vol. XXV, 1931, pp. 589–614 and 881–905; vol. XXVI, 1932, pp. 642–59 and 828–45; vol. XXVII, 1933, pp. 885–98; vol. XXVIII, 1934, pp. 23–39; vol. XXX, 1936, pp. 585–613 and 903–23. These articles provide a detailed study of the principal governmental organs, as they operated under the Constitution of 1889.

McLaren, Walter Wallace, "Japanese Government Documents," edited with an introduction, *Transactions of the Asiatic Society of Japan,* 1914, XLII. This is an extremely valuable collection of translations of documents relating to the Restoration and subsequent developments.

Quigley, Harold S., *Japanese Government and Politics, An Introductory Study,* New York, 1932. This is the standard work in English on the Japanese governmental system.

Reischauer, Robert Karl, *Japan, Government, Politics,* New York, Nelson, 1939. The first part of this valuable little book contains a concise summary of historical developments.

Takeuchi, Tatsuji, *War and Diplomacy in the Japanese Empire,*

University of Chicago Press, 1935. Part I of this study deals with the organization of the government.

Translations of the Constitution of 1889 are found in McLaren, Quigley, and Takeuchi.

## Yearbooks

*The Japan Year Book, 1933–1941,* The Foreign Affairs Association of Japan.

*The Japan-Manchukuo Year Book, 1934–1940,* The Japan-Manchukuo Year Book Co. The 1941 edition of this series appeared under the title *Far Eastern Year Book.*

# CHAPTER 24

# POLITICAL DEVELOPMENTS
# FROM THE RESTORATION
# TO WORLD WAR II

THE modern constitutional structure of the Japanese government was established during the Restoration period upon the foundations of feudal experience. The contemporary substance of that structure is the product not only of these factors, which were discussed in the preceding chapter, but of subsequent political developments. These developments, extending from the Restoration in 1867 down to World War II, form the content of the present chapter.

## THE ELDER STATESMEN, 1867–1918

It has been described how the Restoration leaders, or elder statesmen, as they frequently are known, devised a form of government which would fit their purpose of ensuring the continuation of their own rule. In the accomplishment of this purpose these men were eminently successful. Until the conclusion of World War I they and their immediate associates monopolized the key advisory posts in the Supreme Command, the Imperial Household and the Privy Council. Seven of the eight prime ministers who held office between 1889 (the year in which the constitution was promulgated) and 1918 were members of the two principal clans in the Restoration movement.[1] These two clans, moreover, monopolized the command positions and the officer ranks of the rapidly developed army and navy. Through

[1] Reischauer, *op. cit.*, p. 107.

employment of repressive police regulations and press laws the narrow ruling oligarchy stifled criticism of government policy and suppressed the activities of nascent political parties. During these years the representatives of the people in the Diet were never able to assume active direction of national affairs. At times criticism and refusal to accept budgetary and legislative proposals caused the ruling oligarchy considerable embarrassment, but the elder statesmen firmly held the reigns of government by dominating the advisory organs. Throughout this period, therefore, the prime minister, who was the nominal head of government, was responsible not to the Diet but to the elder statesmen in the Supreme Command, the Imperial Household and the Privy Council.

**Achievements of the Elder Statesmen.** Under the leadership of the elder statesmen, Japan experienced exceptional national growth and progress. As indicated in the last chapter, she deliberately applied the technological developments of the western world to her own requirements. With the expansion of modern industry her cities grew rapidly and her total population, which had remained relatively stable around twenty-five million during the two and a half centuries of Tokugawa rule, passed the fifty-million mark by 1920. Within a little more than two generations Japan, already seeking imperial advantages in Asia, defeated China and Russia in war and emerged with the colonies of Formosa and Sakhalin and valuable railway, mining, and other economic concessions in southern Manchuria. To these she soon added the colony of Korea by annexation.

Japan's industrial and colonial expansion produced many significant changes in her national life. Certainly the very rapid transition from the small, isolated feudal nation found by Commodore Perry into the modern major power of the twentieth century was one of the outstanding national achievements of the time. But these changes, great as they were, must not obscure the more important fact that basically the old structure of Japan, handed down from the feudal past, remained at the heart of the whole pattern of political, economic, and social organization. It has been pointed out how the tradition of rule by a relatively small group, firmly established in the shogunate era, was carried forward by the elder statesmen and was perpetuated in the new organs of government. Technological developments were utilized to build up the industrial resources and military defenses of the nation, but the standard of living of the mass of the people—and their opportunities for political experience— hardly rose above the extremely low level of feudal times. By reason of the peculiar nature of the Restoration, whereby a small group engineered the shift to new leadership, the expanding economy of the nation was controlled by a small number of wealthy family combinations with close connections in government circles. This again emphasized the vast difference between the ruling oligarchy and the mass of the people. Likewise the social pattern of old Japan was carried forward with its exaggeration of unquestioned loyalty to superior authority, class distinction, and special privilege for the few.

## The Principal Political Groups

Prior to World War I no separate political group successfully challenged the supremacy of the elder statesmen and their immediate associates. In the generation following the war, on the other hand, numerous elements played major roles in political affairs. Before continuing the discussion of political developments, brief discussions of each of these principal groups should be given, in order that their composition and political outlook may be defined.

**The Militarists.** The militarists were the heirs of the feudal lords and warriors who ruled Japan in premodern times and of the Restoration clansmen who instituted conscription and built the modern army and navy. By reason of the constitutional and administrative separation of the supervision of military affairs from the rest of the government, they possessed a real advantage over other groups at all times. The principal objectives of the latter-day successors of the earlier militarists were control of the government at home by the military hierarchy and establishment of Japanese hegemony throughout East Asia. By taking the nation into war against China and finally against the United Nations, they achieved the former and came dangerously close to achieving the latter. The militarists always were extremely nationalistic and antidemocratic, and suppressed even the slightest manifestations of liberalism. They exploited the ancient concepts of the divine origin of the Japanese nation and of absolute imperial authority to demand the complete obedience of all subjects of the emperor and the humble subservience of all conquered peoples. The militarists, however, did not always constitute a unified, homogeneous group, for within the army and navy circles there were marked differences between diverse cliques. More extreme elements, reflecting sympathy for small shopkeepers, poorly paid industrial workers, and impoverished peasants, directed vitriolic attacks upon capitalists and politicians, upon whom they blamed the economic ills of the country. They sought complete state control of the national economy, as well as conquest of overseas sources of raw materials and markets for Japanese goods. Recognizing the inability of the armed forces to direct the national economy without the cooperation of business management, and understanding the dependence of the war machine upon industrial output, more hardheaded and realistic militarists were willing to come to terms with business leaders. Without the support of business they could not have secured domination of the government.

**The Zaibatsu.** A striking feature of the Japanese economy was the monopolistic control exercised by a half-dozen huge family-holding combines, of which the Mitsui and Mitsubishi were the largest and best known. These wealthy combinations generally are identified by the Japanese term *Zaibatsu*, which literally means "money clique." Not only did these organizations produce the bulk of Japan's manufactured goods, but through their ownership of banks, insurance companies, trading concerns, and shipping lines, they dominated the whole national economic system. During the 1920's, when the Zaibatsu asserted its interests through the political parties, it resisted the attempts of the militarists to run the government. The Zaibatsu feared the state socialism which was vigorously expounded by the military extremists and the terroristic methods which they employed to achieve their ends. But the rapid expansion of heavy industry after 1931 brought about a basis for cooperation between these outwardly antagonistic groups. Armament expenditures and government-guaranteed investments in new war industries and colonial developments yielded high profits and a willingness of the Zaibatsu to support the military program. During the 1930's, moreover, several rival industrial groups grew up outside of the family combines, largely as the result of army connections. The Zaibatsu, in other words, accepted the militarists in self-interest; it was profitable for them to do so.

Closely associated with the Zaibatsu in the political arena was the large landowning class. Although this group at times differed with business elements on matters of economic policy, its members generally shared the same conservative political outlook, particularly in respect to social and economic reforms, whether suggested by the left or by the extremists among the militarists.

**The Bureaucrats.** Since the seventh century, when a civil service system was modeled upon the Chinese, a permanent bureaucracy has been influential in Japanese politics. The modern civil service, numbering about a half million in peacetime, was a well-trained and homogeneous official caste, proud and jealous of its prerogatives and aware of the influence which it possessed by reason of its knowledge of administrative procedures. It was extremely contemptuous of liberal tendencies and of the political aspirations of the common people, whom it considered utterly unqualified for self-government, a view which was reflected in its lack of respect for members of the lower house of the Diet. Some among the career officials advanced into Cabinet posts and membership in the Privy Council, the Imperial Household, and the House of Peers. During the 1920's the bureaucrats, for the most part, found it to their advantage to side with the Zaibatsu on matters of national policy. In more recent years they shifted their allegiance to the militarists, whose program of a controlled economy and colonial development offered bigger and better opportunities for government jobs. Certain able bureaucrats furnished the brains for the army's elaborate schemes of industrial and colonial expansion, and the rank-and-file civil servants prattled the nationalistic exhortations of the militarists in the best parrot fashion. Their significance continued to lie in their monopoly of administrative know-how, without which no other group could operate the government.

**The Superpatriots.** In feudal times terrorism and force were common political devices, and they have been common in modern times as well. An outstanding feature of recent political history was the influence of superpatriotic, ultranationalistic, and militaristic gangs and societies. Their growth was greatly stimulated by the disillusionment of the depression years, but many of them were established before the turn of the century. By the mid-1930's they numbered between two and three hundred, and ranged in membership from Cabinet ministers, high army and navy officers, and bureaucrats to fanatical hoodlums. The most widely known outside Japan was the notorious Black Dragon Society, which was founded to agitate for the war against Russia in 1904. Although differing widely in their methods and objectives, these heterogeneous organizations exhalted imperial absolutism, denounced parliamentarism and democracy, and fostered militarism and foreign aggression. Several of these groups were responsible for the assassinations of 1931 and 1932 which helped to terminate party government, and others had a strong influence upon the army officers who initiated the insurrection of February 1936. The army officer who was responsible for the infamous attack upon the USS *Panay* in 1937 later became the organizer of a nationalistic youth society.

**The Political Parties.** Political parties first developed after the Restoration. These early parties were not parties in the usual western sense, however, but relatively small groups of professional politicians held together by loyalty to a single leader and a common desire to share the spoils of office rather than by faith in certain political principles. Party growth, moreover, was severely retarded by the government program of repression of freedom of speech, press, and assembly. Following World War I, largely as a consequence of the support of the Zaibatsu, the political parties emerged as a major force in politics. For the first time the prime minister was selected from the leading party, and the Diet, in which party influence was concentrated, assumed a prominent role in the determination of national affairs. With the liberalization of the election laws and the introduction of universal manhood suffrage in 1925, the two principal parties, the *Seiyukai* and the *Minseito,* tended to become instruments for the expression of popular interests. But although their leaders gave lip service to liberal political doctrines, the parties remained closely associated with the Zaibatsu and the aristocratic elements in the bureaucracy and court circles and even, to a degree, with certain of the militarists and ultranationalists. Generally the parties favored limited social and economic reforms, enlargement of the authority of the Diet, and the restriction of the political influence of the civil and military bureaucracies. The Seiyukai was inclined toward conservatism in domestic politics and imperialistic expansion abroad, while the Minseito was more liberal and internationalistic in outlook, having sponsored manhood suffrage, partial reform of the House of Peers, and ratification of the London Naval Treaty. But throughout their history the parties continued to be weakened by the limitations of the constitutional system, by restrictions upon freedom of expression, by lack of clear political doctrines, and by internal corruption and quarrels. With the rise of the militarists in the 1930's, the parties gave up their limited independence without an earnest struggle and fell into line with the new dispensation. In 1940 they submitted supinely to government-directed dissolution.

**Popular Movements.** Popular movements representing the interests of the common people never had much chance of survival as a consequence of the severely repressive policy of the government, expressed in many forms but none so effectively as the brutal methods employed by the police against liberal leaders. Nevertheless during the 1920's a number of farm and labor political groups, including a small Communist party, were active in national politics. Various attempts to form a united Farmer-Labor party were made, but without permanent success, largely because of government suppression. After the rise of military influence following the Manchurian affair in 1931, those popular groups which remained either shifted to the opposite pole of extreme nationalism or suffered elimination as a result of even more severe government controls. In spite of the failure of these popular movements to achieve much success, due credit must be given to the courage of their leaders to operate at all in the face of tremendous odds.

## GOVERNMENT BY NEGOTIATION AND COMPROMISE

The militarists, Zaibatsu leaders, large landowners, bureaucrats, superpatriots, and party politicians thus constituted the principal political groups. National politics was largely a struggle between and among these elements to influence the government and to secure the acceptance of their views. It will be remembered, moreover, that due to the retarded development of popular participation in political affairs, public opinion did not have a marked effect upon politics. Thus these various groups did not attempt to achieve their ends by manipulation of public opinion but rather by dominating or controlling an organ or agency within the government itself. The Japanese constitutional structure with its diffusion of authority among numerous organs lent itself to this practice. Because of this diffusion it was possible for different groups to entrench themselves in different parts of the governmental structure: the military in the Supreme Command; Zaibatsu and the bureaucracy in the Imperial Household and the Privy Council; and the parties in the Diet. This in effect gave each group the power of veto over the formulation of national policy, for the agreement of each of these organs was required before the government could act.

**Necessity for Compromise.** Thus it was essential that the different groups negotiate among themselves and work out a compromise reasonably satisfactory to all concerned. This situation led to a great deal of behind-the-scenes political maneuvering and bickering among the leaders of the various groups, who most frequently were the real rulers of the nation, while the public officeholders out front acted merely upon the basis of decisions reached outside official channels. The consequence of this system of politics, derived from indirect rule and dependent upon the achievement and maintenance of compromise agreements between diverse elements, was a high degree of political instability. At any time any element could threaten the government by independent action, as the military did in 1931 when they launched the attack upon Manchuria without the sanction of the Cabinet. Actually the advantage usually fell to the militarists in time of crisis because of the special privileges granted to them within the framework of the government. Thus the political system of Japan, and the constitution in which it was reflected, placed serious obstacles in the way of the political maturity of the Japanese nation and of the development of popular government by its people. And because of this instability Japan was a constant threat to the peace of her neighbors and ultimately of the whole world.

This, then, was the manner in which the various political groups operated, sometimes for and sometimes against each other. The remainder of this chapter will contain an outline of their struggles during the period extending from World War I to the outbreak of World War II.

## THE PERIOD OF PARTY RULE, 1918–32

World War I brought a change in the complexion of Japanese political development. Japan entered the conflict against Germany but her military participation was negligible. Taking advantage of the preoccupation of the manufacturing countries of Europe with the war, Japanese trade and industry experienced a remarkable boom. As a consequence, the process of industrialization, which had commenced with the Restoration, was greatly accelerated, and the Zaibatsu for the first time became a leading factor in political affairs. This situation soon brought changes in the composition of national leadership.

**Influence of the Zaibatsu.** Trade and industry had been close to the government ever since the Osaka merchants backed the Restoration financially, but industrial leaders were no more than the junior partners of the elder statesmen. With the stimulation of war profits, however, these leaders reached out for a major role in the direction of national affairs. Finding their road to power blocked by the control which the elder statesmen still exercised in the advisory organs, they threw their support to the political parties, which up to this time had never been more than small groups associated with a prominent political figure. Now, with the financial backing of business, the parties broadened their organization and became of major consequence. In 1918, Hara, a strong party leader, became prime minister, the first commoner to hold the position.

**Party Leadership.** From 1918 to 1922 and from 1924 to 1932 the political parties supplied the prime ministers of Japan. And since the parties controlled the lower house of the Diet, the practice developed that the prime minister should command the support of a majority of that body. Thus a system of parliamentary government came into being, and with it a degree of responsibility on the part of the prime minister and his Cabinet to the lower house. In 1925, moreover, universal male suffrage was instituted, and other steps were taken pointing toward constitutional democratic government. Such was the trend but it was only a trend. The constitutional limitations upon the Diet, such as the restrictions upon its financial powers, obstructed the growth of true parliamentary responsibility. A more serious obstacle was the existence of the advisory organs with which the Cabinet shared the responsibility of policy formulation. And so long as the supervision of the armed forces remained separated from that of the rest of the government through the unique arrangements which granted to the high military officials independent access to the emperor, every Cabinet was at their mercy in a showdown.

National policies during the 1920's reflected the interests of the Zaibatsu for the most part. Foreign trade was promoted, military expenditures were curtailed, and peaceful relations with the rest of the world were encouraged. The passage of a limited amount of social legislation demonstrated the beginnings of wider popular participation in government. The acceptance of the naval treaties of 1922 and 1930 indicated that the armed forces were being held in balance. Only during a brief interlude from 1927 to 1929 did they gain the upper hand under the premiership of the notorious General Baron Tanaka, who assumed the presidency of the Seiyukai.

## THE STRUGGLE FOR POLITICAL CONTROL, 1932–36

The relative stability of the 1920's was preserved only so long as the combination of the Zaibatsu and political parties was maintained in power. Conditions which culminated with the impact of the great depression in the early 1930's shattered that combination and opened the way for a military dictatorship. The parties had been discredited by a series of sensational scandals and by bitter internal bickering and intrigue. Economic distress and unrest produced widespread discontent and disillusionment with the capitalists and their party henchmen. The situation was ripe for vigorous new leadership to make a challenge. Extremists within the army took full advantage of the situation to launch the conquest of Manchuria on their own authority in September 1931. In the months of unrest which followed, fanatics within the army and the superpatriotic societies made repeated threats upon members of the Cabinet and business leaders. By May of the following year the head of the Mitsui interests and the last two party prime ministers were eliminated by the assassin's bullet. Party rule, with its hope of parliamentary democratic government, was ended.

**Coalition Government.** A military dictatorship was not established quickly. Although the Zaibatsu and the parties no longer were strong enough to dominate the government, they still had many friends in the Imperial Household and in other advisory positions, placed there in the preceding decade. Conservative elements within the army and navy, moreover, opposed the radical demands of the military extremists. For the next four years coalition Cabinets, representing business, the parties, the bureaucracy, and the armed forces, directed national affairs. The army secured a free hand to consolidate its conquests in Manchuria (where it tried out its ideas of state socialism) and to penetrate into North China, but the coalition of conservative elements maintained control of domestic affairs in Tokyo. Economic recovery eliminated the unrest of the early 1930's.

**The 1936 Insurrection.** By 1936 the trend actually was away from military rule. Elections for the lower house of the Diet, held in mid-February, resulted in a victory for the Minseito party, whose members opposed the extreme features of the militarists' policy, indicating popular disfavor with the aggressive attitude of the army. Cabinet responsibility to the Diet might have been reasserted, but the extremists once more took things into their own hands. On February 26, 1936, a military insurrection broke out in Tokyo, and with it the assassination of several high officials in the government including the lord keeper of the privy seal and the finance minister. The prime minister escaped only because of mistaken identity. Although the insurrection was broken up, it enabled the army to dominate the government. The extremists were discredited temporarily by the failure of the plot, but their strongest opponents had been eliminated by assassination or intimidation. Less extreme elements within the army took advantage of the situation to attract to themselves leading segments of the Zaibatsu and the bureaucracy and to gain a controlling position.[2] The outbreak of war with China a year later, which was a consequence of this

[2] On the consequences of the 1936 insurrection see T. A. Bisson, *Japan in China*, ch. 6.

internal situation in Japan, placed the nation on a war footing
and permitted the army to employ wartime controls to solidify
its grip.

## THE RISE OF A MILITARY DICTATORSHIP, 1936–41

Significant changes within the Zaibatsu played an important
part in the rise of the militarists to power after 1936. In the
1920's Japanese industry had been geared largely to foreign
markets, and business leaders accordingly favored international
peace and friendship. But during the 1930's, after the Manchurian affair, the rapid expansion of heavy industries greatly
strengthened groups in the business community which stood to
benefit from the militarists' program of arms expansion and
foreign conquest. By 1936 these heavy industrialists carried
greater weight in political counsels than their light-industry associates. Thus the ranks of the Zaibatsu were divided and the
huge financial and industrial combinations no longer presented
a united front against the militarists. Important segments of the
business community now threw in their lot with the army. In
similar fashion, supporters of the militarists program appeared
in increasing numbers in the bureaucracy.

**Opposition to a Military Dictatorship.** Even after 1936 conservative elements within business, the bureaucracy, and the
political parties resisted full military control with some success,
and they were able to force certain compromises upon the militarists. It was not so much that they opposed the policy of
Asiatic expansion, but rather that they were reluctant to yield
up to the army the control of the nation's economy, and that they
feared the consequences of war with the British Empire, the
United States, and the Soviet Union. This situation was reflected by the succession of relatively moderate prime ministers
who held office between 1936 and 1941. It was only after Japan's
high military command was convinced that Hitler would crush
all opposition in Europe and after Prince Konoye, the last of the
moderate prime ministers, failed to secure American acceptance

of the conquest of China that the militarists came out from behind the cloak of a moderate and placed one of their own men at the head of the government. In October 1941 General Tojo, a full general on the active list and a leader among the extremists for more than ten years, formed a Cabinet, just two months before the attack upon Pearl Harbor.

**Composition of the Tojo Government.** So by the autumn of 1941, ten years after the Manchurian affair, the extremist military elements finally achieved control of the government. It must not be supposed, however, that they alone ruled Japan. Closely associated with them remained the Zaibatsu and the bureaucracy. The militarists called the tune in so far as international and strategic affairs were concerned, but the Zaibatsu and the bureaucracy retained a strong hand in political and economic policy. The shift to a war economy after 1936 naturally brought about an increasing volume of government controls over the economy. The army wanted to administer these controls but the Zaibatsu, upon whom the army was dependent for war production, successfully resisted these attempts and managed to dominate the agencies of control which were established. Thus, as Japan entered full-scale war against the United States and the British Empire in December 1941, her government was in the hands of a coalition of militarists, the Zaibatsu, and bureaucrats.[3]

## FEATURES OF THE MILITARY DICTATORSHIP

Following the outbreak of the China war in 1937 Japan quickly experienced a drastic program of government-dictated regimentation. The press, radio, motion pictures, and theater were subjected to even greater suppression than before, and the small popular political parties, farmers' groups, and trade unions were crushed or forced to conform to the official line. Such freedom of thought as remained in the universities and schools was now obliterated. In order to secure the maximum organiza-

[3] See T. A. Bisson, *Japan's War Economy*.

tion and sacrifice of the people, the old Shinto doctrines were exploited to the fullest and the masses were propagandized on the divine mission of the nation to establish a New Order in Greater East Asia. As the total resources of the country were geared to the war effort, production of civilian consumer goods was pared to the bone, and the people were forced to undergo many hardships.

**The Imperial Rule Assistance Association.** In 1940 the political parties suffered the consequences of the military dictatorship. In that year the government, under the direction of Prince Konoye, established the Imperial Rule Assistance Association to provide a single organization by which to secure the complete unity of the nation. The IRAA replaced the political parties, which were disbanded under government direction. It absorbed into its ranks all existing patriotic societies, youth organizations, labor unions, and trade associations, and it rapidly assumed the functions of a single national party under government control, headed by the prime minister. Branches were set up in almost every city, town, and village, through which government propaganda reached down to neighborhood and block associations and thence to the last individual. The IRAA gave the people the illusion of participation in government affairs. Actually it was an instrument of complete government control which ordered the people what to do rather than responding to their needs and wishes.

## WARTIME DEVELOPMENTS

Wartime conditions brought many changes to Japan but no fundamental revisions in the governmental system. The complete subordination of the Diet, control of the press, radio, and other media of expression, and ruthless employment of the civil and military police, effectively eliminated all signs of protest against the government. In 1942 a branch organization of the IRAA, the Imperial Rule Assistance Political Society, was set up to control the Diet election of that year. Approximately 80 per cent of those elected to office were candidates "recommended" by the Tojo Cabinet. IRAPS ensured the subservience of the Diet to the government through a steering committee and other guiding committees. For example, interpellations could be made only upon the approval of the steering committee. In this way the official government line was followed without resistance. In April 1945 the Imperial Rule Assistance Association was reorganized under the name Political Association of Great Japan, and placed under the headship of General Minami, one of the leaders of the extremist element in the army. This step was part of the government's attempt to obtain total resistance of the whole nation against the increasing tempo of the American military offensive and the expected assault upon the home islands.

During the war the government continued to operate along well-established lines. When General Tojo was forced by reversals in the western Pacific to relinquish his leadership in the spring of 1944, the accepted formal procedure was followed in the selection of his successor. The lord keeper of the privy seal was received by the emperor to discuss the new Cabinet. He was accompanied by the living former prime ministers, thus reverting to an early practice whereby a selected group of the elder statesmen advised the emperor on all important national affairs. The choice of General Koiso, whose interests were similar to those of his predecessor, and four other senior army and navy officers for the key Cabinet posts assured the continuation of military domination of Japan.

## CONCLUSION

Japan's wartime government was sometimes characterized as a copy of the totalitarianism of Nazi Germany. More accurately it represented a reversion to Japan's own totalitarianism of the feudal past. The dictatorship of the modern militarists presented striking similarities to the highly centralized, authoritarian regime of the Tokugawa shoguns. Modern institutions of government, such as the Cabinet and the Diet, were molded in such a way as to permit the continuation down to the present of the age-old tradition of government by a narrow bureaucratic oligarchy, chiefly military in composition. The limited parliamentarism of the 1920's was but an interlude in this process.

## READINGS

Allen, G. C., *Japan the Hungry Guest*, New York, 1938. This is an excellent study of social and economic developments.

Bisson, T. A., *Japan in China*, New York, 1938. Chapters VI, VII, and X of this book include an excellent exposition of the trends toward totalitarianism in Japan up to and including the first year of the war with China. The remainder of the book considers the development of Japanese aggression in Manchuria and China.

————, *Shadow Over Asia*, Foreign Policy Association, New York, 1941. This little pamphlet contains a concise and readable summary account of the rise of militant Japan.

————, *Japan's War Economy*, Institute of Pacific Relations, New York, 1945. The struggle of the Zaibatsu and the military for control of Japan's wartime economy forms the central theme of this valuable book.

Borton, Hugh, *Japan Since 1931, Its Political and Social Developments,* Institute of Pacific Relations, New York, 1940. This comprehensive study includes treatment of the extension of government control over the national economy and the mobilization of public opinion. It provides a valuable study of the period in which the militarists were rising to a dominant position in Japanese affairs.

Byas, Hugh, *Government By Assassination*, New York, 1942. For an account of the activities of the superpatriotic, fanatical terrorists of Japan, this book is outstanding.

Chamberlin, William H., *Japan Over Asia*, 2d rev. ed., Boston 1939. This book provides a careful analysis of Japan's Asiatic expansion.

Colegrove, Kenneth W., *Militarism in Japan*, World Peace Foundation, Boston, 1936. For the role of the militarists and their fanatical associates in political affairs, this source is valuable,

Embree, John F., *Suye Mura, A Japanese Village,* University of Chicago Press, 1939. This is a study of a contemporary rural community, its social, political, economic, and religious organization.

————, *The Japanese Nation, A Social Survey,* New York, 1945. This little book is a most useful reference source on modern Japan. It includes detailed information on economic, political, social, and cultural matters; a selected bibliography, a glossary of Japanese terms, and a translation of the constitution of 1889.

Fortune, vol. XIV, September 1936; vol. XXIX, April 1944. These two issues are devoted entirely to Japan. They contain some excellent articles and are well illustrated.

Grew, Joseph C., *Ten Years in Japan,* New York, 1944. The selections from the diaries and private papers of the former American ambassador to Japan afford interesting reading and an insight into political developments during his term of service.

Holtom, Daniel C., *Shinto and Japanese Nationalism,* University of Chicago Press, 1943. This little book, by an outstanding scholar, explains the role of Shinto in totalitarian Japan.

Lamott, Willis, *Nippon: The Crime and Punishment of Japan,* New York, 1944. This is a provocative analysis of the forces in militaristic Japan, by a long-time resident.

Lory, Hillis, *Japan's Military Masters,* New York, 1943. This is a readable account of the Japanese army, its organization, and its role in national affairs.

Maki, John M., *Japanese Militarism, Its Cause and Cure,* New York, 1945. For an analysis of the force of militarism in Japanese historical and contemporary development, this book is particularly recommended.

Mitchell, Kate L., *Japan's Industrial Strength,* Institute of Pacific Relations, New York, 1941. This books contains a detailed account of Japan's prewar industrial position.

Roth, Andrew, *Dilemma in Japan,* Boston, 1945. This book is particularly valuable for its discussion of peasant, labor, and other popular movements in prewar Japan, and of the part which they might play in the development of democratic tendencies.

Russell, Oland D., *The House of Mitsui,* Boston, 1939. This is a popular history of the rise of Japan's greatest Zaibatsu combine.

Schumpeter, Elizabeth B., ed., *The Industrialization of Japan and Manchukuo, 1930–1940*, New York, 1940. Part II of this volume, "Japanese Industry: Its Organization and Development to 1937," by G. C. Allen, contains an excellent account of the organization and operation of the Zaibatsu combines.

Tanin, O., and E. Yohan, *Militarism and Fascism in Japan*, New York, 1934. In this book, two Soviet authors given an extremely useful and provocative analysis of the forces which contributed to the rise of a military dictatorship.

# CHAPTER 25

# JAPAN UNDER ALLIED ADMINISTRATION

THE crushing defeat of Japan by the combined resources and efforts of the Allied powers necessarily produced tremendous changes in that country. Her navy and air force were largely destroyed, her cities laid waste, her people uprooted and made destitute. But defeat in itself did not produce any immediate changes in Japan's political leadership or in the structure of her government. By accepting surrender, August 1945, before her home islands were invaded, Japan ended the war with her political system largely intact. Changes in that system were to occur only under the direction of alien occupation forces.

## CHANGES IN WARTIME LEADERSHIP

Japan's wartime government, as pointed out in the preceeding chapter, consisted of a coalition of military extremists, representatives of the Zaibatsu, and nationalistic bureaucrats. The succession of defeats suffered by Japanese forces, commencing with the battle of Midway in June 1942, threatened the dominant role of the military extremists among these three elements, but there was no organized attempt on the part of groups outside of the coalition to gain control of the government. Rather changes occurred within the coalition itself whereby conservative military figures and representatives of the Zaibatsu and of the bureaucracy achieved greater influence at the expense of the military extremists. This situation was fully developed with the formation of the Suzuki Cabinet in April 1945, following American landings on Okinawa. This Cabinet was composed of experienced senior statesmen who directly represented conservative military, business, and bureaucratic interests.

**The Surrender Cabinet.** It was the Suzuki Cabinet which accepted the surrender of the country four months later. This Cabinet had initiated peace talks in July 1945 through the Soviet government, hoping to bring about a negotiated peace by which Japan might avoid invasion and further destruction and escape from the folly of her aggressive warfare with a part of her empire. But destruction of Hiroshima and Nagasaki by atomic weapons and the entry of the Soviet Union into the war in the Pacific obliterated any hope of a negotiated peace, and hastened the already inevitable surrender. Another new Cabinet was established between the acceptance of surrender and the formal signing of surrender documents on September 2, 1945. Except for the extraordinary fact that a prince of the imperial blood, Prince Higashikuni, was named prime minister, the rest of this Cabinet possessed the same conservative complexion of its predecessor.

Thus when the American occupation forces entered Japan and placed the Japanese government under their authority, the country was ruled by the same sort of narrow oligarchy that had dominated political affairs throughout its modern history. True, extremists had been forced from positions of influence by the consequence of military disaster, but otherwise the internal political situation presented a remarkable degree of continuity. It is interesting to compare conditions in the surrendered Japan of 1945 with certain of those following the emergence of the country from feudalism and isolation after the Meiji Restoration seventy-eight years before. It will be recalled that the Restoration very largely represented a shift of authority from one ruling oligarchy to another not greatly dissimilar in social and political outlook from the first, and that it did not constitute a social and political revolution resulting from the protests of large, well-organized masses of people. The consequence of this situation, it will be recalled, was the perpetuation of autocratic government under the leadership of a relatively small group. Likewise,

Japan weathered the severe storms of defeat and surrender without experiencing an internal political upheaval. The duly constituted and responsible authorities did not lose their control of the established organs of government and administration. By the normal processes by which political leadership is confirmed and exerted they removed from their midst those elements of the military hierarchy most responsible for the failures of the war. Thus, as already stated in the first paragraph of this chapter, Japan managed to emerge from the destruction of war with her political system largely intact. The contrast with the situation in Germany is obvious.

**The Role of the Emperor in the Surrender.** Not only was Japan's political system relatively undamaged, but the role of the imperial institution was not impaired by the developments terminating hostilities. In spite of the serious decline in civilian morale following the destruction of the nation's cities, the emperor escaped the criticism of the people. Toward the end of the war the responsible statesmen who accepted the inevitability of defeat associated themselves with the emperor and the advisory organs close of the Imperial Household. These leaders drew the emperor to their side. Following the dropping of the atomic bombs on Hiroshima and Nagasaki and the entry of the Soviet Union into the war, Prime Minister Suzuki used the fear of further atomic destruction to bring Emperor Hirohito himself into the surrender discussions. The emperor acted as arbiter between those elements favoring capitulation and the die-hard militarists who demanded continued resistance until something less drastic than unconditional surrender could be obtained. With the added influence of the emperor, the conflict was resolved with the acceptance of the Allies' terms of unconditional surrender.[1]

The leaders of the surrender movement attempted to preserve the imperial institution from the threat of abolition by the Allies.

[1] A. W. Burks, "Survey of Japan's Defeat," *Far Eastern Survey,* Aug. 14, 1946, 248–250. For a discussion of the economic factors contributing to Japan's collapse see J. B. Cohen "The Japanese War Economy, 1940–1945," *ibid.*, Dec. 4, 1946, 361–370.

They announced Japan's willingness to accept the Potsdam ultimatum "with the understanding that the said declaration does not comprise any demand which prejudices the prerogatives of his Majesty as a sovereign ruler." This condition the Allies declined to accept, the American reply specifying that after the surrender the emperor was to be subject to the Supreme Commander and that the ultimate form of the Japanese government should be determined by the people themselves at some time in the future.[2] Nevertheless, in the surrender process the position and person of the emperor remained of great symbolic significance, further strengthened by statements avoiding reference to defeat but crediting the emperor with the restoration of peace. During the period of crisis just before the formal surrender the prestige of the imperial institution was utilized to bolster up the Cabinet. An imperial prince, closely related to the emperor, was named prime minister for a short period. When the surrender came, the emperor, for the first time in Japanese history, addressed a personal radio message to the people, appealing to them to accept the new conditions, but assiduously avoiding reference to surrender. "Having been able to safeguard and maintain the structure of the imperial state," the emperor declared, "we are always with you, our good and loyal subjects, relying on your sincerity and integrity."[3]

Like the statesmen of the Meiji Restoration, the political leaders of Japan in 1945 utilized the emperor as a symbol and device of unity and control to lead the nation through the disruption and humiliation of unconditional surrender. The manner in which the people accepted the situation and in which the armed forces obeyed the imperial command was evidence not only of their discipline and submissiveness, but of the entrenched position of the political leadership and the institutions of government, including the imperial institution.

[2] The documents relating to the surrender of Japan will be found in Department of State, *Occupation of Japan, Policy and Progress,* Publication 2671, Far Eastern Series 17, Washington, 1946.

[3] Masuo Kato, *The Lost War,* p. 246.

**The Lack of Organized Opposition.** There was no organized opposition of any significance to the surrender. War Minister Anami, the leader of the group that had favored continued resistance until better terms might be secured, committed suicide following the emperor's decision to end the war, removing a possible source of danger to the surrender Cabinet. On the eve of the emperor's broadcast to the nation a number of general staff officers planned to seize control of the government and demand that the emperor continue the war, but the attempt to prevent the broadcast failed and the ringleaders committed suicide. In the two weeks before the formal surrender more than 1000 officers and soldiers chose death rather than surrender. The military extremists had lost control of the government and of the nation. The Japanese people, moreover, were more than ready to end the war. They were desperately weary of the suffering of wartime conditions which had commenced with the invasion of Manchuria in 1931. They had lost faith in the leadership that had taken them into war against the armed might and resources of the United States.

## TERMS OF SURRENDER

Prior to the final surrender of Japan, the allied nations indicated the broad outlines of the policy they proposed to adopt toward the defeated enemy. At Cairo, in December 1943, President Roosevelt, Prime Minister Churchill, and Generalissimo Chiang Kai-shek proclaimed the policy of unconditional surrender and the stripping of Japan of territorial conquests acquired during her modern history. At Potsdam, in July 1945, the United States, Great Britain, and China issued a proclamation, to which the Soviet Union subsequently adhered, calling upon Japan to surrender and setting forth minimum surrender terms. The Potsdam Declaration included the following terms: (1) unconditional surrender of all armed forces; (2) elimination for all time of the authority and influence of the leaders responsible for Japan's militarism and aggression; (3) limitation of Japanese

sovereignty to the home islands; (4) complete disarmament of
Japanese military forces; (5) punishment of all war criminals;
(6) removal of all obstacles to the revival and strengthening of
democratic tendencies among the Japanese people, establishment
of freedom of speech, religion, and thought, and recognition of
respect for fundamental human rights; (7) establishment, in
accordance with the freely expressed will of the Japanese people,
of a peacefully inclined and responsible government; (8) retention by Japan of peacetime industries but elimination of those
which would enable her to rearm for war, Japan to be permitted
peaceful access to foreign raw materials; (9) Allied occupation
of Japanese territory until there should be convincing proof of
the destruction of Japan's war-making power and of the achievement of Allied objectives.[4]

**The Surrender.** Japan surrendered unconditionally on September 2, 1945, in simple but formal ceremonies on the deck of the
U.S.S. *Missouri* in Tokyo Bay. The Japanese representatives
undertook for the emperor, the Japanese government, and their
successors to carry out the provisions of the Potsdam Declaration,
and to issue whatever orders and to take whatever action might
be required by the Supreme Commander for the Allied Powers,
or by any other designated representative of the Allied Powers,
to give effect to that Declaration. They agreed that the authority
of the emperor and the Japanese government to rule would be
subject to the Supreme Commander, who would take such steps
as he might deem proper to effectuate the terms of the surrender.
The Japanese surrender was accepted in behalf of all of the
victorious nations by General of the Army Douglas MacArthur,
who was designated Supreme Commander for the Allied Powers
by the President of the United States. Representatives of nine
allied nations accepted for their governments separately.

[4] Department of State, *Occupation of Japan, Policy and Progress*, p. 59.
For a very revealing account of the relationship between the Potsdam
Declaration and the dropping of the atomic bombs, see H. L. Stimson,
"The Decision to Use the Atomic Bomb," *Harper's Magazine*, February
1947, CXCIV, 97–107.

## STATUS OF THE JAPANESE GOVERNMENT

Thus, although the authority of the Supreme Commander was paramount, the victors chose to administer Japan by indirect means. They did not propose to assume the task of governing Japan themselves. The Japanese government retained its usual administrative functions, and the occupation forces exercised control by issuing directives to that government. General MacArthur was ordered by the United States government to use the Japanese government to the extent that such an arrangement produced satisfactory results, but he was authorized to employ other measures of enforcement, including the use of force, if necessary.

**Contrast with Germany.** The contrast with methods employed by the Allies in the occupation of Germany will be noted immediately. In Germany the existing national government virtually collapsed with defeat, and the Allied nations established direct rule of the country through their own military governments. No national government of Germany was permitted. Germany, moreover, was divided into four zones, each governed by a separate allied power. In Japan the old political system remained in operation, and was merely placed under the authority and supervision of a single Allied commander, General Douglas MacArthur. In other words, the reforms called for in the Potsdam Declaration were to be executed by the Japanese government itself, although the occupation forces were to direct that government toward their achievement.

## THE RESPONSIBILITIES OF THE UNITED STATES AND THE OTHER ALLIES

From the outset the United States, because of its leading role in the Pacific war, assumed the primary responsibility for the occupation of Japan and the administration of surrender terms. American troops made the first landings and received the surrender and disarming of Japanese forces throughout the Japanese homeland. The general headquarters of the Supreme Commander remained an American command, responsible to the United States government in Washington. Directives providing basic policy toward Japan were transmitted to the Supreme Commander from his superiors in Washington.

**Allied Authority.** Yet the Supreme Commander acted in behalf of the other Allied nations as well as for the United States. As the consequence of a compromise reached at the Moscow Conference of Foreign Ministers in December 1945, these nations obtained certain authority in respect to the formulation of policy toward Japan, if not in its execution. Eleven Allied nations are represented on the Far Eastern Commission, which meets in the former Japanese embassy in Washington. This Commission has the power to define major policies toward Japan by a majority vote, including the affirmative vote of the United States, Soviet Union, Great Britain, and China. The United States retained the authority to issue interim directives to the Supreme Commander on urgent matters, but the Far Eastern Commission subsequently may review these directives and also may review actions of the Supreme Commander involving policy decisions within the jurisdiction of the Commission. The Supreme Commander may act on his own authority if he deems it necessary, except in matters affecting the fundamental structure of the Japanese government or of the occupation regime, which are prerogatives of the Far Eastern Commission. The Commission, however, does not communicate directly with the Supreme Commander; its decisions are transmitted through the United States government. An Allied Council, composed of an American (the Supreme Commander, who is represented by his deputy), a Russian, a Chinese, and a member representing Great Britain, Australia, New Zealand, and India, sits in Tokyo. The Council is authorized to advise the Supreme Commander on policy matters, but it has no executive powers, and because of disagreement among its members has had little authority.[5]

[5] Department of State, *Occupation of Japan, Policy and Progress,* pp. 7–9, 67–73.

Certain of the Allies share the responsibilities of occupation with the American forces. British Commonwealth troops, composed of elements from Great Britain, Australia, New Zealand, and India, occupy the island of Shikoku and a part of western Honshu. Plans for Chinese and Philippine participation in the occupation were delayed because of internal conditions in each of these countries. The Soviet Union has not chosen to send occupation troops to Japan, declining to accept arrangements whereby all occupation units are placed under American command and whereby they are limited to purely occupation duties, not participating in policy matters. The Soviet Union, as well as the other Allies, however, maintains liaison officers at the general headquarters of the Supreme Commander in Tokyo, and also cooperates in a limited number of staff functions of that headquarters, principally the prosecution of General Tojo and other individuals charged with war crimes.

**American Objectives.** The United States thus assumed the principal burden of formulation and implementation of occupation policy and administration. The objectives which the United States government set for its forces were expressed in a basic directive to Supreme Commander MacArthur prepared by the State, War, and Navy Departments and made public by the White House on September 22, 1945. This document declared that the two ultimate objectives of the United States, to which policies of the Supreme Commander must conform, were; first:

to insure that Japan will not again become a menace to the United States or to the peace and security of the world.

and, second:

to bring about the eventual establishment of a peaceful and responsible government which will respect the rights of other states and will support the objectives of the United States as reflected in the ideals and principles of the Charter of the United Nations. The United States desires that this government should conform as closely as may be to principles of democratic self-government but it is not the responsibility of the allied powers to impose upon Japan any form of government not supported by the freely expressed will of the people.[6]

## THE PROGRAM OF DEMILITARIZATION

The first task of the occupation forces, in addition to providing for their own welfare and security in an alien country, was the disarmament of the former enemy's military machine. Within a few months 3,000,000 Japanese troops were demobilized and sent to their homes, while the repatriation of some 4,000,000 troops overseas was virtually completed by the end of 1946, with the exception of those troops which surrendered to the Soviet Union in Manchuria and Korea. Military headquarters and the War and Navy Ministries were abolished, the latter merely continuing restricted operations for purposes of demobilization. Shortly after the surrender, the Japanese government abolished conscription for military service. What little was left of the navy and air force was scrapped, although some naval vessels first were employed in repatriation service. All production of munitions and implements of war was prohibited, as was civil aviation. The Japanese turned over remaining military equipment to the occupation forces. Weapons and matériel were destroyed (except those retained by Allied personnel as war trophies), while supplies of food, clothing, automotive equipment and the like were turned back to the Home Ministry for distribution to the civilian population. Within the surprisingly short space of a few months, Japan was stripped of such physical means for making war as had remained in her possession upon surrender.

**Trial of War Criminals.** At Potsdam the Allied leaders declared that stern justice would be meted out to all Japanese war criminals. Soon after the occupation began, the Supreme Commander ordered the Japanese government to apprehend and turn over to Allied authorities specified individuals wanted under these terms.

---

[6] *Ibid.,* pp. 73–81. The substance of this directive was sent to General MacArthur on August 29, 1945.

Military courts soon commenced the tedious process of trying the large number of Japanese charged with criminal acts against Allied prisoners of war. Similar trials were conducted in the liberated areas of Asia, the most publicized being the trials of Generals Yamashita and Homma in the Philippines.

In the spring of 1946 the trial of twenty-eight high ranking Japanese officials for crimes of aggression and crimes against humanity got under way in Tokyo before a special international military tribunal, composed of eleven justices each representing an Allied nation. Those indicted included representatives of the principal groups which had participated in the rise of a military dictatorship, with the exception of the Zaibatsu. Foremost among these individuals were General Tojo and numerous other military extremists, including Generals Araki and Minami, leaders of the extremists at the time of the Manchurian incident and the 1936 insurrection, and Colonel Hashimoto of the *Panay* incident. Nationalistic bureaucrats were represented by Naoki Hoshino, the principal architect of schemes for an army-dominated war economy; Okinobu Kaya, former finance minister and supporter of similar military plans; Mamoru Shigemitsu, career diplomat and signer of the surrender document; and Yosuke Matsuoka, former foreign minister and principal perpetrator of Japanese adherence to the Axis. (Matsuoka subsequently died in a Tokyo hospital after a long illness.) Baron Kiichiro Hiranuma, former prime minister and president of the Privy Council, represented the notorious superpatriotic, militaristic societies; he had been president of one such organization. Even the court circle failed to escape the stigma of militaristic complicity. Marquis Koichi Kido, lord keeper of the privy seal, and one of the emperor's closest wartime advisers, also was indicted. Prince Konoye, three-time prime minister and immediate predecessor of General Tojo in that office, chose suicide rather than surrender as a war-criminal suspect. Early plans to bring to trial leaders among the Zaibatsu were dropped, reportedly over the protests of the Soviet Union. Although some of these extremist leaders had ceased to have direct influence in the government as a result of the disastrous consequences of their policies of aggression, their indictment before the international tribunal removed all of them as possible threats to Allied objectives.

**The Elimination of Militaristic Controls.** Further elimination of militaristic leaders and organizations and the devices through which their influence had been exerted, was ordered in a series of sweeping directives to the Japanese government. Within a few months the Japanese were told to cancel all laws limiting freedom of speech, thought, assembly, and religion, including laws restricting discussion of the emperor and the imperial institution, and all laws discriminating against any person because of race, creed, or political opinions. Freedom of the press, radio, and motion pictures was proclaimed. The official government-controlled Domei news agency was abolished and the government was ordered to disassociate itself completely from all news gathering and distributing organizations. Plans were prepared to divorce the Japan Broadcasting Corporation from state ownership and control. The infamous *Kempei Tai,* or military police, Japan's Gestapo, and the *Tokokka,* or special "thought control" police, organizations which had participated in the ruthless suppression of liberal tendencies during the past two decades, were ordered abolished. The incumbent home minister and prefectural police chiefs were removed from office. Likewise, the Black Dragon society and other militaristic, terroristic, and ultranationalistic societies were outlawed.[7]

**Disestablishment of State Shinto.** Exploitation of the myths and dogmas of Japan's indigenous religion, Shinto, particularly those emphasizing blind loyalty to the emperor and Japan's divine mission of conquest, was one of the most effective devices by which her militaristic leaders secured and maintained domination of the nation. On December 15, 1945, the Supreme Commander acted to terminate this situation. On that day he directed the Japanese government to end all government financial and

[7] It should be noted that these orders and those described below were based on directives from the United States government to the Supreme Commander.

other support of the Shinto cult. The directive further prohibited teaching of Shinto in all educational institutions, and freed all individuals from any compulsion to believe in, or to profess to believe in, the Shinto faith. It forbade the propagation of "militaristic and ultranationalistic ideology not only to Shintoists but also to followers of all religious sects, creeds, or philosophies," including the myths of divine origin and superiority of the emperor and Japanese people. The directive also prohibited any government official, including the emperor, from taking part in any Shinto function or ceremony in his official capacity. Two weeks later, on January 1, 1946, following an understanding with the Supreme Commander's headquarters, the emperor issued a remarkable imperial rescript in which he declared that "the ties between us and our people . . . are not predicated on the false conception that the emperor is divine and the Japanese people are superior to other races and are fated to rule the world." [8]

**The Elimination of Militarism in the Schools.** The militaristic practices which characterized the Japanese educational system were the subject of early directives from the Supreme Commander. Military training and teaching of militaristic doctrines were prohibited. The emperor's picture was ordered removed from classrooms and Shinto shrines from school properties. Courses in Japanese history, geography, and "morals" were suspended until new programs of study and new textbooks could be prepared under supervision of the Supreme Commander's headquarters. The Japanese Ministry of Education was directed to remove all teachers with militaristic and ultranationalistic views, and when this program lagged, occupation authorities themselves ordered the removal of undesirable teachers when their continued presence in the school system came to attention.

**The "Purge" Directive.** One of the most drastic of the Supreme Commander's directives was the so-called "purge" directive of January 4, 1946. This directive, which the Japanese called the

[8] Department of State, *Occupation of Japan, Policy and Progress,* pp. 133–35.

"MacArthur typhoon," ordered the government to exclude from office in the Cabinet, advisory organs, and Diet, in the higher grades of the civil service, and in prefectural governorships, all persons who had participated actively in leading the nation to war. The directive specifically enumerated persons in the following broad categories: (1) war criminals; (2) career military and naval personnel, including members of the Board of Fleet Admirals and Field Marshals, Supreme War Council, Imperial General Headquarters, army and navy general staffs, and the Supreme Council for Direction of the War (a wartime agency of the highest government figures); commissioned officers in the regular army, navy, and special volunteer reserve; commissioned and non-commissioned officers, enlisted men, and civilian employees who served with the Kempei Tai (military police), naval police, thought-control police, and other secret intelligence and military and naval police organizations; and persons who served as minister, vice-minister, parliamentary vice-minister, councilor, and chief secretary of the war and navy ministries; (3) influential members of ultranationalistic, terroristic, and secret patriotic societies; (4) persons influential in the activities of the Imperial Rule Assistance Association, Imperial Rule Assistance Political Society, and the Political Society of Great Japan; (5) officers of financial and development organizations involved in Japanese expansion; (6) governors of occupied territories; and (7) persons who denounced or contributed to the seizure of opponents of the militaristic regime, or who instigated or perpetrated an act of violence against such opponents, or who played an active and predominant government part in the Japanese program of aggression, or who by speech, writing, or action showed themselves by their activities to be exponents of militant nationalism and aggression.

In consultation with representatives of the Supreme Commander, the Japanese government implemented the last category by defining as active exponents of militant nationalism persons who had held certain high positions in the government during the period from the outbreak of war in China in 1937 to the surrender in 1945. These positions included Cabinet posts, the lord keeper of the privy seal, positions of responsibility in government-owned or controlled corporations and in the military administrations of occupied territories, and persons identified with certain specified programs of suppression of liberalism. The "purge" directive imposed upon the Japanese government a large and difficult administrative job of screening incumbent and prospective officeholders, as did the directive calling for elimination of militaristically inclined teachers. It was a job which was still far from completed after more than a year of occupation. But these directives did have the immediate effect of removing the more conspicuously undesirable persons in the government and of preventing others from securing public office. It thus had a marked influence upon the composition of national leadership.

**Reparations.** The Potsdam Declaration called for the exaction from Japan of just reparations. It was recognized that reparations should be demanded not only as a means of compensating in small part the victims of Japan's aggressions, but also of eliminating her war-making potential in the future. The amount and kind of reparations, provisions for which will be made in the peace terms imposed upon Japan, were still undetermined at the end of 1945, because of the failure of the Far Eastern Commission to come to agreement on preliminary plans. Some indication of the American position was made several months after the surrender by Ambassador Edwin W. Pauley, the President's special representative on reparations. Mr. Pauley recommended that the bulk of Japan's foreign assets, including Japanese-owned properties in China, Manchuria, and other Asiatic countries, be confiscated and used for reparations payments, and that most of Japan's steel, shipbuilding, and chemical plants, half of her thermal electric plants, and machine-tool industries, and certain other specified industrial facilities, such as those for aluminum production, be confiscated and applied to reparations. He recommended that property of the Zaibatsu should be taken first, and that property of the emperor and the imperial family should not be exempt from seizure. Mr. Pauley based his recommendations on the proposition that Japan's economy should be pared back to that required to satisfy her normal prewar civilian, non-military consumption.

## THE PROGRAM OF REORIENTATION

The occupation of Japan, as determined by the Potsdam Declaration and subsequent directives to the Supreme Commander, imposed upon him two distinct obligations, one of immediate concern, the other of long-range responsibility. The first of these obligations stemmed directly from the most pressing of Allied war aims, namely the destruction of the power of the former enemy to make war again. It entailed the elimination of features of Japanese society which the allies believed responsible for Japan's militarism and aggression, and which, if permitted to remain, would constitute a menace to the peace and security of the world. The measures which the Supreme Commander ordered in fulfilment of this first obligation have been described in the section of this chapter just completed. These measures were executed vigorously and dramatically, winning for General MacArthur much deserved credit. This aspect of the occupation was largely a matter of surgery, the cutting away of the cancerous growth of militarism throughout the body politic.

The second obligation of the Supreme Commander was dictated by the long-range aims declared at Potsdam and in the basic American directive of August 1945. It will be recognized that the achievement of these ultimate aims could not be secured by the mere issuing of directives prohibiting undesirable practices and influences. The hoped-for changes in Japan, changes essential to the achievement of Allied objectives, could come only through positive reconstruction and reorganization of the whole social, economic, and political fabric of the nation, leading to the development of democratic tendencies and the eventual establishment of government according to the freely expressed will of the people. Merely to state the problem indicates its immensity and complexity. The history of the world demonstrates the difficulties involved in the establishment of responsible popular government in any country. Very few people have achieved this level of political attainment. The Japanese statesmen who engineered the surrender and accepted the occupation could hardly be expected to provide the initiative and leadership necessary for the growth of Japan along new and untried lines of political development, for as already indicated, the government of postsurrender Japan rested in the hands of representatives of the same narrow oligarchical interests that dominated the country throughout its modern history. Accordingly, if changes were to be made, they had to be made under the guidance of occupation authorities. The situation required much more than outlawing certain pernicious features of Japanese life; it demanded inspired leadership and painstaking encouragement of the faint sparks which might be kindled into the steady flame of the democratic spirit.

**Administrative Problems.** The achievement of these long-range objectives presented serious administrative and political problems. Japan was a badly defeated nation, whose cities were burned and shattered, whose foreign commerce was destroyed, whose industries were almost completely shut down. Even under the most favorable productive conditions, the population faced malnutrition and disease for many years to come. Japan needed internal stability and order to achieve economic recovery. Yet the accomplishment of needed political changes involved dynamic revolutionary forces—forces which potentially might threaten not only the maintenance of stability, but also the security of the occupation itself. It was the delicate task of the Supreme Commander to achieve a balance between demands for stability and the equally pressing demands for revolutionary change. Likewise, it was imperative that complete deterioration of the economic situation be prevented, lest food shortages and unemployment precipitate mass disorders which might threaten the security of the occupation troops. Thus much of the effort of the Supreme Commander's headquarters was devoted of necessity to supervising the attempts of the Japanese government to improve the food situation, prevent runaway inflation, and provide employment. The Supreme Commander secured limited imports of food supplies from the United States to tide Japan over the period of most severe shortages. Devotion of attention to these problems of immediate concern limited that available for supervision of long-range reforms.

**Release of Political Prisoners.** Within the first year of the occupation a very considerable start toward reconstruction and reform was made. One of the first steps was an order directing the Japanese government to release political prisoners. The government accordingly freed 32,000 political prisoners, and restored the civil rights of over 60,000 others who had been released previously. This action resulted in the liberation of many courageous leaders who had been jailed and maltreated for their opposition to militarism and totalitarianism during the previous two decades. It provided them with the opportunity to renew their political activities and to exert their advanced ideas toward the reform of political institutions and the organization of like-minded people, counterbalancing to a degree the marked conservatism of the dominant national leadership.

**Free Flow of Information.** Another early step taken by the Supreme Commander's headquarters was the encouragement of the free flow of accurate information to the people. Newspapers were instructed to publish full information about Japan's actions in Asia, about the war, and about other countries, information previously withheld from them. They were directed to explain to their readers the meaning of programs initiated by the Supreme Commander. Likewise, occupation authorities worked with radio, theatre, and motion-picture people toward the production of new features stressing democratic principles and ideals.

**Elevation of Women.** From the start, occupation forces encouraged the liberation of Japanese women, using the prestige and authority of General MacArthur to weaken the old traditions which held women in a subordinate position. Early in the occupation the Supreme Commander directed the government to extend the voting franchise to women. This was done and in April 1946, for the first time in Japanese history, women went to the polls. The turnout was surprising, women constituting nearly one-half of those voting. And in that election, thirty-nine women were elected to the lower house of the Diet, the largest number of women in any national legislative body in the world. Another symbolic act in behalf of women occurred when the government was directed to abolish licensed prostitution and to abrogate all contracts binding women involuntarily in this trade.

**Educational Reform.** The educational system of Japan afforded the occupation authorities an effective means of directing the reorientation of the Japanese people along the lines prescribed by Allied objectives. Japan always has been proud of her high literacy rate and has assigned a considerable portion of her national income to the education of her children. In the pages above it was described how the Supreme Commander acted to free the schools of controls by which militaristic leaders perverted the schools for purposes of mass indoctrination. Subsequently occupation headquarters commenced a more difficult long-range program. A special mission of prominent American educators spent a month in Japan advising occupation officials charged with this responsibility. Their recommendations called for a thorough overhauling of the whole educational system, divorcing it from all but nominal connection with the national government.[9]

One year later very little had been done toward the application of these recommendations, although new textbooks and new courses of study had been approved to replace those prescribed in early directives. Unfortunately the agencies responsible for reform of the educational system were seriously understaffed. The principal attention of the Japanese Ministry of Education and of occupation authorities during the first year was devoted to the new textbooks, and to screening teachers under the directive calling for the elimination of persons with militaristic tendencies.

[9] Department of State, *United States Education Mission to Japan,* Publication 2579, Far Eastern Series 11, Washington, 1946.

However, in October 1946 it was announced that of the more than 500,000 teachers in the country, only 16,000 had been screened, and of these only 331 had been removed, indicating that the Japanese had failed to carry out the intent of the directive. It was reported that the Supreme Commander's headquarters was disturbed by this situation.[10]

**Local Government Reform.** In Chapter 23 it was pointed out that the central government of Japan exercises very rigid control over units of local government. The Meiji leaders established this system to secure the unified administrative structure which they desired for their purposes, and, similarly, centralized controls were extended by Japan's wartime leaders as instruments of totalitarian dictatorship. The occupation authorities took steps to terminate this situation and to introduce democratic elements into the operation of local government. The Japanese government was directed to weaken the ties binding local government to national authority. In September 1946 the Diet enacted legislation providing for popular election, rather than Home Ministry appointment, of prefectural governors, city mayors, and town and village headmen. Shortly thereafter it was announced that the "purge" directive of January 4, 1946, would be applied to these officers. The first elections under these new provisions were scheduled for the spring of 1947.

## REFORM OF THE NATIONAL ECONOMY

How closely the economic structure of Japan was associated with her political system was described in Chapters 23 and 24. Concentration of the wealth of the nation in the hands of a relatively small group contributed to domination of the government by a narrow ruling oligarchy. This situation resulted in the subordination of the mass of the people, rendering virtually impossible the growth of popular government. Consequently economic as well as political reforms were planned by the occupation forces to achieve a peaceful and responsible government. The

[10] *New York Times,* October 21, 1946.

basic American directive of August 1945 to the Supreme Com mander emphasized this program. It provided that "Encouragement shall be given and favor shown to the development of organizations in labor, industry, and agriculture, organized on a democratic basis," and that "Policies shall be favored which permit a wide distribution of income and of the ownership of the means of production and trade." The directive further stated that "Those forms of economic activity, organization, and leadership shall be favored that are deemed likely to strengthen the peaceful disposition of the Japanese people, and to make it difficult to command or direct economic activity in support of military ends."

**Land Reform.** The Supreme Commander initiated steps toward the enforcement of economic reform during the early months of the occupation Thus, in November 1945, his headquarters issued a basic directive on land reform. This directive informed the Japanese government that the peasants must be freed from the burdens of intense overcrowding on the land, feudal absentee ownership, oppressive debt, discriminatory taxation, and authoritarian government controls. The directive ordered the government to draw up plans which would provide for farm credit at reasonable rates, protection of farmers against exploitation by processors and distributors, stabilization of farm prices, diffusion of technical and other information to farmers, and encouragement of agricultural cooperatives free from domination by nonagricultural interests. Compliance with this directive was the subject of protracted negotiation between occupation authorities and the Japanese government. Finally, in September 1946, the Diet accepted the government's land reform bill, which provided for purchase by the government of acreage held by large landowners and for its resale to tenants on a long-term basis. The measure represented but a start toward the realization of the requirements of the Supreme Commander's basic land reform directive.

**Organization of Labor.** The rights of the laboring classes also received attention in early directives. As already indicated in

Chapter 24, the labor movement in Japan had been subjected to repressive government measures, and unionization as a consequence made very little headway before the war. In December 1945, upon the initiative of occupation authorities, the Diet enacted legislation removing restrictions upon the organization of labor and recognizing specifically the right to organize and to bargain collectively, following the pattern of the American National Labor Relations Act. Japanese working people, including women, responded quickly to the new freedom. Within six months an estimated 2,800,000 members had joined over 3000 unions, and the number continued to increase. Strikes for higher wages and better working conditions became commonplace, and Japanese workers developed a new technique in dealing with recalcitrant employers. When demands were turned down they locked the management out of the plants and assumed operating control themselves until agreement was reached. In some instances production was higher than normal during these periods of employee control. With the continuation of food shortages and the evils of serious inflation, labor leaders became even more insistent. Strikes and protests against the incumbent government became more frequent. During the latter half of 1946 the prestige and influence of the occupation forces were employed to curtail the spread of strikes and of the political influence of unions. The Supreme Commander issued a statement that strikes inimical to the objectives of the occupation would not be tolerated. In September the Diet passed a law, introduced by the government with the approval if not the encouragement of occupation headquarters, which restricted government transport and other workers by requiring them to submit disputes to compulsory arbitration.

**Reform of the Zaibatsu.** As a part of the policy of promotion of democratic forces by means of economic reform, the basic American directive of September 1945, ordered the Supreme Commander "To favor a program for the dissolution of the large industrial and banking combinations which have exercised control of a great part of Japan's trade and industry." Thus the

United States government took the position that for the Zaibatsu to retain its monopolistic control of Japan's economy would constitute a serious obstacle to the development of democratic tendencies. In the first part of this chapter it was indicated that the Zaibatsu retained a leading role in the direction of public affairs throughout the war and into the postsurrender period. Likewise, the Zaibatsu retained its dominant position in finance, commerce, and industry. True, many of the physical assets of the Zaibatsu were destroyed by B-29 raids, and by the loss of overseas property in Japan's lost territories. Yet the Zaibatsu fared no worse than other groups and relatively its position was favorable.[11]

**Plans for Partial Dissolution.** When it became known that occupation policy would be directed toward the dissolution of the large industrial and financial combinations, certain Zaibatsu interests made gestures toward voluntary compliance, the sincerity of which may readily be questioned. A considerable number of the officers of the larger companies, including members of the controlling families, resigned their official positions. Following conferences with occupation authorities, a voluntary dissolution plan was submitted by the top holding company of the Yasuda combine on behalf of itself and of the Mitsui, Mitsubishi, and Sumitomo interests. These four are the largest Zaibatsu combinations. The Supreme Commander approved the Yasuda plan in November 1945, with the understanding "that full freedom of action is retained by the Supreme Comander to elaborate or modify the proposed plan at any time and to supervise and review its execution." At the same time the Supreme Commander directed the Japanese government to present further plans for dissolution of these huge combinations, and to present plans for the abrogation of legislative and administrative measures fostering private monopoly. These plans were to include provisions for the elimination of private monopolies and restraints of trade, undesirable interlocking directorates, and un-

[11] Corwin D. Edwards, "The Dissolution of the Japanese Combines," *Pacific Affairs*, September 1946, pp. 227–40.

desirable corporate security ownerships for the segregation of banking from commerce, industry, and agriculture, and for equal competitive opportunity.

Under the Yasuda plan the top holding companies of the four largest combines will transfer their security holdings and other property to a liquidating commission to be established by the Japanese government. The holding companies will then be dissolved. The liquidating commission will hold these properties until they are sold to new owners. Zaibatsu stockholders will be compensated by payments in blocked government bonds, which may not be cashed or transferred for ten years. Members of the Zaibatsu families will resign all official connections in banking and industry, and will transfer to the liquidating commission all shares which they hold in companies affiliated with or controlled by these combines. Likewise, officials appointed by the controlling families or by the holding company will resign. The dominant bank in each combine will cease to control its subsidiary banks.

Until such time as plans could be approved, temporary stop-gap measures were directed by the Supreme Commander to bring the Zaibatsu concerns under occupation control. By June 1946 twenty-nine Zaibatsu holding companies and 719 of their subsidiaries were placed on a restricted list, which meant that they were required to provide extensive information about their assets and liabilities, their corporate connections, and the holders of their securities. Their bank accounts and the accounts of certain of their executives were frozen to prevent unauthorized transactions, and new investments by members of Zaibatsu families were forbidden.

In July 1946 the Supreme Commander approved the program of the Japanese government for dissolving the Zaibatsu, based very largely upon the Yasuda plan. It will be recognized that this program alone is insufficient to destroy the power of the Zaibatsu. If such power is to be destroyed, further action will be necessary to reach beyond the top holding companies and to eliminate the many special privileges which the Zaibatsu possess in finance and in relations with the government—preferential subsidies and

trade preferences, favorable inheritance and income tax regulations. Moreover, definite policies providing an alternative to
Zaibatsu ownership are essential. As late as one year after the
commencement of the occupation, no decision had been made on
the disposition of Zaibatsu holdings by the liquidating commission.[12]

## CONCLUSION

This concludes the discussion of Allied policy toward Japan.
It has been seen that the Supreme Commander directed the efforts of his administration along two lines. In the first place,
Japan was disarmed and a program of demilitarization was inaugurated. By the end of the first year of occupation this aspect
of the Allied task was very largely completed. In the second place,
the Supreme Commander outlined a broad program of reform,
designed to achieve the long-range objectives set by Allied authorities. It was clearly understood that its success in the end
would depend upon the Japanese people themselves.

## READINGS

The student seeking further information concerning Japan under
Allied administration must rely largely upon articles published in
current newspapers and magazines. The *Far Eastern Survey,* published by the American Council, Institute of Pacific Relations, New
York, has carried a series of detailed and specialized reports which
are particularly recommended. Other periodicals specializing on
Japan and other areas of the Far East include *Amerasia, Asia and the
Americas, Far Eastern Quarterly,* and *Pacific Affairs.* Very few reports of the Supreme Commander for the Allied Powers have been
given general distribution.

Department of State, *Occupation of Japan, Policy and Progress,*
Publication 2671, Far Eastern Series 17, Washington, 1946.

[12] See Department of State, *Report of the Mission on Japanese Combines,* Publication 2628, Far Eastern Series 14, Washington, 1946.

This pamphlet contains the principal documents and a summary account of occupation policy.

Johnstone, Anne and William, *What Are We Doing With Japan?*, Institute of Pacific Relations, New York, 1946. In a concise pamphlet, the authors review terms of surrender, division of administrative responsibility, and policy directives issued during the first half-year of occupation.

Johnstone, William C., *The Future of Japan*, New York, 1945. Written in anticipation of the surrender of Japan, this book deals with the important issues relating to allied policy toward the enemy.

Hart, Richard, *Eclipse of the Rising Sun*, Foreign Policy Association, New York, 1946. This pamphlet considers Japan's surrender, Allied surrender terms, and the first half-year of occupation. It includes a summary of the new constitution.

Kato, Masuo, *The Lost War, A Japanese Reporter's Inside Story*, New York, 1946. This is an account of Japan's war years, of the surrender, and of the first days of the occupation, by one of the country's leading journalists.

Supreme Commander for the Allied Powers, *Summation of Non-military Activities in Japan*, Tokyo, published monthly (mimeographed). These monthly reports, although devoid of any critical interpretation of the occupation, contain a wealth of factual information.

# CHAPTER 26

# THE RESPONSE TO OCCUPATION POLICY

THE preceding chapter was concerned with the formulation and execution of Allied policies for a defeated Japan. The time has come to consider the manner in which the Japanese people and their government responded to these policies. It will be recognized that the objectives of the occupation could not be achieved overnight, for the Allied program represented an attempt to reverse conditions and to change institutions of long standing, conditions and institutions deeply rooted in Japanese life. A review of the feudalistic political principles inherited by Japan from her earlier history, described in Chapter 23, will demonstrate that these heritages constituted an extremely serious obstacle to the development of popular government.

## REACTIONS TO THE OCCUPATION

**The People.** The reaction of the Japanese people to the Supreme Commander's administration was heartening. The people responded quickly to the new opportunities afforded by the removal of repressive controls. Newspapers expressed themselves with amazing frankness, bookstores were flooded with thousands of political pamphlets ranging from extreme right to extreme left, many freely discussing the status of the emperor and other issues which formerly were strictly prohibited. Labor unions grew rapidly, and demonstrations of workers became a frequent sight in the cities of the country. The great mass of people naturally was preoccupied with the problems of livelihood, but it was clear that even the severe measures of Japan's totalitarian dictatorship had not destroyed the inherent demands of her people for freedom of expression and political opportunity.

**Political Leadership.** After one year of occupation, Japan's government, on the other hand, remained in the hands of conservative bureaucratic and business interests. Militarists were eliminated or withdrew promptly as a consequence of occupation; those who did remain were caught by the purge directive. But the government remained the affair of the two other principal political elements. Shortly after the occupation began, a Cabinet was formed under the leadership of Baron Shidehara, former foreign minister and leader in the Minseito party. Shidehara, who was associated with the Mitsubishi interests by marriage, was acceptable to the occupation authorities because of his known opposition to the militarists before and during the Manchurian incident of 1931. His Cabinet represented the familiar business and bureaucracy combination.

**Political Parties.** The surrender very quickly produced a resurgence of activity by party politicians. Even before the formal surrender on September 2, the Cabinet dissolved the Political Association of Great Japan, the wartime successor to the Imperial Rule Assistance Association. Within a few months four principal political parties and a large number of parties of lesser importance had been organized. These parties were similar to the first parties which had come into existence after the Meiji Restoration, that is, they were composed of small groups of party leaders or influential government figures, held together by personal friendship and loyalty and a common desire to secure the spoils of office. One year after their initial organization, these parties still lacked extensive party machinery and broad membership.[1]

The Liberal party (*Jiyuto*) was the most influential of the new parties. Its original membership was composed of former members of the old Seiyukai, drawn together by Ichiro Hatoyama, a

[1] General Headquarters, Supreme Commander for the Allied Powers, Government Section, *Japanese Political Parties*, 2 vols. (mimeographed), Tokyo, 1946.

professional politician with long experience in the Diet, one-time Cabinet secretary under the notorious Baron Tanaka, and subsequently minister of education. This group reportedly had close connections with both Mitsui and Mitsubishi interests, with the bureaucracy, and with the Imperial Household. The party's platform, after the necessary support of the Potsdam Declaration, advocated the maintenance of the emperor system, the establishment of a democratically responsible government, and the guarantee of civil liberties. It also proposed the stabilization of the national economy by individual initiative, free financial activity, and reconstruction of agricultural, commercial, and industrial enterprises.

The Progressive party (*Shimpoto*) was very similar to the Liberal party in composition and outlook, although its leaders were personal rivals of Hatoyama and others among the Liberals. The original party consisted of a merger of professional politicians and bureaucrats who had belonged to the former Minseito and Seiyukai. This group likewise possessed ties with business interests. The original Progressive party was severely hit by the Supreme Commander's purge directive. Almost all of its leading figures, and all but twenty-three of the 273 members of the Diet who had associated with it, were disbarred from office by this directive. Nevertheless, the party managed to hold together under new leadership, and Baron Shidehara was persuaded to accept the party presidency. The platform of the Progressives was similar to that of the Liberal party, and likewise featured support of the imperial system. The student will recognize that the names selected by the founders for these two parties were designed to appeal to American ears. (Early in 1947 the Progressive party was renamed the Democratic party.)

The Social Democratic party (*Shakaito*) was the third major party. It was a loosely organized combination of politicians of divergent views, and represented a bridge between the extreme conservatives on the right and the communists on the left. The party nucleus consisted of former members of several small peasant and labor parties which had opposed the rise of the military dictatorship and which had been broken up by police suppression. Although the party's left wing contained former members of the Communist party, its right wing possessed the greatest influence. Due to the influence of this right wing, the party declined the overtures of the Communists to form a "democratic front" alliance.

The platform of the Social Democratic party presented a broad appeal agreeable to both the right and left elements. It included democratization of the constitutional system, government assistance to labor and agriculture, and unemployment, health, and old age insurance, and other forms of social legislation.

The Communist party of Japan (*Kyosanto*) originally was founded in 1922. It was an illegal organization and during the 1920's and 1930's did not number more than 100 active members. But in spite of severe government suppression, it did have some influence. This influence was exerted through members who permeated peasant and labor organizations and other popular movements. During the period of 1932–34 alone, over 70,000 suspected communists were arrested by the police and no less than 7000 were jailed, although almost all of these persons were punished for other than proved communist connections.

The Supreme Commander's directive releasing political prisoners opened the way for a reorganization of the Communist party. In December 1945 the party held what it called its fourth national party convention, emphasizing continuity with its prewar existence. Kyuichi Tokuda, who had spent seventeen years in jail, was named secretary-general. Because of a widespread belief that the party advocated violence and overthrow of the emperor system, and because of common suspicion that it had ties with the Soviet Union, relatively few members were attracted to the party. But by the use of clever publicity, including mass demonstrations, the party secured a great deal of popular attention, and its influence appeared to be in excess of its real strength.

In January 1946 Communist party headquarters were joined by Sanzo Nosaka, a Japanese communist who, under the assumed name of Okano, had worked among Japanese prisoners of war captured by the Chinese communists. Nosaka declared that conditions in Japan were not suitable for the immediate application of communism. He advocated abandonment of the theory of an aggressive proletarian revolution in favor of parliamentary action through nonviolence. He also toned down the party's persistent opposition to the emperor system. Perhaps as a consequence of Nozaka's moderating influence, the Communists attracted an increasing number of members, the enrollment reaching 20,000 by June 1946, and the circulation of the party newspaper, *Red Flag*, rising to 300,000.

The principal activities of the Communist party were directed toward the spread of communist doctrines through various popular movements. Because of the inherent conservatism of the peasant population and the stronger position of the Social Democratic party among peasant groups, the Communists made more headway in the cities than in the rural areas. In the cities they exerted considerable influence within the rapidly growing labor movement. This influence was checked, however, by the strong position against violence and mass demonstrations taken by the Supreme Commander in May 1946. It was generally recognized that the Supreme Commander's action was directed primarily against the Communist minority in the labor movement. In spite of a belief among some Japanese that the Communist party received financial support from the Soviet Union, intensive research by occupation authorities and by Japanese investigators failed to substantiate this claim. About a quarter to a half of the party's income was derived from the sale of its publications.[2]

The Communist platform, like those of the other Japanese parties, was full of generalities and lacking in precise detail. It demanded the abolition of the emperor system and the establishment of a republic, extensive agrarian reforms, nationalization of Zaibatsu interests, and government assistance to workers.

**The April 1946 Election.** On April 10, 1946, the Japanese people, including the newly enfranchised women, conducted the

[2] General Headquarters, Supreme Commander for the Allied Powers, Government Section, *Japanese Political Parties*, 1946, vol. II, p. 12.

first national election following the surrender, voting for members of a new lower house of the Diet. The results of the election demonstrated that conservative elements dominated public affairs at that time. The two conservative parties, the Liberals and Progressives, together polled more than 40 per cent of the vote, securing 139 and 93 seats respectively. Moreover, a large portion of the more than 100 minor party and independent members who were elected associated themselves with these major conservative parties. The Social Democrats elected 92 members. The Communists trailed with 5. The conservative parties scored heavily in rural areas, while the Social Democrats and Communists obtained the greater portion of their votes in the cities.[3]

Shortly after the April election, the Shidehara Cabinet resigned. Six weeks were required to form a new cabinet. With 139 members, the Liberals became the plurality party, but they lacked a clear majority. After some delay, agreement was reached between the Liberals and Progressives whereby the two groups were to form a Cabinet, headed by the Liberal Party leader, Hatoyama. This move, however, did not meet with the approval of the Supreme Commander. It was found that Hatoyama clearly came within the terms of the purge directive by reason of previous activities as a proponent of totalitarian principles. The Japanese government should have prevented him from running in the election; but nevertheless he polled a large number of votes. The Supreme Commander directed the Japanese government to bar him from all public office, without further delay.

Subsequently a coalition Cabinet, composed of representatives of the two conservative parties, was formed by Shigeru Yoshida, a career diplomat and personal friend of the deposed Hatoyama. Yoshida also became president of the Liberal party. Baron Shidehara, president of the Progressive party, remained in the Cabinet as a minister of state. The new Cabinet reflected the dominant business and bureaucratic interests.

[3] See Department of State, *Occupation of Japan, Policy and Progress*, pp. 24–26, 136–45.

Prime Minister Yoshida was selected after the usual conferences between leading figures in the principal advisory organs of government. He was nominated, according to custom, by the emperor. But at this time these political maneuverings were freely reported and discussed in the press, and the public was given a valuable lesson in the problems and responsibilities of selecting political leadership.

## CHANGES IN THE STRUCTURE OF GOVERNMENT

It was widely recognized by the leading American officials that changes would have to be made in the structure of government if a peaceful and progressive Japan were to be achieved. The Japanese government itself made a few gestures in this direction in the early months of the occupation. It abolished outright the Greater East Asia Ministry and the Ministry of Munitions. The Board of Information, in which had been concentrated all wartime propaganda and censorship agencies, was eliminated and its component parts were returned to the ministries in which they originally had been located. After the arrest of Marquis Kido, lord keeper of the privy seal during the war years, as a war criminal, the government abolished that office and announced that the Imperial Household Ministry would be reduced in size and function. But aside from these relatively minor changes, Japan's political leaders initiated no further steps toward revamping the structure of government.

**The Emperor.** One of the most controversial issues concerning treatment of Japan which was discussed prior to the actual surrender of the country related to the status of the emperor. Some argued that it would be impossible to achieve a peaceful and democratic Japan so long as the imperial institution survived. These people pointed to the manner in which the emperor and the Shinto myths surrounding his person had been exploited by Japan's military leaders. Others argued that the emperor, as a symbol of national unity and stability, could be used properly as a vehicle for the establishment of a new system of government.

The language of the Potsdam Declaration and of subsequent pronouncements permitted a wide choice of action in dealing with the emperor. The basic American directive of August 1945, which instructed the Supreme Commander to exercise his authority through the Japanese governmental machinery and agencies, including the emperor, made this clear. This directive stated that "This policy . . . does not commit the Supreme Commander to support the emperor or any other Japanese governmental authority in opposition to evolutionary changes looking toward the attainment of United States objectives. The policy is to use the existing form of government in Japan, not to support it." [4]

Although the matter became a subject of open discussion, there was no serious movement on the part of the Japanese people to eliminate the emperor. It has already been noted that the surrender was handled in such a way as to enhance the prestige of the imperial system. Subsequently the Japanese government very carefully cultivated popular favor toward the emperor. Hirohito began a series of informal public appearances, visiting farms and factories, schools and private homes. He was photographed speaking with average citizens and emphasis was placed upon the fact that he shared the privations of his subjects. The emperor's rescripts and statements were now made in the colloquial language, rather than in the classical style as formerly. The Liberal and Progressive parties took a strong stand in favor of the emperor system, a position shared by most of the leaders of the Social Democratic party. Only the Communists demanded the abolition of the whole imperial system and the establishment of a republic, a position which probably lost them votes in the April election. The people responded to the new approach. They greeted the emperor enthusiastically, crowding around him informally.

**The Imperial Family.** Although the manner in which the Supreme Commander handled his relations with the Japanese government favored the retention of the emperor, certain steps

[4] *Ibid.*, p. 75.

were taken to abolish the autocratic features of the imperial system. Thus the special privileges possessed by members of the imperial family were abolished. Imperial princes were deprived of the usual monetary grants from the public treasury, and their personal holdings were subjected to taxation. The vast properties held by the imperial family were turned over to the state to be administered in the public interest. An American woman journeyed to Japan to become the tutor of the crown prince.

## THE CONSTITUTION OF 1946

The Japanese government through which the Supreme Commander administered Japan for more than one year operated under the Constitution of 1889. The provisions of this constitution were discussed in Chapter 23. Shortly after the surrender, government spokesmen commenced discussions of constitutional revision. Prince Konoye, for example, prepared one draft, but this and others presented to the Supreme Commander were found to offer very little improvement over the existing document. These men could not be expected to propose extensive changes on their own initiative. Finally, after close consultation with occupation headquarters, the Shidehara Cabinet, through the emperor, presented to the Japanese people on March 6, 1946, the draft of an entirely new constitution.[5] Although the document was far in advance of the proposals made by the government and by the political parties up to that time, it was accepted with only minor change by the new Diet during its sessions in the summer of 1946. Only the Communist members declined to vote for the new instrument of government, basing their position on the fact that it provided for the retention of the emperor.

On November 3, 1946, Emperor Hirohito issued an imperial rescript promulgating the new constitution of Japan.[6] A few

[5] For a description of the drafting procedure see D. N. Rowe, "The New Japanese Constitution," *Far Eastern Survey,* January 29, 1947, 13–17; February 12, 1947, 30–34.

[6] *New York Times,* November 4, 1946.

days later celebrations were held throughout the nation, honoring the new basic law. The emperor, empress, and crown prince appeared at the celebration before the imperial palace in Tokyo, which was attended by an estimated 200,000 persons.

The constitution of 1946 represents a complete revision of the constitution of 1889. This situation is emphasized in the preamble, which begins with the declaration:

We, the Japanese people, acting through our duly elected representatives in the National Diet, determined that we shall secure for ourselves and our posterity the fruits of peaceful cooperation with all nations and the blessings of liberty throughout this land, and resolved that never again shall we be visited with the horrors of war through the action of government, do proclaim that sovereign power resides with the people and do firmly establish this Constitution. Government is a sacred trust, the authority for which is derived from the people, the powers of which are exercised by the representatives of the people, and the benefits of which are enjoyed by the people. This is an universal principle of mankind upon which this Constitution is founded. We reject and revoke all constitutions, laws, ordinances, and rescripts in conflict herewith.[7]

Thus the new document made a sharp break with the past. It terminated the sovereign prerogatives of the emperor, providing the legal basis for the elimination of that feature of the old constitutional system which had been most effectively exploited by the ruling oligarchy for its own purposes. The new constitution vested full sovereignty in the people of the nation.

**The Emperor.** Under the new constitution, the emperor loses the sovereign prerogatives and the exhalted religious authority which he formerly possessed. He is, according to the constitution, "the symbol of the State and of the unity of the people, deriving his position from the will of the people with whom resides sovereign power" (Article I). Moreover, it is clearly recognized that the emperor may act only with the approval of the Cabinet. The constitutions states in Articles III and IV that:

[7] *Official Gazette*, English Edition, Extra, November 3, 1946, Government Printing Bureau, Tokyo.

The advice and approval of the Cabinet shall be required for all acts of the Emperor in matters of state, and the Cabinet shall be responsible therefor.

The Emperor shall perform only such acts in matters of state as are provided for in this Constitution, and he shall not have powers related to government.

The constitution terminates the independent status which the imperial institutions formerly possessed by granting to the Diet full authority over the Imperial House Law (Article II). Likewise the Diet is given full control of imperial income and expenditures (Article VIII).

**Contrast with British King.** It will be recognized that the new constitution reduces the emperor of Japan to a status very similar to that of the British king. Each of these monarchs has lost all authority to govern, but each remains the symbolic head of the nation. The draftsmen of the constitution modeled the practices of the emporor after British customs, but the student will recognize that accepted developments and principles in Great Britain and Japan are vastly different. The British Crown was reduced to its present status as early as the seventeenth century, but not until considerable blood, including royal blood, had been shed. As a counterbalance to royal authority, the British, over a period of many centuries extending as far back as Magna Carta, developed the rights and prerogatives of the people's representatives in Parliament. Japan does not possess a similar tradition of parliamentary authority. The new constitution makes the Diet the supreme governing body, but only time and experience will eliminate the authority and prestige of the imperial institution, as required in the new basic law. Japan, lacking the experience of open revolt against imperial authority, requires a clear and precise understanding of the limitations upon such authority.

**Renunciation of War.** Article IX is a unique feature of this constitution. This article states:

. . . the Japanese people forever renounce war as a sovereign right of the nation and the threat or use of force as a means of settling international disputes . . . land, sea, and air forces, as well as other war potential, will never be maintained. The right of belligerency of the state will not be recognized.

**Bill of Rights.** Chapter 3 of the Constitution, consisting of thirty articles, contains an extensive list of the rights and duties of the people. The constitution of 1889 also granted certain rights to the people, but these rights were restricted by the provisions that each was subject to revision according to the law. In practice the people of Japan possessed few, if any, civil liberties until the Supreme Commander issued his directives on this subject. The new constitution recognizes civil liberties as an absolute right.

The list of these liberties enumerated in Chapter 3 of the constitution includes the following: equality under law; no discrimination because of race, creed, sex, social status, or family origin; no extension of the peerage and no inheritance of titles of nobility; the inalienable right to choose public officials and to dismiss them; secrecy of the ballot; the right of peaceful petition; prohibition of involuntary servitude except as punishment for crime; freedom of religion and of religious organization, with a prohibition of government support for any religion; freedom of assembly, association, press, and all other forms of expression; freedom of occupation, and of emigration and expatriation; academic freedom; equality of each sex in marital relations, including property rights, inheritance, choice of domicile, and divorce; free public education; the right to work, with prohibition of exploitation of child labor; right of workers to organize and to bargain collectively; inviolability of private property as defined by law and in conformity with the public welfare; no person to be deprived of life or liberty, except according to processes established by law; no search or seizure without warrant; and the right of a speedy and public trial by an impartial tribunal in all criminal cases.

Chapter 3 thus constitutes a broad recognition of the civil liberties and the rights of the Japanese people. It prohibits all of those features of militaristic Japan which the Supreme Commander banned in the series of directives which were issued during the early months of the occupation and which were described above in Chapter 25.

**The Diet.** The new constitution establishes the Diet as "the highest organ of state power," and "the sole law-making organ of the State" (Article XLI). Thus it appears to be the purpose of this chapter of the constitution to provide a legislative body similar in authority to the British Parliament. The Diet consists of two houses, the House of Representatives and the House of Councilors. The members of each of these houses are elected by the people, those of the lower house for a four-year term, those of the House of Councilors for six years, half being elected every three years.

The House of Representatives is superior in authority to the House of Councilors. The constitution provides that a bill which is passed by the House of Representatives, but which is rejected by the House of Councilors, becomes a law when passed a second time by the House of Representatives by a majority of two-thirds or more of the members present. Moreover, if the House of Councilors fails to take action within sixty days, the decision of the House of Representatives is final. Likewise, when the House of Councilors rejects a budgetary bill of the House of Representatives, or treaty, or fails to act within thirty days on either of these matters, the decision of the House of Representatives will be considered the final decision of the Diet (Articles LIX-LXI).

The Cabinet may dissolve the lower house and call a general election, which must be held within forty days. During this interval the House of Councilors must be closed, except that the Cabinet may in time of national emergency call it into special session. Measures enacted at this emergency session become null and void, however, unless accepted by the new lower house within ten days after the opening of the next regular session of the Diet (Article LIV).

The financial powers of the Diet are set forth in Chapter 7 of the constitution. The Diet possesses full authority over national finances, and no taxes may be imposed or expenditures made without its approval (Articles LXXXIII-LXXXIV). Likewise, all property of the Imperial Household, other than hereditary estates, is declared to be the property of the state. All allowances for the support of the Imperial Household must be appropriated by the Diet (Article LXXXVIII).

**The Cabinet.** Chapter 5, which provides for the Cabinet, again shows a parallel with British practice. This chapter clearly establishes the principle that the Cabinet is responsible to the representatives of the people in the Diet. According to Article LXVI, "the Cabinet, in the exercise of executive power, shall be collectively responsible to the Diet." Article LXVII states that "the Prime Minister shall be designated from among the members of the Diet by a resolution of the Diet." In the event that the House of Representatives and House of Councilors disagree, the decision of the former shall be the decision of the Diet. The members of the Cabinet other than the Prime Minister are appointed by the Prime Minister; a majority must be Diet members.

The principle of parliamentary responsibility is further strengthened by the provision that "If the House of Representatives passes a non-confidence resolution, or rejects a confidence resolution, the Cabinet shall resign en masse, unless the House of Representatives is dissolved within ten days" (Article LXIX). It is also provided that "when there is a vacancy in the post of Prime Minister, or upon the convocation of the Diet after a general election, the Cabinet shall resign en masse" (Article LXX).

The constitution enumerates the functions which the Cabinet performs in addition to its regular administrative duties. These include the management of foreign affairs; conclusion of treaties, conditional upon Diet approval; preparation of the budget for presentation to the Diet; and enactment of Cabinet orders necessary to carry out the provisions of the constitution and of the law.

**The Judiciary.** Chapter 6 makes provision for the judiciary. This chapter establishes the independence of the courts, and introduces the American principle of judicial review into Japanese government. Article LXXXI states: "The Supreme Court is the court of last resort with power to determine the constitutionality of any law, order, regulation or official act." Judges of the Supreme Court are appointed by the Cabinet. However, Article LXXIX follows a procedure used in the State of California whereby the appointment of Supreme Court judges is reviewed by the people at the next general election, and at subsequent intervals of ten years. Judges of the inferior courts are appointed, for ten year terms, by the Cabinet from a list of persons nominated by the Supreme Court (LXXX).

**Other Provisions.** In a concluding chapter recognition is given to the principle of local autonomy, and provision is made for popular election of local executives (Chapter 8). Amendments to the constitution are initiated by the Diet, by a concurring vote of two-thirds of all members of each house. The proposal is then submitted to the people for ratification, which requires an affirmative vote of a majority of all votes cast (Chapter 9).

The new constitution of Japan became effective six months after its promulgation by the emperor, or on May 3, 1947.

**Significance of the New Constitution.** The new constitution represented a major step toward the achievement of allied objectives in Japan. It will be noted that it did away with those features of the old constitutional structure which blocked the way for democratic government. Gone were the independent advisory organs, the Privy Council, the Imperial Household ministers, and the Supreme Command. Gone were the peerage and the conservative House of Peers. Gone also were those organs through which irresponsible militarists were able to operate the so-called "dual government." In their stead, the responsibility of the Cabinet to the representatives of the people in the Diet was clearly enunciated.

**1947 Election.** On February 7, 1947, General MacArthur ordered the Japanese government to hold a new election for members of the Diet "as soon as practicable" after the close of the Diet session in April. The order was issued at a time when labor and radical groups directed vigorous attacks upon the Yoshida

Cabinet, blaming it for the country's social and economic ills. These protests, coupled with strikes and threats of disorder, indicated a growing restlessness and a popular demand for new leadership. The Supreme Commander's order pointed to this situation, stating: "But because important changes have occurred since the last general election, [and] since the people's wishes may also well have changed . . ., a new expression of national opinion is necessary. Therefore the new election now will be held." [8] Likewise, elections required by the new constitution were scheduled for April. The people were to vote for prefectural governors and other local executives and for the members of the new upper house of the Diet. These elections, national and local, promised to bring about a shift of national leadership away from the conservative outlook of the Yoshida government.

## CONCLUSIONS

It is too soon to evaluate Japan's response to Allied administration of Japan. Such an evaluation must wait until the withdrawal of occupation troops. Only at that time can an observer determine whether the reforms ordered by the Supreme Commander will endure. With respect to the new constitution, the student will recognize, of course, that no constitution can work, no matter how good it is, unless the people understand their responsibilities as well as their rights, and unless statesmen provide positive leadership. Moreover, as even these brief chapters reveal, the achievement of Allied objectives in Japan rests not so much upon manipulation of the constitutional system as it does upon extensive changes in Japan's feudalistic social and economic structures. Inasmuch as surrender left Japan's old ruling classes in control, it is not likely that such changes will take place upon the initiative of the Japanese government. With the successful promulgation of the new constitution, therefore, the Supreme Commander still faced the larger task of producing the much needed social and economic changes.

[8] *New York Times,* February 8, 9, 1947.

## READINGS

*Fortune,* March 1947, XXXV, "The U. S. Does A Job." The Mac-Arthur program receives warm praise in this article.

Haring, Douglas G., ed., *Japan's Prospect,* Harvard University Press, 1946. This symposium includes chapters by nine recognized authorities on fundamental problems of Japan's postwar reconstruction.

LaCerda, John, *The Conqueror Comes to Tea,* Rutgers University Press, 1946. In this book an American correspondent in Japan reports on the reactions of Japanese and American troops to the occupation.

Imperial Japanese Government, *Official Gazette,* Tokyo, 1946–——. Under date of April 4, 1946, the Japanese government commenced the publication of an English-language edition of this official publication containing text of all ordinances and official announcements.

Rosinger, Lawrence K., "Will U. S. Occupation Bring Fundamental Changes to Japan?", *Foreign Policy Bulletin,* October 18 and 25; November 1, 1946. The author, in three articles, questions the wisdom of certain American policies. Compare these with the *Fortune* article.

See also the references for Chapter 25.

# CHINA

# CHAPTER 27

# THE CHINESE REVOLUTION AND THE ESTABLISHMENT OF THE NATIONAL GOVERNMENT

THE story of contemporary politics in China is the story of the struggles of a persevering and stouthearted people against tremendous odds to maintain a government capable of performing the responsibilities of a twentieth century state. Chapter 23 described how China's smaller neighbor, Japan, was able to emerge from long, self-imposed isolation and to adjust quickly to the modern world in which she suddenly found herself. China, during the nineteenth century, likewise faced the problems of similar adjustment. But China did not possess the sort of internal organization which would enable her to withstand the pressures of the western nations. Consequently she came dangerously close to losing her political independence altogether. Her difficulties in large measure may be traced to the impact of the West's technologically advanced culture upon her own existing political, economic, and social systems. The student of Chinese affairs, accordingly, will find it to his profit to examine China's ancient form and practice of government and certain of the events of the last century which bear upon the attempts of the Chinese people to convert that government into a modern republic.

## THE EMPIRE

At the end of the nineteenth century China was nearing the conclusion of more than two thousand years of monarchical government. The emperor possessed absolute political authority which he exercised through appointed councilors and other high officials. The principal functions of the imperial government, which were carried out by administrative boards, consisted of the raising of revenue, the performance of ceremonial rites, the provision of national defense, the prosecution of justice, and the maintenance of canals, highways, public buildings, and other public works.

**The Imperial Government.** The imperial government was highly decentralized, and the provinces into which the country was divided were semi-autonomous in authority. In each province the emperor was represented by an appointed viceroy or governor. After a general policy was determined upon in Peking (since 1928, Peiping), the national capital, it was transmitted to the provincial governors, who frequently modified it according to local customs and conditions or according to their own sympathies or those of other provincial officials.

The provinces, of which there were eighteen during most of the nineteenth century, were in turn subdivided into smaller administrative units, including circuits and *hsien,* or counties. The county magistrates, numbering over 1400, were the most important administrative officers of the whole system, since they were the connecting links between the imperial government and the people. The magistrate collected taxes, registered land, served as police judge, coroner, prosecuting attorney, sheriff, jail warden, and public works commissioner.[1]

**The Civil Service.** The civil service system was one of the outstanding achievements of ancient China. Civil officials were scholar-bureaucrats, men of prestige, advanced learning, and social attainment. They received appointment on the basis of a well-developed examination system, graded for the different levels of government. In theory at least, these examinations were open to all comers, candidates without material advantages competing on equal terms with those from aristocratic families. Successful candidates commenced their services at the local level,

[1] A concise description of imperial China is given in H. M. Vinacke, *A History of the Far East in Modern Times,* ch. 1.

and advanced by examination and merit to the higher administrative positions. Thus the officialdom of imperial China was selected from among the best-educated people of the nation.

In practice, however, the civil service system had many shortcomings. Nepotism and other forms of favoritism undermined the principle of advancement by merit. But the principle weakness was that the educational standards by which scholars were trained were utterly unsuited to modern world conditions. These standards placed an exaggerated emphasis upon the past. Students were rated according to their ability to reproduce the sayings and principles found in the classical literature of China. Their outlook was narrowed to the past experience of the nation, a situation favoring stability and maintenance of the established social and political order, but one which prevented flexibility of administration and discouraged the exercise of creative talents and experimentation. Officials were not prepared to handle the complex problems arising out of new conditions of society, particularly those brought about by China's contacts with the materially advanced western civilization of the late nineteenth century.

**Geographical Factors.** The geography of China, in the past as well as in the present, exercised a strong conditioning effect upon the form of government. The Chinese people and their political institutions cannot be considered apart from their physical surroundings. In few countries is the association between land and people so close.

Territorially China is one of the largest countries in the world, totaling more than 4,000,000 square miles and exceeding by one-fifth the combined areas of the United States and Alaska. This vast area extends from the maritime provinces of Siberia on the extreme northeast to French Indochina and Burma on the south, and to Afghanistan and Russian Turkestan on the west. Within this land presently live approximately 500,000,000 people, the greater portion of whom are crowded on the plains and lowlands of the coastal and central regions.

China presents a great variety of geographical features, ranging from lofty and rugged mountains in the southwest to low-lying plains in the north, from wooded interiors to desert wastes, from cold and dry zones in the north and west to hot and humid subtropical coastal regions in the south. These geographical diversities are reflected in the people and their customs. North Chinese are tall and lanky, and customarily are believed to be taciturn and unemotional; their countrymen in the south are short and chubby, and excitable. Local differentiation is most notably demonstrated in a bewildering variety of dialects and languages. Under such conditions of territorial and physical diversity in a country in which even today transportation and communication facilities are very limited, it is understandable why a pattern of society developed in which the authority of the central government, while theoretically extensive, actually was severely restricted in practice. A high degree of local autonomy was the only practical solution to this situation under the traditional imperial system.

**The Confucian Ideal.** Confucianism, the principal philosophical system of imperial China, likewise contributed to this pattern of limited governmental authority. According to Confucian ideology, the ideal society would be achieved through the setting of the perfect model by the ruler. Thus government officials should be concerned with maintaining their leadership by example rather than by establishment of controls over the people; they should provide models of propriety in their private and public lives rather than interfere in the lives of their subjects. Confucianism thus placed strong emphasis upon the performance of ceremonial functions by the scholar-bureaucrats, and stressed tradition and convention.[2]

## GOVERNMENT OF LIMITED POWERS

Actually the government of imperial China left most phases of the people's lives untouched. It was not designed to perform many of the functions which in the western world are carried

[2] P. M. A. Linebarger, *Government in Republican China*, ch. 1.

out by government. In China these functions were performed, if performed at all, by nonpolitical institutions. China was then, as it is today, an agricultural country in which almost all of the people lived in rural villages. Within each village there were few tasks for government, since the principal needs of the people were served by the traditional social units of which the village was composed. The family (which consists of several related "families" in the western sense) formed the basic social unit, and regulated the relationships of individuals within the group. Inter-family relations were adjusted by a village council of elders, which was made up of heads of households or of a few other persons recognized for their leadership. A village headman was selected from the council. The family elders and the village council dispensed local justice and disciplined offenders. Among artisans, traders, and merchants disputes were settled and commercial practice determined by the guilds into which they were organized. The imperial government reached into the village only in the person of the county magistrate, to whom the headman transmitted taxes owed by the members of the community. The governmental system developed in China over the centuries thus was one of strict limitations upon its objectives and the extent of its operations.[3]

In summary, imperial China lacked a governmental system in the western sense. Yet it must not be concluded that the government was entirely negative in its operation. As already indicated there were significant nonpolitical devices for achieving social control. Moreover, aside from the lack of strong, central authority, there were numerous factors producing unity and homogeneity. In spite of regional differences, China possessed a remarkable degree of cultural uniformity, the product of one of the oldest and most bountiful civilizations of the world. Local habits and customs were of minor significance in comparison with the homogeneity of the Chinese people. In large measure the imperial government, and particularly its scholar-bureauc-

[3] For further discussion of this situation see D. N. Rowe, *China Among the Powers*, ch. 8.

racy, was the vehicle by which the culture of China was transmitted. The imperial government thus was the symbol and instrument of Chinese cultural unity.

## THE IMPACT OF THE WEST

The imperial system of government served China well for many centuries. Neighboring states looked to China as the center of civilization, and paid tribute to her monarchs. Although the country was invaded numerous times and its government was taken over by the invading people, these conquerors were of a lower cultural development and were eventually assimilated by the Chinese, upon whom they left little permanent imprint.

**Western Imperialism.** In the end, however, the internal stability of China was shattered by the impact of western imperialism. For several centuries the traders and missionaries of Europe had demanded the right of entry and commerce, but the officials of the reigning Manchu dynasty, convinced of the superiority of Chinese culture, refused to open the country. When the showdown came during the nineteenth century the loosely organized, conservative, decadent, and corrupt political organization of the imperial government was not equipped to withstand the superior force and organized skill of the technologically advanced western nations. For the first time in her history China faced a culture more materially advanced than her own. The existing political system was utterly incapable of organizing the country's resources to withstand the encroachments of alien forces. Governmental authority—weakened by familism and localism, hidebound by traditionalism and conservatism, spread thin over a wide and complex geographical area, and exercised by bureaucrats preoccupied with the niceties of ceremonial performances—was not suited to the problems now facing the country.

**National Humiliation.** China suffered one national humiliation after another. Internal rebellions, brought on by the pressures of the West, further weakened her. She was defeated in war by the British and French and by her neighbors the Japanese, who had adopted the methods of the West with relative ease. She was forced to accept treaties and agreements which reduced her to a semicolonial status, and to yield to the western nations the right to maintain foreign settlements and concessions in her principal cities, to maintain garrisons in her cities and gunboats on her rivers, and to try their own nationals charged with crime in China in their own courts under their own law (extraterritoriality). China lost the right to fix her tariff, and had to agree to the operation of her customs and postal services by foreign directors. Finally, the western nations carved out leased territories and spheres of interest for themselves. China was saved from complete dismemberment and loss of political sovereignty only by the balance of power among the western nations, which prevented any one nation from gaining a preponderant advantage at the expense of the others.

## THE TASKS OF REVOLUTION

China entered the twentieth century facing tremendous tasks of reorganization and reconstruction if she were to retain her integrity as a nation in the modern world in which she found herself. Each of these tasks was revolutionary in scope, involving the breaking away from established ways, the destruction of vested interests, and the exercise of positive and vigorous action on the part of an effective, modern government. In the political field she had to throw off the limitations of her old form of government. In their stead she had to establish a strong central political authority capable of undertaking the defenses of the nation against foreign aggression, instituting long over-due internal reforms, and providing the requirements of a twentieth-century state. This political system had to be organized according to the principles of popular government. Economically she had to raise herself above the primitive agricultural and handicraft level of the past and terminate the economic colonialism imposed upon her by the western powers. She had to reform her ancient agricultural system, eliminate the heavy burdens borne by the peasants, and introduce modern methods of production which would provide economic security for the toiling masses. Socially she had to adjust her ancient civilization to the impacts of an alien world, salvaging all the traditional fine qualities and adjusting them to new circumstances.

The student will note the contrast with the experience of Japan. Japan was able to bridge the gap from isolation to the modern state quickly and effectively because of the compact, well-disciplined nature of her society. But the progress of China has been discouragingly slow, and the adjustment has been extremely difficult. Lacking the characteristics and institutions which would have permitted her to organize herself quickly to meet new conditions, she has instead been going through a protracted, tedious process of disintegration and reconstruction out of which a pattern for the modern state is beginning to emerge.

## THE REVOLUTION OF 1911

The Manchu dynasty failed to resist the encroachments of foreign imperialism and to solve the economic and social problems arising from the opening of China to foreign trade. A number of able statesmen in the imperial government inaugurated a program of gradual reform during the first decade of the present century. But this movement did not ameliorate the fundamental problems besetting the nation. The weaknesses of the imperial system finally led to its downfall. Conditions were ripe for exploitation by extreme revolutionary leaders.

The revolution of October 1911, which terminated imperial authority, was brought about by the agitation of revolutionary groups under the leadership of Dr. Sun Yat-sen. These groups had been active for many years in organizing insurrection against the government. The revolution itself was a series of rebellions of provincial troops and officials, directed in large measure by the revolutionists. Representatives of the revolting provinces met in a national convention in Nanking and named Sun Yat-sen the first president of a new provisional republican government. Dr. Sun had been traveling abroad in behalf of the revolutionary movement at the time of the successful break, and he returned to China for his inaugural on January 1, 1912.

The revolutionists, however, were not strong enough to assume political control of the whole nation. In Peking the imperial court finally abdicated its authority, but it first placed dictatorial powers in the hands of one of its trusted officials, General Yuan Shih-kai. The troops under General Yuan's command were superior in military strength to the revolutionary armies. Neither the revolutionists nor General Yuan, however, possessed the financial and material resources to continue civil war. Consequently a compromise was worked out. General Yuan accepted the Republic, while Dr. Sun resigned the provisional presidency to which he had been elected. General Yuan then succeeded him as president of the Republic. But within a short time General Yuan ousted Sun Yat-sen and the revolutionists from the Peking government and established an even more dictatorial regime than the monarchy which had preceded it. In the summer of 1913 the revolutionary movement was driven underground after an abortive attempt to gain control by the use of force against General Yuan.

## The War Lords, 1912–28

The Revolution of 1911 brought an end to the decadent Manchu dynasty but it did not provide the internal stability and national strength which China desperately needed. On the contrary, the years from 1912 to 1928 were filled with civil war, economic dislocation, and continued national humiliation. The country was far from ready for the representative democratic government which the revolutionists had hoped to establish, and in many respects the four-year rule of Yuan Shih-kai differed little from what had gone before. The provinces retained a large measure of autonomy, including control of their own provincial troops. By building up these troops and by retaining provincial revenues, the governors were able to challenge the authority of the Peking government when they had a mind to, and to run their own affairs pretty much as they pleased.

**Provincial War Lords.** The regime of General Yuan Shih-kai was terminated in 1916 by his death. In the years which followed, the national government in Peking exercised little control over the nation, and civil war engulfed much of the land. Political authority rested in the hands of the autonomous provincial war lords. The power and influence of each of these war lords varied with the military strength and financial resources at his disposal. Certain war lords banded together and secured control of the national government, profiting by the revenues available to that government. But this coalition was unstable, and was succeeded by others in rapid succession. As a consequence the national government was controlled successively by different cliques of provincial military leaders. At the same time provincial leaders continued to make war on each other and upon whatever clique happened to control the national government.

During these years China continued to suffer national disgrace. There was no central authority capable of providing internal order and external security. Economic and social reforms were impossible under such conditions. It was during this period, moreover, that Japan took advantage of the chaotic nature of Chinese affairs to further her own selfish interests. She pressed upon China the notorious Twenty One Demands, extending her economic grip upon the rich areas of Manchuria.

## SPREAD OF NATIONAL REVOLUTION

Although warlordism and civil strife drained the resources of the country, the spirit of national revolution continued to swell. Intellectuals and students, particularly those who had studied abroad or in western-supported educational institutions in China, were aroused by western democratic thought and by Russian communism. Militant student and labor groups demonstrated against officials who yielded to Japanese demands, and appealed for the termination of the unequal treaties and of other forms of foreign intervention in Chinese affairs.

**Assistance of the Soviet Union.** In the early 1920's the Nationalist movement centered in the southern city of Canton, where Sun Yat-sen and his revolutionary party, the *Kuomintang* (literally National People's Party), secured control of the provincial government. In 1923 the movement gained new vigor with the acceptance of aid from the Soviet Union. Under the direction of the able Soviet agent, Michael Borodin, the Kuomintang, which had hitherto consisted largely of intellectuals bound together by personal loyalty to Dr. Sun, was reorganized on a broader basis to provide a more effective appeal to peasants and workers. Members of the relatively small Chinese Communist party were admitted to membership in the Kuomintang, which thereby benefited considerably from their advanced organizing abilities.

## THE "THREE PRINCIPLES OF THE PEOPLE"

**Nationalism.** The political teachings of Sun Yat-sen (particularly the *San Min Chu I*, or Three Principles of the People) now became the accepted doctrine of the Nationalist revolutionary cause, and provided the material for extremely effective appeals for wide popular support. Dr. Sun's Three Principles were nationalism, popular sovereignty, and economic security. First of all, he declared, China's salvation depended upon the development of a spirit of nationalism upon which could be constructed a strong national state, capable of throwing off the yoke of foreign political and economic domination. "If we do not earnestly promote nationalism and weld together our four hundred millions into a strong nation," Sun proclaimed to his disciples, "we face tragedy and the loss of our country and the destruction of our race." [4] He felt that the Chinese people should extend to the nation the same degree of loyalty which they already extended to the family and to the clan.

[4] *China Handbook, 1937–1943*, p. 67.

**Popular Sovereignty.** Sun Yat-sen's second principle called for government by the people. But he distinguished between the mass of the people and those of superior wisdom, vision, and foresight—the experts to whom the actual administration of the government should be entrusted. The people should exercise ultimate political control indirectly by means of the right of suffrage, the recall of officials, and the initiative and referendum.

**Economic Security.** The principle of economic security represented a recognition that China could not have progressive, modern government unless her basic economic problems were solved. Dr. Sun advocated the equalization of land holdings, the control of private capital, government encouragement of food production, and other reforms designed to alleviate the distressing poverty of the country, particularly among the agricultural population. He also demanded the end of foreign domination of China's economy.

**The Three Stages of Development.** After the Revolution of 1911 Sun Yat-sen and the other revolutionists had demanded the immediate establishment of representative democratic government. Subsequent experience demonstrated to them that the entrenched war-lord system, mass poverty, illiteracy, and lack of a substantial middle class rendered the attainment of this advanced stage of political development an extremely difficult task. Full democracy could be achieved only by progressive advancement through three stages: first, a period of military rule, during which the forces of the national revolution would achieve national unity by conquest of the war lords and other opponents of the cause; second, a period of political tutelage, in which the Kuomintang, as the party of the revolution, would have the sole authority of government; and third, a period of full democracy. Democratic government should be established first at the local level, then, as the people became more experienced, at the provincial level, and finally at the national level, with the operation of constitutional national government.

Sun Yat-sen died in 1925, before his dream of a unified, democratic China could be realized. He immediately became the symbol of the national revolution and his teachings the official credo of the cause. In a certain sense Sun Yat-sen in death has been utilized by the Kuomintang in much the same way that the Japanese militarists employed the emperor as a device to cultivate inner discipline and intense, unquestioned loyalty to the authority of government, government in China meaning the authority of the Kuomintang.

### POLITICAL REORGANIZATION OF THE KUOMINTANG

During the Canton period the Kuomintang became a highly organized and effective instrument of propaganda and revolution. The Kuomintang was revolutionary not only in its theoretical objectives but in its methods of operation. It was dedicated to the achievement of its aims by forceful overthrow of the war lords and other elements standing in the way of progress and change. It accepted the aid of the Soviet Union and admitted Chinese Communists to its ranks. It spread revolutionary doctrines, particularly among students, organized peasant and labor unions, and attacked the interests of foreign powers in China. These political activities aroused a new national consciousness and a new feeling of common unity and interest among the inarticulate masses. The middle 1920's were marked by political upheaval, widespread strikes among urban workers, stirrings among the peasants, and bitter demonstrations against foreign controls, all of which were encouraged by the Kuomintang and its Communist associates.

### MILITARY REORGANIZATION AND THE NORTHERN CAMPAIGNS

In addition to its political revitalization, the Kuomintang initiated military reorganization of immediate practical significance to the success of the Nationalist movement. General Chiang Kai-shek was responsible in large measure for this achievement. Chiang, whose association with Sun Yat-sen had begun before

1911, utilized Soviet advisers in organizing the beginnings of a modern army, trained in revolutionary techniques and instilled with loyalty to himself and the Nationalist cause. The existence of this military strength placed the Nationalist revolution on a new basis. The Kuomintang was now strong enough to challenge the war lords at their own game of civil war. Accordingly, in July 1926, under the command of Chiang Kai-shek, the Canton forces commenced the famous northern campaigns to free China from the war lords and to establish the Kuomintang in the national capital. These campaigns constituted the so-called Nationalist revolution.

Within a year the Nationalist armies swept north from Canton and established themselves over all of the area south of the Yangtze valley. The campaign was rendered relatively easy by reason of the fact that the way had been well prepared by the revolutionary doctrines of the Kuomintang party. The Nationalist revolution was on its way to success.

In the meantime, however, a deep rift developed within the ranks of the revolutionists. Alarmed by strikes and peasant uprisings, and fearful of losing their leadership, Chiang Kai-shek and conservative figures within the Kuomintang struck against those leaders responsible for the revolutionary aspects of the whole nationalist movement. They ousted the Communists and their sympathizers within the party and turned to conservative provincial, landowning, and commercial interests for support. Recognizing the success of the Nationalist armies, these latter interests were in a position to offer such support. Chiang Kai-shek and his associates received valuable financial assistance from wealthy banking and merchant leaders in Shanghai which assured him control of national affairs. Instead of crushing the remaining war lords, Chiang came to terms with them. While the Kuomintang party was still pledged to the fulfillment of the revolutionary doctrines proclaimed by Sun Yat-sen, within a short time it came to represent not the forces of the revolutionary movement, but the very elements which most strongly opposed any basic alteration of the existing economic and social structures.

Subsequent developments relating to the party schism will be considered in the two chapters which follow.

**Establishment of the Nanking Government.** With the backing of wealthy, propertied interests of Shanghai and other coastal cities, General Chiang Kai-shek in 1928 established the national capital of China in Nanking, in the lower Yangtze valley. This government was soon recognized by the foreign powers, thus adding to its prestige and influence. In 1928 Peking was abandoned by its last war-lord ruler and was occupied by Chiang's troops. Shortly thereafter Chang Hsueh-liang, the war lord of Manchuria, pledged allegiance to the Kuomintang, thus extending the authority of the Nanking government to the three eastern provinces. By 1928 all China was nominally under the control of the government of Chiang Kai-shek and the Kuomintang in Nanking, the new capital of the Chinese Republic.

## CONCLUSION

The establishment of the Nanking government was a mark of considerable progress in China's troubled path toward political maturity. It represented the achievement of the objective which had been lost in the revolution of 1911, the successful creation of a government based upon revolutionary doctrines and pledged to the fulfillment of these doctrines. This new government possessed certain resources which would enable it to undertake the huge tasks which it faced. It had secured the recognition of the foreign powers, it had an effective military force and it had the support of influential business and landowning interests. But its authority still was limited, for in many provinces local political and military leaders remained virtually independent, recognizing the superiority of Nanking in theory, but accepting the orders of Nanking only when compatible with their own self-interests. Nevertheless the Nanking government offered great hope for the future. It was yet to be seen whether its leaders would remain faithful to the principles of the revolution, and would carry out much needed reforms.

## Readings

*Bibliographies*

   Gardner, Charles S., comp., *A Union List of Selected Western Books on China*, American Council of Learned Societies, Washington, 1938.

   Goodrich, L. C., and H. C. Fenn, *A Syllabus of the History of Chinese Civilization and Culture*, 2d ed., China Society of America, New York, 1934.

   Pritchard, E. H., ed., *Bulletin of Far Eastern Bibliography*, vols. 1–5, 1936–40, Washington, American Council of Learned Societies; continued in *The Far Eastern Quarterly*.

*History and Civilization*

   Cressey, George B., *China's Geographic Foundations*, New York, 1934. This is a standard reference work.

   Buck, Pearl, *The Good Earth*, New York, 1931. This Nobel prize winning novel is highly recommended as an introduction to the study of contemporary China.

   Goodrich, L. Carrington, *A Short History of the Chinese People*, New York, 1943. This is one of the most readable, most compact, and most authoritiative general histories available in English.

   Holcombe, Arthur N., *The Chinese Revolution*, Harvard University Press, 1930. For a concise account of the rise of the nationalist movement this small book is particularly valuable.

   Lattimore, Owen and Eleanor H., *The Making of Modern China*, New York, 1944. This short but lucid introductory history of China is recommended for a beginner in Chinese studies.

   Latourette, Kenneth S., *The Chinese, Their History and Culture*, 6th ed., rev., New York, 1946. This is a good, general history.

   Lin Yutang, *My Country and My People*, rev. ed., New York, 1939. Lin Yutang's interpretation of his own people has become a classic.

   MacNair, Harley F., *China in Revolution*, University of Chicago Press, 1930. This is an excellent brief treatment of the nationalist revolution.

   ———, ed., *China*, University of California Press, Berkeley and Los Angeles, 1946. This recent symposium contains contributions by recognized authorities on Chinese historical and political development, philosophy and religion, the arts, literature and education, and economics and reconstruction.

Pott, W. S. A., *Chinese Political Philosophy*, New York, 1925. This essay provides a concise interpretation of the doctrines underlying Chinese political organization.

Linebarger, Paul M. A., *The Political Doctrines of Sun Yat-sen*, Johns Hopkins Press, 1937. This is a scholarly analysis.

Linebarger, Paul M. W., *Sun Yat-sen and the Chinese Republic*, New York, 1925. This authorized biography was written too early for an objective interpretation of the great nationalist leader.

Sharman, Lyon, *Sun Yat-sen: His Life and Its Meaning*, New York, 1934. This is the most critical but at the same time the least biased of the biographies available.

Sun Yat-sen, *San Min Chu I: The Three Principles of the People*, translated by Frank W. Price, New York, 1943. The famous lectures of the Nationalist leader are available in English in a standard translation, first published in Shanghai in 1927.

*Handbook*

Chinese Ministry of Information, *China Handbook, 1937–1943, A Comprehensive Survey of Major Developments in China in Six Years of War*, New York, 1943. Although adhering strictly to the official position on all matters, this government publication is valuable for its wealth of factual information.

# CHAPTER 28

# POLITICAL DEVELOPMENTS AND
# WAR WITH JAPAN

WITH the establishment in 1928 of the Nanking government, most frequently referred to as the National government, China had an opportunity to go ahead with plans for the reorganization of the governmental structure and for the institution of economic and social reforms. In large measure the opportunity was destroyed by dislocations of civil war and foreign aggression. Yet in the years between the establishment of the capital at Nanking and the termination of the war with Japan in 1945 considerable progress was made. A pattern of government and administration was developed which well may form the foundation for future constitutional reforms. This chapter considers that pattern of government, and also the principal political issues and developments which occupied these seventeen years.

## THE STRUCTURE OF GOVERNMENT

The structure of government in Kuomintang China was erected by Chiang Kai-shek and his associates in the years following the removal of the capital to Nanking. It is derived from a combination of traditional experience and contemporary political doctrines, many of them emanating from the teachings of Sun Yat-sen. It will be recalled that Dr. Sun taught that China should progress from military rule to political tutelage and thence to popular government. Upon the occupation of Peking and the establishment of the new government in Nanking, the leaders of the Kuomintang declared that the period of military rule was terminated. China then entered the period of political tutelage, the second stage of national progress envisaged by Sun Yat-sen.

The practical implications of the doctrine of political tutelage must be kept clearly in mind in proceeding with an analysis of the political structure of modern China. According to this doctrine the Kuomintang has exclusive responsibility and authority for the government of the Chinese people. This arrangement is to exist until such time as the people are capable of wider participation in political affairs, a time to be determined presumably by the Kuomintang itself. The legal basis of this situation was proclaimed by the party in various organic laws dating back to 1925, and in a provisional constitution of 1931. Thus the Kuomintang not only is China's sole legal political party, but also it is the actual government of China. The party runs the affairs of the nation, while the formal organs of government merely provide the administrative machinery through which policies are put into operation.

The student should note the use of certain terms relating to government in China. The terms National government and Central government, as frequently used, refer to the Kuomintang and the formal organs of government together in the collective sense, to distinguish them from the government of Communist China. But the term National government also is applied in the narrow sense to the formal organs of government alone, to distinguish them from the party machinery of the Kuomintang. In the discussion of the structure of government which follows, the party machinery will be considered first.

**Organization of the Kuomintang.** The membership of the Kuomintang totals no more than several million in a nation of approximately 500,000,000 persons. Control within the party is firmly held by a small group which dominates the principal party organs. In theory the highest organ of the Kuomintang is the Party Congress. This body assembles at infrequent intervals, usually once every two or three years. Consequently the real power of the party rests in the Central Executive Committee, a group of 120 members, which meets in plenary session at least once every six months. The Standing Committee of the Central

Executive Committee is composed of fifteen members, all high party figures. It is in continuous session and is the seat of all party authority. The members of the Central Executive Committee are elected by the Party Congress, but since the Congress is dominated by the Committee, the latter is virtually a self-perpetuating group. A Central Supervisory Committee, also elected by the Congress, is charged with the responsibility of inspecting and checking party affairs, but in practice it has had little independence and has not been effective.

**Supreme National Defense Council.** The principal political organ of China is the Supreme National Defense Council,[1] a fairly small group of the highest Kuomintang and military leaders and administrative officials. The Supreme National Defense Council was established after the outbreak of war with Japan. It replaced a peacetime agency of the Kuomintang known as the Central Political Committee, the powers of which were similar but not so extensive. The Supreme National Defense Council translates the general policies of the party into direct action. Its powers are very broad. It initiates government policies, determines the basic principles of legislation and finance, formulates important plans concerning military affairs, and appoints high administrative officials. The Supreme Council possesses wide emergency powers, enabling it to issue orders to other departments of the Kuomintang and to subordinate departments of the government. In other words, it is the highest directing agency.

In addition to retaining within its own structure the highest political organs of the state, the Kuomintang also engages in numerous functions which are governmental in nature. If it were not for the one-party nature of Chinese politics, these functions would be performed by the government rather than by a political party. The Central Training Institute, which operates under the direct supervision of the Central Executive Committee, for example, conducts the training of party workers and of teachers in

[1] In preparation for the operation of the new constitution the Central Executive Committee of the Kuomintang voted in March 1947 to abolish the Supreme National Defense Council and to transfer its functions to an enlarged Council of State (page 397).

all political, military, economic, and educational organs of the country. According to an official party statement, the Committee places special emphasis upon "thought training." [2] Since the party has a monopoly of government, the Central Training Institute is strategically placed, for it is concerned with the training of government officials as well as loyal party leaders, and the program which it conducts follows strict party lines. Another party organization of extraparty significance is the Ministry of Information, a propaganda organ. In a country where broad powers of censorship are exercised by government, this board determines not only what the people shall hear and be permitted to say, but also what the outside world shall learn through official channels. Here again, it is important to notice that the function of publicity and censorship is directed by a party organ, and that administrative officials within the government merely carry out the orders of the party.

**Territorial Organization.** Below this top level of national agencies, the Kuomintang is highly organized vertically, reflecting the early Soviet influence. Within the province, county, district and subdistrict there are congresses, executive committees, and standing committees corresponding to their national counterparts. In theory the National Party Congress represents these local units under a system whereby the congress of each unit selects delegates to the next highest level. Actually, the local units are very largely dominated by the national leadership of the party, just as the National Party Congress is dominated by the relatively few members of the Central Executive Committee and its Standing Committee. Policies determined by national headquarters are enforced through local party officials and through the use of all of the party's resources, including appointment to public office, disbursement of supplies and services, and the operation of the party's weapons of propaganda and censorship. Thus the Kuomintang is a highly centralized organization, pyramiding from many small local units to national headquarters at the top, but effectively dominated and controlled by that headquarters.

[2] *China Handbook,* 1937–1943, p. 47.

## THE NATIONAL GOVERNMENT

**Military Affairs Commission.** The administrative machinery of government, called the National government, operates under the control and supervision of the Kuomintang. The National government functions through a Military Affairs Commission and five *yuan* (departments). The Military Affairs Commission is charged with the administration of the nation's military forces, including operations, training, supplies, and transport. The Ministry of War is under its jurisdiction. The Military Affairs Commission has branched out into other fields, such as propaganda, social work, education, and certain economic matters relating to national defense. This situation makes it of political as well as military significance, interposing an obstacle in the way of civil administration of these affairs. Its membership is designated by the Supreme National Defense Council, to which it is responsible, and consists of high officers of the armed forces.

**The Five Yuan.** The division of the National government into five yuan is based upon the teachings of Sun Yat-sen. The Executive Yuan, which is the largest and most important, is the executive arm of the government, and is composed of the heads of various ministries and commissions, such as Foreign Affairs, Finance, Education, and Communications. It has authority over bills submitted to the Legislative Yuan, the budget, declarations of war and peace, the appointment of administrative and judicial personnel, and other executive matters. The Executive Yuan takes orders from the Central Executive Committee of the Kuomintang, which selects its president and members, and from the Supreme National Defense Council. Upon occasion the president, or chairman, of the Executive Yuan is referred to as the prime minister of China. While this official is chief among the various ministers of the Executive Yuan and may be an influential figure by reason of his position in the party, he is not, as head of this organ, the principal official of government.

The other four yuan have not attained significant proportions. The Legislative Yuan is not a legislative body in the accepted sense, but largely a bill-drafting agency with no independent authority. The Judicial Yuan supervises the Ministry of Justice and the national courts. The Examination Yuan corresponds to the United States Civil Service Commission, but in practice has very limited authority, since the recruitment, training, and placing of administrative personnel remains largely a party matter. The Control Yuan, derived from past Chinese practice whereby independent officials made reports on the activities of the civil bureaucracy, is responsible for the impeachment of officials and the auditing of records and accounts. As in the case of the Examination Yuan, its operations are limited so long as the Kuomintang retains its monopoly of the National government.

**Generalissimo Chiang Kai-shek.** The Kuomintang and National government cannot be understood apart from the personality of Generalissimo Chiang Kai-shek. In the scope of his authority Chiang possesses dictatorial powers. He holds or has held at one and the same time all of the important positions in the party and the government, including chairman of the Central Executive Committee, president of the Supreme National Defense Council, president of the Military Affairs Commission, president of the Executive Yuan, and commander in chief of the armed forces. In 1938 he was honored with the director-generalship of the Kuomintang, a position of broad personal power which had not been filled since the death of Sun Yat-sen thirteen years before. Following the death of the venerable President Lin Sen in 1943, the Central Executive Committee elected Chiang president of the National government for a three-year term, re-electing him again in 1946. Whereas the presidency of China had been a mere formal position similar to the presidency of the French Republic, it then was endowed with wide powers.

**Council of State.** The National government is given a certain degree of administrative unity by the Council of State. This organ, directly under the President, possesses formal rather than administrative authority. It is composed of high administrative officials, and serves as a channel through which instructions from the Supreme National Defense Council are transmitted to the National government for action.[3]

**People's Political Council.** China has no representative political organ of government. In 1938, after the outbreak of war with Japan, the People's Political Council was created through action of the Kuomintang, to provide for the expression of views on matters of national concern. Although the Kuomintang exercises effective control over the selection of the members, nonparty members are included, and the Council has produced some outspoken criticism of the government. But it has only advisory powers and it has not instituted any significant political, military, or economic measures.

**Local Government and Courts.** The province, hsien (county), and village remain the basic units of government as under the imperial system, and within them the old tradition of regional and local autonomy lingers. The village retains much of its ancient character and organization. The trend, however, has been toward national centralization of local government. Before the outbreak of war in 1937 the National government at Nanking gradually extended its influence over the provinces, several in the lower Yangtze valley being ruled directly, while others followed national directives at least in form. After the removal of the capital to Chungking with the coming of the war, the strategic interior provinces of Szechwan and Yunnan were brought under the direct control of the central authorities. The complete plan of the Kuomintang for local reform, which is only partially in operation, would establish a pattern similar to that found in Japan, in which the provinces and lesser units serve as administrative units of the central government. There would be a popular assembly of limited power at each level of government.

The judiciary is the least developed branch of government in China. Most disputes are settled still by extragovernmental means, such as the family and the guild. In the smaller hsien the magistrate serves as judicial officer, sometimes with the

[3] See footnote 1, page 394.

assistance of a judge; in the larger hsien there is a separate court. Progress in the reorganization of a national judicial system, composed of district courts, provincial high courts, and a national Supreme Court, was retarded by war.

## PROGRESS UNDER THE NANKING GOVERNMENT, 1928–37

Although the National government at Nanking resembled its predecessors in many respects, its establishment in 1928 was an extremely important advance in the political reconstruction of China. Generalissimo Chiang Kai-shek, its leader, was primarily a militarist, whose influence depended upon the troops at his command. In order to win and maintain wider support, Chiang found it necessary to bargain and compromise with provincial war lords, who thus were able to retain command of their own troops and to maintain a considerable degree of autonomy in their own areas. Chiang's acceptance of the financial backing of the Shanghai bankers made it certain that the government would proceed toward reform conservatively and cautiously. But in other significant features Nanking marked a striking departure from the past. The armies of Generalissimo Chiang owed allegiance not to a provincial war lord, but to the nation itself. In addition to its strong military character, the government gathered about it an increasingly competent group of civil officials and administrators, many of them foreign-educated. It secured a wide following among small merchants, landowners, local gentry, intellectuals, overseas Chinese, and the politically active student class.

**Progress and Achievement.** For the first time in its modern history China had a government with the foresight, leadership, and administrative ability to undertake the reforms which the country so desperately needed. Within the short space of ten years, from the end of the northern campaigns to the outbreak of war with Japan in 1937, substantial progress was made in training and equipping a national army, extending railways, highways, and air transportation, and providing the beginnings of modern health and educational facilities. A national banking and currency system was set up successfully. Under the personal direction of Chiang Kai-shek the New Life Movement indoctrinated the people with a sense of social and political morality, opening up new horizons of national strength and unity. The foreign powers recognized the progress being made in China by making loans for economic reconstruction, granting tariff autonomy, and promising to end extraterritoriality and other treaty privileges.

**Agrarian Problem.** It must not be overlooked, however, that the National government accomplished very little toward the alleviation of China's chronic economic problem—the destitution of her farmers, who comprise almost three-quarters of the working population. Although a few improvements were instituted with the aid of League of Nations experts, little actually was done to provide relief from the high rents, burdensome taxes, and usurious interest rates which bind the peasant to eternal poverty. In large part this failure was dictated by the simple fact that the government depended for support upon the people who had the greatest interest in the continuation of the status quo, namely, provincial and local officials, landlords, bankers, and local gentry. It will be recognized that the whole character of the Kuomintang changed from that of its earlier revolutionary outlook. The activities and methods of the conservative leadership which dominated the party machinery after 1928 indicated that its greatest concern was the maintenance of its own entrenched position. Two specific examples might be cited as illustrations of this condition. The Kuomintang established a secret police organization similar to the notorious thought control police of Japan. This organization employed brutality and star-chamber methods against critics of the party. Likewise the party set up the so-called San Min Chu I Youth Corps along the lines of the youth programs of totalitarian Germany and Italy. The Corps operated in the sole interests of the party, as a device to combat liberal tendencies among the youth of the nation.

The failure of the National government to inaugurate effective internal reforms was the consequence also of military considerations. The government devoted most of its energy and resources to the development of its military strength. Nanking was at no time secure against the threat of civil war, and, of greater significance, it lived in the broadening shadow of Japanese aggression. In 1931 Japan conquered Manchuria and in succeeding years prior to the renewal of armed hostilities in 1937, she extended her domination over large portions of North China by intimidating and controlling local officials. Japan made clear her intention to establish hegemony throughout the rest of China at the earliest opportunity.[4]

## THE CHINESE COMMUNISTS

How the Kuomintang accepted the support of the Soviet Union and admitted the small Communist party of China into membership in the Kuomintang was told in Chapter 27. This policy contributed much to the preparations for and the success of the northern campaigns in 1926 and 1927. Chiang Kai-shek, it will be remembered, subsequently shifted his political ground, accepting the support of conservative interests centered in Shanghai, and drove the Communists and other leftist elements from the party and the government. The failure of Nanking to solve the agricultural problem in the following years opened the way for the Communists to reorganize their activities among peasants and workers and to challenge effectively the authority of the Kuomintang. Between 1927 and 1931 the Communists built up the famous Red army out of deserters from the Nationalist troops and partisan bands, and established a soviet type of government in the southeast provinces of Hunan and Kiangsi. Within the area under their control they instituted a program of land distribution, under which large holdings were expropriated and divided among poorer peasants. They employed mass education and other forms of political indoctrination to secure wide popular following among the poverty-stricken masses. By the employment of guerrilla tactics, the Red army time and again

[4] See T. A. Bisson, *Japan in China*, chs. 1–4.

turned back attempts by the Nationalist forces to wipe out the Communists.

The troops of Generalissimo Chiang Kai-shek never were able to subjugate the soviet area. But in 1934, after mobilizing nearly 1,000,000 men and employing his new foreign-trained air force, Chiang finally forced the Red army to abandon its base in the south and to retreat in the famous "Long March" across the great expanse of China to the relatively poor northwest province of Shensi. Here a new soviet government was established.[5]

**The United Front.** The anti-Communist campaigns of the government were unpopular with many Chinese, who felt that the government should subordinate its differences with this group of fellow Chinese in order to lead a united resistance against the rising menace of Japan. During 1935 and 1936 students and other liberal groups organized public demonstrations in the principal cities of the nation against the the government's policy of compromise. Many of these demonstrations were ruthlessly suppressed by the police under the orders of Nanking. The movement nevertheless reached nation-wide proportions and affected the troops which had been sent against the Communists in the northwest. The Communists themselves appealed to the Kuomintang to end the civil war and take up resistance against Japan. Reflecting the united front tactics which at that time motivated the actions of leftist groups in other countries, the Communists revealed a willingness to suspend land expropriation and other extreme features of their reform program in order to join forces with the Kuomintang against the common enemy, Japan. Finally a compromise was worked out, but not until after Chiang Kai-shek was kidnaped and held captive at Sian, in December 1936, by officers of the troops which had been ordered by him to eliminate the Red army. During the crucial two weeks in which he was a prisoner, Chiang finally was persuaded by these officers to accept a united front. Thus, on the eve of war with Japan and largely as a direct result of

[5] See Edgar Snow, *Red Star over China,* for a description of the Long March and other Communist developments.

the threat of that war, internal unity was at last achieved in China.[6]

## CHINA AT WAR, 1937–45

Japan renewed open warfare in July 1937. In a little more than a year China lost her principal cities, almost all of her railways, most of what little industry she had, and large sections of her territory. The National government fled from Nanking to Hankow, and finally to Chungking, far in the interior.

China's continued resistance throughout the eight years of war and suffering provided convincing evidence of the political progress of the country and of the rising spirit of nationalism— the first of Sun Yat-sen's principles. The people and their leaders remained united against the enemy and scorned his peace overtures. Only one leader of national prominence, Wang Ching-wei, a former close associate of Sun Yat-sen and Chiang Kai-shek, went over to the Japanese. Wang headed the puppet government established by the Japanese in Nanking. Further recognition of China's achievements and of her role as an ally was accorded by the United States and the other United Nations when extraterritoriality and other special rights were given up in 1943.

**Political Disunity.** But although the Chinese were united in resistance against the foreign invader, they were unable to maintain the political united front which had been forged on the eve of the war. During the first two years of war the Kuomintang and Communists subordinated their political differences to the bigger job of fighting the enemy. But after the war bogged down into a stalemate, repeated contentions seethed under the surface of common unity. In spite of outward acceptance of the authority of the National government, the Communists continued to maintain an autonomous government and an independent army in the northwest. The Kuomintang, on the other hand, did not

[6] Documents relating to the creation of the United Front will be found in L. K. Rosinger, *China's Wartime Politics, 1937–1944,* pp. 94–103.

institute any substantial political and economic reforms nor did it allocate arms and other resources to the Red army, which carried a heavy share of the fighting against the Japanese. On numerous occasions armed hostilities occurred between National and Communist troops. Moreover, the political differences were not limited to those between the Kuomintang and the Communists. Moderate groups became increasingly dissatisfied with Kuomintang leadership during the war years, including some within the Kuomintang itself. These elements were alienated by the suppression of civil liberties, rigid control of popular expression of political views, and other authoritarian measures practised by the Kuomintang leaders, as well as by inept and corrupt political and military administration.

## Is China a Dictatorship?

This summary description reveals that the government of Kuomintang China has exhibited many features of an authoritarian dictatorship. Control of the government has been retained by a single party which has tolerated no opposition and which itself has been dominated by a relatively small ruling oligarchy. This oligarchy has represented the interests of national and provincial militarists, bureaucrats, and wealthy commercial and landowning classes. It has provided no effective means for representatives of the mass of the people to have their say and to participate in public affairs. To ensure its position this oligarchy, moreover, has employed censorship, propaganda, privilege, and even terrorism.

The question naturally arises whether this government should be called a dictatorship, in view of these conditions. In the sense that it has been government by a narrow ruthless oligarchy, motivated in large measure by its own self-interest, tolerating no opposition, and utilizing all the resources at its disposal to suppress such opposition, the rule of Generalissimo Chiang Kai-shek clearly has been a dictatorship. As such it has been operating in direct contradiction to Sun Yat-sen's advocacy of popular government, however appealingly party leaders may have rationalized their position by claims that popular government can not be instituted before the people of China are ready for it.

In a more practical sense, however, the government of Kuomintang China has not been a dictatorship. A dictatorship, strictly speaking, is a government which can apply its authority at will. Chiang's government has not been able to do this; its authority has not been unlimited. On the contrary, many phases of Chinese life have remained beyond the reach of government, as they did under the empire. And in many provinces, aside from those within the orbit of Communist influence, the Kuomintang has had to bargain with strong provincial military and political figures, who have retained much local autonomy. It is not that the Kuomintang has not wished to exercise absolute authority in all matters; it is simply that it has not possessed the ability to do so. Its power has been spread thin over the vast geographical expanse of China. The party and its National government are still without the administrative machinery and the technical resources of a modern state. China remains for the most part a primitive agricultural nation in which most of the people dwell in small rural villages. In these villages, as already indicated, much of the ancient pattern of life remains.

## CONCLUSION

As the war with Japan drew to a close, China still faced tremendous tasks of political, economic and social reconstruction. The political unity of the early years of the war was largely shattered, with only the continued presence of the invader on Chinese soil preventing civil war from breaking forth in renewed fury. Still remaining was the job of broadening the base of government to permit greater participation by the people in public affairs, and of creating effective administrative services capable of mobilizing the full resources of the nation and undertaking long overdue reforms. The suffering and destitution of war left a heavy mark upon the Chinese people. The liberation of the country from the Japanese would free the land from the invader and would offer the opportunity of renewed progress toward the accomplishment of the heavy tasks of revolution. Would China be able to take advantage of this opportunity, or would she lapse into the protracted agony of civil war?

### READINGS

*The Structure of Government*

Linebarger, Paul M. A., *Government in Republican China,* New York, 1938. This scholarly study is recommended particularly for its emphasis upon the doctrines underlying political development and organization.

―――――――――, *The China of Chiang Kai-shek, A Political Study,* World Peace Foundation, Boston, 1941. This is the most comprehensive discussion of the governmental system of China available in English.

*Political Development*

Bisson, T. A., *Japan in China,* New York, 1938. In the course of tracing Japanese aggression in China, this valuable book considers internal political developments in China.

Carlson, Evans F., *The Chinese Army,* Institute of Pacific Relations, New York, 1940. The short analysis of the organization of the Chinese army is well done. The book also contains an interesting account of techniques of resistance developed by the Chinese, written by a Chinese author.

―――――――――, *Twin Stars over China,* New York, 1940. This is the story of the famous marine raider's experiences with the Chinese guerrilla forces.

Chiang, May-ling Soong, *China Shall Rise Again,* New York, 1940. The vitality and optimism of China's "First Lady" are reflected in this collection of wartime articles and speeches.

Hu Shih, *The Chinese Renaissance,* University of Chicago Press, 1934. The spirit of revolutionary China is caught in this little book by one of its intellectual leaders.

Institute of Pacific Relations, comp., *Agrarian China, Selected Source Materials from Chinese Authors,* University of Chicago Press, 1938. This is an excellent reference work.

Quigley, Harold S., "China Today," *International Conciliation*, no. 404, October 1944, pp. 591–626. For a concise summary of contemporary political, economic, and social trends this pamphlet is excellent.

Snow, Edgar, *Red Star over China*, New York, 1938. This highly readable account of the story of Chinese communism has become a classic of American journalism.

Tawney, R. H., *Land and Labor in China*, London, 1932. This is a balanced and comprehensive discussion of modern economic and social problems.

Taylor, George E., *The Struggle for North China*, Institute of Pacific Relations, New York, 1940. This is an excellent account by a competent observer of the political, economic, and social aspects of Chinese resistance behind Japanese lines.

*Chiang Kai-shek*

Berkov, Robert, *Strong Man of China, The Story of Chiang Kai-shek*, Boston, 1938. This is a reasonably objective biography of Chiang, covering his prewar career.

Chiang Kai-shek, *The Collected Wartime Messages of Generalissimo Chiang Kai-shek, 1937–1945,* compiled by the Chinese Ministry of Information, New York, 1946.

———, *China's Destiny*. Two editions of this controversial book now are available in English. The translation authorized by the Chinese Ministry of Information was published by Macmillan, an unauthorized translation by Roy, both in 1947.

Tong, Hollington K., *Chiang Kai-shek*, 2 vols., Shanghai, 1937, This is the authorized biography, by an official of the government information service.

# CHAPTER 29

# THE ELEMENTS OF CIVIL CONFLICT

THE liberation of Chinese territory from the yoke of the Japanese invader might have offered China a glorious opportunity to advance toward the goals of the revolution. These are the goals proclaimed by Sun Yat-sen and accepted by all political groups—the goals of national unity, popular government, and economic security.

**Renewal of Civil Conflict.** But instead of bringing the objectives for which the Chinese people have suffered and for which they yearn, Japan's surrender in August 1945 plunged China once again into bitter civil strife. The reasons for this fratricidal conflict are complex, and information coming from all sources in China has been highly colored by censorship and bias. Consequently a fair and complete interpretation of the troubled events and contentious issues cannot be given until impartial reports are available and more of the facts are known. Yet the student can understand the basic elements in this struggle if he will examine the composition and outlook of each of the groups and factions which strive to influence and control Chinese national affairs. The Kuomintang and the Communists, the principal groups, already have been discussed in previous chapters. Within the Kuomintang there are distinct factions, and between the two extremes of Kuomintang and Communist party there are numerous liberals and moderates, who reject the authoritarian practices of the parties to their right and left.

## COMPOSITION OF THE KUOMINTANG

The Kuomintang is composed of many factions, each with its own interests and attitudes, yet for the most part closely associated in the final formulation of party policies and programs. The Kuomintang, of course, is not to be considered similar to a national party in the United States. Unlike the American party, it is highly centralized in its organization, open to an extremely small fraction of the total national population, and dominated from the top down by a relatively small ruling hierarchy. It has no concern with "getting out the vote," and all that that phenomenon implies in American politics. But in respect to the assortment of intraparty factions and individual personal leaders which make up the whole party, the Kuomintang does resemble an American party. It takes many pieces to make up the whole patchwork of the American party, including prominent individuals with personal followings, city and state machines, affiliated business, labor and farm interests, public office seekers, rank and file party members, and also, in varying degrees, independent voters. The Kuomintang likewise is composed of diverse and separate elements, including professional politicans, military figures, administrative officials, bankers, commercial leaders, landowners, local gentry, intellectuals, students, and overseas Chinese. At times these elements appear to be strange political bedfellows. All of these elements officially are pledged to the program of Sun Yat-sen. Actually they accept fundamentally different interpretations of that program.[1]

**Chen Clique.** One of the most influential factions within the party is that which is headed by the Chen brothers, Chen Li-fu and Chen Kuo-fu, and which is sometimes referred to as the "CC Clique." These men have been closely associated with control of the Kuomintang since before the death of Sun Yat-sen, and they reputedly are held in high esteem by Generalissimo Chiang Kai-shek. Chen Kuo-fu for many years has been a key officer on the Generalissimo's personal staff and was until 1944 minister of organization of the Kuomintang, a post which he relinquished to Chen Li-fu at that time. Previously Chen Li-fu long had served as minister of education and as director of the

[1] For discussion of the composition of the Kuomintang see T. H. White and A. Jacoby, *Thunder Out of China*, ch. 7.

all-important Central Training Institute. The strength of the Chen clique, aside from its close association with Chiang Kai-shek, lies in its control of party machinery and patronage, its influence within the party and government bureaucracy, and its use of the party secret police.

The Chen clique is extremely nationalistic, antiliberal, and antiwestern in outlook. Its members have been responsible, for example, for rigid control of thought and ruthless suppression of liberal tendencies among teachers and students in China's schools and colleges. The Chen clique is preoccupied with the maintenance by the party of its monopolistic control of the government and is unyielding in its bitter opposition to the liberalization of the party organization, or the broadening of control of national affairs to permit participation by non-Kuomintang parties. It has been responsible, accordingly, for suppression of criticism of the party leadership, denial of civil liberties, and the employment of the nation's educational system to project a jingoistic, antiforeign nationalism. Theodore White, a competent observer of Chinese affairs, characterizes the Chen group as "a corrupt political clique that combines some of the worst features of Tammany Hall and the Spanish Inquisition." [2]

**The Military.** A second faction within the Kuomintang, likewise possessing considerable influence, is the military group. In a nation which has experienced over thirty years of civil and foreign war, militarism remains a principal source of political power. Since the rise of the nationalist revolution in the middle 1920's, the exercise of military power has been one of the Kuomintang's principal methods of operation. Leading military figures rank high in party councils, and lesser members of the armed forces have been tied in closely with the party machinery. At times the party has assigned organizers to field units, following a practice employed in the Soviet Union.

The militarists are divided into two groups, the military bureaucracy headed by General Ho Ying-chin, and the so-called Whampoa clique. General Ho is the most influential militarist,

[2] T. H. White, " '*Life*' Looks at China," *Life*, May 1, 1944.

aside from Generalissimo Chiang Kai-shek himself, and with the Generalissimo and Chen Li-fu is one of the three most powerful men in China. For fourteen years, until 1944, he was minister of war. For a short time he represented his government on the Military Staff Commission of the United Nations, but early in 1947 he returned to China to participate in the civil war against the Communists. General Ho is the recognized leader among the old-line military administrators, men who adhere to strict party discipline and who oppose bitterly compromises with the Communists and other non-Kuomintang groups. They support the party dictatorship, the suppression of liberal tendencies, and the maintenance of the economic and social status quo. Above all, they insist upon the maintenance of strong, military power under exclusive command of Kuomintang leadership. They regard the National army as the possession of the party.

The Whampoa clique takes its name from the Whampoa Military Academy, which was established under the personal direction of Generalissimo Chiang Kai-shek during the Canton period of Kuomintang reorganization. This institution trained many of the officers who commanded the Nationalist troops during the northern campaigns of 1926–28. At the conclusion of war with Japan over two thirds of all divisions of the National army of China were commanded by Whampoa officers.[3] Politically the Whampoa clique's outlook is similar to that of General Ho and the military bureaucrats. But whereas the latter are preoccupied with retaining their entrenched power, the Whampoa officers, younger and less conservative, favor the elimination of corruption and favoritism in the army, and of antiquated methods of training, organization, and combat. Prominent among such officers is General Chen Cheng, who succeeded General Ho Ying-chin as minister of war in 1944 and chief of staff in 1946. General Chen worked with American officers in the inauguration of reforms in the Chinese army. But such men are overshadowed in political affairs by the well-organized and disciplined followers of General Ho.

[3] White and Jacoby, *op. cit.*, p. 101.

**Provincial Militarists.** Provincial armies still compose a large part of the military strength of China. In varying degrees the provincial leaders who command these troops retain independent political authority, measured largely in terms of their relative military strength, much as during the years which followed the collapse of the imperial government in 1911. These provincial leaders, for the most part, recognize the supremacy of the National government and of its military command, but because of their local strength, they in turn exert considerable influence upon central politics. Some of them hold positions in the party or in the government. Their influence is, with a few exceptions, conservative and antiliberal. The continued existence of such provincial military leaders naturally constitutes a threat to national unity and to the growth of popular civil government.

**Personal Leaders.** Another principal group within the Kuomintang is made up of prominent party figures who have gained positions of leadership by reason of individual achievement and connections within the government. Each of them retains a personal following, and at times their interests run counter to each other. One such person is H. H. Kung, who is married to a sister of Madam Chiang Kai-shek. Kung has held high positions in the government, including the presidency of the Executive Yuan and the post of minister of finance, but his influence within the party rests in large measure upon his dominance in national financial affairs. Kung has exerted a conservative influence in party circles. His brother-in-law, T. V. Soong, who is well known abroad, likewise has held high financial responsibilities, but more recently has been concerned with China's diplomatic responsibilities. He is more progressive in his outlook than Kung, who frequently has been considered his political rival.

**Political Science Clique.** Still another group of individuals within the party which can be singled out for separate consideration is the so-called Political Science clique. This is a middle-of-the-road group of administrators and business men, many of whom received their education abroad. Its members, who favor the introduction of modern governmental and business methods, hold important administrative positions. But since they are chiefly interested in improving the techniques of government, their influence upon policy is limited.

**Liberal and Moderate Elements.** Liberal and moderate elements within the Kuomintang are not well organized, although they possess a courageous advocate in the person of Sun Fo, son of the founder of the party. Sun Fo has held numerous posts in the government, most recently that of president of the Legislative Yuan. As a leader among intellectuals, professional people, and civil servants, Sun has been prominent in the movement for constitutional government and broader popular participation in public affairs. During the war years he was an outspoken critic of the dictatorial practices of the right-wing Kuomintang leadership. His demands for democratization of processes within the party and for extensive civil liberties for the people stand in sharp contrast to the practices of the Chen and military factions. Large numbers of rank and file civil employees of the government share similar views. Likewise some of the middle-class elements which support the government are outraged by the reactionary, totalitarian methods of the dominant Kuomintang officials. These groups, however, are not in a position to exert influence upon the party, possessing neither military strength nor material resources.

## GENERALISSIMO CHIANG KAI-SHEK

Just as the effectiveness of an American national party is destroyed if it cannot pull together its many diverse elements under decisive central leadership, so the Kuomintang depends upon the authority and prestige of its great leader, Generalissimo Chiang Kai-shek. The Generalissimo is the undisputed leader among party factions and in the whole nation. He is first of all a military commander. As such he organized the forces which fought victoriously in the northern campaigns, and made possible the establishment of the Nanking government under Kuomintang leadership. Chiang's military power figured prominently in his dealings with provincial leaders, by which he extended Nanking authority over a broad geographical area. Likewise as a military commander, Chiang determined the strategy of stalemate which brought about the deterioration of Japan's forces during the long years of war.

But Generalissimo Chiang rapidly became much more than a military leader. After the invasion of Chinese territory by Japan, he rose to the challenge which faced him. He became not only the commander of China's forces of defense, but the symbol of resistance and of the will for national survival. Throughout the war he remained steadfastly and unhesitatingly opposed to any sort of compromise with the enemy, although at times less courageous elements in the government might have accepted terms. Clearly, in the hour of crisis, Chiang mounted above personal interest and partisan motive, assuming a positive role of national leadership. Even the Communists, against whom Chiang had directed his best troops, recognized him as the only statesman capable of uniting the nation against the aggressor. When the Generalissimo was held captive at Sian in December 1936, it was they who counseled his release.

Chiang Kai-shek thus supplies the cohesive element which binds together the divergent factions of the Kuomintang and the National government into a workable ruling group. As commander in chief he is responsible for unity of military command. But more important than this, as chief of state, he is a highly talented political leader. Skilled in the fine arts of political maneuver, he pulls together the component elements among his following in mutual self-interest. In a sense he is a creature of these component elements, for Chiang, just as a national political figure in the United States, must recognize the special interests of the organized groups upon whom he depends for support. Yet at the same time, by reason of his tremendous prestige and the intense personal loyalty which he commands, he rises above the selfish interests of any single group within the party.

Generalissimo Chiang Kai-shek's political and social views are clouded in the mystery which still surrounds his person and his activities, and are further obscured by the bias of many of the reports which have been circulated about him. Certainly he is deeply concerned with the welfare of his country and its people, a motive which transcends any thoughts of personal aggrandizement. His attitude toward government, however, is strongly flavored by traditional Chinese political philosophy and experience. Chiang's outlook accords with the ancient concept that the country should be governed by an authoritarian ruler. This ruler establishes his right to govern not by reference to the wishes of the people, but by the example of right conduct which he personally exhibits. He maintains his rule through the unquestioned loyalty of his ministers and subjects. Chiang Kai-shek is not a democrat in the western sense.[4]

## COMMUNIST CHINA

There are two Chinas, Nationalist and Communist, each with its own territory, government, and military forces. Preceding chapters have described how the small Chinese Communist party was received into a working alliance with the Kuomintang during the critical years of the national revolution, how that alliance was shattered following the establishment of the Nanking government, and how a second working arrangement again was hammered out in 1937 on the eve of war with Japan. It will be recalled, however, that the united front, while never openly denounced by either party to the agreement, nevertheless was threatened repeatedly by failures on each side to abide by its terms and by resulting armed hostilities, some of them reaching the scale of major military operations.

By the time of Japan's surrender in the summer of 1945, the Chinese Communists controlled an area in the northwest, centered in Shensi province and extending eastward behind the Japanese lines. In this area live an estimated 30,000,000 to 90,-000,000 people. Here the Communists operated their own soviet

[4] For a more critical appraisal of Chiang see White and Jacoby, *op. cit.*, ch. 8.

government, with headquarters at Yenan; instituted economic and social reforms; organized schools; issued currency; and maintained a field army of an estimated 200,000 to 500,000 troops. The Red army successfully defended this area against the Japanese throughout the war, and inflicted considerable damage upon the enemy, particularly in harassing and delaying maneuvers.

**Communist Program.** Communism in China owed its start to the inspiration and encouragement of the Soviet Union. Its leaders today are strict Marxist doctrinaires. The Soviet Union, however, has maintained a formally correct attitude toward the Chinese Communists and has extended little if any direct material aid to the Chinese party, at least according to reports made as late as the summer of 1946. Chinese Communism, in its application, has developed a remarkably indigenous character, best described as agrarian equalitarianism. Although adhering to Marxist polemics in their theoretical discussions, the Communist leaders have worked out a pragmatic program deeply rooted in Chinese needs and traditions, and tested in almost two decades of civil war and resistance to foreign aggression. They accept the basic teachings of Sun Yat-sen, but declare that China must be organized and governed in the interests of the peasantry and the working people, not for and by the wealthy landlords and money lenders, the privileged gentry, and the entrenched military and civil bureaucracy. Their program is directed toward alleviation of the hardships of the impoverished toiling masses. In the areas under their control they have divided large landholdings, reduced rentals and interest rates, and introduced limited features of mass participation in government. But like the Kuomintang, the Communist party adheres strictly to one-party rule. In its areas it tolerates no organized opposition, and employs propaganda, censorship, espionage, terrorism, and other devices to maintain its control.

**Communist Leadership.** Leadership of the Communist party rests in the hands of men who have held top positions since the split with the Kuomintang in 1927. The head of the Party is

Mao Tse-tung, party chairman. Mao became a radical at an early age and served in the Kuomintang during the revolution of the 1920's. He opposed the policies of Chiang Kai-shek even before the break in 1927, and subsequently rose quickly to become the recognized political leader of the Communist movement. Chu Teh is the military genius of the party. He joined the revolution in 1926 and served as a political officer in the Kuomintang armed forces, but with Mao Tse-tung he was driven from that party. General Chu soon became the military leader of the Red army and is credited with advancing the tactics which enabled the Communists to stand off the superior forces of the National troops during the long civil war. Chu Teh led the Red army on its famous "Long March" from Kiangsi to Shensi, and during the war with Japan directed the guerrilla resistance of the Red army's partisan bands against the invader. A third Communist leader of importance is General Chou En-lai, known abroad through his wartime role of principal liaison officer between the Communist and Kuomintang governments. Chou once served under Chiang Kai-shek in the Whampoa Military Academy, and is one of several Whampoa men who deserted their former colleagues after the shift of the Kuomintang to the right.[5]

## LIBERAL AND MODERATE ELEMENTS

The Kuomintang and the Communists are not the only political groups in China. Between the extreme right of the former and the extreme left of the latter there stands a largely unorganized body of individuals which rejects the methods of the major parties and seeks a middle-road solution of China's problems. This body is composed of many elements of varying shades of opinion. Its ranks include journalists, professors, students, lesser government officials, small businessmen, nonpartisan liberals, and a few army officers and provincial political leaders. Perhaps the most prominent figure within this group is Madam

[5] Further readings on the Communists are suggested at the end of this chapter.

Sun Ching-ling, the widow of Sun Yat-sen. Although a sister of Madame Chiang Kai-shek, Madam Sun has been outspoken in her criticism of Kuomintang policies. (Sun Fo is the son of Sun Yat-sen by an earlier marriage.)

**Intellectual and Student Movement.** The intellectual and student movement deserves special mention. Intellectual leaders and students traditionally have played an active part in Chinese public affairs. Scholarship was the foundation upon which the ancient imperial civil service was erected. In modern times intellectuals and students have had important roles in the overthrow of the Manchu dynasty, the organization of opposition to the war lords and foreign imperialism, the spread of the nationalist movement, and the maintenance of resistance against Japan. Students educated abroad have applied their talents to the problems of statecraft. Outstanding contributions have been made by such men as Hu Shih and James Y. C. Yen. The literary renaissance led by Hu Shih and the mass education and rural reconstruction movements of James Yen stimulated a large segment of the Chinese population to political thinking and active participation in political affairs. Reflecting their desire to blend the best of western and Chinese experience, China's intellectuals and students constitute a strong force for social and economic reform and the establishment of constitutional democratic government.

The obstacles standing in the path of liberals and moderates in China have been numerous and difficult. Most of these individuals, as members of the relatively small middle class, were hit severely by the runaway inflation of the war years. Many writers and professors were impelled to find employment as manual laborers in order to provide for themselves and their families, leaving little time and even less energy to engage in political activities. More serious has been the systematic campaign of repression waged by the National government and by reactionary right-wing leaders of the Kuomintang. For brief periods liberals have been granted relative freedom in expressing their views. But rigid denial of freedom of speech, of assembly, and of the press has been the general rule, and even more extreme measures, including murder, have been employed to destroy liberal criticism. These repressive measures differ from those employed by the military dictators of Japan only in degree.

**National Salvation Movement.** In spite of these obstacles the voices of the liberals and moderates have been heard, at times with considerable effect. During 1936–37 students and professors organized effective demonstrations against the Nanking government's policy of compromise and appeasement toward Japan. The National Salvation Movement, which emerged from these protests, spread rapidly to the principal cities of the country and won the support of merchants and businessmen and of a widening group of provincial leaders. The Movement was responsible in part for the stiffened attitude which the government finally adopted just prior to the renewal of armed hostilities with Japan in 1937. It likewise added impetus to the final establishment of the united front at that time.

**Democratic League.** During the war years liberal and moderate elements continued to agitate for political and economic reforms. Although much of the leadership was provided by separate individuals, a number of small extralegal parties sought to influence government policy. In 1941 these parties came together to form the Federation of Chinese Democratic Parties, also known as the Democratic League. The principal efforts of this loose coordinating group were directed toward termination of one-party rule, and broadening the government to permit participation by the Communist and other non-Kuomintang parties. The Democratic League advocated rapid advancement toward constitutional reforms which would enable such a coalition government to function and to progress toward democratic rule. The League struck out vigorously against the corruption and maladministration of the Kuomintang, and demanded the inauguration of civil liberties and revision of the tax structure to relieve the peasant and worker of inequities, shifting the burden of government to those with the ability to pay.[6]

[6] L. K. Rosinger, *China's Crisis,* ch. 8.

## ISSUES IN THE CIVIL CONFLICT

While China continued to face the aggressions of Japan, all parties, in theory at least, formally espoused the principle of national unity. But the termination of the conflict in 1945, instead of bringing immediate peace to China, brought a renewal of open struggle between the forces of the National government and the Communists. To understand the reasons for this unfortunate situation, it may be helpful to return briefly to an examination of the principal differences between the two major parties during the war period.

**Conditions of National Unity.** When the Kuomintang and Communists established the united front in 1937 each party agreed to certain conditions. For their part the Communists avowedly abandoned their policy of overthrowing the Kuomintang by force and of replacing it by a soviet-type government. Likewise they gave up forcible confiscation of land from landlords. Of more immediate concern, they agreed to abolish their autonomous government and their separate Red army, placing both under national authority. In return the Kuomintang agreed that the full national effort would be employed to resist Japanese aggression, and that immediate steps would be taken toward constitutional, democratic government and social and economic reforms.

**Mutual Distrust.** Fulfillment of these conditions was an extremely difficult matter. It readily can be appreciated that long years of civil war had produced bitterness and animosity on each side, which could not be brushed aside casually. The National government, for example, had offered large ransoms for capture of Mao Tse-tung, Chu Teh, and other Communist leaders. Although the pressures of common defense against the enemy finally brought the two parties together, old hatreds and suspicions naturally remained. Neither party trusted the other. One of the fundamental sources of continuing trouble was the unwillingness of either party to proceed with its part of a bargain until it was certain that the other would do likewise. The Communists, for example, agreed to abolish the Red army as a separate fighting institution and place it under national command. But to them the Red army was essential to their welfare and to their very existence as a distinct factor in national affairs. Its exploits in the field of combat had made possible the creation of the first soviet government and the protection of Communist territories against civil and foreign enemies. Consequently they would yield control over the Red army only if they were given demonstrable evidence of the good faith of the Kuomintang. They demanded adequate representation in the military organs of the National regime, to which the Red army would be subordinated. Likewise, they agreed to place their government under National control, but again would do so only if granted satisfactory opportunity for participation in a national coalition government.

The leaders of the Kuomintang, on the other hand, were unwilling to give the Communists any positions of responsibility and trust in the National government until they had abandoned both the Red army and their political autonomy. To these leaders the issue was clear: the Communists were nothing more than rebels, rebels employing force to overthrow the legitimate government of China. As such they deserved no right to expect participation in the government. Such participation was contrary to the tenet that the Kuomintang itself possessed the sole right to govern the country during the period of political tutelage. The Communist army as a rebel outfit was not entitled to receive national supplies, even though it might be withstanding Japanese forces.

In actual practice, moreover, the Kuomintang leadership failed to institute effective reforms. It did set up the Peoples Political Council as an assembly of opinion, but this body was not broadly representative, nor did it have more than advisory power. Instead of providing wider opportunities for popular participation in government, the Kuomintang suppressed freedom of speech, assembly, and the press, terrorized liberal critics, and placed the educational institutions of the country in an intellectual strait jacket. In the economic field, little was done to seek a solution to China's greatest problem, her decadent, oppressive agrarian system.

Liberal and moderate elements, both in the Kuomintang itself and in such groups as the Democratic League, protested repeatedly against this situation. They deplored the failure of the government to carry out needed reforms. They demanded a termination of the corrupt and incompetent administration which characterized every phase of public affairs. Most of them recognized that political and economic progress could be made only by terminating the Kuomintang dictatorship. Consequently they urged the Kuomintang to accept the Communists and the minor parties in a reformed national government.

## The Contrast of Opposing Ideologies

From this summary account it will be observed that the gulf separating the Kuomintang and the Communists was deeper than the issues relating directly to the subordination of the Communist government and army to national control. Each of these parties stood for a distinct economic and political philosophy.

Following the establishment of government at Nanking in 1928, and particularly in 1939 after the disasters of two years of war with Japan, the Kuomintang reflected the interests of the forces opposed to fundamental reforms. During the Nanking period, prior to the Japanese invasion, the conservative influence of this support was modified by the progressive outlook of certain Kuomintang statesmen and of forward-looking business elements in the port cities. But when the government was forced to withdraw to the far interior, it was cut off from these influences. It now found it necessary to rely more and more upon reactionary provincial politicians, who responded to the interests of the land-owning gentry. Furthermore the suffering and destitution of the long war years made it almost inevitable that corruption and maladministration should render extremely difficult the maintenance of a liberal, progressive outlook.

**Communists Assume the Revolutionary Leadership.** While the Kuomintang leadership became more conservative and cautious, the Communist party pushed forward as the proponent of the revolution. Lacking material resources and located in poor and barren territory, the Communists had little to build with except that most numerous and most neglected of all China's resources, the Chinese peasant. Accordingly, the Communist program was based upon the mobilization of the peasant masses. But mobilization of the masses required an all-out attack on the agrarian problem. If the Communists could free the peasant from the shackles which bound him to the land, they could capitalize upon China's greatest need as the means to power. Thus in the areas under its control, the Communist party followed measures which would stimulate peasant support, including reduction of the costs of production, improved methods of cultivation, education and mass propaganda devices, and organized resistance against the depredations of the Japanese troops. Most of all, the Communists depended upon peasant mobilization for their military strength. They organized partisan bands, fighting units composed of local peasants, men who supported themselves on the land but fought in the common cause within their own areas. The promise of economic security made it worth while for these men to fight.

Communist mobilization of the peasant masses was a cause of particular antagonism among Kuomintang leaders. Such mobilization constituted a direct challenge to the old, established order, the order upon which depended the local landlords and local politicians. Moreover, the mobilization of partisan fighting units threatened the military supremacy of provincial military leaders. This situation was largely responsible for the National government's action in maintaining some of its best fighting units as a blockade between Communist areas and the rest of China.

## THE RENEWAL OF OPEN CONFLICT

Japan surrendered to the United Nations in August 1945 before her troops were driven from the large areas of China which they occupied. This unexpected development immediately presented the National government with a serious problem, the problem of recovering the former Japanese-occupied zones before the Communists could take them over. The Communists were in a particularly advantageous position to do just that. During the war years they had achieved marked success in organizing so-called border governments within the areas occupied by the enemy. While the Japanese held the cities and lines of communication, the partisan armies of the border governments operated throughout the hinterland, strategically located in north and central China. The National government, largely for political reasons, had not organized behind-the-lines partisan bands in any number. Moreover, the National government was more distantly located from the key cities and railroads. If unopposed upon Japan's surrender the Communist partisan armies, under the coordinated command of General Chu Teh, would have found it relatively simple to spread out and gain full control of these areas. This is exactly what the Communist forces proceeded to do, in open disregard of the order of Generalissimo Chiang Kai-shek to hold their positions until National troops could receive the surrender of the Japanese.

The situation turned rapidly into a race between Communist and National troops for possession of former occupied territory. In north China the Communists held the strategic advantage and soon gained control of large areas, including many of the principal rail lines. The National government, however, secured central China, and the important northern cities of Peiping and Tientsin. The rapid movement of National troops in American transport planes and vessels contributed materially to this success. Thus the end of 1945 found China sharply divided, territorially as well as ideologically. The country was liberated from the Japanese, but it now faced the crisis of civil strife.

**Postwar Economic Development.** Another source of concern for elements outside of the dominant Kuomintang group was related to the National government's preparations for postwar industrial and commercial reconstruction. Under the leadership of party and government officials, the government inaugurated a program to place China's economic development under rigid state control. It established government owned and operated companies in the major fields of industrial and commercial enterprise, including steel, petroleum, sugar, textiles, chemicals, flour, shipping, trucking, and many others. Once these organizations were established, private interests were obstructed by prohibitory or restrictive laws and regulations. Likewise, following Japan's surrender, the government converted former enemy enterprises erected in occupied territory into government monopolies. The consequences of this policy were widespread, and if continued promised to destroy China's small middle class. If the government's economic program were to be continued, not only would China lose the moderating political influence of this group, but she would follow the path by which Japan, during the last century, erected a political system dominated by the militarists, bureaucracy, and Zaibatsu.[7]

## EXTERNAL FACTORS

The internal situation in China at the termination of hostilities with Japan was complicated by reason of external factors. Other nations were concerned lest events in that troubled land upset their own interests and security. The United States played the major role in the defeat of Japan, and its troops were now stationed throughout the Far East. Likewise, the Soviet Union, after a late entry into the war in the Far East, occupied Manchuria and northern Korea, having crushed the Japanese troops in these areas.

**Position of the United States.** During the war the United States had furnished an increasing supply of military and lend-lease assistance to China. Although this aid was extended to the National government, as the recognized government of China, American policy had attempted, without success, to promote

[7] On this situation see Chen Han-seng, "Monopoly and Civil War in China," *Far Eastern Survey*, October 9, 1946, 305–10.

agreement between the government and the Communists. It was
hoped to bring together the military strength of the two factions
in order to increase China's contribution to ultimate victory.

When the dangers of full-scale civil conflict in China became
apparent after the Japanese surrender, the United States assumed an even greater part in attempts to reach a peaceful
solution. In November 1945 President Truman appointed General of the Army George Marshall as his special envoy to China.
In a public statement on December 15, Mr. Truman outlined
the principles of American policy toward China which General
Marshall would follow. He declared that a strong, united, and
democratic China was of the utmost importance to the success of
the United Nations and for world peace, and that the United
States government accordingly believed it essential that a cessation of hostilities be arranged between the armies of the National
government and the Chinese Communists. Likewise a national
conference of representatives of major political elements should
be arranged to bring about the unification of China. The President stated that while the United States government properly
recognized the National government as the only legal government in China, it strongly advocated that the national conference agree upon arrangements which would terminate one-
party government and give other political elements fair and effective representation in that government. With the institution of
a broadly representative government, autonomous armies should
be eliminated as such, and all armed forces in China integrated
effectively into the National army. Although the American government disavowed any form of intervention in China's internal
affairs, the President declared that as China moved toward peace
and unity, the United States would be prepared to assist the
National government in economic rehabilitation and the establishment of a modern military organization.[8]

On December 27, 1945, the foreign ministers of the United
States, Great Britain, and the Soviet Union, then meeting in
Moscow, issued a statement along similar lines. They declared

[8] Department of State *Bulletin*, December 16, 1945, XIII, pp. 945–46.

that: "They were in agreement as to the need for a unified and democratic China under the National government, for broad participation by democratic elements in all branches of the National government, and for a cessation of civil strife. They affirmed their adherence to the policy of noninterference in the internal affairs of China."[9]

General Marshall, after a hurried flight to China, brought representatives of the Kuomintang, the Communist Party, and minor parties into direct negotiation in a Political Consultative Conference. In February 1946 his headquarters announced that an agreement had been reached. It was reported that liberal and moderate elements in the Kuomintang and the Democratic League had been influential in securing compromise. By terms of the agreement, Communists and other minor parties would be admitted to a coalition government and the Red army would be integrated with the National army. Cease-fire teams, composed of Nationalist, Communist, and American officers, were dispatched to the field to secure the termination of hostilities between the opposing forces. Without waiting for the fulfillment of these terms, the United States government proceeded to carry out agreements for assistance to the National government, including a loan for the purchase of cotton, technical advice for the improvement of agriculture, sale of surplus military supplies in the Pacific theatre at reduced cost, and training of additional Chinese troops. American armed forces, chiefly marines, were landed in North China immediately after Japan's collapse. The United States government announced that this action was required to assist the Chinese National government in undertaking the surreder of Japanese troops. In addition to completing this task successfully, the presence of American forces materially assisted the National government in securing control of strategic areas prior to Communist occupation.[10]

[9] Department of State *Bulletin,* December 30, 1945, XIV, 1030–31.
[10] For a concise summary of the Marshall mission and of American policy, see the statement of President Truman issued in December 1946, *ibid.,* December 29, 1946, XVI, 1179.

The agreement negotiated by General Marshall in February 1946 was not carried out. When the agreement was placed before the Central Executive Committee of the Kuomintang in March, it was bitterly attacked by conservative members, who again declined to give up one-party rule. And again they refused to admit Communists to a coalition government while the Red army continued in possession of large areas of territory. For their part, the Communists strongly resisted the efforts of the National government to recover north China and Manchuria.

**Position of the Soviet Union.** The actions of the Soviet Union in Manchuria played into the hands of these conservative Kuomintang elements. In an agreement of alliance and friendship with China which was announced in August 1945, the Soviet Union pledged itself to respect the sovereignty and territorial integrity of China and not to interfere in the internal affairs of the country. In an accompanying note it declared that its moral and material aid would be given entirely to the National government as the central government of China, continuing the policy which it had followed during the war years. At the same time China granted to the Soviet Union important economic and strategic rights in Manchuria.[11] But the action of Soviet troops in Manchuria following the surrender of Japan aroused the suspicions and hostility of the National government. Before withdrawing from Manchuria these troops removed Japanese industrial equipment and other resources, claiming them as spoils of war. The Chinese government had counted on acquiring these properties, which were located in territory seized by Japan from China. Moreover, many Chinese believed that the deployment of Soviet troops contributed to the subsequent occupation of large parts of Manchuria by Communist forces before Nationalist forces could reach that part of China.

With the abrogation of the February agreement, hostilities between National and Communist units continued. The Communists sought to hold the territory they had secured following

[11] The texts of the treaty and of attached agreements are given in H. L. Moore, *Soviet Far Eastern Policy, 1931–1945*, pp. 265–77.

Japan's surrender, intent on maintaining a strong military base in the event of failure to reach political agreement with the National government. National forces advanced from coastal ports to seize railways and strategic positions. General Marshall returned to China in the summer of 1946 in the hope of finding new conditions of agreement, but in August he and United States Ambassador Stuart reluctantly announced that a settlement of outstanding issues between China's opposing factions seemed impossible. In December General Marshall terminated his special mission. Upon leaving China he issued a statement remarkable among state papers for its plain speaking and frankness. Because this statement so clearly and precisely reviews the factors standing in the way of internal peace in China, the principal parts of it are herein reproduced:

In the first place, the greatest obstacle to peace has been the complete, almost overwhelming suspicion with which the Chinese Communist Party and the Kuomintang regard each other. . . .

I think the most important factors involved in the recent breakdown of negotiations are these: On the side of the National Government, which is in effect the Kuomintang, there is a dominant group of reactionaries who have been opposed, in my opinion, to almost every effort I have made to influence the formation of a genuine coalition government. This has usually been under the cover of political or party action, but since the Party was the Government, this action, though subtle or indirect, has been devastating in its effect. They were quite frank in publicly stating their belief that cooperation by the Chinese Communist Party in the government was inconceivable and that only a policy of force could definitely settle the issue. This group includes military as well as political leaders.

On the side of the Chinese Communist Party there are, I believe, liberals as well as radicals, though this view is vigorously opposed by many who believe that the Chinese Communist Party discipline is too rigidly enforced to admit of such differences of viewpoint. Nevertheless, it has appeared to me that there is a definite liberal group among the Communists, especially of young men who have turned to the Communists in disgust at the corruption evident in the local governments—men who would put the interest of the Chinese people above ruthless measures to establish a Communist ideology in the immediate future. The dyed-in-the-wool Communists do not hesitate at the most drastic measures to gain their end as, for instance, the destruction of communications in order to wreck the economy of China and produce a situation that would facilitate the overthrow or collapse of the Government, without any regard to the immediate suffering of the people involved. They completely distrust the leaders of the Kuomintang and appear convinced that every Government proposal is designed to crush the Chinese Communist Party. . . .

However, a very harmful and immensely provocative phase of the Chinese Communist Party procedure has been in the character of its propaganda. I wish to state to the American people that in the deliberate misrepresentation and abuse of the action, policies, and purposes of our Government this propaganda has been without regard for the truth, without regard whatsoever for the facts, and has given plain evidence of a determined purpose to mislead the Chinese people and the world and to arouse a bitter hatred of Americans. . . . In the interest of fairness, I must state that the Nationalist Government publicity agency has made numerous misrepresentations, though not of the vicious nature of the Communist propaganda. . . .

Sincere efforts to achieve settlement have been frustrated time and again by extremist elements of both sides. The agreements reached by the Political Consultative Conference a year ago were a liberal and forward-looking charter which then offered China a basis for peace and reconstruction. However, irreconcilable groups within the Kuomintang, interested in the preservation of their own feudal control of China, evidently had no real intention of implementing them. Though I speak as a soldier, I must here also deplore the dominating influence of the military. Their dominance accentuates the weakness of civil government in China. At the same time, in pondering the situation in China, one must have clearly in mind not the workings of small Communist groups or committees to which we are accustomed in America, but rather of millions of people and an army of more than a million men.

I have never been in a position to be certain of the development of attitudes in the innermost Chinese Communist circles. Most certainly, the course which the Chinese Communist Party has pursued in recent months indicated an unwillingness to make a fair compromise. It has been impossible even to get them to sit down at a conference table with Government representatives to discuss given issues. . . .

Between this dominant reactionary group in the Government and the irreconcilable Communists who, I must state, did not so appear last February, lies the problem of how peace and well-being are to be brought to the long-suffering and presently inarticulate mass of the people of China. . . . The salvation of the situation, as I see it, would be the assumption of leadership by the liberals in the Government and in the minority parties, a splendid group of men, but who as yet lack the political power to exercise a controlling influence. Successful action on their part under the leadership of Generalissimo Chiang Kai-shek would, I believe, lead to unity through good government.[12]

Shortly after General Marshall's departure from China the Department of State announced that the United States government had decided to terminate its connection with the special agencies which had been established for the purpose of mediating the issues of the civil conflict and of ending armed hostilities. It was indicated at the same time that most of the remaining American troops in China would be withdrawn.[13]

## THE CONSTITUTIONAL ISSUE

Before this chapter is concluded, consideration should be given to another issue which has figured in the differences between the Kuomintang, minor parties, and the Communists, This is the issue of constitutional government. The development of constitutional government has been an issue of Chinese politics since the overthrow of the imperial system in 1911. The revolutionists who founded the Republic regarded the adoption of a constitution as one of their principal aims, believing constitutionalism to be a prerequisite of modern government. Likewise the Kuomintang accepted constitutional rule as the ultimate objective, to be reached upon advancement from military rule, through tutelage, to popular government. Warlordism, civil strife, and Japanese aggression blocked the achievement of this goal. With the surrender of Japan it again became a matter of immediate concern. It will be recalled that the Democratic League and other liberal elements had been particularly articulate in demanding the early establishment of constitutional government.

Since 1931 China has operated under a provisional constitu-

[12] Department of State *Bulletin,* January 19, 1947, XVI, 83.

[13] *Ibid.,* February 9, 1947, XVI, 258; *New York Times,* January 30, 1947.

tion, formulated by the Kuomintang. In 1932 the Central Executive Committee of the Party announced plans to establish a permanent constitution. It was expected that a national congress would be held in 1935 to adopt the constitution, but delays followed. In 1936 the Legislative Yuan of the National government published a draft constitution, upon which it had deliberated for three years, and this draft was formally promulgated by the National government as the official draft. In spite of pledges to proceed with its adoption, the government took the position that the war with Japan necessitated postponement. Finally, in May 1945, the Sixth National Party Congress of the Kuomintang adopted a resolution providing that in the following November the government was to convene a national Congress to adopt and promulgate the permanent constitution. It was planned to hold this Congress while hostilities against Japan continued.

Japan's surrender brought open renewal of civil strife, as already explained. One of the issues which the Communists raised in negotiations for a settlement of differences was the postponement of the national Congress scheduled for November. The Communists objected because they believed that they would not receive adequate representation in the Congress. The delegates to the Congress had been selected prior to the war, when it was originally planned to convene the body, and no new selection had been made. Consequently the Congress was postponed until May 1946, and then until November of that year.

**Constitutional Assembly.** In the meantime, the Kuomintang acceded to the demands of liberal elements and of the Communists for revision of the 1936 draft constitution. This draft had proposed a form of government in which far-reaching powers were lodged in the president of the Republic, including the authority to issue ordinances under emergency conditions to be determined by himself. There was to be no strong legislative or representative organ. By thus concentrating the powers of government in the president, and by granting very little governing authority to the people's representatives, the draft constitution would have enabled the perpetuation of one-party rule, and would have minimized the influence of opposition elements.[14]

The agreement to revise the draft constitution was one of the achievements of the People's Consultative Conference, which, it will be recalled, was established as a consequence of General Marshall's mediation. Thus when the National Assembly finally met in November 1946 to adopt the constitution, a somewhat liberalized version of the original draft was presented to the delegates by Generalissimo Chiang Kai-shek. But by this time, however, the intensity of the civil conflict had increased, and the Communists and most of the minor parties associated with the Democratic League now refused to participate in the deliberations.

The National Constitutional Assembly convened in Nanking in November 1946. Most of the 2050 delegates were elected in 1936 when initial plans were made by the Kuomintang for the adoption of the draft constitution. The Assembly was, therefore, almost entirely a Kuomintang body. The Communists and minor parties remained away, charging that the Kuomintang was violating its agreements by unilaterally calling the Assembly before setting up a genuine coalition government. Nevertheless the Assembly proceeded, under the vigorous leadership of Generalissimo Chiang Kai-shek, to deliberate upon and to approve the draft which was submitted to it. The Generalissimo effectively opposed the attempts of conservative "old-guard" elements of his party to abandon the revisions which had been incorporated into the original 1936 draft, and of certain moderate elements who favored arrangements which they felt were necessary to prevent domination of the new government by the well-organized Chen brothers' clique. The constitution was approved in the end by an almost unanimous vote on Christmas Day. It was announced that the new national charter would come into force one year later and that national elections preparatory to the establishment of a government under the constitution would be completed by the end of September 1947. The present National government was instructed to enact regulations for these elections and to revise

[14] *China's Draft Constitution*, Chinese News Service, New York.

or eliminate all laws conflicting with the new constitution.[15]

**The 1946 Constitution.** The constitution as finally approved is a very long document, containing 165 articles in all.[16] It provides for a continuation of the president and the division of the government into the five yuan, as advocated by Dr. Sun Yat-sen. It follows the plan of the 1936 draft in granting broad responsibilities to the president of the republic. In addition to the usual powers of a chief of state, he is authorized in times of emergency, during the recess of the Legislative Yuan, to issue emergency decrees "expedient and necessary to cope with the situation." He must, however, submit such a decree to the Legislative Yuan within one month, and in the event that the Legislative Yuan refuses approval, the decree becomes null and void (Article 43). The president is elected by a National Assembly, a large body whose members are selected by provincial and other units of local government, and which meets only for this purpose or for the recall of the president, and for consideration of amendments to the constitution. The president is elected for a term of six years and is eligible for re-election for a second term.

The Executive Yuan is the highest administrative organ of the republic. In composition and operation it continues the experience of the Nanking and Chungking periods, being made up of the president (or chairman), the vice-president, the heads of various ministries, and a number of members without portfolio. The president of the Yuan is appointed by the president of the Republic with the consent of the Legislative Yuan. The Executive Yuan is responsible for the preparation of the annual budget, legislative proposals, and administrative reports (Chapter V).

The Legislative Yuan is granted more authority and dignity than in the 1936 draft. It is an indirectly representative body, with members selected by the provinces and other territories and by the professions and other occupational groups for three-year

[15] *New York Times,* November 4, 16, 31; December 3, 5, 17, 18, 22, 25, 26, 30, 1946.
[16] *The Constitution of the Republic of China,* Chinese News Service, New York, January 11, 1947.

terms. It meets semiannually for sessions of three months. The Legislative Yuan is given limited control over the Executive Yuan in provisions which introduce into Chinese government certain elements of the parliamentary system. It can interpellate members of the Executive Yuan and can, if it objects to an important policy of the Executive Yuan, by resolution request the Executive Yuan to alter the policy. The Executive Yuan may then, with the approval of the president of the Republic, request the Legislative Yuan to reconsider this action. But if the Legislative Yuan upholds its original vote by a two-thirds majority, the president of the Executive Yuan shall either abide by the decision or resign (Article 57, paragraph 2). Likewise, the Executive Yuan can request the Legislative Yuan to reconsider a resolution relating to a statutory, budgetary, or treaty bill. If the Legislative Yuan upholds its original resolution by a two-thirds vote, the president of the Executive Yuan shall either abide by the decision or resign (paragraph 3). These provisions were not included in the 1936 draft constitution.

The Judicial Yuan is the highest judicial organ, and "shall attend to the adjudication of civil, criminal, and administrative suits and to disciplinary measures against public functionaries." According to Article 78, it has the power "to interpret the constitution and also the power to unify the interpretations of laws and decrees." The Examination Yuan, following past intentions, attends to matters relating to the civil service. It is composed of members appointed by the president of the republic with the consent of the Control Yuan (Chapter VIII). The Control Yuan likewise carries forward provisions of earlier laws (Chapter IX). It is composed of members elected by provincial and local councils for six-year terms, and acts as a sort of investigatory body, somewhat similar in function in a much broader field to the Inspector General of the United States army. It has the right to impeach officials and to make audits.

Chapter XII of the constitution provides for universal suffrage and for secret ballot. Article 136 of this chapter declares that the people's exercise of their two rights of initiative and referendum shall be stipulated by law, thus enacting one of the principles advocated by Dr. Sun Yat-sen.

The constitution contains a bill of rights of fourteen articles (Chapter II), guaranteeing equality of all persons, racial groups, and of each sex regardless of party affiliation. It includes an extensive list of civil liberties. According to Article 23, however: "No one of the liberties and rights enumerated in the preceding articles may, except as warranted by reasons of preventing infringement of the liberties of other persons, averting an imminent crisis, maintaining social order or advancing public interest, be restricted by law."

Fundamental national policies are set forth in considerable detail in the thirty-two articles of Chapter XIII. These policies include equitable distribution of land, control of capital, protection and limitation of private property, government management of public utilities and other monopolistic enterprises, state supervision of education and the appropriation of a minimum of 15 percent of the national budget, 25 percent of the provincial budget and 35 percent of the hsien budget for educational and cultural purposes, opportunity of employment for all persons capable of work, protection of women and child labor, and establishment of social insurance. Articles 139 and 140 are of particular interest in the light of past policies and practices of the Kuomintang and Communist Party. These articles declare:

No political party or faction or individual may make use of armed force as an instrument in a political struggle for power.
No military man in active service may concurrently hold a civil office.

The constitution thus provides an opportunity for a government very much different from that which has been given to China so far by either the Kuomintang or the Communists. An appraisal of this new government will not be possible until its extensive provisions have actually been put to test. Since the present government of the Kuomintang is charged with the responsibility of enacting the regulations necessary to place the new constitutional system in operation, the success of the national charter will depend upon the leadership of Chiang Kai-shek and his associates and their ability to terminate civil strife. For so long as China remains divided in war, the achievement of the high ideals of the constitution will be impossible.

## CONCLUSION

China still faces the basic problems which have confronted her since the overthrow of the imperial system. She still must establish a system of strong, centralized and united government capable of providing economic security for the mass of the people without destroying the opportunity for political freedom. Neither of her major parties has demonstrated the ability or the willingness to achieve this end. The Kuomintang, preoccupied with the continuation of its own authority as the sole governing party, has neglected to solve the basic agrarian problem, and its plans for industrial and commercial reconstruction promise to develop China's resources in the interests of the ruling bureaucracy and their favored associates. In order to preserve its own control, the Kuomintang has crushed its opponents. The Communists, intent upon creating a strong foundation for their own rule, have held out the opportunity of economic security, but likewise have threatened to destroy political freedom. In the end there is little choice between the totalitarianism of the right and the totalitarianism of the left. The interests and policies of the Kuomintang point toward the sort of political and economic structure found in modern Japan, a society composed of a small ruling oligarchy and a mass of poverty ridden peasants and workers, while the Communist program would impose upon China a party dictatorship cut from the Soviet pattern.[17]

## READINGS

Forman, Harrison, *Report from Red China*, New York, 1945. This is the personal report by a competent journalist of a visit to the Chinese Communist area.

[17] For further interpretation of these conditions see J. K. Fairbank, "Our Chances in China," *Atlantic Monthly*, September 1946, 37–42.

Lin Yutang, *The Vigil of a Nation*, New York, 1945. For the orthodox, Nationalist interpretation of the Communist problem, contrast this book with Forman or Stein.

Rosinger, Lawrence K., *China's Wartime Politics, 1937–1944*, Princeton University Press, 1944. The documentary appendix of this book, which includes a translation of the proposed draft constitution, is particularly valuable.

———————, *China's Crisis*, New York, 1945. This book, bitter in its criticism of Kuomintang China, is representative of the liberal attitude toward the government of Chiang Kai-shek.

Rowe, David Nelson, *China Among the Powers*, New York, 1945. China's position, in terms of military power and economic and political organization, is thoroughly examined in this scholarly study.

Stein, Guenther, *The Challenge of Red China*, New York, 1945. This is a carefully prepared and readable interpretation of Communist China, by a first-hand observer.

Sun Fo, *China Looks Forward*, New York, 1944. In this collection of speeches and articles prepared during the war years, the son of the founder of the Republic offers some vigorous criticism of Kuomintang policies, and suggests a path for the future.

White, Theodore H., and Annalee Jacoby, *Thunder Out of China*, New York, 1946. This is the best of the recent books on China, written by the former China correspondents of *Time* magazine.

### Constitutional Government

Pan Wei-tung, *The Chinese Constitution, A Study of Forty Years of Constitution-Making in China*, Institute of Chinese Culture, Washington, 1945. This is a study of the origins and historical development of constitutionalism in China; it includes the draft constitution of 1936.

### Notes on Other Sources

For further information on contemporary developments in China the student may turn to several periodicals specializing on Far Eastern topics. Particularly recommended are *Amerasia, Asia and the Americas, Far Eastern Quarterly, Far Eastern Survey,* and *Pacific Affairs*. The Chinese News Service, an official Chinese agency in New York, publishes *The China Magazine*, a monthly.

# APPENDIX

## THE CONSTITUTION OF
## THE FRENCH REPUBLIC [1]

### PREAMBLE

On the morrow of the victory of the free peoples over the regimes that attempted to enslave and degrade the human person, the French people proclaims again that every human being, without distinction of race, religion or belief, possesses inalienable and sacred rights. It solemnly reaffirms the freedoms of man and of the citizen consecrated by the declaration of rights of 1789 and the fundamental principles recognized by the laws of the Republic.

It proclaims, moreover, as particularly necessary in our time, the following political, economic and social principles.

The law guarantees to women in all domains equal rights with those of man.

Anyone persecuted because of his acts in favor of liberty has the right of asylum on the territories of the Republic.

Every one has the duty to work and the right to obtain employment. No one may suffer in his work or his employment by reason of his origins, his opinions or his beliefs.

---

[1] From the *New York Times*, September 21, 1946. Adopted by a popular referendum October 13, 1946, by a vote of approximately 9,200,000 to 7,790,000, it has since served as the constitutional basis of French government, but may be subject to amendment during the course of the next few years.

439

Every man may defend his rights and interests by trade-union action and may join the union of his choice.

The right to strike is exercised within the framework of the laws that govern it.

Every worker, through his delegates, participates in collective bargaining on working conditions as well as in the management of business.

All property and all businesses whose exploitation has acquired the characteristics of a national public service or a monopoly in fact should become the property of the community.

The nation assures to the individual and to the family the conditions necessary to their development.

It guarantees to all, and notably to the child, to the mother and to aged workers, protection for health, material security, rest and leisure.

Every human being who, by reason of his age, physical or mental condition or economic situation, finds himself incapable of work has the right to obtain from the community the means of decent living.

The nation proclaims the solidarity and equality of all French citizens with regard to the burden resulting from national calamities.

The nation guarantees equal access of the child and the adult to instruction, to vocational training and to culture. The organization of free and secular public education at all stages is a duty of the state.

The French Republic, faithful to its traditions, conforms to the rules of international law. It will undertake no war with a view to conquest and will never employ its forces against the liberty of any people.

On condition of reciprocity, France consents to the limitations of sovereignty necessary to the organization and defense of peace.

France forms with the peoples overseas a union founded on the equality of rights and duties without distinction of race or religion.

The French Union is composed of nations and peoples placing in common, or coordinating, their resources and their efforts to develop their civilization, to increase their well-being and to assure their security.

Faithful to her traditional mission, France proposes to guide the peoples for whom she has assumed responsibility toward freedom to govern themselves and democratically to manage their own affairs; putting aside all systems of colonization founded on arbitrary power, she guarantees to all access to public office and the exercise of the individual or collective rights and liberties proclaimed or confirmed above.

# INSTITUTIONS OF THE REPUBLIC

## TITLE 1. SOVEREIGNTY

Article I. France is a republic—indivisible, secular, democratic and social.

Article II. The national emblem is the tri-color flag—blue, white and red—in three vertical bands of equal dimensions.

The national hymn is the "Marseillaise."

The motto of the republic is: "Liberty, Equality, Fraternity."

Its principle is: government of the people, for the people and by the people.

Article III. The national sovereignty belongs to the French people.

No section of the people nor any individual may assume its exercise.

The people in constitutional matters act by the vote of their representatives and by the referendum.

In all other matters they exercise sovereignty through their deputies in the National Assembly, elected by universal, equal, direct and secret suffrage.

Article IV. Under conditions determined by the law, all French nationals who are majors of both sexes enjoying their civil and political rights are voters.

## TITLE 2. THE PARLIAMENT

Article V. The Parliament is composed of the National Assembly and the Council of the Republic.

Article VI. The duration of the powers of each Assembly, its mode of election, the conditions of eligibility, the basis of ineligibilities and incompatibilities are fixed by the law.

However, the two chambers are elected on a territorial basis—the National Assembly by universal direct suffrage, the Council of the Republic by the communal and departmental units by universal indirect suffrage.

The Council of the Republic is renewable, one half at a time.

Nevertheless, the National Assembly may itself elect by proportional representation councilors whose number shall not exceed onesixth of the total number of members of the Council of the Republic.

The number of members of the Council of the Republic may not be less than one-third or more than half the number of members of the National Assembly.

Article VII. War may not be declared without a vote of the National Assembly and concurrence in advance by the Council of the Republic.

Article VIII. Each of the two Chambers is the judge of the eligibility of its members and of the regularity of their election; it alone may receive their resignations.

Article IX. The National Assembly convenes by right in annual session on the second Tuesday of January.

The total duration of interruptions of the session may not exceed four months. Any adjournments of sittings of more than ten days are considered as interruptions.

The Council of the Republic sits at the same time as the National Assembly.

Article X. The sittings of the two Chambers are public. Reports of debates in extenso, as well as the parliamentary documents, are published in the Official Journal. Each of the two Chambers may convene as a secret committee.

Article XI. Each of the two Chambers elects its secretariat each year at the beginning of the session in accordance with the proportionate representation of the party groups.

When the two Chambers meet together to elect the President of the Republic, their secretariat is that of the National Assembly.

Article XII. When the National Assembly is not sitting, its secretariat, checking on the actions of the Cabinet, may convoke the Parliament; it must do this on the request of one-third of the deputies or on that of the Premier.

Article XIII. The National Assembly alone may vote the laws. It may not delegate this right.

Article XIV. The Premier and members of Parliament have the initiative in legislation.

Bills and Proposed laws formulated by the members of the National Assembly are tabled with its secretariat.

The proposals framed by the members of the Council of the Republic are tabled with its secretariat and transmitted without rebate to the secretariat of the National Assembly. These may not be received when they would have as a consequence the reduction of receipts or the creation of new outlays.

Article XV. The National Assembly studies the projects and proposals submitted it in its committees, of which it fixed the number, composition and competence.

Article XVI. The budget proposal is submitted to the National Assembly.

This law must include only strictly financial dispositions.

An organic law will regulate the method of presentation of the budget.

Article XVII. The Deputies of the National Assembly possess the initiative in expenditures.

However, no proposal for increasing expenditures or creating new expenditures may be presented during the discussion of the budget or of prospective or supplementary credits.

Article XVIII. The National Assembly supervises the accounts of the nation.

In this it is assisted by an accounting court. The National Assembly may entrust to the accounting court any inquiries or studies connected with public revenues and expenses or the management of the treasury.

Article XIX. Amnesty may be accorded only by law.

Article XX. The Council of the Republic examines proposed laws voted on first reading by the National Assembly.

It gives its opinion at the latest within two months after a measure is sent to it by the National Assembly.

When a budget law is involved, this delay is reduced, if desirable, to such an extent as not to exceed the time expended by the National Assembly in its examination and vote. When the National Assembly has decided on an urgent procedure, the Council of the Republic gives its advice in the same time as that provided for discussion in the National Assembly in settlement of the matter. The delays provided in the present article are suspended during interruptions of the session. They may be prolonged by a decision of the National Assembly.

If the advice of the Council of the Republic conforms, or if it has not been given within the period provided in the preceding part, the law is promulgated as voted by the National Assembly.

If its advice does not conform, the National Assembly examines the project or proposal for a law in a second reading. It determines definitively and in sovereign right the amendments submitted by the Council of the Republic, accepting or rejecting them in whole or in part. In case of total or partial rejection of these amendments, the vote in the second reading takes place by public ballot by an absolute majority of the members composing the National Assembly, when the vote on the whole has been expressed by the Council of the Republic under the same conditions.

Article XXI. No member of Parliament may be prosecuted, arrested, detained or judged on the basis of opinions or votes expressed by him in the exercise of his functions.

Article XXII. No member of Parliament may, during his term of office, be prosecuted or arrested for a criminal offense except with the authorization of the Chamber to which he belongs, except in case of a major crime. The detention or prosecution of a member of Parliament is suspended if the Chamber to which he belongs requests it.

Article XXIII. Members of Parliament receive compensation fixed in relation to a grade of civil servants.

Article XXIV. No one may belong at the same time to the National Assembly and the Council of the Republic. Ministers of Parliament may not be members of the Economic Council or of the Assembly of the French Union.

## Title 3. The Economic Council

Article XXV. An Economic Council whose status is fixed by law examines and advises on proposed laws in its domain. These proposed laws are submitted to it by the National Assembly before the Assembly discusses them.

The Economic Council may also be consulted by the Cabinet. It must be so consulted on the adoption of a national economic plan for the full employment of men and the rational use of material resources.

## Title 4. Diplomatic Treaties

Article XXVI. Diplomatic treaties duly ratified and published have the force of law, even when contrary to domestic French laws, requiring for their application no legislative acts beyond those necessary to insure their ratification.

Article XXVII. Treaties relative to international organization, peace treaties, commercial treaties, treaties that involve state finances, those relating to the status of persons and to the property rights of French citizens abroad and those that modify French internal laws as well as those that involve the cession, exchange or addition of territory do not become definitive until after having been ratified by a law.

No cession, no exchange and no addition of territory is valid without the consent of the interested populations.

Article XXVIII. Diplomatic treaties duly ratified and published having an authority superior to that of internal laws, their provisions may not be abrogated, modified or suspended without a previous regular denunciation notified through diplomatic channels. When one of the treaties mentioned in Article XXVII is involved, except commercial treaties, the denunciation must be authorized by the National Assembly.

## Title 5. The President of the Republic

Article XXIX. The President of the Republic is selected by the Parliament. He is elected for seven years. He is eligible for re-election only once.

Article XXX. The President of the Republic appoints in the Cabinet the Councilors of State, the Grand Chancellor of the Legion of Honor, Ambassadors and envoys extraordinary, members of the Superior Council and of the Committee of National Defense, rectors of universities, prefects, chiefs of central administration, general officers and representatives of the Government in overseas territories.

Article XXXI. The President of the Republic is kept informed of international negotiations.

The President of the Republic accredits Ambassadors and envoys extraordinary to foreign powers; foreign Ambassadors and envoys extraordinary are accredited to him.

Article XXXII. The President of the Republic presides over the Cabinet. He causes to be established and has custody of the reports of the sittings.

Article XXXIII. The President of the Republic presides with the same attributes over the Superior Council and the Committee of National Defense and assumes the title of chief of the armies.

Article XXXIV. The President of the Republic presides over the Superior Council of the Magistracy.

Article XXXV. The President of the Republic exercises the right of pardon in the Superior Council of the Magistracy.

Article XXXVI. The President of the Republic promulgates the laws within ten days after the transmission of a law definitively adopted to the Government. This delay is reduced to five days if urgency is declared by the National Assembly.

Within the period fixed for promulgation the President of the Republic may, in a message, ask the two Chambers for a new deliberation, which may not be refused.

In default of promulgation by the President of the Republic within the limits fixed by the present Constitution, it shall be accomplished by the President of the National Assembly.

Article XXXVII. The President of the Republic communicates with Parliament by messages addressed to the National Assembly.

Article XXXVIII. Each official action of the President of the Republic must be countersigned by the Premier and by a Minister.

Article XXXIX. Fifteen days at least, and thirty days at most, before the expiration of the powers of the President of the Republic, Parliament elects a new President.

Article XL. If in the application of the preceding article the election takes place when the National Assembly is dissolved in conformity with Article LI, the powers of the President in office are extended until the election of a new President. Parliament will elect this new President within ten days after the election of a new National Assembly.

Article XLI. In case of disability noted by a vote of Parliament or in case of vacancy through death, resignation or any other cause, the President of the National Assembly provisionally assumes interim functions of the President of the Republic. He will be replaced by a Vice-President.

A new President of the Republic is elected within ten days, except under the conditions mentioned in the preceding article.

Article XLII. The President of the Republic may be tried only in case of high treason.

He may be placed under accusation by the National Assembly and arraigned before the High Court of Justice under the conditions provided in Article LVII below.

Article XLIII. The function of the President of the Republic is incompatible with any other function.

Article XLIV. Members of families having reigned in France are ineligible for the Presidency of the Republic.

## Title 6. The Cabinet

Article XLV. At the opening of each Legislature, the President of the Republic, after the customary consultations, designates the Premier.

The latter may not constitute his Cabinet until invested with the confidence of the Assembly expressed by a public vote of an absolute majority of the Deputies, except if *force majeure* prevents the meeting of the National Assembly.

The same procedure is followed during the sitting of the Legislature in case of vacancy through death, resignation or any other cause, with the exception cited in Article LII below.

No ministerial crisis occurring within fifteen days of the nomination of the Ministers will count for the application of Article LI.

Article XLVI. The Premier and the Ministers chosen by him are named by a decree of the President of the Republic.

Article XLVII. The Premier assures the execution of the laws. He appoints all civil and military officials except those referred to in Articles XXX, XLVI and LXXXIV.

The Premier assures the high direction of the armed forces and coordinates the putting into operation of the national defense.

The acts of the Premier mentioned in the present article are countersigned by the interested Ministers.

Article XLVIII. The Ministers are collectively responsible to the National Assembly for the general policy of the Cabinet and individually for their personal actions.

They are not responsible to the Council of the Republic.

Article XLIX. A question of confidence may not be placed except after deliberation by the Cabinet; it may not be placed except by the Premier.

The vote on a question of confidence may not take place until a whole day after it has been placed before the Assembly. It takes place by public vote.

Confidence may not be refused to the Cabinet except by an absolute majority of the Deputies of the Assembly.

This refusal entails the collective resignation of the Cabinet.

Article L. The voting of a motion of censure by the National Assembly entails the collective resignation of the Cabinet.

This vote cannot occur until a full day after the deposit of the motion. It takes place by public ballot.

The motion of censure may not be adopted except by an absolute majority of the Deputies of the Assembly.

Article LI. If in the same period of eighteen months two Ministerial crises occur under the conditions mentioned in Articles XLIX and L, the dissolution of the National Assembly may be decided by the Cabinet after the advice of the President of the Assembly. The dissolution shall be pronounced in conformity with this decision by a decree of the President of the Republic.

The dispositions of the preceding paragraph are applicable only after the expiration of the first eighteen months of the legislature.

Article LII. In case of dissolution, the Cabinet, except the Premier and the Minister of the Interior, remains in office for the dispatch of current affairs.

The President of the Republic designates the President of the National Assembly as Premier. The latter designates a new Minister of the Interior in agreement with the secretariat of the National Assembly. He designates as Ministers of State members of the groups not represented in the Government.

General elections take place at least twenty days and not more than thirty days after the dissolution.

The National Assembly convenes by right on the third Thursday after its election.

Article LIII. The Ministers have access to the two Chambers and their committees. They must be heard when they request it.

They may have themselves invited to participate in discussions before the Chambers by committee members designated by decree.

Article LIV. The Premier may delegate his powers to a Minister.

Article LV. In case of vacancy through death or for any other reason, the Cabinet designates one of its members to exercise provisionally the functions of Premier.

## Title 7. The Penal Responsibility of Ministers

Article LVI. Ministers are responsible penally for crimes and offenses committed in the exercise of their functions.

Article LVII. Ministers may be placed under accusation by the National Assembly and ordered before the High Court of Justice.

The National Assembly decides by secret ballot and in accordance with an absolute majority of the members of which it is composed, except those who are participating in the prosecution in the inquiry or in judgment.

Article LVIII. The High Court of Justice is elected by the National Assembly at the opening of each legislature.

Article LIX. The organization of the High Court of Justice and its procedure are determined by a special law.

## Title 8. The French Union

### SECTION 1. PRINCIPLES

Article LX. The French Union is formed on the one hand by the French Republic, which includes metropolitan France and the departments and territories overseas; and on the other hand by the territories or associated states.

Article LXI. The situation of the associated states in the French Union depends for each of them on the act that defines its relations with France.

Article LXII. The members of the French Union place in common their entire means for guaranteeing the whole of the Union. The Government of the Republic assumes the coordination of these means and the direction of policy suitable for preparing and assuming this defense.

## SECTION 2. ORGANIZATION

Article LXIII. The central organs of the French Union are: The Presidency, the High Council and the Assembly.

Article LXIV. The President of the Republic is the President of the French Union, whose permanent interests he represents.

Article LXV. The High Council of the French Union is composed, under the presidency of the President of the Union, of a delegation of the French Government and the representation that each of the associated States has the power to accredit to the President of the Union.

It has the function of assisting the Government in the general conduct of the Union.

Article LXVI. The Assembly of the French Union is composed half of members representing metropolitan France and half of members representing the overseas departments and territories and the associated States.

An organic law shall determine the conditions under which the different parts of the populations will be represented.

Article LXVII. The members of the Assembly of the Union are elected by territorial assemblies with respect to overseas departments and territories; they are elected in metropolitan France to the number of two-thirds by members of the National Assembly representing the home country and to the number of one-third by members of the Council of the Republic representing the home country.

Article LXVIII. The associated States may designate delegates to the Union Assembly within the limits and conditions fixed by an internal law and act in each State.

Article LXIX. The President of the French Union convokes the Assembly of the French Union and closes its sessions. He must convoke it on the demand of half its members.

The Assembly of the French Union may not sit during interruptions of sessions of Parliament.

Article LXX. The rules of Articles VIII, X, XXI XXII and XXIII are applicable to the French Union under the same conditions as to the Council of the Republic.

Article LXXI. The Assembly of the French Union receives projects or proposals that are submitted for its opinion by the National Assembly or the Government of the Franch Republic or the governments of associated States.

The Assembly is qualified to pronounce on resolutions submitted to it by one of its members and, if they are taken into consideration, to instruct its secretariat to transmit them to the National Assembly. It may make proposals to the French Government and to the High Council of the French Union.

To be admissible, the resolutions referred to in the preceding paragraph must relate to legislation concerning overseas territories.

Article LXXII. In the overseas territories the legislative power belongs to Parliament as concerns criminal legislation, the regime of public liberties and political and administrative organization.

In all other matters French law is applicable in the overseas territories only by special order or if it has been extended by decree to the overseas territories after consultation with the Assembly of the Union.

Moreover, as an exception to Article XIII, special dispositions may be applied by edict to each territory by the President of the Republic in the Cabinet with the advice of the Assembly of the Union.

### SECTION 3. DEPARTMENTS AND OVERSEAS TERRITORIES

Article LXXIII. The legislative regime of the overseas departments is the same as that of metropolitan departments save for exceptions fixed by law.

Article LXXIV. The overseas territories are endowed with special status taking into account their special interests in the general interests of the Republic.

This status and the interior organization of each overseas territory or each group of territories are fixed by law after the advice of the Assembly of the French Union and consultation with the territorial assemblies.

Article LXXV. The respective status of members of the Republic and of the French Union are susceptible to evolution.

Modifications of the status and passage from one category to another within the framework set by Article LX may result only from a law voted by Parliament after consultation with the territorial assemblies and the Assembly of the Union.

Article LXXVI. The representative of the Government in each territory or group of territories is the depository of the powers of the Republic. He is the chief of the administration of the territory.

He is responsible for his acts to the Government.

Article LXXVII. In each territory an elected assembly is instituted. The electoral regime and the composition and competence of the Assembly are fixed by law.

Article LXXVIII. In groups of territories the management of common interests is confided to an Assembly composed of members elected by the territorial Assemblies. Its composition and powers are fixed by law.

Article LXXIX. The overseas territories elect representatives to the National Assembly and the Council of the Republic under conditions determined by law.

Article LXXX. All natives of overseas territories have the status of citizens with the same standing as French citizens of metropolitan France or of overseas territories. Special laws will establish the conditions under which they will exercise their rights of citizenship.

Article LXXXI. All French natives and natives of the French Union are citizens of the French Union, which assures them the enjoyment of the rights and liberties guaranteed by the preamble of the present Constitution.

Article LXXXII. Those citizens who have not French civil status will preserve their personal status as long as they have not renounced it. This status cannot in any case constitute a motive for refusing or limiting the rights and liberties pertaining to the status of French citizen.

## Title 9. The Superior Council of the Magistracy

Article LXXXIII. The Superior Council of the Magistracy is composed of fourteen members: the President of the Republic, presiding; the Keeper of the Seals or Minister of Justice, vice president; six persons elected for six years by the National Assembly by a two-thirds majority and chosen outside its membership, and six alternates elected under the same conditions; six persons designated as follows: four magistrates elected for six years each, representing a category of magistrates under conditions prescribed by law, and four alternates elected under the same conditions; two members designated for six years by the President of the Republic outside Parliament and the magistracy but from the judiciary professions, and two alternates designated under the same conditions.

The decisions of the Superior Council of the Magistracy are taken by a majority. In case of a tie vote, that of the President is deciding.

Article LXXXIV. The President of the Republic appoints magistrates from a list submitted by the Superior Council of the Magistracy, except those of the public prosecutor's office.

The Superior Council of the Magistracy assures, in conformity with the law, the discipline of its magistrates, their independence, and the administration of judiciary tribunals. The presiding magistrates are not removable.

## Title 10. Local Government Units

Article LXXXV. The French Republic, one and indivisible, recognizes the existence of local government units. These units are communes, *departements* and overseas territories.

Article LXXXVI. The framework, the scope and the eventual regrouping of communes, departments and overseas territories are fixed by law.

Article LXXXVII. Local government units freely administer themselves through Councils elected by universal suffrage. The execution of the decisions of these Councils is assured by their Mayors or their Presidents.

Article LXXXVIII. The coordination of the activities of state officials, the representation of the national interests and the administrative supervision of local government units are assured within the departments by the delegates of the Government designated by the Cabinet.

Article LXXXIX. Organic laws will extend departmental and municipal liberties; they may provide for certain large town structures and manners of functioning that differ from those of small communes and that entail special dispensations for certain departments; they will determine the conditions of application of Articles LXXXV–LXXXVIII above.

Laws will likewise determine the conditions under which local services of central administrations will function in order to bring the administration closer to the people.

## Title 11. The Revision of the Constitution

Article XC. Revision takes place in the following manner:

Revision is to be decided by a resolution adopted by an absolute majority of the members composing the National Assembly.

The resolution stipulates the object of the revision.

After at least three months it undergoes a second reading under the same conditions, unless the Council of the Republic, to which the resolution has been referred by the National Assembly, has adopted by an absolute majority the same resolution.

After the second reading, the National Assembly drafts a bill for the revision of the Constitution. This bill is submitted to Parliament and voted by a majority in the manner of an ordinary law.

It is submitted to a referendum unless it has been adopted on a second reading by the National Assembly by a majority of two-thirds or been voted by a majority of three-fifths by each of the two houses.

No constitutional revision touching the existence of the Council of the Republic can be made without the concurrence of that Council or resort to a referendum.

The bill is promulgated as constitutional law by the President of the Republic within eight days of its adoption.

Article XCI. The constitutional committee is presided over by the President of the Republic.

It includes the President of the National Assembly, the President of the Council of the Republic, seven members elected by the National Assembly at the beginning of each annual session by proportional representation of groups and chosen outside its membership, and three members elected under the same conditions by the Council of the Republic.

The constitutional committee determines whether laws voted by the National Assembly entail a revision of the constitution.

Article XCII. In the period allowed for the promulgation of the law, the committee receives a joint request from the President of the Republic and the President of the Council of the Republic, the Council having decided by an absolute majority of its members. The committee examines the law, strives for agreement between the National Assembly and the Council of the Republic and, if it does not succeed, takes its decision within five days from its receipt of the request. This period may be reduced to two days in case of urgency.

It is competent to decide on the possibility of revision of only Titles 1 to 10 of the present Constitution.

Article XCIII. A law that, in the opinion of the committee, entails a revision of the Constitution is sent back to the National Assembly for further consideration.

If Parliament adheres to its original vote, the law may not be promulgated until the Constitution has been revised in the manner provided in Article LXXXII.

If the law is considered in conformity with the provisions of Titles 1 to 10 of the present Constitution, it is promulgated within the period provided in Article XXXVI, which period is prolonged by the addition of the periods provided in Article XCII above.

Article XCIV. In case of the occupation of all or part of the metropolitan territory by foreign forces, no procedure of revision may be started or continued.

Article XCV. The republican form of government may not be the subject of a proposal of revision.

## TITLE 12. TEMPORARY PROVISIONS

Article XCVI. A secretariat of the National Constituent Assembly is charged with assuring the permanence of national representation until the meeting of the deputies of the new National Assembly.

Article XCVII. In case of exceptional circumstances, the deputies belonging to the National Constituent Assembly may, until the date provided in the preceding article, be called into session by the secretariat either on their own initiative or at the request of the Government.

Article XCVIII. The National Assembly will meet with full authority on the third Thursday after the general elections. The Council of the Republic will meet on the third Tuesday after its election. The present constitution will take effect from that date.

Until the meeting of the Council of the Republic, the organization of public powers will be determined by the law of Nov. 2, 1945, the National Assembly having the attributes conferred by that law on the National Constituent Assembly.

Article XCIX. The Provisional Government formed under Article XCVIII will hand its resignation to the President of the Republic on his election by Parliament under the conditions fixed by Article XXIX above.

Article C. The secretariat of the National Constituent Assembly is charged with preparing the meeting of the Chambers created by the present constitution and providing for them, before the meeting of their respective secretariats, the meeting places and administrative facilities necessary to their functioning.

Article CI. During a period of not more than one year dating from the meeting of the National Assembly, the Council of the Republic may officially deliberate when two-thirds of its members have been proclaimed elected.

Article CII. The first Council of the Republic will be renewed entirely in the year after the renewal of the municipal councils, which shall take place within one year dating from the promulgation of the constitution.

Article CIII. Until the organization of the Economic Council and during a maximum period of three months dating from the meeting of the National Assembly, the application of Article XXV of the present constitution shall be suspended.

Article CIV. Until the meeting of the Assembly of the French Union and during a maximum period of one year dating from the

to in accordance with the Imperial House Law passed by the Diet.

Article III. The advice and approval of the Cabinet shall be required for all acts of the Emperor in matters of state, and the Cabinet shall be responsible therefor.

Article IV. The Emperor shall perform only such acts in matters of state as are provided for in this Constitution and he shall not have powers related to government.

The Emperor may delegate the performance of his acts in matters of state as may be provided by law.

Article V. When, in accordance with the Imperial House Law, a Regency is established, the Regent shall perform his acts in matters of state in the Emperor's name. In this case, paragraph one of the preceding article will be applicable.

Article VI. The Emperor shall appoint the Prime Minister as designated by the Diet.

The Emperor shall appoint the Chief Judge of the Supreme Court, as designated by the Cabinet.

Article VII. The Emperor, with the advice and approval of the Cabinet, shall perform the following acts in matters of state on behalf of the people:

Promulgation of amendments of the Constitution, laws, cabinet orders and treaties.

Convocation of the Diet.

Dissolution of the House of Representatives.

Proclamation of general election of members of the Diet.

Attestation of the appointment and dismissal of Ministers of State and other officials as provided for by law, and of full powers and credentials of Ambassadors and Ministers.

Attestation of general and special amnesty, commutation of punishment, reprieve, and restoration of rights.

Awarding of honors.

Attestation of instruments of ratification and other diplomatic documents as provided for by law.

Receiving foreign ambassadors and ministers.

Performance of ceremonial functions.

Article VIII. No property can be given to, or received by, the Imperial House, nor any gifts can be made therefrom, without the authorization of the Diet.

## CHAPTER 2. RENUNCIATION OF WAR

Article IX. Aspiring sincerely to an international peace based on justice and order, the Japanese people forever renounce war as a sovereign right of the nation and the threat or use of force as means of settling international disputes.

In order to accomplish the aim of the preceding paragraph, land, sea, and air forces, as well as other war potential, will never be maintained. The right of belligerency of the state will not be recognized.

## Chapter 3. Rights and Duties of the People

Article X. The conditions necessary for being a Japanese national shall be determined by law.

Article XI. The people shall not be prevented from enjoying any of the fundamental human rights. These fundamental human rights guaranteed to the people by this Constitution shall be conferred upon the people of this and future generations as eternal and inviolate rights.

Article XII. The freedoms and rights guaranteed to the people by this Constitution shall be maintained by the constant endeavor of the people who shall refrain from any abuse of these freedoms and rights and shall always be responsible for utilizing them for the public welfare.

Article XIII. All of the people shall be respected as individuals. Their right to life, liberty, and the pursuit of happiness shall, to the extent that it does not interfere with the public welfare, be the supreme consideration in legislation and in other governmental affairs.

Article XIV. All of the people are equal under the law and there shall be no discrimination in political, economic, or social relations because of race, creed, sex, social status or family origin.

Peers and peerage shall not be recognized.

No privilege shall accompany any award of honor, decoration or any distinction, nor shall any such award be valid beyond the lifetime of the individual who now holds or hereafter may receive it.

Article XV. The people have the inalienable right to choose their public officials and to dismiss them.

All public officials are servants of the whole community and not of any group thereof.

Universal adult suffrage is guaranteed with regard to the election of public officials.

In all elections, secrecy of the ballot shall not be violated. A voter shall not be answerable, publicly or privately, for the choice he has made.

Article XVI. Every person shall have the right of peaceful petition for the redress of damage, for the removal of public officials, for the enactment, repeal or amendment of laws, ordinances or regulations and for other matters; nor shall any person be in any way discriminated against for sponsoring such a petition.

Article XVII. Every person may sue for redress as provided by law from the State or a public entity; in case he has suffered damage through illegal act of any public official.

Article XVIII. No person shall be held in bondage of any kind. Involuntary servitude, except as punishment for a crime, is prohibited.

Article XIX. Freedom of thought and conscience shall not be violated.

Article XX. Freedom of religion is guaranteed to all. No religious organization shall receive any privileges from the State, nor exercise any political authority.

No person shall be compelled to take part in any religious act, celebration, rite or practice.

The State and its organs shall refrain from religious education or any other religious activity.

Article XXI. Freedom of assembly and association as well as speech, press and all other forms of expression are guaranteed.

No censorship shall be maintained, nor shall the secrecy of any means of communication be violated.

Article XXII. Every person shall have freedom to choose and change his residence and to choose his occupation to the extent that it does not interfere with the public welfare.

Freedom of all persons to move to a foreign country and to divest themselves of their nationality shall be inviolate.

Article XXIII. Academic freedom is guaranteed.

Article XXIV. Marriage shall be based only on the mutual consent of both sexes and it shall be maintained through mutual cooperation with the equal rights of husband and wife as a basis.

With regard to choice of spouse, property rights, inheritance, choice of domicile, divorce and other matters pertaining to marriage and the family, laws shall be enacted from the standpoint of individual dignity and the essential equality of the sexes.

Article XXV. All people shall have the right to maintain the minimum standards of wholesome and cultured living.

In all spheres of life, the State shall use its endeavors for the promotion and extension of social welfare and security, and of public health.

Article XXVI. All people shall have the right to receive an equal education correspondent to their ability, as provided by law.

All people shall be obligated to have all boys and girls under their protection receive ordinary education as provided for by law. Such compulsory education shall be free.

Article XXVII. All people shall have the right and the obligation to work.

Standards for wages, hours, rest and other working conditions shall be fixed by law.

Children shall not be exploited.

Article XXVIII. The right of workers to organize and to bargain and act collectively is guaranteed.

Article XXIX. The right to own or to hold property is inviolable.

Property rights shall be defined by law, in conformity with the public welfare.

Private property may be taken for public use upon just compensation therefor.

Article XXX. The people shall be liable to taxation as provided by law.

Article XXXI. No person shall be deprived of life or liberty, nor shall any other criminal penalty be imposed, except according to procedure established by law.

Article XXXII. No person shall be denied the right of access to the courts.

Article XXXIII. No person shall be apprehended except upon warrant issued by a competent judicial officer which specifies the offense with which the person is charged, unless he is apprehended, the offense being committed.

Article XXXIV. No person shall be arrested or detained without being at once informed of the charges against him or without the immediate privilege of counsel; nor shall he be detained without adequate cause; and upon demand of any person such cause must be immediately shown in open court in his presence and the presence of his counsel.

Article XXXV. The right of all persons to be secure in their homes, papers and effects against entries, searches and seizures shall not be impaired except upon warrant issued for adequate cause and particularly describing the place to be searched and things to be seized, or except as provided by Article XXXIII.

Each search or seizure shall be made upon separate warrant issued by a competent judicial officer.

Article XXXVI. The infliction of torture by any public officer and cruel punishments are absolutely forbidden.

Article XXXVII. In all criminal cases the accused shall enjoy the right to a speedy and public trial by an impartial tribunal.

He shall be permitted full opportunity to examine all witnesses, and he shall have the right of compulsory process for obtaining witnesses on his behalf at public expense.

At all times the accused shall have the assistance of competent counsel who shall, if the accused is unable to secure the same by his own efforts, be assigned to his use by the State.

Article XXXVIII. No person shall be compelled to testify against himself.

Confessions made under compulsion, torture or threat, or after prolonged arrest or detention shall not be admitted in evidence.

No person shall be convicted or punished in cases where the only proof against him is his own confession.

Article XXXIX. No person shall be held criminally liable for an act which was lawful at the time it was committed, or of which he has been acquitted, nor shall he be placed in double jeopardy.

Article XL. Any person, in case he is acquitted after he has been arrested or detained, may sue the State for redress as provided by law.

## Chapter 4. The Diet

Article XLI. The Diet shall be the highest organ of state power, and shall be the sole law-making organ of the State.

Article XLII. The Diet shall consist of two Houses, namely the House of Representatives and the House of Councilors.

Article XLIII. Both Houses shall consist of elected members, representative of all the people.

The number of the members of each House shall be fixed by law.

Article XLIV. The qualifications of members of both Houses and their electors shall be fixed by law. However, there shall be no discrimination because of race, creed, sex, social status, family origin, education, property or income.

Article XLV. The term of office of members of the House of Representatives shall be four years. However, the term shall be terminated before the full term is up in case the House of Representatives is dissolved.

Article XLVI. The term of office of members of the House of Councilors shall be six years, and election for half the members shall take place every three years.

Article XLVII. Electoral districts, methods of voting and other matters pertaining to the method of election of members of both Houses shall be fixed by law.

Article XLVIII. No person shall be permitted to be a member of both Houses simultaneously.

Article XLIX. Members of both Houses shall receive appropriate annual payment from the national treasury in accordance with law.

Article L. Except in cases provided by law, members of both Houses shall be exempt from apprehension while the Diet is in session, and any members apprehended before the opening of the session shall be freed during the term of the session upon demand of the House.

Article LI. Members of both Houses shall not be held liable outside the House for speeches, debates, or votes cast inside the House.

Article LII. An ordinary session of the Diet shall be convoked once per year.

Article LIII. The Cabinet may determine to convoke extraordinary sessions of the Diet. When a quarter or more of the total members of either House makes the demand, the Cabinet must determine on such convocation.

Article LIV. When the House of Representatives is dissolved, there must be a general election of members of the House of Representatives within forty (40) days from the date of dissolution, and the Diet must be convoked within thirty (30) days from the date of the election.

When the House of Representatives is dissolved, the House of Councilors is closed at the same time. However, the Cabinet may in time of national emergency convoke the House of Councilors in emergency session.

Measures taken at such session as mentioned in the proviso of the preceding paragraph shall be provisional and shall become null and void unless agreed to by the House of Representatives within a period of ten (10) days after the opening of the next session of the Diet.

Article LV. Each House shall judge disputes related to qualifications of its members. However, in order to deny a seat to any member, it is necessary to pass a resolution by a majority of two-thirds or more of the members present.

Article LVI. Business cannot be transacted in either House unless one-third or more of the total membership is present.

All matters shall be decided, in each House, by a majority of those present, except as elsewhere provided in the Constitution, and in case of a tie, the presiding officer shall decide the issue.

Article LVII. Deliberation in each House shall be public. However, a secret meeting may be held where a majority of two-thirds or more of those members present passes a resolution therefor.

Each House shall keep a record of proceedings. This record shall be published and given general circulation, excepting such parts of proceedings of secret session as may be deemed to require secrecy.

Upon demand of one-fifth or more of the members present, votes of the members on any matter shall be recorded in the minutes.

Article LVIII. Each House shall select its own president and other officials.

Each house shall establish its rules pertaining to meetings, proceedings and internal discipline, and may punish members for disorderly conduct. However, in order to expel a member, a majority of two-thirds or more of those members present must pass a resolution thereon.

Article LIX. A bill becomes law on passage by both Houses, except as otherwise provided by the Constitution.

A bill which is passed by the House of Representatives, and upon which the House of Councilors makes a decision different from that of the House of Representatives, becomes a law when passed a second time by the House of Representatives by a majority of two-thirds or more of the members present.

The provision of the preceding paragraph does not preclude the House of Representatives from calling for the meeting of a joint committee of both Houses, provided for by law.

Failure by the House of Councilors to take final action within sixty (60) days after receipt of a bill passed by the House of Representatives, time in recess excepted, may be determined by the House of Representatives to constitute a rejection of the said bill by the House of Councilors.

Article LX. The budget must first be submitted to the House of Representatives.

Upon consideration of the budget, when the House of Councilors makes a decision different from that of the House of Representatives, and when no agreement can be reached even through a joint committee of both Houses, provided for by law, or in the case of failure by the House of Councilors to take final action within thirty (30) days, the period of recess excluded, after the receipt of the budget passed by the House of Representatives, the decision of the House of Representatives shall be the decision of the Diet.

Article LXI. The second paragraph of the preceding article applies also to the Diet approval required for the conclusion of treaties.

Article LXII. Each House may conduct investigations in relation to government, and may demand the presence and testimony of witnesses, and the production of records.

Article LXIII. The Prime Minister and other Ministers of State may, at any time, appear in either House for the purpose of speaking on bills, regardless of whether they are members of the House or not. They must appear when their presence is required in order to give answers or explanations.

Article LXIV. The Diet shall set up an impeachment court from among the members of both Houses for the purpose of trying those judges against whom removal proceedings have been instituted.

Matters relating to impeachment shall be provided by law.

## Chapter 5. The Cabinet

Article LXV. Executive power shall be vested in the Cabinet.

Article LXVI. The Cabinet shall consist of the Prime Minister, who shall be its head, and other Ministers of State as provided for by law.

The Prime Minister and other Ministers of State must be civilians.

The Cabinet, in the exercise of executive power, shall be collectively responsible to the Diet.

Article LXVII. The Prime Minister shall be designated from among the members of the Diet by a resolution of the Diet. This designation shall precede all other business.

If the House of Representatives and the House of Councilors disagree and if no agreement can be reached even through a joint committee of both houses, provided for by law, or the House of Councilors fails to make designation within ten (10) days, exclusive of the period of recess, after the House of Representatives has made designation, the decision of the House of Representatives shall be the decision of the Diet.

Article LXVIII. The Prime Minister shall appoint the Ministers of State. However, a majority of their numbers must be chosen from among the members of the Diet.

The Prime Minister may remove Ministers of State as he chooses.

Article LXIX. If the House of Representatives passes a nonconfidence resolution, or rejects a confidence resolution, the Cabinet shall resign en masse, unless the House of Representatives is dissolved within ten (10) days.

Article LXX. When there is a vacancy in the post of Prime Minister, or upon the first convocation of the Diet after a general election of members of the House of Representatives, the Cabinet shall resign en masse.

Article LXXI. In the cases mentioned in the two preceding articles, the Cabinet shall continue its functions until the time when a new Prime Minister is appointed.

Article LXXII. The Prime Minister, representing the Cabinet, submits bills, reports on general national affairs and foreign relations to the Diet, and exercises control and supervision over various administrative branches.

Article LXXIII. The Cabinet, in addition to other general administrative functions, shall perform the following functions:

Administer the law faithfully; conduct affairs of State.

Manage foreign affairs.

Conclude treaties. However, it shall obtain prior or, depending on circumstances, subsequent approval of the Diet.

Administer the civil service in accordance with standards established by law.

Prepare the budget, and present it to the Diet.

Enact cabinet orders in order to execute the provisions of this Constitution and of the law. However, it cannot include penal provisions in such cabinet orders unless authorized by such law.

Decide on general amnesty, special amnesty, commutation of punishment, reprieve, and restoration of rights.

Article LXXIV. All laws and cabinet orders shall be signed by the competent Minister of State and countersigned by the Prime Minister.

Article LXXV. The Ministers of State, during their tenure of office, shall not be subject to legal action without the consent of the Prime Minister. However, the right to take that action is not impaired hereby.

## Chapter 6. Judiciary

Article LXXVI. The whole judicial power is vested in a Supreme Court and in such inferior courts as are established by law.

No extraordinary tribunal shall be established, nor shall any organ or agency of the Executive be given final judicial power.

All judges shall be independent in the exercise of their conscience and shall be bound only by this Constitution and the laws.

Article LXXVII. The Supreme Court is vested with the rule-making power under which it determines the rules of procedure and of practice, and of matters relating to attorneys, the internal discipline of the courts and the administration of judicial affairs.

Public procurators shall be subject to the rule-making power of the Supreme Court.

The Supreme Court may delegate the power to make rules for inferior courts to such courts.

Article LXXVIII. Judges shall not be removed except by public impreachment unless judicially declared mentally or physically incompetent to perform official duties. No disciplinary action against judges shall be administered by any executive organ or agency.

Article LXXIX. The Supreme Court shall consist of a Chief Judge and such number of judges as may be determined by law; such judges excepting the Chief Judge shall be appointed by the Cabinet.

The appointment of the judges of the Supreme Court shall be reviewed by the people at the first general election of the House of Representatives following their appointment, and shall be reviewed again at the first general election of the House of Representatives after a lapse of ten (10) years, and in the same manner thereafter.

In cases mentioned in the foregoing paragraph when the majority of the voters favors the dismissal of a judge, he shall be dismissed.

Matters pertaining to review shall be prescribed by law.

The judges of the Supreme Court shall be retired upon the attainment of the age as fixed by law.

All such judges shall receive, at regular stated intervals, adequate compensation which shall not be decreased during their terms of office.

Article LXXX. The judges of the inferior courts shall be appointed by the Cabinet from a list of persons nominated by the Supreme Court. All such judges shall hold office for a term of ten (10) years with privilege of reappointment, provided that they shall be retired upon attainment of the age as fixed by law.

The judges of the inferior courts shall receive, at regular stated intervals, adequate compensation which shall not be decreased during their terms of office.

Article LXXXI. The Supreme Court is the court of last resort with power to determine the constitutionality of any law, order, regulation or official act.

Article LXXXII. Trials shall be conducted and judgment declared publicly. Where a court unanimously determines publicity to be dangerous to public order or morals, a trial may be conducted privately, but trials of political offenses, offenses involving the press, or cases wherein the rights of people as guaranteed in Chapter 3 of this Constitution are in question, shall always be conducted publicly.

## Chapter 7. Finance

Article LXXXIII. The power to administer national finances shall be exercised as the Diet shall determine.

Article LXXXIV. No new taxes shall be imposed or existing ones modified except by law or under such conditions as law may prescribe.

Article LXXXV. No money shall be expended, nor shall the State obligate itself, except as authorized by the Diet.

Article LXXXVI. The Cabinet shall prepare and submit to the Diet for its consideration and decision a budget for each fiscal year.

Article LXXXVII. In order to provide for unforeseen deficiencies in the budget, a reserve fund may be authorized by the Diet to be expended upon the responsibility of the Cabinet.

The Cabinet must get subsequent approval of the Diet for all payments from the reserve fund.

Article LXXXVIII. All property of the Imperial Household shall belong to the State. All expenses of the Imperial Household shall be appropriated by the Diet in the budget.

Article LXXXIX. No public money or other property shall be expended or appropriated for the use, benefit or maintenance of any religious institution or association, or for any charitable, educational or benevolent enterprises not under the control of public authority.

Article XC. Final accounts of the expenditures and revenues of the State shall be audited annually by a Board of Audit and submitted by the Cabinet to the Diet, together with the statement of audit, during the fiscal year immediately following the period covered.

The organization and competency of the Board of Audit shall be determined by law.

Article XCI. At regular intervals and at least annually the Cabinet shall report to the Diet and the people on the state of national finances.

## CHAPTER 8. LOCAL SELF-GOVERNMENT

Article XCII. Regulations concerning organization and operations of local public entities shall be fixed by law in accordance with the principle of local autonomy.

Article XCIII. The local public entities shall establish assemblies as their deliberative organs, in accordance with law.

The chief executive officers of all local public entities, the members of their assemblies, and such other local officials as may be determined by law shall be elected by direct popular vote within their several communities.

Article XCIV. Local public entities shall have the right to manage their property, affairs and administration and to enact their own regulations within law.

Article XCV. A special law, applicable only to one local public entity, cannot be enacted by the Diet without the consent of the majority of the voters of the local public entity concerned, obtained in accordance with law.

## CHAPTER 9. AMENDMENTS

Article XCVI. Amendments to this Constitution shall be initiated by the Diet, through a concurring vote of two-thirds or more of all the members of each House and shall thereupon be submitted to the people for ratification, which shall require the affirmative vote of a majority of all votes cast thereon, at a special referendum or at such election as the Diet shall specify.

Amendments when so ratified shall immediately be promulgated by the Emperor in the name of the people, as an integral part of this Constitution.

## CHAPTER 10. SUPREME LAW

Article XCVII. The fundamental human rights by this Constitution guaranteed to the people of Japan are fruits of the age-old struggle of man to be free; they have survived the many exacting tests for durability and are conferred upon this and future generations in trust, to be held for all time inviolate.

Article XCVIII. This Constitution shall be the supreme law of the nation and no law, ordinance, imperial rescript or other act of government, or part thereof, contrary to the provisions hereof shall have legal force or validity.

The treaties concluded by Japan and established laws of nations shall be faithfully observed.

Article XCIX. The Emperor or the Regent as well as Ministers of State, the members of the Diet, judges, and other public officials have the obligation to respect and uphold this Constitution.

## CHAPTER 11. SUPPLEMENTARY PROVISIONS

Article C. This Constitution shall be enforced as from the day when the period of six months will have elapsed counting from the day of its promulgation.

The enactment of laws necessary for the enforcement of this Constitution, the election of members of the House of Councillors and the procedure for the convocation of the Diet and other preparatory procedures necessary for the enforcement of this Constitution may be executed before the day prescribed in the preceding paragraph.

Article CI. If the House of Councilors is not constituted before the effective date of this Constitution, the House of Representatives shall function as the Diet and until such time as the House of Councilors shall be constituted.

Article CII. The term of office for half the members of the House of Councillors serving in the first term under this Constitution shall be three years. Members falling under this category shall be determined in accordance with law.

Article CIII. The Ministers of State, members of the House of Representatives and judges in office on the effective date of this Constitution, and all other public officials who occupy positions corresponding to such positions as are recognized by this Constitution shall not forfeit their positions automatically on account of the enforcement of this Constitution unless otherwise specified by law. When, however, successors are elected or appointed under the provisions of this Constitution they shall forfeit their positions as a matter of course.

# THE CONSTITUTION OF
# THE REPUBLIC OF CHINA [1]

## PREAMBLE

The National Assembly of the Republic of China, by virtue of the mandate received from the whole body of citizens, in accordance with the teachings of Dr. Sun Yat-sen, founder of the Republic of China, and in order to consolidate the power of the state, safeguard the rights of the people, ensure social security and promote the welfare of the people, hereby adopt this Constitution to be promulgated and enforced throughout the land for faithful and perpetual observance by all.

### CHAPTER 1. GENERAL PROVISIONS

Article 1. The Republic of China, founded on the San Min Chu I (Three People's Principles), is a democratic republic of the people, for the people and governed by the people.

Article 2. The sovereignty of the Republic of China resides in the whole body of citizens.

Article 3. Persons possessing the nationality of the Republic of China are citizens of the Republic of China.

Article 4. The territory of the Republic of China comprises its original areas. It shall not be altered except by resolution of the National Assembly.

Article 5. All racial groups of the Republic of China shall enjoy equality.

Article 6. The national flag of the Republic of China shall have a red background with a blue sky and a white sun in the upper left corner.

### CHAPTER 2. RIGHTS AND DUTIES OF THE PEOPLE

Article 7. All citizens of the Republic of China, irrespective of sex, religion, race, class or party affiliation shall be equal before the law.

---

[1] Unofficial translation released by Minister of Information, Nanking, January 4, 1947, special release of Chinese News Service, New York, January 11, 1947. Adopted by the National Assembly on December 25, 1946, and promulgated by the National Government on January 1, 1947, to become effective on December 25, 1947.

Article 8. Freedom of person shall be guaranteed to the people. No person may, except in case of *flagrante delicto* as otherwise provided for by law, be arrested or detained except through a judicial or a police organ in compliance with legal procedure. No person may be tried or punished except by a law court in accordance with legal procedure. Any arrest, detention, trial or punishment, if conducted not in accordance with legal procedure, may be refused.

When a person is arrested or detained on suspicion of having committed a crime, the organ responsible therefore shall in writing inform the said person and his designated relatives or friends of the reason for the arrest or detention, and shall, within twenty-four hours, turn him over to a competent court for trial. The said person, or any other person, may petition the competent court to demand from the organ concerned the surrender, within twenty-four hours, of the said person to the court for trial.

The court may not reject the petition mentioned in the preceding section, nor shall it order the organ concerned to make an investigation and report first. The organ concerned may not refuse to execute or delay in executing the writ of the court for surrender of the said person for trial.

When a person is arrested or detained illegally he or any other person may petition the court for investigation. The court may not reject such a petition, and shall, within twenty-four hours, make the investigation with the organ concerned, and proceed with the case in accordance with law.

Article 9. No person may, except those in active military service, be subject to trial by a military court.

Article 10. The people shall have the freedom of domicile and of change of domicile.

Article 11. The people shall have the freedom of speech, academic instruction, writing and publication.

Article 12. The people shall have the freedom of secrecy of correspondence.

Article 13. The people shall have the freedom of religious belief.

Article 14. The people shall have freedom of assembly and of association.

Article 15. The right of existence, the right of work and the right of property shall be guaranteed to the people.

Article 16. The people shall have the right to present petitions, file complaints or institute legal proceedings.

Article 17. The people shall have the right of election, recall, initiative and referendum.

Article 18. The people shall have the right to take public examinations and to hold public offices.

Article 19. The people shall have the duty of paying taxes in accordance with law.

Article 20. The people shall have the duty of performing military service in accordance with law.

Article 21. The people shall have the right and duty of receiving citizen's education.

Article 22. All other liberties and rights of the people that are not inimical to social order or public interest shall be guaranteed under the Constitution.

Article 23. No one of the liberties and rights enumerated in the preceding articles may, except as warranted by reason of preventing infringement of the liberties of other persons, averting an imminent crisis, maintaining social order or advancing public interest, be restricted by law.

Article 24. Any public functionary who, in violation of law, infringes upon the liberties or rights of any person shall, besides being subject to disciplinary measures in accordance with the law, be responsible under criminal and civil laws. The injured person may, in accordance with law, claim indemnity from the state for damage sustained.

## CHAPTER 3. THE NATIONAL ASSEMBLY

Article 25. The National Assembly shall, in accordance with provisions of this Constitution, exercise political power on behalf of the whole body of citizens.

Article 26. The National Assembly shall be composed of the following delegates:

(1) One delegate to be elected by every hsien, municipality or area of an equivalent status. In case the population exceeds 500,000 an additional delegate shall be elected for every additional 500,000. What constitutes an area equivalent to a hsien or to a municipality shall be determined by law.

(2) Delegates to be elected by Mongolia; four from every league and one from every special banner.

(3) The number of delegates to be elected from Tibet shall be determined by law.

(4) The number of delegates to be elected by various racial groups in the border regions shall be determined by law.

(5) The number of delegates to be elected by Chinese nationals residing abroad shall be determined by law.

(6) The number of delegates to be elected by occupational groups shall be determined by law.

(7) The number of delegates to be elected by women's organizations shall be determined by law.

Article 27. The function and powers of the National Assembly shall be as follows:

(1) Election of the President and the Vice-President.

(2) Recall of the President or the Vice-President.

(3) Amendment of the Constitution.

(4) Ratification of amendments to the Constitution proposed by the Legislative Yuan.

With respect to the exercise of the powers of initiative and referendum, besides what is stipulated in the preceding third and fourth sections, the National Assembly shall institute measures pertaining thereto and enforce them, after the said two powers shall have been exercised in one half of the hsien and municipalities of the whole country.

Article 28. Delegates to the National Assembly shall be elected every six years.

The terms of the office of the delegates to each National Assembly shall terminate on the day of convocation of the next National Assembly. Incumbent government officials may not be elected delegates to the National Assembly in constituencies where they hold office.

Article 29. The National Assembly shall be summoned by the President to meet ninety days prior to the date of expiration of the term of each presidency.

Article 30. The National Assembly may, in any of the following circumstances, convene in extraordinary session:

(1) When, in accordance with the provisions of Article 49 of this Constitution, it is necessary to hold a supplementary election of the President and the Vice-President.

(2) When, in accordance with a resolution of the Control Yuan, an impeachment against the President or the Vice-President is instituted.

(3) When, in accordance with a resolution of the Legislative Yuan, an amendment to the Constitution is proposed.

(4) When it is convened upon a petition of over two-fifths of the delegates of the National Assembly.

When an extraordinary session is called in accordance with the preceding first or second section, the president of the Legislative Yuan shall issue the notice of convocation; when called in accordance with the preceding third or fourth section, such session shall be summoned by the President of the Republic.

Article 31. The National Assembly shall meet at the seat of the Central Government.

Article 32. No delegate to the National Assembly shall be held responsible outside the Assembly for opinions he may express or for votes he may cast in sessions of the Assembly.

Article 33. While the Assembly is in session, no delegate to the National Assembly shall, except in case of *flagrante delicto,* be arrested or detained without the permission of the National Assembly.

Article 34. The organization of the National Assembly, the election and recall of delegates to the National Assembly, and the procedure of the exercise of the functions and powers of the National Assembly shall be prescribed by law.

## CHAPTER 4. THE PRESIDENT

Article 35. The President is the head of the state and represents the Republic of China in official foreign relations.

Article 36. The President shall command the land, sea and air forces of the whole country.

Article 37. The President shall, in accordance with law, promulgate laws and issue mandates with the countersignature of the president of the Executive Yuan or of both the president of the Executive Yuan and the heads of ministries or commissions concerned.

Article 38. The President shall, in accordance with the provisions of this Constitution, exercise the powers of conclusion of treaties, declaration of war and making of peace.

Article 39. The President may, in accordance with law, declare martial law with the approval or confirmation of the Legislative Yuan. When the Legislative Yuan deems it necessary it may, by resolution, request the President to rescind such law.

Article 40. The President shall, in accordance with law, exercise the power of granting general amnesties, pardons, remission of sentences and restitution of civil rights.

Article 41. The President shall, in accordance with law, appoint and remove civil and military officers.

Article 42. The President may, in accordance with law, confer honors and award decorations.

Article 43. In case a natural calamity, an epidemic or a serious national financial or economic change necessitates emergency measures to be taken, the President, during the recess of the Legislative Yuan, may, by resolution of the Executive Yuan Council, and in accordance with the emergency decrees law, issue an emergency decree expedient and necessary to cope with the situation.Such a decree shall, within one month after issuance, be presented to the Legislative Yuan for confirmation; in case the Legislative Yuan dissents, the said decree shall immediately become null and void.

Article 44. In case of any difference of opinion arising among the different Yuan that is not covered by this Constitution, the President may summon a meeting of the presidents of the Yuan concerned for consultation to settle the difference.

Article 45. Any citizen of the Republic of China having attained to the age of forty years may be eligible to the office of the President or the Vice-President.

Article 46. The election of the President and the Vice-President shall be prescribed by law.

Article 47. The term of office of the President and the Vice-President shall be six years. They may be elected for a second term.

Article 48. The President shall, at the time of his inauguration, take an oath as follows:

"I do solemnly and sincerely swear before the people of the whole country that I will observe the Constitution, faithfully perform my duties, and promote the welfare of the people, safeguard the security of the state and will not betray the trust of the people. Should I break my oath, I shall be willing to submit myself to [such] severe punishment [as] the state may decree."

Article 49. In event of the President's office becoming vacant, the Vice-President shall succeed to the presidency until the expiration of the presidential term. In case both the President's and the Vice-President's office become vacant, the president of the Executive Yuan shall discharge the duties of the President's office. In accordance with the provisions of Article 30 of this Constitution, an extraordinary session of the National Assembly shall be convened for the purpose of holding a supplementary election of the President and the Vice-President, who shall hold office until the completion of the unfinished term of the former President.

In case the President becomes unable to attend to office due to a cause, the Vice-President shall discharge the duties of his office. In case both the President and the Vice-President become unable to attend to office, the president of the Executive Yuan shall discharge the duties of the President's office.

Article 50. The President shall retire from office on the day his term expires. If by that time the succeeding President shall not have yet been elected or, if already elected, both the President and the Vice-President shall not have been inaugurated, the president of the Executive Yuan shall discharge the duties of the President's office.

Article 51. The period for the president of the Executive Yuan to discharge the duties of the President's office shall not exceed three months.

Article 52. The President, except in case of commitment of rebellion or treason, shall not, without having been recalled or released from office, be liable to criminal prosecution.

## Chapter 5. Administration

Article 53. The Executive Yuan is the highest administrative organ of the state.

Article 54. The Executive Yuan shall comprise a president, a vice-president, a number of heads of various ministries and commissions and a number of executive members without portfolio.

Article 55. The president of the Executive Yuan shall be appointed by the President of the Republic with the consent of the Legislative Yuan. During the recess of the Legislative Yuan, if the president of the Executive Yuan resigns or if his office becomes vacant, the vice-president of the Yuan shall discharge the duties of the office of the president of the Executive Yuan. The President of the Republic shall, within forty days, request the Legislative Yuan to summon a meeting to consent to his nominee [for] the presidency of the Executive Yuan.

Pending the consent of the Legislative Yuan to the said nominee, the vice-president of the Executive Yuan shall discharge the duties of the office of the president of the Yuan.

Article 56. The vice-president, the heads of the various ministries and commissions and the executive members without portfolio of the Executive Yuan shall be appointed by the President of the Republic upon the recommendation of the president of the Executive Yuan.

Article 57. The Executive Yuan shall be responsible to the Legislative Yuan in accordance with the following provisions:

(1) The Executive Yuan has the responsibility to present to the Legislative Yuan its administrative policies and its adminstrative reports. Legislative members have, in the sessions of the Legislative Yuan, the right to interpellate the president and the heads of the various ministries and commissions of the Executive Yuan.

(2) If the Legislative Yuan dissents to any important policy of the Executive Yuan, it may, by resolution, ask the Executive Yuan to alter such policy. With respect to such resolution, the Executive Yuan may, with the approval of the President of the Republic, request the Legislative Yuan for reconsideration. If, in reconsideration, two-thirds of the attending members of the Legislative Yuan uphold the original

resolution, the President of the Executive Yuan shall either abide by the same or resign from office.

(3) If the Executive Yuan deems a resolution passed by the Legislative Yuan on a statutory, budgetary or treaty bill [unsuitable] for execution, it may, with the approval of the President of the Republic, request, within ten days after the delivery of the said resolution to the Executive Yuan, [that] the Legislative Yuan . . . reconsider [the resolution]. If, in reconsideration, two-thirds of the attending members of the Legislative Yuan uphold the original resolution, the President of the Executive Yuan shall either abide by the same or resign from office.

Article 58. The Executive Yuan shall have an Executive Yuan Council to be composed of its president, the vice-president, the heads of the various ministries and commissions and the executive members without portfolio of the Executive Yuan, with the Yuan president as chairman.

Prior to the submission to the Legislative Yuan of any statutory or budgetary bill or any bill concerning declaration of martial law, granting of general amnesty, declaration of war, conclusion of peace, treaties or other important affairs, or concerning matters of common concern to the various ministries and commissions, the president and the heads of the various ministries and commissions of the Executive Yuan shall present the same to the Executive Yuan Council for discussion and decision.

Article 59. The Executive Yuan shall, three months before the beginning of every fiscal year, present to the Legislative Yuan the budget for the following fiscal year.

Article 60. The Executive Yuan shall, within four months after the end of every fiscal year, present the budget statement to the Control Yuan.

Article 61. The organization of the Executive Yuan shall be prescribed by law.

## CHAPTER 6. LEGISLATION

Article 62. The Legislative Yuan is the highest legislative organ of the state to be constituted of legislative members elected by the people. It shall exercise the legislative power on behalf of the people.

Article 63. The Legislative Yuan shall have the power to decide upon statutory or budgetary bills or bills concerning martial law, general amnesty, declaration of war, conclusion of peace, treaties and other important affairs of state.

Article 64. Members of the Legislative Yuan shall be elected in accordance with the following provisions:

(1) Those elected by provinces and by municipalities under the direct jurisdiction of the National Government; five from each province or municipality with a population of less than 3,000,000; and, in case of a population exceeding 3,000,000, one additional member for every additional 1,000,000 persons.

(2) Those elected by Mongolian leagues.

(3) Those elected by Tibet.

(4) Those elected by various racial groups in border regions.

(5) Those elected by Chinese nationals residing abroad.

(6) Those elected by occupational groups.

The election of the legislative members and the allotment of the number of legislative members in the preceding second to sixth sections shall be determined by law.

The number of women members in the various items of the first section shall be determined by law.

Article 65. Members of the Legislative Yuan shall serve a term of three years, and are re-eligible. The general election shall be completed within three months prior to the expiration of each term of office.

The Legislative Yuan shall comprise a president and a vice-president to be elected by and from among the legislative members.

Article 67. The Legislative Yuan may organize various committees.

Such committees may invite government officials and private persons concerned to be present at their meetings for consultation.

Article 68. The Legislative Yuan shall hold two regular sessions every year, to be convened by itself. The first session shall last from February to the end of May, and the second session from September to the end of December. When necessary, a session may be extended.

Article 69. In any of the following circumstances, the Legislative Yuan may hold an extraordinary session:

(1) At the request of the President of the Republic.

(2) Upon the petition of more than one fourth of the legislative members.

Article 70. The Legislative Yuan shall not make proposals for an increase in the expenditures listed in the budget presented by the Executive Yuan.

Article 71. At the meetings of the Legislative Yuan, the presidents of the various Yuan concerned and the heads of the various ministries and commissions concerned may be present to present their opinions.

Article 72. Statuory bills passed by the Legislative Yuan shall be sent to the President of the Republic and to the Executive Yuan. The President shall, within ten days after their receipt, promulgate them. The President may proceed with them in accordance with the provisions of Article 57 of this Constitution.

Article 73. No member of the Legislative Yuan shall be held responsible outside of the Yuan for opinions he may express and votes he may cast in sessions of the Yuan.

Article 74. No legislative member may, except in case of *flagrante delicto*, be arrested or detained without the permission of the Legislative Yuan.

Article 75. No legislative member may concurrently hold a public office.

Article 76. The organization of the Legislative Yuan shall be prescribed by law.

## CHAPTER 7. JUDICIARY

Article 77. The Judicial Yuan is the highest judicial organ of the state and shall attend to the adjudication of civil, criminal and administrative suits and to disciplinary measures against public functionaries.

Article 78. The Judicial Yuan shall have the power to interpret the Constitution and also the power to unify the interpretations of laws and decrees.

Article 79. The Judicial Yuan shall comprise a president and vice-president, who shall be appointed by the President of the Republic with the consent of the Control Yuan.

The Judicial Yuan shall have a number of grand judges to attend to matters stipulated in Article 78 of the Constitution, who shall be appointed by the President with the consent of the Control Yuan.

Article 80. Judges shall be independent of party affiliations and shall, in accordance with law, have independence in the exercise of their functions, subject to no interference of any kind.

Article 81. The judges shall hold office for life. No judge may be removed from office unless he shall have been subject to criminal or diciplinary punishment or shall have been declared to be under interdiction. No judge may, except in accordance with law, be suspended, transferred or have his salary reduced.

Article 82. The organization of the Judicial Yuan and the law courts of various grades shall be prescribed by law.

## Chapter 8. Examination

Article 83. The Examination Yuan is the highest examination organ of the state and shall attend to matters relating to examination, employment, registration and ranking, checking of records, scaling of salaries, promotion and transfers, safeguarding of tenures, commendation, compensation, retirement, pension system, etc.

Article 84. The Examination Yuan shall comprise a president and a vice-president and a number of examination members who shall be appointed by the President with the consent of the Control Yuan.

Article 85. In the selection of public functionaries, the system of examinations by open competition shall be enforced, quotas of candidates shall be prescribed severally according to provinces and areas, and examinations shall be held in designated districts. No person may be appointed to a public office without having passed an examination.

Article 86. The following qualifications shall be determined and registered through examination by the Examination Yuan in accordance with law:

(1) Qualifications for appointment as public functionaries.

(2) Qualifications for practice in specialized professions and as technicians.

Article 87. The Examination Yuan may, with respect to matters under its charge, present statutory bills to the Legislative Yuan.

Article 88. Examination members shall be independent of party affiliation and shall, in accordance with law, have independence in the exercise of their functions.

Article 89. The organization of the Examination Yuan shall be prescribed by law.

## Chapter 9. Control

Article 90. The Control Yuan is the highest organ of control of the state and shall exercise the powers of consent, impeachment, ratification and auditing.

Article 91. The Control Yuan shall be composed of control members, to be elected by provincial and municipal councils, the local district councils of Mongolia and Tibet, and overseas Chinese communities. The allotment of their respective numbers shall be made in accordance with the following provisions:

(1) Five members from every province.

(2) Two members from every municipality under the direct jurisdiction of the Central Government.

(3) Eight members from Mongolian leagues and banners.

(4) Eight members from Tibet.

(5) Eight members from Chinese nationals residing abroad.

Article 92. The Control Yuan shall comprise a president and a vice-president, to be elected by and from the control members.

Article 93. Control members shall serve a term of six years and are re-eligible.

Article 94. When the Control Yuan exercises the power of consent in accordance with the Constitution, it shall do so by resolutions of a majority of its attending members.

Article 95. The Control Yuan, in the exercise of its censorial powers, may request the Executive Yuan and its ministries and commissions to present to it for perusal orders issued by them and related documents.

Article 96. The Control Yuan, according to the nature of the work of the Executive Yuan and its ministries and commissions, may appoint severally a number of committees to investigate their administration with the view of finding out whether or not there is any violation of law or any neglect of duty on the part of the Executive Yuan and of its ministries and commissions.

Article 97. The Control Yuan may on the basis of the investigations and resolutions of its committees, propose measures of rectification, to be sent to the Executive Yuan and its ministries and commissions concerned, with request to effect improvement.

When the Control Yuan deems a public functionary in the central or a local government guilty of neglect of duty or violation of law, it may propose measures of rectification or institute an impeachment. If the criminal law is involved, the case shall be turned over to a law court.

Article 98. Any impeachment by the Control Yuan against a public functionary of the central or a local government shall be instituted upon the proposal of more than one control member and the endorsement, after due consideration, of more than nine control members.

Article 99. In the institution of impeachment against personnel of the Judicial Yuan or of the Examination Yuan for neglect of duty or violation of law, the provisions of Articles 95, 97, and 98 shall be applicable.

Article 100. Any impeachment against the President or the Vice-President by the Control Yuan shall be instituted upon the proposal of more than one-fourth, and the endorsement, after due consideration, of the majority, of the entire membership of the Yuan, and the same shall be brought before the National Assembly.

Article 101. No control member shall be held responsible outside the Yuan for opinions he may express or for votes he may cast in sessions of the Yuan.

Article 102. Without the permission of the Control Yuan, no control member may be arrested or detained except in case of *flagrante delicto*.

Article 103. No member of the Control Yuan may concurrently hold a public office or carry on a professional practice.

Article 104. In the Control Yuan, there shall be an auditor-general, who shall be appointed by the President of the Republic with the consent of the Legislative Yuan.

Article 105. The auditor-general shall, within three months after the presentation of the budget statement by the Executive Yuan, complete the auditing thereof in accordance with law, and submit an auditing report to the Legislative Yuan.

Article 106. The organization of the Control Yuan shall be prescribed by law.

## CHAPTERS 10 AND 11

[These chapters, containing Articles 107 to 128 inclusive, provide for the division of authority between the central and local governments and for the establishment of local self-government by law. Certain enumerated matters, including foreign affairs, national defense, currency, weights and measures, and foreign trade, are placed under the jurisdiction of the central government. Certain other matters, including education, public utilities, water conservancy, the census, police, and public health, are under the jurisdiction of the central government, but may be delegated to provincial and hsien governments. Still other matters are assigned to the provincial and hsien governments alone. In case of any jurisdictional dispute, the issue is to be settled by the Legislature Yuan.

In each province and hsien, according to provisions to be enacted by law, there is to be a popular assembly, an elected governor, and an elected district magistrate, and provision for recall, initiative and referendum.]

## CHAPTER 12. ELECTION, RECALL, INITIATIVE
### AND REFERENDUM

Article 129. The election stipulated in the Constitution, except when otherwise provided for by the Constitution, shall be [by] universal, equal and direct suffrage and by secret ballot.

Article 130. Any citizen of the Republic of China having attained the age of twenty years shall have the right of election in accordance with law. Unless otherwise provided by the Constitution and laws, any citizen having attained to the age of twenty-three years shall have the right of being elected in accordance with law.

Article 131. All candidates in the election stipulated in the Constitution shall openly campaign for election.

Article 132. Coercion or inducement shall be strictly forbidden in elections. Suits arising in connection with elections shall be tried by the court.

Article 133. A person elected may, in accordance with law, be recalled by his constituency.

Article 134. In the elections, the minimum number of women to be elected shall be fixed, and measures pertaining thereto shall be prescribed by law.

Article 135. Measures with respect to the number and election of representatives of citizens in interior areas whose conditions of living and habits are peculiar shall be prescribed by law.

Article 136. The people's exercise of their two rights of initiative and referendum shall be stipulated by law.

## Chapter 13.

[This chapter, containing six parts and a total of thirty-two articles, sets forth the fundamental national policies of the Republic. These policies include: observance of treaty obligations and of the United Nations Charter, equitable distribution of land ownership, control of capital, protection and limitation of private property, government management of public utilities and other enterprises of a monopolistic nature, public support of educational, cultural, and scientific developments, opportunity for employment, special protection of women and children, and social security.

Articles of particular interest to the student of government are as follows:]

### PART I. NATIONAL DEFENSE

Article 138. The land, sea and air forces of the whole land shall, independent of individual, regional or party affiliation, be loyal to the state and shall protect the people.

Article 139. No political party or faction or individual may make use of armed force as an instrument in a political struggle for power.

Article 140. No military man in active service may concurrently hold a civil office.

## PART 3. NATIONAL ECONOMY

Article 142. National economy shall be based on the Principle of the People's Livelihood for equitable distribution of land ownership and control of capital in order to obtain a well balanced development of public economy and private livelihood.

Article 143. All land within the territory of the Republic of China shall in principle belong to the whole body of citizens. Private ownership of land, acquired by the people in accordance with law, shall be protected and restricted by law. Privately owned land shall be liable to taxation according to its value and the government may buy such land according to its value.

Mines imbedded [in] the land and natural power which may be economically utilized for public benefit shall belong to the state and shall in no wise be affected by the people's acquisition of the right of ownership over such land.

If any land has an increase in its value, not through the exertion of labor and the employment of capital, the state shall levy thereon an increment tax, the proceeds of which shall be enjoyed by the people in common.

In the distribution and adjustment of land, the state shall, as of principle, assist self-farming landowners and persons who make use of the land by themselves, and shall also regulate their appropriate areas of operation.

## PART 4. SOCIAL SECURITY

Article 153. The state, in order to improve the livelihood of laborers and farmers and to increase their productive technical skill, shall enact laws and carry out the policy for their protection. Women and children engaged in labor shall, according to their age and physical condition, be accorded special protection.

Article 155. The state, in order to promote social welfare, shall enforce a social insurance system. To the aged, the infirm and the crippled among the people who are unable to earn a living, and to victims of unusual calamities, the state shall extend appropriate assistance and relief.

## PART 5. EDUCATION AND CULTURE

Article 159. Citizens shall have equal opportunity to receive education.

Article 160. All children of the school age from six to twelve years shall receive primary education free and those who are poor shall be supplied with textbooks by the government. All citizens beyond school age who have not received primary education shall receive supplementary education free, and shall also be supplied with textbooks by the government.

Article 162. All public and private educational institutions in the country shall, in accordance with law, be subject to state supervision.

Article 165. The state shall safeguard the livelihood of those who work in the education fields of sciences and arts, and shall, in accord with the development of national economy, raise their scale of treatment from time to time.

## PART 6. BORDER REGIONS

Article 168. The state shall accord legal protection to the status of the racial groups in the border regions, and shall render special assistance to their undertakings of local self-government.

## CHAPTER 14. ENFORCEMENT AND AMENDMENT OF THE CONSTITUTION

Article 170. The term "law," as used in the Constitution, denotes a law that shall have been passed by the Legislative Yuan and promulgated by the President.

Article 171. Laws in contravention to the Constitution shall be null and void. When doubt arises as to whether or not a law is in contravention to the Constitution, interpretation thereon shall be made by the Judicial Yuan.

Article 172. Ordinances in contravention of the Constitution or of laws shall be null and void.

Article 173. The power to interpret the Constitution resides in the Judicial Yuan.

Article 174. Amendments to the Constitution shall be made in accordance with one of the following procedures:

(1) Upon the proposal of one-fifth of the total number of the representatives of the National Assembly and by a resolution of three-fourths of the representatives present at a meeting having a quorum of two-thirds of the entire Assembly, an amendment may be made

(2) Upon the proposal of one-fourth of the members of the Legislative Yuan and by a resolution of three-fourths of the members present at a meeting having a quorum of three-fourths of the members of the Yuan, an amendment may be drawn up and submitted to the National Assembly for ratification. Such a proposed amendment to the Constitution shall, six months before the coming into session of the National Assembly, be publicly published.

Article 175. Matters provided by the Constitution which require procedures of enforcement shall be prescribed by law.

The preparatory procedure for the enforcement of the Constitution shall be decided upon by the National Assembly which shall have instituted the Constitution.

# INDEX

Administrative boards
England, 17, 31
Soviet Union, 200
Administrative courts
France, 143–44
Japan, 306
Admiralty, Lords of the, 17
Aldermen (England), 96–97
Allied Control Commission (Germany), 250
Allied Council for Japan, 336
Allied Military Government (Italy), 250–51
Allied occupation. See Occupation, Allied
Anami, General Korechika, 333
Anglo-Saxon kingdoms, kingship, 15; local government, 93–94
Appeal court. See Court of Appeals
Araki, General Sadao, 339
Army
China, Communist (Red), 401, 402, 403, 404, 416, 417, 420, 427, 428, 430; National, 388, 399, 402, 404, 410–12, 417, 424, 426, 427, 436
France, 158–59
Italy, 238, 239
Japan, 300, 302–03, 312, 333, 338
Soviet Union, 179
Assembly, Constituent (France), Third Republic constitution, 124–27; after World War II, 161, 163–64
Assembly, Legislative (France), 164
Assembly, National
China, 434
Italy, 252–53
Assembly, National Constitutional (China), 432–33
Assize courts (England), 86–87
Attlee, Clement, 29, 70, 71
Australia, and Japan, 336, 337; member of British Commonwealth, 104; parliament, 24
*Avanguardista* (Fascist organization), 239

Axis, formation of, 249; members of, 5, 339

Badoglio, Pietro, 238, 249–51
*Bakufu,* 292
Baldwin, Stanley, 107, 108, 109, 110
*Balilla* (Fascist organization), 239
Barons, English, 18. See also Peerage
Barristers, 88
Beaconsfield, Lord. See Disraeli, Benjamin
Bevin, Ernest, 29–30
Bicameralism
England, early development, 18–19
France, as political issue, 152–64; Third Republic, 152–53
Italy, under the *Statuto,* 226–28
Japan, 304, 367
Soviet Union, 197
Bidault, Georges, 168
"Big Five," 4
"Big Four," 4
Bill of Rights
China, 436
Japan, 366–67
Bills
England, passage of, 54–57; types of, 54–55
Japan, 367
Black Dragon Society, 315, 340
Black Shirts, 234
Blitzkrieg in France, 158–59
Board of Trade (England), 31–32, 96
Boards, Administrative. See Administrative boards
Bolsheviks, effect of revolution on Italy, 233; origin of, 175–76; recognition of, 190
Bonomi, Ivanoe, 251
Boroughs (England), 94
Bourbon monarchy (France), 119, 122, 125
British Empire-Commonwealth, history, 101–03; imperial relations, 105; types of territories, 103–04
Brown, Clifton, 59
Brown Shirts, 270